Western Frontiersmen Series
XXVIII

# FRONTIER DIPLOMATS

## The life and times of Alexander Culbertson and Natoyist-Siksina'

by
Lesley Wischmann

THE UNIVERSITY OF OKLAHOMA PRESS
Norman

Library of Congress Cataloging-in-Publication Data

Wischmann, Lesley.
   Frontier diplomats : Alexander Culbertson and Natoyist-Siksina' among the Blackfeet / by Lesley Wischmann

     p. cm.— (Western frontiersmen series)
     Originally published: Spokane, Wash. : Arthur H. Clark Co., 2000 in series: Western Frontiersmen series ; 28.
     Includes bibliographical references and index.
     ISBN 978-0-8061-3607-3 (paper)
     1. Culbertson, Alexander, 1809–1879. 2. Natoyist-siksina' 1825–1893. 3. Fur traders—Missouri River Valley—Biography. 4. Indian traders—Missouri River Valley—Biography. 5. Married people—Missouri River Valley—Biography. 6. Frontier and pioneer life—Missouri River Valley. 7. Fur trade—Missouri River Valley—History—19th century. 8. Indians of North America—Missouri River Valley—History—19th century. 9. Missouri River Valley—History—19th century. 10. Missouri River Valley—biography. I. Title. II. Series.

F598.C97 W57 2000
978'.02'0922—dc21
[B]                                                                                  00-024060

The paper in this book meets the guidelines for permanence and durability of the Committee on Production Guidelines for Book Longevity of the Council on Library Resources, Inc.

Originally published as *Frontier Diplomats: The Life and Times of Alexander Culbertson and Natoyist-Siksina'* by the Arthur H. Clark Company, copyright 2000 by Lesley Wischmann. Paperback edition publshed 2004 by the University of Oklahoma Press, Norman, Publishing Division of the University by arrangement with the Arthur H. Clark Company. All rights reserved. Manufactured in the U.S.A.

To My Parents:
WILLIAM JOHN WISCHMANN II (1917–1977)
who taught me to love history and
RITA WALLACE WISCHMANN (1920–1998)
who taught me to love words
as well as my brother,
WILLIAM JOHN WISCHMANN III (1945–2000)
who was my first hero

# Contents

Acknowledgments . . . . . . . . . 9
Introduction . . . . . . . . . 13
1: "Pleased that I was so manly" . . . . . . . 25
2: "If you will send Traders, we will treat them well" . . . 35
3. "This is your land" . . . . . . . . 49
4: "You are too diffident of your own powers" . . . . 59
5: "Nothing but melancholy wrecks of human life". . . . 67
6: "Let your heart be liberal" . . . . . . . 77
7: "Be without a woman at this moon of next summer" . . . 85
8: "No one can ask for more politeness" . . . . . 97
9: "I am going to kill you" . . . . . . . 109
10: "The ground has been made good again" . . . . 119
11: "When a Nation becomes addicted to drinking" . . . 127
12: "For the love of God, do not abandon these souls!" . . . 141
13: "lending influence to perpetuate superstitions". . . . 149
14: "the ball passing a few inches to the right of Culbertson's face" 161
15: "without a single flower to speak pleasant things to you" . 171
16: "a trifling compensation for this right of way" . . . 185
17: "We do not want your land" . . . . . . 199
18: "What will become of the aborigines?" . . . . . 209
19: "these hitherto neglected tribes" . . . . . . 221
20: "gradually reclaim the Indians from a nomadic life". . . 243
21: "the Buffalo will not continue forever". . . . . 255
22: "to help stabilize the family" . . . . . . 269
23: "the strength and importance of the white man" . . . 285
24: "provoked by numerous injustices and misdeeds" . . . 299
25: "a fresh and furious war has broken out" . . . . 313
26: "Tell Baker to strike them <u>Hard</u>" . . . . . . 327
27: "We will remain and see the whole affair through" . . 341
28: "they yielded the palm to Madame" . . . . . 357
Epilogue: "Whatever is kept in memory still endures" . . 371
Bibliography . . . . . . . . . 377
Index . . . . . . . . . . 391

# Illustrations

| | |
|---|---|
| Alexander Culbertson | 234 |
| Natawista | 234 |
| Rocky Spring Presbyterian Church | 235 |
| Alexander Culbertson, Natawista, and son Joe | 235 |
| Jane Culbertson | 236 |
| Joseph Culbertson | 236 |
| Possible photo of Natawista or Jane Culbertson | 236 |
| John Culbertson | 237 |
| Frances Culbertson | 237 |
| Julia Culbertson | 237 |
| Seen From Afar | 238 |
| Rev. Pierre Jean De Smet | 238 |
| Malcom Clarke | 238 |
| Ft. Union by Karl Bodmer | 239 |
| Travellers meeting Minatarre Indians by Karl Bodmer | 239 |
| Fort Benton, 1867 | 240 |
| 1855 Treaty Council sketched by Sohon | 240 |
| "Barter for a Bride" by John Mix Stanley | 241 |
| "The Last of Their Race" by John Mix Stanley | 241 |
| Home where Culbertson died, 1879 | 242 |
| Gravestone of Alexander Culbertson | 242 |
| Natawista's Grave | 242 |

# Acknowledgments

People often say that being a writer must be "fun." Interesting, yes. Challenging, yes. Rewarding, yes. But fun? Not usually. However, it is fun to finally be able to thank all those who made this book possible.

It is no exaggeration to say that this book would not have happened without three people: my second cousin, Helen Wallace Mann, whose research established my Culbertson ancestry; my mother, Rita Wallace Wischmann, who told me the story of the first Alexander Culbertson; and, Carla Davidson, senior editor of *American Heritage* magazine, who suggested me for the Lewis and Clark article that led me to the fur trader, Alexander Culbertson.

I am also deeply indebted to numerous librarians and archivists: Dorothy O'Day, Peoria Historical Society; Larry Jones, Idaho Historical Society; Karen Deller, Special Collections, Cullom-Davis Library, Bradley University; Dean Calimer, Treva Lawyer, and Evelyn Dice, Kittochtinny Historical Society in Chambersburg, Pennsylvania; Kathryn Otto, Ellie Arguimbau, and Robert M. Clark, Montana Historical Society; Kirsten Hammerstrom, Missouri Historical Society; Nancy Merz, Jesuit Missouri Province Archives; Karen Fitz, Alma, Nebraska, Public Library; Connie Horton, Dan Calkins, and Donna Dietz, Harlan County (Nebraska) Courthouse; Eleanor Baldwin, Culbertson (Montana) Public Library; Clara Rowlen, Federal Records Center, Kansas City, Missouri; and, Lisa Ervan, Central Wyoming College.

I am also grateful to Tracy Potter, formerly of North Dakota Tourism, who gave me my first opportunity to visit that wonderful state, and Bonnie Barsness who allowed me to linger at Fort Union National Historic Site. Patty Sundheim, formerly of Fort Union, encouraged this project from the beginning and pointed me in the right direction to get started. Likewise, Paul Hedren, former Superintendent of Fort Union, was always there when I needed advice or encouragement.

Many people shared generously with me of their own research: Robert Utley; Ernest Kuhl; Joel Overholser; Jack Holterman, whose earlier book on the Culbertsons served as a road map; Wayne York; Vince Santucci; Adrienne Stepanek; Bill Gwaltney; Stan Gibson; Henry Case; David Kanouse; Joe Horse Capture; Rosemary Wimberly; Hugh Dempsey; Bill Swagerty; Sarah Boehme; the late Charles E. Hanson, Jr. of the Museum of the Fur Trade; John Lepley; Conni St. Pierre; Alvin and Ellen Barlow; Hugh Welch; John Davis; Bob Watson; and, Bob Gibson, John Mix Stanley researcher.

I would also like to thank Pearl Bantam of Orleans, Nebraska, and Peggy McGeachin Vestal for helping me track down information about Culbertson's final years. In addition, I cannot overlook the hospitality of Joey Wheeler who welcomed me into her Orleans home, previously owned by Julia and George Roberts. My thanks also to R.E.M. for "Electrolite," without which Chapter Thirteen might never have been completed.

Very special words of thanks must go to the descendants of Alexander Culbertson and Natawista: Gloreen Culbertson Strausser and George H. R. Taylor, as well as his late wife, Valorie, who shared generously of their family stories. Their ancestors would be proud. I regret my inability to locate any descendants of Jack's or Fannie's.

Every writer depends on friends to offer encouragement and support when spirits flag. For their various contributions, I thank: Vanette Schwartz, Deb Kalvee, Kay Threlkeld, Roger Blair, Susan Badger Doyle, Will Bagley, Sara Bettencourt, Emmanuelle Vital, Anne Stratton, Susan Wozny, Margaret Susong, and Dr. Kenneth Robertson. Thanks also to my sister, Conny Wischmann, for loving me every day of my life.

This book was greatly improved by those who read it in manuscript form, including: Paul Hedren, Stan Gibson, Bill Swagerty, Hugh Dempsey, Gail and Muriel Carbiener, and the "other" Charles Hanson. Charles, a dear friend and exceptional librarian, knew little about the fur trade and his comments were invaluable in keeping the text clear and crisp. Many thanks also to Sheree Deaderick for her careful proofreading of the galley proofs.

Words are insufficient to express the debt I owe to Doreen Chaky. In addition to providing constant encouragement, Doreen was an unflag-

# ACKNOWLEDGMENTS                                           11

ging and unpaid research assistant. Without her, several obscure sources would never have been found. And, when all that was done, she read the entire manuscript and offered outstanding suggestions on improving it. I hope that, one of these days, we will actually meet!

Another person deserving special recognition is my dear sister, Margaret Mathews. Living east of the Mississippi, she greatly prizes her trips out west. Yet she never complained when I insisted on itineraries that accommodated my research needs. Thanks, pigpen! This book entitles you to one research-free western trip.

Every writer deserves a librarian for a spouse. I am lucky enough to have one: Larry Jansen. Larry's contributions to this book, and my physical and mental well-being, are legion. He was research assistant, cook, chauffeur, reader, editor, critic, sounding board, financial supporter, and computer wizard. No matter where my research took us, I could count on Larry to be an assistant, when needed, and to entertain himself when necessary. How many other people could amuse themselves for hours in a dozen tiny towns like Alma, Nebraska, without complaint? I am truly blessed to have Larry as my life's partner.

Finally, I have nothing but praise for my editor and publisher, Bob Clark. From my first contact with him, he has been enormously supportive. I especially appreciated his understanding when family crises interfered with my ability to meet his deadlines. His critiques made this an eminently better work. Every first-time book author should be so lucky as to have an editor such as Bob.

No doubt I have forgotten someone and to you, I apologize. And, of course, any errors are mine alone.

GUIDE TO ABBREVIATIONS USED IN FOOTNOTES:

| | |
|---|---|
| CDL, BU: | Cullom-Davis Library, Bradley University, Peoria, IL |
| ExDocs: | Executive Documents |
| FRC, KC | National Archives, Federal Records Center, Kansas City |
| FtLar: | Fort Laramie National Historic Site, Fort Laramie, WY |
| FtU: | Fort Union National Historic Site, Williston, ND |
| GTOH: | George Taylor Oral History, Idaho Historical Society, Boise, ID |
| KHS: | Kittochtinny Historical Society, Chambersburg, PA |
| KP, UCLA: | Kessler Papers, William Andrews Clark Memorial Library, UCLA, CA |
| MC: | Manuscript Collection |
| MF: | Microfilm |
| MHSC: | *Contributions to the Montana Historical Society* |
| MiscDocs: | Miscellaneous Documents |
| MoHS: | Missouri Historical Society, St. Louis, MO |
| MtHS: | Montana Historical Society, Helena, MT |
| NAM: | National Archives Microfilm |
| NDHS: | North Dakota Historical Society, Bismarck, ND |
| OPL: | Cordelia B. Preston Memorial Library, Orleans, NE |
| PDT: | *Peoria Daily Transcript* |
| PPL: | Peoria Public Library, Peoria, IL |
| SC: | Small Collections |
| VF: | Vertical File |

# Introduction

Ironically, the genesis of this book lies in bad history. I grew up primarily in Pittsburgh and Cincinnati and every summer my family visited my grandmother at her cottage on the New Jersey shore, requiring a day-long journey across the Pennsylvania Turnpike. To alleviate the boredom of four young children, my parents devised a series of landmarks, games, rituals, and stories to pass the time. As we approached Sideling Hill tunnel, my mother would tell my favorite story.

During the French and Indian War—which, Mom would remind us, occurred before the Revolutionary War—the Delaware Indians attacked McCord's Fort near present-day Chambersburg, Pennsylvania. After killing a score of people, the Indians took an equal number of women and children hostage. News of the assault spread quickly to the surrounding villages where militias were raised to rescue the captives. One of our ancestors was placed in charge of a militia unit that rode out after the Delawares. Near Sideling Hill, they engaged the warriors in battle and our ancestor was killed. His name was Alexander Culbertson.

In the fall of 1988, I was commissioned to write an article on the Lewis and Clark expedition. By then, nearly twenty years had passed since my last family vacation trek across the Pennsylvania Turnpike, and the rituals, games, landmarks, and stories had receded into my subconscious. They would be resurrected, however, by a small booklet on the Upper Missouri Wild and Scenic River published by the Bureau of Land Management.

While the booklet revealed nothing new about the Corps of Discovery, it did contain several references to a nineteenth century fur trader named Alexander Culbertson. I immediately recognized the familiar name, remembering that ancestor of mine killed by the Delaware Indians at the

Battle of Sideling Hill. While two thousand miles and one hundred years separated the two men, I felt certain there had to be a connection and set out to discover it.

At the time, I knew precious little about the fur trade and most of what I thought I knew turned out to be wrong. Having come of age during the 1960s, I too readily embraced the thesis that the fur traders were largely to blame for the denigration of Indian culture and decimation of the buffalo herds. As a result of this superficial understanding, I was, frankly, less than thrilled to have discovered a potential link between my family and a prominent fur trader.

Nevertheless, I pursued my research. I mentioned Culbertson to several friends who had an interest in the fur trade. In response, they forwarded material from their personal libraries. While pursuing other projects, I checked the indexes of fur trade and western history books for references to Culbertson. Although my limited knowledge of the fur trade meant not knowing the best resources to consult, in the long run this worked to my advantage.

Had I been doing similar research on several contemporaries of Culbertson's—such as Kenneth McKenzie, David Mitchell, or James Kipp—my search probably would have been truncated, as the lives and careers of these men were much better documented than that of Culbertson. In fact, that lack of coverage raised my interest level. The only reference to Culbertson in the one-volume reprint edition selected from LeRoy Hafen's ten-volume work, *The Mountain Men and the Fur Trade of the Far West*, mentioned that he had been a partner in the American Fur Company. Why, I wondered, was a Company partner so overlooked?

In general, where Culbertson was concerned, I found short paragraphs dealing with specific incidents, such as his handling of the 1837 smallpox epidemic or his actions in the aftermath of the 1844 massacre at Fort McKenzie. I soon realized that most of these incidents revealed a common theme: the close interaction of Culbertson with his Indian trading partners. None of the Culbertson vignettes seemed to concern the inner workings of the AFC. Was this, perhaps, a reason that traditional fur trade histories gave him short shrift?

Eventually, I found Hiram Martin Chittenden's short biographical sketch of Alexander Culbertson in *The American Fur Trade of the Far West*. According to Chittenden, Culbertson was born in Chambersburg, Penn-

# INTRODUCTION

sylvania, of Scots-Irish heritage.[1] With this confirmation of my initial hunch, I turned to the authoritative genealogy of the Culbertson clan: Lewis Culbertson's *Genealogy of the Culbertson and Culberson Families*. There, I found that the fur trader was the son of Joseph, grandson of Robert, and great-grandson of Joseph. The elder Joseph, an Irish immigrant, had been either the brother or cousin of "my" Alexander Culbertson, killed in the French and Indian War.[2]

But Lewis Culbertson's book also contained a surprise: my ancestor, Nancy Agnes Culbertson, daughter of Samuel Culbertson and Rebecca Officer, was not mentioned at all. According to our family history, this Samuel Culbertson had been the grandson of Alexander of French and Indian War fame. Lewis Culbertson disagreed. Several more months of research finally established that the Samuel Culbertson who married Rebecca Officer had been "Tanner Sam" of Cumberland County, Pennsylvania, not the Samuel Culbertson of Franklin County, Pennsylvania, that my grandfather's cousin had claimed in her application for membership in the Daughters of the American Revolution. Either cousin Helen had been sloppy in her research or simply chose the most illustrious of the numerous Samuel Culbertsons in the region as her ancestor. In any case, since the DAR did not verify applications very carefully in the early 1900s, her error went unchallenged.

As a result, my mother told the story of our courageous "ancestor," Alexander Culbertson, and the raid on McCord's Fort, twice a year, every year, during my entire childhood. This bit of false family history had led me to the fur trader, Alexander Culbertson. Now that I had established that our relationship was distant, at best, it was time to move on to other topics that interested me much more than the nineteenth century fur trade.

Except, by then, my curiosity had been whetted. What I had learned contradicted most of what I thought I knew about fur traders. Culbertson's life and relationship with the upper Missouri Indians seemed to contain tantalizing clues about a cross-cultural society I never knew existed. In addition, I had come across several interesting tidbits about Culbertson's Indian wife. To my surprise, I found myself drawn to their story. Over the next six years, my research would take me to Pennsylvania, Illi-

---
[1]Chittenden, *American Fur Trade*, Vol. 1, p. 386.
[2]Lewis Culbertson, pp. 254-255 and pp. 266-269.

nois, Missouri, Nebraska, North Dakota, South Dakota, Montana, and Canada, and reveal the compelling story of a fascinating couple living in a complex society on the edge of the frontier.

Very little new material has been published about the fur trade in recent years. This may be due, in part, to the prevalence of those erroneous attitudes about the role of the fur trade in the development of the West which I possessed at the beginning of this study. Early fur trade historians, such as Chittenden, Hafen, and Bernard De Voto, tended to lump the traders together with fur trappers and mountain men, stressing their rugged individualism, entrepreneurial attitudes, and independent spirit. This analysis coincided nicely with how, until recently, Americans liked to view themselves and their history. They had come from across the seas to found a new country, tame the wilderness, spread civilization, and settle a continent. The concept of manifest destiny made this not only right but obligatory.

Then, thorny issues about how these new immigrants had treated the native inhabitants of the Americas surfaced and it was no longer so easy to look upon those who spread "civilization" across the continent as unabashed heroes. The fur traders fell victim to this new analysis, causing many to denigrate them for having contributed to the destruction of western Indian culture. Ironically, this condemnation stemmed, at least in part, from the analysis of those early fur trade enthusiasts who stressed the adventurous nature of the traders and the entrepreneurial spirit of their enterprise. But was this an accurate depiction?

Surprisingly, the answer to this may be inherent in the term "fur trade." While traditional historians stressed the business mechanics—how many robes were sold, at what prices, for how much profit—it is self-evident that "trade" requires at least two willing partners. And, despite the fact that many historians had virtually ignored the Indian side of the equation, the fur trade was most definitely a partnership between Indians and whites, a partnership which led to a mutually beneficial cooperative society. Attempting to understand the life of a fur trader without examining his relationship to his trading partners would be a superficial examination at best.

This necessity for more fully examining partnership became abundantly clear as I researched the life of Alexander Culbertson. Although he became an extremely successful fur trader, the evidence suggests that Culbertson was not a particularly shrewd businessman. Rather, his achievements appear to have resulted primarily from his respectful relationship with the upper Missouri Indians, especially the Blackfeet.

On any number of occasions, when others suggested a rash approach designed to show the superiority of the white man, Culbertson opted instead for a moderate course—counseling with the Indians, listening to their grievances, and mediating the troubles. This approach, no doubt, saved many lives, but it risked marking Culbertson as weak in the eyes of other, more aggressive whites. Nonetheless, Culbertson was so effective that he usually muted criticism from his superiors and underlings alike. In this way, Culbertson was less an entrepreneur, less a businessman, than a diplomat and emissary between two cultures.

What in Culbertson's background or character led him to this course of action? There seemed to be little in his childhood to suggest his future understanding attitude toward the natives. He was, after all, named for a Culbertson luminary who died at the hands of the Delaware Indians. Moreover, during Culbertson's youth, "Indian Captivity Narratives," small books detailing the ordeals of whites taken hostage by Indians during the eighteenth century, were extremely popular in the East. It is very likely that the young Culbertson, growing up in a literate household, was exposed to these tales.

Most likely, he also heard the story of Mary Jemison, taken captive from a nearby settlement at the time of the raid which led to the death of the elder Alexander Culbertson. Mary Jemison's story was somewhat unique, though, in that she chose to stay with the Indians after being located by her family.[3] Jemison's story, if known, may have meliorated Culbertson's impressions of the Indians but it seems unlikely that one such tale could have overcome all the other negative concepts that he likely received as a youth. It is also possible that Culbertson's stepmother, the devout Frances Stuart Culbertson, instilled in him a certain missionary zeal which stressed cooperation and understanding between cultures. It seems more likely, however, that Culbertson's attitudes were shaped by his own experiences on the upper Missouri.

---

[3]Frances Roe Kestler, *The Indian Captivity Narrative: A Woman's View* (NY: Garland Publishing, 1990).

When Culbertson first arrived on the upper Missouri in 1833, the American Fur Company still had a tenuous association with the Blackfeet, widely regarded as the fiercest of the upper Missouri tribes. Fort McKenzie, the post serving the Blackfeet, had only been established in 1832. When Culbertson left Fort Union with trader David Mitchell that next summer, the ability of the AFC to maintain their trading position among the Blackfeet remained in doubt. But, within three years, Culbertson had made the Blackfeet trade one of the most profitable interests of the AFC empire. Apparently, he accomplished this less through any consummate business acumen and more by communicating with and understanding the Blackfeet.

Those first three years, during which Culbertson did not once leave the Blackfeet country, did much to shape his future attitudes. During that time, he endured a fierce intertribal raid as well as near-starvation and mutiny when the Crows laid siege to Fort McKenzie. However, the two most significant events in shaping Culbertson's responses and demeanor probably occurred in 1837 and 1838.

In 1837, the deadly smallpox epidemic swept the upper Missouri. Culbertson did all in his power to prevent the disease from spreading to the Blackfeet but could not persuade them of its dangers. As a result, it has been estimated that the tribe lost two-thirds of its population. And while many other traders waited at their forts to learn what had occurred among the tribes, Culbertson rode out into the countryside to discover the fate of the Blackfeet. The sight that greeted him in the Piegan camp at Three Forks haunted him the rest of his life. When the Blackfeet, their society in tatters, turned to Culbertson for assistance in rebuilding their lives, he joined with them in a partnership to create a community that could thrive into the future.

The following year, after Culbertson's underlings killed a Blood chief who had attacked their boss, the brothers of the deceased man threatened to kill Culbertson. When, soon after that, the Blood elders invited Culbertson to their encampment, everyone, including Culbertson, suspected a trap. Nonetheless, he realized that he could never carry on an effective trade with the Bloods while living in fear of them. Thus, Culbertson accepted their invitation, thereby demonstrating precisely the kind of bravery that the tribe expected from their own members. Whether consciously or not, Culbertson had adopted exactly the right strategy to honor the Blood chiefs and to convince them that he was a worthy partner. The meeting, which passed uneventfully, established a deep and lasting bond between Culbertson and the Bloods. In the ensuing years, Culbertson would often advise other white men to follow what appeared to be a more dangerous, but less aggressive, course of action, knowing that this would garner the respect of the Indians.

In this way, Culbertson presented the Indians with a positive model of white men. For the Blackfeet, this was especially important since they well remembered their first encounter with white Americans—when Meriwether Lewis killed a Piegan during his return journey in 1806. Culbertson showed the Blackfeet a different example, one that believed in moderation and temperate action.

Culbertson not only understood the Indian way of life, but also openly respected their culture and lifestyle. His reputation as an honest broker enabled him to negotiate the end of the 1833 Crow siege of Fort McKenzie, helped him re-establish the Blackfeet trade after the massacre at Fort McKenzie, convinced the upper Missouri delegation to accompany him to the Fort Laramie Treaty Conference in 1851, facilitated the safe passage of the 1853 Northern Pacific Railroad Survey, and contributed to the successful negotiation of the 1855 Blackfeet Treaty. The Blackfeet, along with the other tribes of the upper Missouri, knew from years of interaction with Culbertson that he could be trusted to speak the truth and to bargain in good faith. When Culbertson vouched for the integrity of other white men, the Indians accepted his representation.

Culbertson's effectiveness in dealing with the Indians helped many other whites see and understand the logic of his approach, as they saw that his manner brought positive results. Father Nicolas Point noted that Culbertson "has made it his rule to act with heroic moderation."[4] The distinguished Jesuit missionary, Pierre De Smet, called Culbertson "a distinguished man, endowed with a mild, benevolent, and charitable temper, though if need be, intrepid and courageous."[5] Washington's Territorial Governor, Isaac Stevens, found that Culbertson exhibited "an

---

[4]Buckley, p. 373.
[5]Chittenden, *De Smet*, Vol. II, p. 653.

ascendancy over these tribes which could only have been gained by a just and decisive course toward them."[6]

Unfortunately for Culbertson and the Indians, other white men turned out to be less trustworthy. Even the U.S. government unilaterally abrogated or failed to ratify treaties negotiated in good faith. Therefore, although Culbertson helped the Indians see that white men could be trustworthy and, for a time, helped other whites see that respect and moderation could be a winning approach in dealing with the Indians, in the end, impatient whites with an overwhelming desire to capture the lands and resources of the Indians swept through the area, erasing the cooperation fostered through Culbertson's careful diplomacy.

Just as Culbertson helped the Indians learn to trust the white man, his stunning Blood wife, Natawista, caused whites to reconsider their preconceived attitudes toward the Indians. Many whites, with little personal experience among the tribes, regarded them as bereft of civilized qualities. In Natawista, they found unexpected attributes.

The naturalist, John James Audubon, called her "handsome and really courteous and refined...."[7] Isaac Stevens believed "she presents the most striking illustrations of the high civilization which these tribes of the interior are capable of attaining."[8] And Elkanah Mackey, a Presbyterian missionary, described Natawista as possessing "a noble, kind and generous heart, quick to detect the wants of those around her and prompt to relieve them."[9]

Unfortunately, Natawista's role is much more difficult to document through the historical record. Nearly all nineteenth century histories were written by white males and, sadly, they did not always feel inclined to record the actions and contributions of a full-blooded Indian woman. That Natawista is mentioned at all, however, provides striking evidence of what a truly impressive individual she must have been. John C. Ewers, the distinguished Smithsonian anthropologist, did not exaggerate when he compared her to Sacagawea, the legendary Shoshone woman who

---

[6]Isaac I. Stevens to Alexander Culbertson, 21 Sep 1853, House ExDocs 1 (33-1) 710, p. 463.
[7]Audubon, Vol. II, p. 111.
[8]Senate ExDocs 1 (33-2) 746, p. 403.
[9]Holterman, p. 127.

# INTRODUCTION 21

accompanied the Lewis and Clark expedition, in furthering relations between the whites and the Indians.[10]

While family oral tradition holds that she almost always traveled with her husband, it is simply not possible to prove this from the historic record. It is frustratingly common for a diarist to record Natawista's presence at the beginning of an expedition, only to ignore her from then on. Most regrettably, her husband did not mention her in his reminiscences. Culbertson apparently felt that including details about his family would diminish the authority of his observations about life among the tribes. It is also possible that, when he reflected on his life with Lieutenant James Bradley in the 1870s, the end of their marriage still caused much pain.

Nevertheless, from the moment we meet the teenaged Natawista in 1843 through John James Audubon until her death on the Blood Reserve in 1893, the picture of her remains remarkably consistent. She is proud and independent, self-assured and confident, discerning and persuasive, intrepid and trustworthy, ebullient and sincere—qualities she shared with her husband. She suffered from no delusions about the treachery with which the tribes, when provoked, might react while recognizing that simple acts of accommodation—such as throwing a feast or distributing small gifts—might ameliorate the tensions. Respecting the sensitivities of both sides, she presented her arguments in a reasoned, rational manner, often convincing white men to follow her admonitions.

As you read this book, I encourage you to imagine the active role that Natawista played in many delicate negotiations, even though her actions are not as well documented as her husband's. Picture her by his side, offering her own interpretations and suggesting alternative courses of conduct for, when her role is recorded, that is what we see. She was one half of an active diplomatic team, building bridges between two cultures and enabling a cooperative community to prosper. Without Natawista, Culbertson almost certainly would not have been as effective.

Finally, I would like to address my research techniques and use of language. Research for this book was conducted in a variety of locations, relying on as many contemporaneous documents as possible. Those doc-

---

[10]Ewers, *Indian Life*, p. 62.

uments, however, frequently contained differing accounts of the same incident. This created the special challenge of trying to decipher the truth. In most cases, it was clear that each account had been given in good faith with different people hearing, and recording, different versions of the same event. Sometimes, the story apparently grew over time and, in those cases, it was fairly easy to accept the earliest record as the most reliable. In other cases, the historical record clearly established one version as more probable than another. Sometimes, however, it was less clear which to believe. In those cases, it was often possible to blend the equally plausible accounts into one version of events and I have done so. When one account had to be chosen over another, variants will be found in the footnotes.

When I began writing this book, I never anticipated that language would become so difficult. Issues ranged from relatively simple questions—such as how to spell "tipi"—to much more difficult ones which arise when writing from historical documents about nineteenth century Indian tribes.

Interestingly, when people learned I was working on a book dealing with the Blackfeet, the first question many asked was whether the proper term is Blackfeet or Blackfoot. During the nineteenth century, this question arose much less frequently as the traders recognized three distinct tribes within the Blackfeet confederacy: the Piegans, the Bloods, and the Northern Blackfoot. In this book, I have preserved those distinctions except when referring to the confederation of the three tribes. Then they are the Blackfeet.

Today, the distinction between Piegans, Bloods, and the Northern Blackfoot is more blurred. The tribe currently residing in Montana are almost always referred to as the Blackfeet, although, in general, they are the descendants of the Piegans. The correct term for them is Blackfeet, whether referring to one or numerous members of the tribe. The members of the tribe now living in Canada—primarily the Bloods and Northern Blackfoot—are referred to as the Blackfoot, both singularly and in a group. And while Piegan is spelled Peigan in Canada, as an American, I have used the former.

A number of other difficulties arose. In general, I have tried to be faithful to the language used by the historical journalists upon whose records I have relied. I have used the term Indian—rather than Native Americans, indigenous peoples, or first nations—because that is the term used in the historical records as well as the preference of many individual tribal members I consulted. Whenever possible, however, I have tried to identify the specific tribe as accurately as the historical record allows. Unfortunately, this is sometimes limited to such generic terms as "Sioux."

Individual Indians have been referred to by their "white" names, since these were much more common in the historical record. However, when an Indian translation of the name exists, even when supplied by contemporary historians, I have included it in the footnotes. A notable exception to this is Natawista. In nearly all of the available records, she is called simply "Mrs. Culbertson," Culbertson's wife, or even his "squaw." I chose to use her own name and, within the family, she was known by the Indian form rather than its English translation, "Holy Snake."

Three terms common in the nineteenth century—squaw, brave, and half-breed—are not used in this text except in quotations, since all are now widely regarded as derogatory. To designate the children of the fur traders and their Indian wives, I have used the term "mixed-blood." I recognize and regret that some might also find this objectionable.

In recounting events of the so-called "Indian Wars" of the 1850s through 1870s, it was necessary to distinguish those Indians who felt themselves in a constant state of war with the whites from those who attempted to negotiate a settlement of the disputes. In keeping with the historical language, again, I have used the term "hostiles" to designate the former. I do so without negative connotation.

I have referred to the American Fur Company post on the Laramie River in what is now Wyoming by its common name, Fort Laramie, even though it was officially Fort John during Culbertson's time. Finally, while it may dismay fur trade "purists," I have used American Fur Company for all the various permutations of the fur trade companies owned principally by Pierre Chouteau. I have done so both for simplicity's sake and because I believe it accurately reflects how Alexander Culbertson viewed his relationship to the Company. Although Culbertson held partnership shares, little in my research suggests that he much concerned himself with the AFC's inner workings or changes. To him, the Company was one entity which underwent subtle and periodic changes. Moreover, this is not a history of the American Fur Company but rather the story of Alexander Culbertson, Natawista, and the society they helped establish on the western frontier, in the hope that it might provide the blueprint for a lasting, shared community between Indians and whites.

# Chapter One

## *"Pleased that I was so manly"*

As an old woman, Frances "Fannie" Culbertson Irvin enjoyed recounting how her beloved father left his boyhood home and journeyed west, ultimately settling on the vast frontier that would become Montana.

According to Fannie, Alexander Culbertson was "only a little boy" of fourteen when he left his Chambersburg, Pennsylvania, home in 1823. For years, he had pestered his father, Joseph, about going west and finally Joseph decided to let his son "test his mettle." But Joseph knew a little more about the real world and so he gave Alexander $100, fully expecting his son to quickly return home, his curiosity overwhelmed by day-to-day survival struggles.

Young Culbertson took his father's money, tucked it away for emergencies, and headed west on the National Road. Alexander traveled by foot, occasionally getting a lift in a lumber wagon. At night, he stopped at farmhouses, bartering his labors for meals and a place to sleep. Usually that worked. But when that strategy failed, Culbertson found shelter under a wagon, a tree, or the stars. Then, in the morning, he began walking again, stopping at the next farmhouse to trade work for breakfast.

The journey went well. As long as he headed west, Culbertson knew he would eventually reach St. Louis. There, he was sure he could find work to support himself until he saved enough to head for the frontier. Even at fourteen, he knew what he wanted.

After several weeks, Culbertson arrived in the bustling town of St. Louis on a hot summer's day. He was dirty, tired, and barefoot. Tall and gangly with clear blue eyes, the boy looked like the many other strays who drifted into town. A solitary fourteen-year-old boy raised few eyebrows back then.

Culbertson, needing work, walked into the first business he saw: the American Fur Company office. When he asked about a job, the man in the office, Pierre Chouteau, AFC head, replied that there was not much work for a boy of Culbertson's size.

"Well," Culbertson replied, "I might black your boots."

The boy's straightforward manner and sincere desire piqued Chouteau's curiosity; he asked Culbertson about himself.

Culbertson replied: "My name is Alexander Culbertson and I am sixteen years old," lying for fear that his real age might work against him. "I started out a-foot from our home in Chambersburg, Pennsylvania. I walked most of the way. Now and then I got a lift in a lumber wagon, and I usually found a pretty good place to sleep. I would stop at farmhouses, and work my way when I could. I was alone and people were pretty good to me. I knew that if I kept traveling this direction, I would get to St. Louis."

Culbertson did not tell Chouteau about his well-respected, reasonably affluent family back east or the $100 tucked in his back pocket. He probably thought Chouteau would sooner hire a waif than a relatively well-educated young man from a socially prominent family who might return home as soon as the novelty of his adventure wore off.

Chouteau, impressed by the boy's pluckiness, decided to give him a chance. Culbertson worked around the office, and performed well, but he wanted a job on the frontier. Soon, Chouteau assigned him to work on the boats that plied the Missouri River in the fur trade. As a cabin boy, Culbertson loaded and unloaded cargo. While more satisfying, this was still not the work Culbertson wanted. Chouteau, however, did not think him ready to go upriver.

Instead, Chouteau promoted him to clerk. Culbertson performed those tasks well, inspiring confidence. And then, finally, Chouteau assigned him to Fort McKenzie, a new American Fur Company post serving the Blackfeet Indians, renowned for their fighting disposition.[1]

At least that's the tale his daughter told. Almost certainly, it is the story she heard from her father who, in the tradition of Indian story-tellers, probably crafted the account to impress his children with the importance of following their dreams. The story, however, contained only the smallest vestiges of truth.

On May 19, 1809, Mary Finley Culbertson gave birth to her third son.[2] Her husband, Joseph Culbertson, represented the third generation of a Scots-Irish pioneer family who staked their claim in the Pennsylvania wilderness during the 1740s. The proud parents named their baby

---

[1] Berglund, SC 414, MtHS.   [2] Lewis Culbertson, p. 268.

Alexander after one of the most distinguished members of the Culbertson clan, Captain Alexander Culbertson.

The first Alexander Culbertson emigrated from County Antrim, Ireland, around 1735. With his brothers Robert and Samuel, Alexander settled in the Cumberland Valley. Joseph Culbertson, either a brother or cousin, joined them several years later and the four planted roots on adjacent tracts of wilderness.[3]

The Scots-Irish immigrants who settled the Cumberland Valley, nearly all Presbyterians, brought with them a tradition of hardscrabble existence. Their ancestors had been sent from the Scottish lowlands to colonize northern Ireland for the English. The Irish deeply resented their presence and, in the mid-1600s, the British persecuted them for their religious faith. When absentee British landlords forced them off their lands, thousands ended up impoverished. Having already forsaken one homeland, many now took their uniquely energetic and restless temperament to the New World.[4]

The Culbertson brothers were drawn to the Cumberland Valley by its gently rolling countryside, numerous streams, powerful waterfalls, abundant forests, bountiful game, and rich soil. Using rough implements, they cleared the trees, removed limestone boulders, broke the land, planted seeds, built homes, harvested crops, and established a community that came to be known as Culbertson's Row.

But the white immigrants were squatters. William Penn had received legal title to thousands of acres through the Royal Charter of 1681, but the lands west of the Susquehanna River, including the Cumberland Valley, still belonged to the Delaware Indians. By the 1750s, through a series of fraudulent legal manipulations, the white settlers obtained what they considered legal title. But the Indians did not agree.[5]

When the French and Indian War broke out, the emigrant Alexander Culbertson joined the military, accompanying Major General Edward Braddock on his doomed 1755 expedition against Fort Duquesne. Subsequently commissioned a captain, Culbertson helped defend his neighbors against Indian raiders.

On August 1, 1755, Culbertson petitioned the provincial government on behalf of his neighbors who lived "in such imminent Peril of being

---

[3]Lewis Culbertson, p. 254.   [4]Havens, pp. 14-19.
[5]Havens, pp. 60-62.

inhumanly Butchered by our Savage neighbors, whose tender Mercies are Cruelty." He beseeched the governor to "strengthen our Hands with a Quantity of Arms and Ammunition" so that the settlers could defend themselves.[6]

Soon enough, the Indians began a series of random attacks against the isolated Cumberland Valley settlers. The government authorized a militia and series of provincial forts; Joseph Culbertson built a large log fort in front of his home, with spring water and space to shelter the Culbertson clan and some neighbors.[7]

On April 4, 1756, the Indians attacked McCord's Fort, four miles from Culbertson's Row, killing more than twenty people[8] and carrying off many more. When the news reached Captain Alexander Culbertson, he raised a company of men and rode west, hoping to rescue the hostages. Three days later, Culbertson met the Indians at Sideling Hill and a fierce battle ensued. Culbertson and most of his men were killed.[9]

Hans Hamilton wrote his superiors with the "Malancoly (*sic*) News" of the battle: "Our men Engaged about 2 hours, being about 36 in Number, & we should have had the better had not thirty Indians come to [the Indians'] Assistance. Some of our men fir$^d$ 24 Rounds a piece, and when their Ammunition fail$^d$, were oblig$^d$ to Fly."[10] Captain Alexander Culbertson's death left a lasting impression on his family.

Captain Culbertson's oldest son, Samuel, became a colonel in the Revolutionary War, fighting alongside his brother and cousins.[11] Before marching out, the men gathered by the spring at old Fort Culbertson, now owned by Joseph's son, Colonel Robert Culbertson.[12] In the custom of their Scots-Irish ancestors, the Culbertsons clasped hands across the water, swore fidelity to the cause of their newly emerging country, and shared a tinful of whiskey from Robert Culbertson's still.[13]

The Alexander Culbertson who would work for the American Fur Company was Colonel Robert Culbertson's grandson. Known to his neighbors as "Curly-headed Bob,"[14] Robert Culbertson fought at the Battles of Trenton and Princeton.[15] Yet his grandson, growing up in the early nineteenth century, had little appreciation for the hard-won tran-

---

[6]Havens, p. 71.     [7]Conrad, p. 175.     [8]Havens, pp. 73-75.
[9]Lewis Culbertson, p. 135.
[10]Hans Hamilton, p. 611. His name also appears as Hance Hamilton.
[11]Lewis Culbertson, p. 138.     [12]Conrad, p. 175.     [13]Lewis Culbertson, p. 156.
[14]Huey, Culbertson Collection, MoHS.     [15]Conrad, p. 175.

quility his ancestors had secured. Surrounded by aging men who told wondrous stories of Indian and Revolutionary War battles, and reared on tales of hardships and deprivations endured and overcome, the boy feared he might perish of boredom.

Where were the opportunities to prove one's valor? Where were the enemies to be vanquished? What renown could possibly come from tilling a field? What would his famous namesake think of his uneventful life? As the young boy studied with his cousins and attended the church his ancestors had built, Alexander felt stifled by stability.

One of young Alexander's favorite relatives was his uncle, John Craighead Culbertson. Despite the tranquil times, John Culbertson had found adventure with the 22nd United States Infantry during the War of 1812. He had been wounded twice—at Lundy's Lane and Chippewa. He had even fought Indians during the Seminole War. In June 1819, John Culbertson became a captain in the United States army.[16]

Six years later, Captain Culbertson ascended the Missouri River with the Atkinson-O'Fallon—or Yellowstone—expedition[17] after the United States government authorized a delegation to negotiate treaties with the upriver Indian tribes who had grown increasingly hostile to white fur traders. General Henry Atkinson led the military contingent, including Culbertson, while Major Benjamin O'Fallon, nephew of General William Clark of the Lewis and Clark expedition, represented the Indian Department.

Between June 9 and October 6, 1825, the commissioners met and negotiated treaties with twelve tribes.[18] The treaties acknowledged the supremacy of the United States, promised United States friendship and protection for the tribes, guaranteed that only properly licensed whites could trade with the tribes at designated locations, provided mutual agreements for the punishment of whites or Indians charged with depredations, and pledged that the Indians would not supply hostile tribes with arms or ammunition.[19] Captain J. C. Culbertson witnessed the treaty

---

[16]Lewis Culbertson, pp. 292-293.

[17]Kennerly, p. 83; Reid and Gannon, p. 25.

[18]The treaties were signed with: the Ponca tribe; the Teton, Yankton and Yantonai tribes; the Blackfeet Sioux and Oglala tribes; the Cheyennes; the Hunkpapas; the Arikaras; the Hidatsas; the Mandans; the Crows; the Oto and Missouri tribes; the Pawnees; and, the Omahas.

[19]Reid and Gannon, pp. 8-9.

with the Mandan tribe on July 30, 1825.[20] The expedition had been conducted primarily to ensure the viability of the fur trade and Culbertson probably met some of St. Louis's capitalist scions during this period.

But more importantly to his impressionable nephew, John Craighead Culbertson was having adventures! Every time John visited Pennsylvania, the young Alexander followed him around, begging to hear his stories. With these tales echoing in his head, Alexander vowed he would soon leave his safe cocoon and go where the Indians lived and adventures awaited.

Alexander Culbertson was seventeen in the summer of 1826 when John Craighead Culbertson returned to Chambersburg. Following an army reorganization, Culbertson had become sutler for the First Infantry.[21] Sutlers followed the army, selling amenities to the troops. While not officially employed by the military, sutlers had to be appointed by the Secretary of War and military regulations controlled their for-profit sales. Sutlers followed their regiment. For John Culbertson, this meant traveling the Gulf of Mexico from Pensacola to New Orleans.

At seventeen, Alexander Culbertson was a man, more than ready to leave home. When John Culbertson offered him an assistant's position, he jumped at the opportunity. Alexander's father, Joseph, gave his blessing and perhaps even that emergency $100.

Alexander's mother could not consent; she had died in childbirth when he was eight years old.[22] The next spring, in April 1818, Joseph Culbertson married Frances Stuart. A deeply pious woman, Frances Stuart Culbertson helped found The Female Missionary Society of Dauphin County which pledged itself to spread the gospel among "those poor savage tribes."[23] On the frontier, her stepson might be able to further that cause.

His last Sunday in the valley, Alexander attended services at Rocky Spring Presbyterian, the quiet country church his family had helped found in the mid-1700s. When the Revolutionary War broke out, the Rev. John Craighead, namesake of Alexander's uncle, had preached a rousing service after which every adult male in the congregation marched

---

[20]Kappler, Vol. II, p. 244.
[22]Lewis Culbertson, p. 268.
[21]Toomer, MF250, Reel 16, MtHS; Kennerly, p. 83.
[23]Holterman, p. 6.

off to war.[24] A decade later, with the war won, the congregants replaced the wood frame church with an appropriately more permanent handmade brick building.

Alexander took his seat in the high-backed wooden pew that bore Col. Robert Culbertson's name on the swinging endgate. Other members of the Culbertson clan occupied several other pews paid for with their family's tithings. The family owned no fewer than four pews. In the very back of the church, the black members sat in a pew reserved for "Africans."

The preacher ascended several steps to the canopied pulpit positioned in the middle of the long wall of the rectangular building. A star in the overhead sounding board symbolically reflected his message.[25] In the winter, heat came from stoves but the building had no external chimneys. When the church was built, memories of Indian raids remained fresh and the congregation knew that they sometimes followed telltale puffs of smoke to an unsuspecting crowd. Therefore, the cautious worshippers ran stovepipes into the attic where a layer of sand smothered the sparks. Late at night, with the congregation safely dispersed, a member returned to open an attic door and vent the smoke.[26]

When the service ended, Alexander walked through the maple trees and down a slight hill to visit the graves of his mother and maternal grandfather, James Finley. He opened the gate, marked Culbertson, in the wrought iron fence and stood next to the raised crypts under the shaggy bark hickory tree to say his goodbyes.[27]

That summer of 1826, Alexander and John Craighead Culbertson headed for the southern frontier where Alexander watched his uncle make shrewd deals and learned the tricks that made John Culbertson suc-

---

[24]Jordan, p. 8.
[25]More than two hundred years later, Rocky Spring Presbyterian Church still stands amid towering maple trees on a slight knoll north of Chambersburg. Maintained primarily by the Daughters of the American Revolution, the church holds one service each year. A devastating storm struck Rocky Spring in early June 1996. The roof was torn off and the 1996 annual service had to be cancelled. However, thanks to contributions from concerned individuals, the church was repaired and the annual service was again held on August 24, 1997. Rocky Spring Trustees to the author, June 1996 and June 1997.
[26]Garber, p. 3; author's personal observations, October 1992.
[27]Author's personal observations, October 1992. Nearby, a large memorial commemorates the Culbertson family and its veterans who fought and died in their country's wars.

cessful. High on that list was the understanding that a trader's greatest commodity was trust. Without trust, no one would trade and, without trade, the trader failed. No matter what else might have to be sacrificed, Alexander resolved to keep his word as good as gold.

In December, six months after leaving home, Alexander Culbertson boarded a small schooner in New Orleans en route to Pensacola. In Mobile Bay, the schooner wrecked. Those aboard floated in the bay for several hours before finally being rescued. At Cantonment Clinch, Culbertson wrote a long letter home describing his perilous escapade. He began by assuring his stepmother that he was "very much pleased" with his new life. To ensure that his uncle would not be unduly blamed, Alexander admitted that John Culbertson "did not like the idea of letting me go for fear of some accident." But Culbertson had ignored his uncle's warnings after learning that no other vessel would be making the trip for at least two weeks. Eventually, his uncle came around, being "very much Pleased that I was so manly."

Conditions, according to Culbertson, were routine until "a gale of wind struck" and "set the boat keel upward," throwing them into the ocean. "O, my Dear Mother," Culbertson asked, "what do you suppose were my thoughts? Every moment, I thought my peace was ended. It was too late then to think of Death." As the crew clung to the capsized craft, they pondered how to reach the small town on shore, about one mile distant.

"Waving [their] hats for help," the castaways finally attracted the attention of the townsfolk shortly before the boat sank. "What a narrow escape we made," Culbertson declared. The men lost everything and Alexander bemoaned the loss of his "fine clothes," boots, and a "fine hat." The townspeople raised $70 to replace the crew's belongings but Culbertson "didn't receive a cent." He thanked the townspeople kindly but refused the money since he was "near my journey's end."

Besides, the young man still had $10 in his pocket which "by chance" he had not lost and he used this to return to Pensacola. There, John Culbertson ordered new clothing for his nephew, including "8 shirts, 3 pr. pantaloons, two coats and three jackets." Alexander assured his stepmother that he was also not without spiritual sustenance since he had "left [his] Bible with Uncle John."[28]

---

[28] Alexander Culbertson, Cantonment Clinch, Pensacola, Alabama, to Frances Stuart Culbertson, 8 Dec 1826. Culbertson Collection, MoHS.

That spring, the First Infantry moved west to Jefferson Barracks, then under construction on the outskirts of St. Louis.[29] The Culbertsons went along and, for the first time, Alexander came within the orbit of the powerful American Fur Company.[30]

In 1827, St. Louis was a bustling town of some seven thousand residents which served as the gateway to several frontiers. Trails led to Santa Fe, to the Platte, to the upper Missouri, and, of course, back east. Full of warehouses, churches, houses of prostitution, shanties, and mansions, St. Louis boasted a diverse population of French, Americans, Mexicans, Spaniards, Creoles, Canadians, Germans, and even Indians. The real power, however, rested with St. Louis's leading family, the Chouteaus, who had built their fortune and fame on the Indian trade.[31]

John and Alexander Culbertson did not remain in St. Louis long, leaving quickly with the First Infantry for Fort Snelling, on the Minnesota frontier. No doubt with his uncle's help, Alexander Culbertson secured a license to trade with the nearby tribes,[32] conducting business from a trading house on the banks of the Mississippi River one mile from Fort Snelling.[33] The Culbertsons traded with both the army and the Indians until 1832 when John Culbertson, then forty years old, decided to retire.[34]

In mid-May 1832, John and Alexander Culbertson left Fort Snelling for St. Louis. John Culbertson carried with him a note for $500 drawn on the account of the Upper Mississippi Outfit of the American Fur Company.[35] When John Craighead Culbertson went to the offices of the AFC to

---

[29]Toomer, MF 250, Reel 16, MtHS, p. 2.

[30]The fur trading companies went through numerous permutations as various competitors entered the field, only to be driven out, merged, or bought out. For simplicity's sake, this book will refer to the fur trading businesses run by the Chouteau family as the "American Fur Company." For a more complete analysis of the various companies operating on the frontier in the 1800s, see Sunder.

[31]Holterman, pp. 9-11.      [32]Taliaferro, p. 249.

[33]Toomer, MF 250, Reel 16, MtHS. Frances "Fannie" Culbertson Irvin claimed that Alexander Culbertson signed his first contract with the AFC in 1829 and served the Company on the Minnesota frontier. A search of the AFC records at the MoHS failed to uncover any evidence of Alexander Culbertson having been on the payroll of the AFC prior to 1833. Furthermore, the draft on behalf of John Craighead Culbertson found in the Chouteau Collection, MoHS, indicates that John Culbertson continued as sutler until 1832.

[34]Lewis Culbertson, p. 268.

[35]H. L. Dousman, Prairie des Chiens, to Pierre Chouteau, Jr., St. Louis, 14 May 1832. Chouteau-Maffitt Collection, MoHS.

collect, his nephew most likely went along. And it was probably then that the AFC offered the young Culbertson a job in the fur trade. But for now, Alexander planned to return to Chambersburg. Preparing for his first visit home in six years, Culbertson bought his stepmother a brass clock decorated with a figure of President George Washington.[36]

Back in Chambersburg, a few things had changed. Culbertson now had a little sister, Anna Mary, the first girl in a family of eight boys.[37] But, at twenty-three, Alexander Culbertson had other young women on his mind. Soon after returning, he began to court Eleanor, or Ellen, Maclay. The Maclays shared much history with the Culbertsons. Ellen's mother was a Culbertson and her great-grandfather was Captain Alexander Culbertson.[38] Although both families encouraged a marriage, it was not to be.

The longer Culbertson remained in the Cumberland Valley, the more he remembered why he had wanted to leave. If anything, the region was even quieter than it had been in his youth. The closest thing to adventure that year was a cholera epidemic.[39]

As winter receded, the old longings stirred. Deep inside, Culbertson knew that a quiet life in Chambersburg could never satisfy him. And he could not forget the possibility of working for the powerful American Fur Company. As much as he loved his family and Ellen, and as much as he would have liked to please them, Culbertson knew his destiny lay on the frontier.

Ellen initially refused to accept his decision. She would wait for him. Or she would accompany him. But Culbertson knew neither would work. He could never promise to return to Chambersburg nor could he take this gentle, refined woman to the wild frontier. Perhaps she could have been satisfied in St. Louis but he had no intention of staying there. No, he told her, the engagement must end.

And end it did. Ellen, however, found her place in the Culbertson family, marrying Alexander's younger brother, Cyrus Duncan, in 1836.[40]

---

[36]Toomer, MF 250, Reel 16, MtHS, p. 2.
[37]Lewis Culbertson, p. 268.
[38]Lewis Culbertson, p. 191.
[39]Holterman, p. 13.
[40]Berglund, SC 414, MtHS, p. 5. This story comes from Fannie Culbertson and may be one of her romantic tales.

Chapter Two

## *"If you will send Traders, we will treat them well"*

Kenneth McKenzie, born in Scotland in 1797, emigrated to the United States around 1817. After clerking for the North West Company, he entered the fur trade on the upper Mississippi, where he almost certainly met Alexander Culbertson,[1] before moving to the upper Missouri. In 1827, he merged his interests with those of the powerful Chouteau family and the hegemony of the American Fur Company over the upper Missouri trade began.[2]

In 1829, McKenzie erected Fort Union near the junction of the upper Missouri and Yellowstone rivers. McKenzie chose a site some three miles above the junction where the river ran close to the bank, offering easy docking for loading and unloading cargo. McKenzie built on the north bank where the prairie extended a mile or more, providing level ground for the Indian encampments McKenzie hoped would be abundant at trading time.[3]

A stout palisade surrounded the quadrangle of buildings housing employee quarters, storerooms, and a retail shop. At the north end stood the impressive Bourgeois's House. Imposing, two-story stone bastions guarded the northeast and southwest corners with a tall flagstaff in the open center court.

In June 1832, the *Yellow Stone* became the first steamboat to reach Fort Union. The Indians, having never seen such a vessel, dubbed it, "Fire Boat that Walks on Water." Pierre Chouteau made the inaugural voyage along with George Catlin, the first American artist to record Indian life

---

[1]The general tone of McKenzie's letters, such as Kenneth McKenzie to Alexander Culbertson, 21 Jan 1834, *Fort Union Letter Books*, MoHS, and his early confidence in Culbertson's abilities suggest that the two had been acquainted for more than the few months Culbertson had been on the upper Missouri.

[2]Hafen, *Mountain Men*, Vol. II, pp. 217-219.    [3]Thompson, p. 12.

on the upper Missouri. Catlin described Fort Union as "the largest and best-built establishment of the kind on the river, being the great or principal head-quarters and depôt of the Fur Company's business in this region."[4]

Despite his remote location, the bourgeois, or head trader, lived "in good and comfortable style." McKenzie, "a kind-hearted and high-minded Scotsman," presided over a table which "groans under the luxuries of the country; with buffalo meat and tongues, with beavers' tails and marrow-fat; but *sans* coffee, *sans* bread and butter. Good cheer and good living we get at it however, and good wine also, for a bottle of Madeira and one of excellent Port are set in a pail of ice every day, and exhausted at dinner."[5] Such bounty would increase now that steamboats could bring supplies to Fort Union.

Alexander Culbertson returned to St. Louis in the winter of 1833 with Edwin Thompson Denig, also from the Cumberland Valley. Denig, three years younger than Culbertson, had a keen interest in nature and anthropology. Possessed of wanderlust, Denig also hoped to find employment with the American Fur Company.

Since the Company needed educated young men for its frontier posts, both quickly found employment. On April 10, 1833, the American Fur Company records credited Denig with a draft of $400 for "Services ending 1 year from date."[6] Culbertson signed on for three years as a clerk.[7]

That spring the American Fur Company expanded their steamboat fleet, sending both the *Assiniboin* and the *Yellow Stone* up the Missouri. The newly acquired *Assiniboin* left St. Louis first, carrying Culbertson, Denig, and another young employee named Alexander Harvey.

Stashed below was Kenneth McKenzie's private still. Although liquor had long been banned on the frontier, the American Fur Company, along with the other traders, routinely ignored the prohibition.

The *Yellow Stone* followed the *Assiniboin* out of St. Louis. She carried the dignitaries: Pierre Chouteau, Kenneth McKenzie, Indian agent John F. A. Sanford, the noted German naturalist and explorer, Maximilian, Prince of Wied-Neuwied, and his artist-companion, Karl Bodmer. At

---

[4]Catlin, Vol. I, p. 21.   [5]Catlin, Vol. I, p. 21.   [6]Denig, p. xiv.
[7]Toomer, MF 250, Reel 16, MtHS, p. 4; Contract of Alexandre (*sic*) Culbertson, 6 Feb 1833. Chouteau-Walsh Collection, MoHS.

# IF YOU SEND TRADERS, WE WILL TREAT THEM WELL    37

Fort Pierre, the *Yellow Stone* turned back and McKenzie, Maximilian, and Bodmer boarded the *Assiniboin* for the remainder of the journey.[8]

Culbertson later told his children that he faced his first test with his new employers when McKenzie boarded the *Assiniboin*. Early in the voyage, all hands had been ordered to shore to cut wood. Culbertson refused since he had been hired as a hunter, not a woodcutter. Even when his superior threatened to report him, Culbertson stood his ground.

The mate took his complaints to McKenzie but the bold defiance of the young man appealed to the older trader and, instead of disciplining him, McKenzie promoted Culbertson to clerk.[9] The incident, while impressing Culbertson's children, probably never happened. The contract Culbertson signed before leaving St. Louis included the very terms he claimed to have been offered later by McKenzie.[10]

When Prince Maximilian boarded the *Assiniboin*, Culbertson got his first glimpse of the Prince. He was decidedly unimpressed. Judging Maximilian to be at least twenty years older than himself, Culbertson described him as being of "medium height, rather slender, sans teeth, passionately fond of his pipe, unostentatious, and speaking very broken English. His favorite dress was a white slouch hat, a black velvet coat, rather rusty from long service, and probably the greasiest pair of trousers that ever encased princely legs."[11]

On June 24, 1833, seventy-five days after leaving St. Louis, the *Assiniboin* reached Fort Union. Maximilian penned a vivid description as the fort came into view: "Fort Union, on a verdant plain, with the handsome American flag, gilded by the last rays of evening, floating in an azure sky, while a herd of horses grazing animated the peaceful scene." James Archdale Hamilton, in charge during McKenzie's absence, fired the cannon to welcome the steamboat.

The employees of Fort Union, "Americans, Englishmen, Germans, Frenchmen, Russians, Spaniards, and Italians, about 100 in number, with many Indians, and half-breed women and children" streamed forth. Inside the palisade, Maximilian noted several tipis around the flagpole, quarters for mixed-blood hunters and their families. The courtyard also

---

[8]Denig, p. xv.　　　　　　　　　[9]Toomer, MF 250, Reel 16, MtHS, p. 4.
[10]Contract, 6 Feb 1833. Chouteau-Walsh Collection, MoHS. The three year contract paid $2,000.　　　　　　[11]Bradley, *MHSC*, Vol. III, p. 206.

contained "about fifty or sixty horses, some mules, and an inconsiderable number of cattle, swine, goats, fowls, and domestic animals," the filth of which annoyed McKenzie.[12]

Soon after the men arrived, the northwest prairie filled with several hundred Indians. The Assiniboines had come to trade. Dogs carried the furs on primitive drags known as travois. Women, children, and dogs surrounded the warriors. Several chiefs led the way. The formation reminded Maximilian of "two bodies of infantry." They fired musket shots and broke into their "original song, consisting of many abrupt, broken tones, like those of the war-whoop...." The group advanced to within about sixty feet of the fort before halting at a small ravine to await the traders' welcome.[13]

The Company did a lucrative trade in buffalo robes that year. Maximilian counted between forty and fifty thousand robes but only twenty-five thousand beaver skins. There was also an assortment of otter, weasel, marten, lynx, red fox, cross fox, silver fox, mink, muskrat, and deer pelts.[14]

Kenneth McKenzie decided to post Alexander Culbertson to Fort McKenzie, the AFC's frontier post serving the Blackfeet, the fiercest tribe on the upper Missouri. For years, McKenzie had tried to establish a Blackfeet trade. In 1830, he persuaded Jacob Berger, a former Hudson's Bay Company trader among the Blackfeet, to try to bring the tribe to Fort Union to trade. McKenzie's employees scoffed at the idea, terming it "the forlorn hope."[15]

But Berger succeeded, bringing more than one hundred Piegans (pronounced pay-GAN), one of three Blackfeet tribes,[16] to Fort Union. McKenzie welcomed them with great celebration, offering presents and promising to build a fort in their country the next fall. McKenzie's success resulted largely from his offer to trade with the Indians: the Indians would collect the furs which the traders would buy. The Blackfeet strongly objected to the free trappers who "destroy everything before them." They had told Agent Sanford: "If you will send Traders into our Country we will protect them & treat them well; but for Trappers—Never."[17]

---

[12]Thwaites, Vol. 22, p. 377.  [13]Thwaites, Vol. 23, pp. 14-15.
[14]Thomas and Ronnefeldt, p. 52.  [15]Ewers, *Blackfeet*, p. 56.
[16]The three Blackfeet subdivisions are: the Piegan or Pikuni; the Blood or Kainah; and, the Siksika, Blackfoot proper, or Northern Blackfoot. For more, see Ewers, *Blackfeet*, p. 5.
[17]Abel, p. 253.

# IF YOU SEND TRADERS, WE WILL TREAT THEM WELL 39

As a result of these contacts, in the fall of 1831, McKenzie dispatched James Kipp, forty-four men, and a keelboat filled with trade goods to establish a Piegan post. Kipp, born near Montreal, had been one of the original members of the Columbia Fur Company. In May 1823, he had built a trading post among the Mandans. After the Columbia Fur Company merged with the AFC in 1828, Kipp moved upriver and began working with Kenneth McKenzie at the fledgling Fort Union.[18]

The Indians arrived to trade as soon as Kipp appeared, but he persuaded them to come back in seventy-five days after he had built a fort. Exactly seventy-five days later, the Piegans returned and, to their amazement, found a completed fort surrounded by a stockade. Kipp named the post Fort Piegan and the trading commenced.

Kipp offered much more for the Piegan pelts than his competitor, the Hudson's Bay Company. In fact, the payment far exceeded market value, but the Company's strategy that season was less about making money and more about undercutting their competition.[19] Of equal importance, and contrary to the law, Kipp kept the liquor flowing. For three days, the Piegans drank to excess. When they sobered up, they sold Kipp 6,450 pounds of beaver furs.

That winter, however, Kipp nearly lost all the pelts when Blood Indians, another Blackfeet tribe, besieged the fort. Kipp held his fire, hoping to win over the Bloods and secure their trade. But after eleven days, with the water supply nearly depleted, Kipp loaded a cannon with grapeshot and fired at a huge cottonwood tree. The explosion sent splintered wood flying, scattering the frightened Bloods.

Soon after, two Blood chiefs returned to Fort Piegan and told Kipp that the Hudson's Bay Company had induced them to attack the new traders. Kipp, however, had won their respect by showing bravery and restraint in defending the fort. Kipp cemented the relationship by agreeing to buy buffalo robes from the Bloods. The Hudson's Bay Company, unable to get the heavy furs to market, refused to trade for them. That winter, the Bloods traded 3,000 buffalo robes for tobacco, alcohol, cloth, knives, guns, gun powder, awls, axes, kettles, mirrors, beads, and other manufactured goods.[20]

In the spring of 1832, as Kipp prepared to take the pelts to Fort Union, he discovered only a few men willing to stay behind. Since this was too

---

[18]Hafen, *Mountain Men*, Vol. II, pp. 201-202.   [19]Thomas and Ronnefeldt, p. 98.
[20]Ewers, *Blackfeet*, p. 58.

small a contingent to maintain the fort, Kipp dismantled and abandoned it. Later, the Indians burned what remained. Thus, despite a successful trading season, the American Fur Company still lacked a post in the Blackfeet territory.

When Kipp reached Fort Union, Kenneth McKenzie immediately dispatched David Mitchell, an AFC clerk, with sixty men and a new supply of trade goods, to re-establish the post.[21] Mitchell, one of the more cultured of the traders, had been born in Virginia in 1806. Coming west in his youth, he quickly gained a solid reputation. When he was transferred to the upper Missouri in 1830, he commanded the generous salary of $700 per year.[22] Six miles above the mouth of the Marias River, Mitchell constructed Fort McKenzie.[23]

On July 6, 1833, McKenzie ordered flags hoisted, guns discharged, and fireworks exploded as David Mitchell, Prince Maximilian, Karl Bodmer, Alexander Culbertson, and some forty hunters, interpreters, and laborers set off for Fort McKenzie aboard the keelboat *Flora*.[24]

The keelboats, stout barges equipped with a keel, mast, and rudder, could sail when the wind cooperated. Most of the time, though, they had to be rowed with long oars, pushed with iron-shod poles, or pulled by men on shore with long stout cords known as cordelles. When water was low, as it was that summer, cordelling became the primary means of progressing. The work was hard, dirty, and tedious.

The *Flora* contained one rear cabin with two bunks for Maximilian, Mitchell, and Mitchell's Indian wife. Culbertson and Bodmer slept on the open deck while most of the crew camped on shore. At night, a rotating guard kept watch.[25]

Sheer misery marked the first ten days. Fighting shallow waters and swift currents, cordellers slogged through muddy water and willow thickets. The *Flora* ran aground, was freed, and ran aground again. Riverbanks collapsed and falling trees nearly crushed the boat. Uprooted trees created huge underwater snags that had to be chopped through to form a passable channel. Violent thunderstorms soaked passengers and baggage. And when the rains stopped, huge clouds of mosquitoes descended. The

---

[21] Bradley, *MHSC*, Vol. III, p. 204.
[23] Ewers, *Blackfeet*, p. 60.
[25] Thomas and Ronnefeldt, p. 74.
[22] Hafen, *Mountain Men*, Vol. II, p. 241.
[24] Thompson, p. 28.

cordelle snapped and the *Flora* nearly sank in a whirlpool. Company veterans could not remember a more difficult voyage upstream.[26]

In early August, the group passed Milk River and entered the country of the Gros Ventres, a nation closely allied with the Blackfeet. Equally fearsome, the Gros Ventres two years earlier had destroyed a Canadian trading post, killing nineteen. In 1832, they had fought a bitter battle with American traders at the rendezvous in Pierre's Hole.[27]

Near Arrow River, the men saw nearly 260 lodges, housing almost the entire Gros Ventre tribe, on the prairie. In the foreground, near the principal chief's tipi, an American flag waved. As the keelboat slowed, several Indians swam out to meet it. One boldly entered Mitchell's cabin. Mitchell dismissed him, making it clear he was not welcome on board. They would visit on shore, Mitchell explained.

The *Flora* saluted the camp with cannon shot and the Indians answered. The crew anchored the keelboat on the far shore to avoid unwanted encounters while Mitchell and his interpreter, Doucette, rowed across to greet the chiefs. After a brief meeting, Mitchell invited eight chiefs back to the *Flora* to smoke pipes and receive gifts.

While Mitchell entertained the chiefs, a number of Indians swam over and boarded the *Flora*. They demanded liquor and gun powder for their furs. Mitchell persuaded the chiefs to get their people to leave but as quickly as some jumped off, others boarded from the opposite side. The situation threatened to get out of control. Finally, Mitchell sent Doucette and others, probably including Culbertson, to shore to trade. When a favorable wind came up, the *Flora* moved off. Doucette would bring the smaller Company boat along and meet them beyond the village.

After a long wait, the small AFC boat came into view; numerous Indians had crowded on board. Mitchell tried to make the best of the situation, using the Indians as cordellers. But as the *Flora* passed into the Stone Walls, a stretch of eroded sandstone cliffs and narrow canyons along the upper Missouri River, Prince Maximilian bemoaned the fact that, due to crowded conditions, "we could not breathe freely enough duly to appreciate the surrounding scenery."[28]

Eventually, Mitchell persuaded the Gros Ventres to disembark and come later to Fort McKenzie to meet with their allies, the Blackfeet, and conduct a proper trade. Not entirely satisfied, the Indians departed. That

---

[26]Thomas and Ronnefeldt, p. 75.   [27]Ewers, *Blackfeet*, p. 60.
[28]Thwaites, Vol. 23, p. 74.

night, the traders kept a vigilant watch lest the keelboat again be overwhelmed.[29]

The next morning, the group continued their journey through the magnificent Stone Walls which Meriwether Lewis had described as "most romantic."[30] According to Maximilian, there was "nothing like it on the whole course of the Missouri; and we did not leave the deck for a single moment the whole forenoon."[31] Three hundred feet high in places, the bluffs rose nearly perpendicular to the river. Bodmer, a careful artist, ran out of paper sketching the towering formation, Citadel Rock.

Centuries of water trickling over the soft white sandstone created fantastic shapes and structures which a little imagination quickly transformed into "colonnades . . . little towers, pulpits, organs with their pipes, old ruins, fortresses, castles, churches. . . ."[32] As the *Flora* moved along, the passengers confronted visions reminding them of "a large blown-up fortress," "white fairy-like castles," and "an ancient Gothic chapel with a chimney."[33] Large herds of bighorn sheep climbed these dream-like formations and "stood on a lofty peak, far beyond the reach of our rifles, while the outlines of their forms were clearly defined against the bright blue sky."[34]

That night, after tying up the keelboat, some of the men climbed the spectacular cliffs: "When standing among the remarkable masses of the sand-stone, we fancied ourselves in a garden laid out in the old French style, where urns, obelisks, statues, as well as hedges and trees clipped into various shapes, surrounded the astonished spectator."[35]

On August 8th, at the Gates of the Stonewalls, the company encountered Seen From Afar,[36] a Blood warrior, and his wife, Pretty Woman. [37] Seen From Afar, named for his frequent distant journeys,[38] probably received that name after he returned from a bold adventure undertaken in his youth to earn a place in council.

Early in the spring, Seen From Afar and at least one other youth had

---

[29]Thwaites, Vol. 23, pp. 71-74.  [30]DeVoto, *Journals*, p. 123.
[31]Thwaites, Vol. 23, p. 77.  [32]Thwaites, Vol. 23, p. 78.
[33]Thwaites, Vol. 23, pp. 78-79 and p. 81.  [34]Thwaites, Vol. 23, pp. 79-80.
[35]Thwaites, Vol. 23, pp. 81-82. This magnificent stretch of river is today preserved in the Upper Missouri Wild and Scenic River.
[36]His Indian name is given as Peenaquim by Dempsey, *Red Crow*, p. 1; as Pinukwiim by Hungry Wolf, *Blood People*, p. 157; as Pi-inakoyim by Holterman, p. 28; as Pe-in-ah Coo-yem by Bradley, *MHSC*, Vol. III, p. 258; as Panarquinimaki in Buckley, p. 347; and, as Penahkwiem by Joseph Culbertson, draft manuscript, KP, UCLA, p. 90. Joe wrongly identifies Seen From Afar as Natawista's father.
[37]Dempsey, *Red Crow*, p. 5.  [38]Hungry Wolf, *Blood People*, p. 157.

# IF YOU SEND TRADERS, WE WILL TREAT THEM WELL

headed south. They were gone for more than a year and many in the tribe assumed they had been killed. But as the tribe gathered on Two Medicine River for the Sun Dance, the young men rode into camp on the first "spotted ponies" ever seen by the Blackfeet. The young men had beautiful wooden saddles decorated with high horns and silver, silver-encrusted bridles, and, on their heads, sombreros with silver and ribbon adornment.

The long journey had taken the youths to the Spanish southwest where, after patient observations, they had stolen the horses, fancy saddles, and sombreros. During the long journey home, they had lost several horses, but still returned with several fine horses. More importantly, the journey earned them the desired council seats. In thanks, Seen From Afar made an offering of his sombrero at the Sun Dance.[39]

The 1833 journey from which Seen From Afar was returning was more modest. The warrior and his wife had wintered with the Mandans in what is now North Dakota. The Mandans had given Seen From Afar, who was deeply religious, a special gift: the Different People Pipe.[40] Pretty Woman also had gifts: a sacred buffalo headdress and special ceremony that would become the foundation of the Blood women's secret Motokiks Society.[41]

Seen From Afar, a peaceable man but fearless warrior, was the son of Two Suns,[42] chief of the Fish Eaters band of the Blood Indians.[43] Mitchell invited the couple on board and Alexander Culbertson met Seen From Afar,[44] beginning a lifelong friendship which would profoundly affect both men.

That Kenneth McKenzie allowed Prince Maximilian to enter the Blackfeet country suggests the Company felt reasonably secure in their

---

[39]Holterman, p. 34; Hugh Welch in correspondence with the author. Welch is an enrolled member of the Blackfeet tribe who spent most of his life on their Montana reservation where he heard many of the old stories from his great-grandmother, Caroline Connoyer, who was born to Black Bear Woman, the sister of Mountain Chief, and a French trapper, in the mid-1840s. The story that Welch heard about "How the Blackfeet got the Pinto Ponies" does not give any names for the involved youth. That this was Seen From Afar is the author's conclusion based on stories of his trip to the Spanish southwest.

[40]Hungry Wolf, *Blood People*, p. 157; Dempsey, *Red Crow*, p. 5, calls it the Longtime Medicine Pipe.

[41]Hungry Wolf, *Blood People*, p. 157; Dempsey, *Red Crow*, p. 5, calls it the *Motoki* society. Both the Different People Pipe and the Motokiks Society remain integral parts of current Blood culture.

[42]Dempsey, *Red Crow*, p. 1, gives his Indian name as Stoó-kya-tosi.

[43]Dempsey, *Red Crow*, pp. 1-3.     [44]Thwaites, Vol. 23, pp. 82-83.

relationship with the tribe. Nonetheless, the AFC had never before maintained a fort among the Blackfeet for a full year and, as they neared Fort McKenzie, David Mitchell had qualms. These increased when no one appeared downstream to welcome the returning traders, as was customary. Mitchell decided to tie up about twelve miles below the fort and reconnoiter the area. Understanding the potential dangers, he directed Culbertson to retreat downriver if he had not returned by midnight.

As the men aboard the *Flora* waited apprehensively, they heard Indian drumming from near Fort McKenzie and the howling of wolves. About 10:30, Mitchell returned but, having lost his way, without news of the fort. The men slept fitfully, wondering what awaited them.[45]

The next morning, in a heavy rain, the *Flora* slowly approached the fort. A small mounted party of Company men soon appeared. All was well, they reported, with a peaceful encampment of Indians awaiting the beginning of trade.[46]

Soon, the fort came into view with more than one thousand Blackfeet encamped on the surrounding prairie. The warriors welcomed the boat with musket fire and war whoops; the *Flora* returned their salute. As the men disembarked, two of the tribe's most distinguished chiefs, Iron Shirt, a Blood,[47] and Bear Chief, a Piegan,[48] greeted them. Bear Chief had "a large crooked nose" and long hair partially hiding his face. On his head, he wore "a round felt hat, with a brass rim, and a silver medal on his breast."[49] A long reception line awaited the newly arrived men.

On August 10, 1833, their first full day at Fort McKenzie, Iron Shirt threw a welcoming feast. His "spacious" tipi, "very clean and tastefully decorated," measured fifteen feet in diameter. The visitors sat on buffalo skins around the center fire as Iron Shirt offered them a tin of pemmican, dry grated meat mixed with sweet berries. What they did not eat, Iron Shirt consumed.

The chief then presented Mitchell a variety of presents, including a scarlet uniform he had received from the English. This signified his willingness now to trade with the Americans. Mitchell accepted the gifts, knowing they obligated him in return. "When the chief began to fill his

---

[45]Thomas and Ronnefeldt, p. 86.    [46]Thomas and Ronnefeldt, p. 98.
[47]Bodmer, p. 240, gives his Indian name as Mehkskehme-Sukahs.
[48]Bodmer, p. 243, gives his Indian name as Ninoch-Kiäiu.
[49]Thwaites, Vol. 23, p. 88.

# IF YOU SEND TRADERS, WE WILL TREAT THEM WELL    45

pipe, made of green talc, we rose and retired (quite in the Indian fashion) in silence, and without making any salutations."[50]

Meanwhile, the other Company men prepared for the traditional Indian reception, a solemn ritual that preceded the opening of trade. With the flag flying, the men fired small cannons to signal their readiness. The Indians responded with songs and weapons of their own and advanced toward the fort. When they reached the gate, it was opened and the cannons fired again. The chiefs and principal warriors entered. Elaborate ceremonies followed, with handshakes, presentation of gifts, offerings of drink and tobacco, and speeches. Throughout, the Indians beyond the gates continued to fire their guns and chant their songs. Finally, after all the bands had been properly received, the trading began.[51]

During his first weeks at Fort McKenzie, Alexander Culbertson had to absorb the daily functioning of the fort, the manner of Mitchell's leadership, his own role in the hierarchy, the customs of the Blackfeet, and the personalities of their chiefs. He needed to understand all this to be the successful trader he so wanted to be.

Fur traders had long since recognized the value of marrying Indian women. Not only did this provide female companionship in a country where white women did not exist but it also forged bonds between the tribe and the Company. Therefore, on the night of August 26, 1833, less than three weeks after arriving, Alexander Culbertson took a Piegan woman "of the family of the White Buffalo" for his wife. The bride, whose name has been lost, gave her husband a rifle with a horse to follow. Culbertson paid his new family $100.[52]

To celebrate the marriage and successful trade, the Piegans indulged in a day of alcohol, song, and dance. Finally, in the early hours of the 28th, they fell drunk and exhausted into their lodges. Their sleep came to an abrupt end at dawn when several hundred Assiniboine warriors charged the encampment. As the Assiniboines swooped down from the bluffs and crossed the valley toward the fort, the Company men rushed to defense.

The garrison manned the guns and fired on the advancing Assini-

---

[50]Thwaites, Vol. 23, pp. 123-124.   [51]Thwaites, Vol. 23, pp. 125-128.

[52]Thomas and Ronnefeldt, pp. 108-109. Considering Culbertson's yearly salary of just over $650, the money almost certainly came from the Company.

boines. Even Prince Maximilian took up arms. Forgetting his gun was already loaded, the Prince rammed another charge into it. Spying an Assiniboine within his range, Maximilian fired but the overloaded weapon threw him against the opposite wall of the bastion where he fell, stunned, to the floor.

Mitchell soon realized that the true object of Assiniboine wrath was not the fort but the Piegans and he ordered the AFC employees to hold their fire. As the Assiniboines neared, the Piegans hurried to the fort for protection. At the gate, Culbertson tried to help them inside but the Piegans blocked their own way by throwing their saddles and furs in first.

Long Hair, an Assiniboine warrior, rushed forward. Killing a Piegan, he demanded that Culbertson move out of the way. Culbertson refused. Although he could easily have killed the young trader, Long Hair saved his wrath for the Piegans. Forty years later, when the aged Long Hair received annuities at Fort Belknap where the equally aging Alexander Culbertson served as interpreter, the two men would laugh about their first meeting.[53]

After the Piegans sent a messenger to a nearby tribal encampment, several hundred additional warriors appeared

> galloping in groups, from three to twenty together, their horses covered with foam, and they themselves in their finest apparel, with all kinds of ornaments and arms, bows and quivers on their backs, guns in their hands, furnished with their medicines, with feathers on their heads; some had splendid crowns of black and white eagles' feathers, and a large hood of feathers hanging down behind . . . the upper part of their bodies partly naked . . . and carrying shields adorned with feathers and pieces of coloured cloth.[54]

As the reinforcements approached, the Assiniboines retreated across the Marias River.

Mitchell decided to battle alongside the Piegans. He and Culbertson joined the Piegans as they rode off after the Assiniboines, now encamped along the bluffs above the Marias. Several hundred Piegans crossed the river. The Assiniboines swiftly descended and engaged them in combat. Fleeing wildly back across the river, the Piegans left behind some fifteen dead comrades.

---

[53]Bradley, *MHSC*, Vol. III, p. 209.  [54]Thwaites, Vol. 23, pp. 150.

The Assiniboines crossed the river and the battle resumed. When Mitchell's and Culbertson's horses were shot out from under them, they withdrew. The Piegans, gathering their forces, ultimately pushed the Assiniboines back across the river. When night fell, the Assiniboines retreated to the Bear Paw mountains, having lost fewer than ten of their warriors while killing nearly forty Piegans.[55]

Maximilian watched in fascinated horror as, early in the fight, the Piegans wreaked vengeance on a fallen Assiniboine: "The men fired their guns at it; the women and children beat it with clubs, and pelted it with stones, the fury of the latter was particularly directed against the privy parts." The Prince wished to add the dead man's skull to his artifacts but "before I could obtain my wish, not a trace of the head was to be seen."[56]

The wounded included Culbertson's new in-law, White Buffalo, who had been shot in the head. His relatives carried him through the fort as they chanted, wailed, cried, and shook rattles to drive out the evil spirits. "He himself, though stupified (*sic*) and intoxicated, sung without intermission...."[57]

The battle over, the Piegans returned to Fort McKenzie to thank Mitchell. Distant Bear,[58] noting that no harm had come to him, attributed his good fortune to having had his portrait painted by Karl Bodmer.[59] For Alexander Culbertson, the honeymoon, in more ways than one, was over.

---

[55]Bradley, *MHSC,* Vol. III, pp. 207-210; Ewers, *Blackfeet,* pp. 62-63. For a contrary account of the number killed on both sides, see the account that Culbertson gave John J. Audubon in Audubon, Vol. II, p. 135, where it is claimed that seven Piegans died with another twenty wounded. This account gives no figures for the Assiniboine dead. Since Culbertson was the source for the mortality figures used by both Bradley and Audubon, it is difficult, if not impossible, to determine which is accurate.

[56]Thwaites, Vol. 23, p. 149.

[57]Thwaites, Vol. 23, p. 148.

[58]Bodmer, p. 249, gives his Indian name as Pioch-Kiäiu.

[59]Thwaites, Vol. 23, p. 152, identifies this individual as Bear Chief whereas Bodmer, p. 249, identifies him as Distant Bear.

# Chapter Three

# *"This is your land"*

In the beginning, all the world was water. Then one day, Napi, the Old Man, became curious about what lay below. He sent various animals down to explore. None found anything. Finally Napi sent down a muskrat. The muskrat remained below so long that Napi feared it had drowned. Eventually the muskrat surfaced, holding a ball of mud. Napi blew on the mud and it grew and grew until it became the whole earth.

Napi traveled across his creation, piling up rocks to make mountains, carving out streams and lakes and rivers, covering the plains with grass, causing berries and roots and trees to grow, creating birds and animals.[1] When he spoke, all his creatures understood him.

But Napi had made mistakes. The bighorn sheep, placed on the prairie, moved awkwardly. So Napi moved them to the mountains where they bounded easily across the cliffs. Napi was satisfied: "This place suits you."

In the mountains, Napi created the antelope. But the antelope ran fast and fell off the cliff. That would not do. So Napi took the antelope to the plains and the animal ran swiftly away. Napi declared, "This is your place."

Then Napi decided to make a woman and a child. He molded two lumps of clay into humans and told the forms, "You must be people." He covered the clay and walked away. The next day, the forms had changed somewhat. Napi covered them again and left. On the second day, and on the third, Napi found more changes. Finally, on the fourth day, Napi told the figures to rise and walk.[2]

Napi, the woman, and her child walked down to the river. The woman asked Old Man, "Will the people live forever?" Napi had not considered

---
[1] Ewers, *Blackfeet*, p. 3.
[2] Grinnell, *Blackfoot Lodge Tales*, pp. 137-138.

this. "We will have to decide," he said. "I will take this buffalo chip and throw it in the river. If it floats, the people will die for four days and then live again. But if it sinks, there will be an end to them."

The woman picked up a stone and said, "No, I will throw this stone. If it floats, the people will live forever. If it sinks, the people must die. That way, they will have sympathy for each other." The woman threw the stone into the river where it sank. "There," said Napi, "you have chosen. The people must die."

A few night laters, the child died. The woman cried and cried. Then she approached Napi: "Let us change this. The law you first made, let that be the rule." "No," replied Napi. "What is decided must be. The child is dead and it cannot be changed."[3]

In the beginning, the people were very poor, without clothing or food. Old Man took them onto the prairie, showed them the roots and berries, told them what to eat, and when to harvest it. In certain months, Napi explained, they could eat the bark of some trees.

Then he taught the people about the animals. "These are your herds," he said. "All these animals—the rats, squirrels, skunks, and beavers—are good to eat." The same was true of the birds. "You need not fear to eat the flesh of these creatures," Old Man declared. Then he explained the power of herbs, that the roots of certain ones, gathered in certain months, could cure sickness.

Great buffalo herds roamed the land. The buffalo had horns, but the people had no weapons. One day, as the people crossed the plains, the buffalo charged. They speared, killed, and ate the people. When Old Man saw the people lying dead, he asked the survivors why they did not eat the buffalo. They replied, "We have no way to kill them." Napi promised to make them a weapon.

He gathered sarvisberry shoots and peeled its bark. He flattened a piece of wood and affixed a string, creating a bow. Napi then plucked

---

[3]Grinnell, *Blackfoot Lodge Tales*, pp. 138-139; Wissler, *Mythology*, pp. 20-21; Hungry Wolf, *Ways*, p. 141; de Jong, p. 29. Wissler, p. 21, also gives a slight variant of this story in which the Old Woman, who had "great power," allowed the buffalo chip to be thrown but turned it into a rock before it hit the water, causing it to sink. Wissler and Hungry Wolf say the child was a daughter; Grinnell says only "child."

feathers from a bird. He split these and attached four to the sarvisberry shoots. But when Napi shot the arrow, it did not fly well. Then he attached three feathers and, this time, the arrow flew straight. Now, he needed an arrow point. After testing different stones, Old Man decided on black flint. Finally, Napi took his weapon and taught the people how to kill the buffalo.

The next time the buffalo charged, the people did not run. Instead, they used Napi's weapon and killed several buffalo. The people were happy. They cut the meat from the carcasses as Napi had taught them and cooked the meat over the fire they had learned to make from punk. From the land, the people gathered stones; they used hard stones to hollow out softer ones and make kettles.[4]

Now the people had weapons and medicine and kettles and fire. They had food in roots and plants and animals. From animal skins, they fashioned clothing and lodges. Napi had taught them how to survive in the land he had created. And so Napi decided it was time to leave, to form other people, and to teach them how to live.

Before he left, Napi marked the ground and told the people, "This is your land. It is full of animals and other things which I have given you. Let no other people come into it. When others cross the line, take your bows and arrows, your lances and your battle axes, and keep them out. If they remain, trouble will come."[5] Napi then disappeared, promising to return some day.[6]

It is tempting, even seductive, to believe that before the white man arrived, Plains Indians lived simple lives of joy and harmony. Unfortunately, this is no more accurate than Alexander Culbertson's fanciful tale of walking west to St. Louis. For the early Plains Indians, life consisted of one long struggle to survive.

In the early days, dogs carried the tribe's possessions on small travois as the nomadic peoples moved from place to place. Many items which would become standard fare in later years—large tipis, lodge furnishings, extra clothing, medicine bundles, dried meat, and wild fruits and vegeta-

---

[4]Grinnell, *Blackfoot Lodge Tales*, pp. 139-141.
[5]Grinnell, *Blackfoot Lodge Tales*, pp. 143-144.
[6]Grinnell, *Blackfoot Lodge Tales*, p. 257.

bles—were excess baggage in those days. What the dogs could not carry the Indian women did, usually on their backs. Since the strongest dog could only haul about seventy-five pounds,[7] the tribes alternated between periods of great feasting and virtual starvation.[8]

Obtaining food consumed nearly all the tribe's energy. Traveling bands could be no smaller than what was needed to kill the buffalo but no larger than what could be sustained by the hunt. Each tribe broke into hunting bands, usually including no more than twenty to thirty families related by blood.[9] Throughout the year, these bands moved constantly in pursuit of prey. In the warmer months, the buffalo grazed on rich, open grasslands; in winter, they sought shelter from the deep snows, subzero temperatures, and fierce winds in wooded valleys. Wherever the buffalo went, the Indians followed.

Weasel Tail, a Blood Indian, remembered his ancestors describing the buffalo hunt before horses and guns. After scouts located the buffalo, the men and women approached from downwind to prevent the animals from picking up their scent. The women then placed their travois upright in the ground and tied them together to create a small, semi-circular fence.

The women and dogs then hid behind the barrier while the tribe's swiftest runners doubled back to drive the herd towards the travois fence. As the buffalo neared the barrier, men closed in from the sides, cutting off their escape. As the women rose up shouting and the dogs began to bark, the buffalo became confused and the men closed in to kill them with lances and arrows. After the kill, the chief counted the dead animals and divided the meat and hides equally among the family groups.[10] Another technique involved stampeding the buffalo over a steep cliff. Some died from the fall while others, injured or stunned, were killed at the base of these so-called "buffalo jumps."[11]

In winter, the Indians camped in a sheltered valley and constructed a rough corral nearby. When the buffalo appeared, the tribe used the same methods of chase and panic to force the animals into the corral. Unfortunately, though, nature did not always cooperate. Sometimes the buffalo failed to appear; other times, shifting winds carried the human scents or

---

[7]Ewers, *Blackfeet*, pp. 10-11.      [8]Dempsey, *Red Crow*, p. 1.
[9]Ewers, *Blackfeet*, p. 10.
[10]Ewers, *Blackfeet*, pp. 11-12; Ewers, *Indian Life*, p. 9.
[11]Dempsey, *Red Crow*, p. 1.

sounds to the animals. Then the Indians suffered terribly. Many winters, if the hunt went badly and winter storms set in, starvation became commonplace.[12]

The buffalo supplied the Indians with more than food. Women used the heavy hides for tipi covers, winter clothing, mittens, moccasins, and bedding. The buffalo's thick neck hide made excellent war shields. Rawhide was used to stitch clothing and lodge covers as well as to bind stones to wooden handles for use as arrows, clubs, knives, mauls, and berry mashers. From soft skins, the women crafted bags known as parfleches for hauling and storing household goods.

The Indians' every need was satisfied by the natural world. Wild plants provided medicine. Sharpened stones and carved animal horns became pipes, eating utensils, knives, scraping blades, arrow points, and lance heads. The Indians crafted cooking pots from the earth's clay and used earth pigments for paints to decorate both their bodies and possessions.[13]

The first major change in Plains Indian culture occurred around 1730 with the introduction of the horse from the Spanish southwest. Exactly how the Blackfeet initially acquired horses is unclear. They may have captured them in battle[14] or, more probably, they gained them through peaceful trade with other tribes.[15] In any case, once the Blackfeet got horses, or "elk dogs,"[16] life became much easier.[17]

Horses could draw large travois and carry much heavier loads than dogs. Possessions became more numerous and a newfound concept of wealth evolved. This, however, created class distinctions among different bands and even within a band.[18] Most significantly, horses allowed hunters to race alongside the buffalo and bring them down with a well-placed arrow. Horses also made it possible to carry stores of dried meat, reducing the threat of starvation.

The arrival of horses greatly increased intertribal warfare. Not only did

---

[12]Ewers, *Blackfeet*, pp. 13-14.   [13]Ewers, *Blackfeet*, pp. 14-15.
[14]Ewers, *Indian Life*, p. 13.
[15]Ewers, *Blackfeet*, p. 23; Kehoe, *North American Indians*, p. 297.
[16]Ewers, *Indian Life*, p. 13; Ewers, *Blackfeet*, p. 22, translates this as "ponokamita."
[17]Ewers, *Blackfeet*, pp. 22-23.
[18]Ewers, *Blackfeet*, p. 18; Kehoe, *North American Indians*, p. 313.

the Indians now have more time to pursue their enemies, they also had an incentive to do so as they sought to acquire more horses. Since horses represented wealth, young men frequently engaged in horse-stealing expeditions to prove their bravery or to acquire the wealth needed to claim a bride.

The tribes drew a bright line between "stealing" from a friend, an act often punishable by death, and "capturing" the goods of an enemy, an act of courage and honor.[19] Of course, one raid usually led to a counter raid. Long before the traders of the American Fur Company arrived on the upper Missouri, tribes had established enemies.

Soon after horses came guns. In 1738, members of Pierre La Vérendrye's overland expedition noted some guns being traded in the Mandan villages.[20] The Mandans lived year-round in six fortified villages on the Missouri near the mouth of Heart River in what is now North Dakota where, in addition to raising crops, they carried on a thriving intertribal trade.[21] As the location of these villages became known, white traders became an increasingly common sight, bringing with them a variety of manufactured goods. In addition to the Mandans' agricultural crops, visiting nomadic tribes came to barter for iron and brass arrowheads, tomahawks, axes, knives, metal cooking pots, awls, buttons, blankets, decorative bracelets, trade cloth, horses, guns, and ammunition.[22]

The Mandans well understood the value of their trading network and the potential competition the white traders represented. To keep the trade for themselves, they warned Europeans against traveling inland, citing the ferocious nature of the nomadic tribes. The strategy succeeded and, for many years, few whites ventured beyond the Mandan villages.[23]

Then in 1804, the Lewis and Clark expedition arrived. Their many charges included learning more about the intertribal trading structure.[24] Most importantly, though, President Thomas Jefferson had charged Lewis with finding "the most direct and practicable water communication across this continent, for the purposes of commerce."[25] Nothing the Mandans told Lewis and Clark could discourage them from continuing their westward trek.

The expedition enjoyed incredible overall success. Their one fatal

---

[19]Dempsey, *Red Crow*, p. 2.  [20]Ewers, *Indian Life*, p. 3.
[21]Kehoe, *North American Indians*, p. 297; Ewers, *Indian Life*, p. 3.
[22]Ewers, *Indian Life*, p. 26.  [23]Ewers, *Indian Life*, p. 58.
[24]Ewers, *Indian Life*, p. 31.  [25]DeVoto, *Journals*, p. xxxvii.

encounter with the Plains Indians, however, would haunt relations between the Blackfeet and the Americans for years to come.

On their 1806 return trip, Lewis and Clark split up to do more extensive explorations in what is now Montana. Clark followed the southerly Yellowstone River while Lewis and nine men took a northerly course. The two groups planned to rendezvous at a designated site farther east.

In mid-July, Lewis and three men set out to try to find the source of the Marias River which Lewis believed would mark the northwestern boundary of the Louisiana Purchase. On horseback, they traveled to Cutbank Creek, deep in Blackfeet country. Determining that the source of the Marias probably lay farther west and intent on keeping the scheduled rendezvous, Lewis decided to turn back. He was also influenced by reports of an apparently recent, large encampment of Indians near the forks of the Marias. "[W]e consider ourselves extreemly (*sic*) fortunate in not having met with these people," Lewis wrote.[26]

Their fortunes soon changed. On July 26, 1806, Lewis descried a group of Indians near the junction of Two Medicine River and Badger Creek. Although considering this "a very unpleasant sight," Lewis approached them "in a friendly manner."[27] Cautiously, the four expedition members met the eight Piegans and shook hands. Although the Indians outnumbered his men, Lewis had little choice but to spend that night with them in the little river valley.

During the evening, Lewis smoked with the Piegans and, using sign language, told them, falsely, that he had sought them out to encourage them to make peace with their neighboring tribes. The evening passed uneventfully but, ever cautious, Lewis posted a man to guard their horses while they slept.

Shortly after dawn, Lewis heard George Drouillard arguing with one of the Indians. "Damn you. Let go of my gun," Drouillard shouted. When the Indian ran, Lewis's men pursued him and, when they caught him, Reuben Fields stabbed him. The wounded Indian ran a short distance, then fell dead. A fracas ensued and Lewis shot and wounded another Piegan. The Indians then rode off, leaving behind some horses,

---

[26]DeVoto, *Journals*, p. 433.     [27]DeVoto, *Journals*, p. 434.

guns, and their dead comrade. Before fleeing, Lewis placed one of the expedition's commemorative medals around the neck of the fallen Piegan "that they might be informed who we were."[28]

Although Lewis believed the Indians to be Gros Ventres, a contemporary Canadian trader, David Thompson, identified them as Piegans. Years later, the Piegans would identify the fallen warrior to Alexander Culbertson and the AFC traders as He That Looks at the Calf.[29] This episode hardened the hearts of the Piegans and the Blackfeet against the American traders whom they called "Big Knives." As a result, for years, they kept their trade with the English, or "Northern White Men."[30]

From their earliest encounters with the Blackfeet, white men recognized them as three separate, albeit affiliated, tribes: the Piegan or Pikuni;[31] the Kainah or Blood;[32] and, Northern Blackfoot, Siksika, or Blackfoot proper.[33] Politically independent, the tribes shared a language, common culture, and often intermarried. They also frequently banded together to wage war on common enemies.

While it became increasingly common to lump the tribes together under the rubric of the Blackfeet nation, the bands maintained a fierce sense of proud independence.[34] And it was a great mistake to assume that they were above internecine quarrels, as David Mitchell learned when he and Alexander Culbertson greeted the assembled tribe at Fort McKenzie in 1833.

Soon after their arrival, Mitchell took aside Bear Chief, the Piegan chief, to present him with gifts designed to show his status as an unwavering friend of the American Fur Company. In addition to a double-barreled shotgun, Mitchell gave the chief a beautiful new uniform and a red felt hat.[35]

Mitchell also presented uniforms to several other chiefs but none so

---

[28]DeVoto, *Journals*, pp. 436-439.  [29]Ewers, *Blackfeet*, pp. 47-48.
[30]Ewers, *Blackfeet*, p. 45.
[31]Also known as Far-Off Robes or Rough-Tanned Robes.
[32]Translated as Many Chiefs.
[33]Schultz, *Signposts*, p. 15. Schultz spells Kainah as "Kai'na." Hungry Wolf, *Indian Tribes*, p. 3, give a fourth subdivision: the South Piegans, also Pikuni, being that part of the tribe which now lives in Montana. In Canada, Piegan is spelled Peigan.
[34]Ewers, *Blackfeet*, p. 5.  [35]Thwaites, Vol. 23, p. 127.

resplendent as that which he had bestowed on Bear Chief. Apparently Mitchell did not anticipate that this lavish gift would evoke jealousy and animosity among the Bloods. But it did. Iron Shirt, the Blood chief who had hosted the feast for Mitchell, Culbertson, and Maximilian, was so angered that he refused even to look at Bear Chief. As the Bloods spoke openly of murder, Bear Chief retreated to Mitchell's room for protection.

The Bloods, apparently deciding it would be imprudent to kill Bear Chief himself, killed his nephew instead before fleeing. The Piegans probably would have gone after the Bloods to avenge their kinsman's death if they had not themselves been attacked by the Assiniboines the next day.[36]

As the winter of 1833 settled in on the upper Missouri, a spectacular event occurred. About 10 p.m. on November 13, shooting stars became visible in the night sky. Over the next few hours, the number of falling stars increased markedly until, by the early morning hours, it has been estimated that they fell at the rate of 10,000 an hour. The celestial spectacle lasted throughout the night and, more slowly, for the next twenty-four hours.[37] The Blood calendar remembered 1833 as "Stars—when they fell."[38]

The Plains Indians, and indeed their more educated white contemporaries, looked upon the display with awe and fear. Many believed that the world was coming to an end. Today, astronomers recognize this display as the Leonides meteor shower. But for the Blackfeet, no such explanation would have sufficed. Indeed, the world they had known was coming to an end.

In the one hundred years since the Blackfeet first acquired horses and guns, much had changed and they had no desire to return to the days when all their energies had been focused on mere survival. The manufactured goods obtained from white men not only simplified their lives, they had become an essential part of their existence. Yet these goods had also brought greed and materialism into their culture. Unwittingly, the tribes had become active players in the very forces that would conspire to destroy the world they had known.

---

[36]Schultz, *Signposts*, pp. 39-41.   [37]Walton-Raji, p. 611.
[38]Hungry Wolf, *Blood People*, p. 197.

Chapter Four

# "You are too diffident of your own powers"

Alexander Culbertson, who so wanted to prove himself an able trader, quickly found himself dissatisfied at Fort McKenzie. Weeks after arriving, in early September, Culbertson wrote Kenneth McKenzie with his grievances.

High on Culbertson's list were the exorbitant prices charged at the Fort McKenzie Company store. Culbertson brazenly suggested that McKenzie either cut the prices or allow a reduction for clerks. McKenzie demurred, suggesting that prices at Fort McKenzie were only "proportionably higher" than at the Company store in Minnesota, reflecting "the risk & difficulty of getting them there." Furthermore, McKenzie noted that Culbertson had been "long enough engaged in the Indian trade to know the general terms on which Merchandise is sold at the various trading posts in the Indian country."[1]

Culbertson's second concern presented a more significant problem. Before McKenzie sent Culbertson to the Blackfeet post, the two had discussed McKenzie's hope that Culbertson would take command of Fort McKenzie the following spring when David Mitchell took the returns to Fort Union. At the time, Culbertson apparently agreed but now he expressed reservations.

McKenzie tried to allay Culbertson's doubts by emphasizing the "entire confidence I know I might repose in you." Surely, McKenzie wrote, "you are too diffident of your own powers," assuring Culbertson that his experience and talents were "fully equal . . . to the charge of an establishment such as Fort McKenzie."

But Culbertson hoped for another assignment, perhaps to Fort Pierre. Although McKenzie found it "as remote from my principle as my practice to press an irksome duty on any gentleman in my employ," he could not accommodate Culbertson because he had no available replacement.

---

[1] Kenneth McKenzie to Alexander Culbertson, 21 Jan 1834. *Fort Union Letter Books*, MoHS.

Acknowledging his "regret" that Culbertson's situation was "less comfortable than you expected and than I wished it to be," McKenzie promised to try "to remedy the evils complained of," believing that Culbertson would find him "just and as liberal as my situation will admit."[2]

That same day, McKenzie wrote David Mitchell, Culbertson's superior, regarding the young trader's dissatisfaction. McKenzie conveyed his complete trust and confidence in Culbertson's abilities, expressing his hope that "the mountains of last fall have dwindled into mole-hills." Still, McKenzie inserted a prayerful hope that Mitchell might "resume your command for one little year more."[3]

McKenzie's plea fell on deaf ears; Mitchell intended to leave Fort McKenzie for good in the spring. By March 1834, it was clear that Culbertson would have to assume command of the Blackfeet post, at least for the summer. McKenzie, anticipating the dissatisfaction this would kindle in his employee, instructed Mitchell to "assure [Culbertson] of my respect & confidence that under his management nothing will be left undone which ought to be done & which he has the means to effect." Finally, and presciently, McKenzie urged Mitchell to "impress on Mr. Culbertson the importance of the adage 'an ounce of precaution is worth a pound of cure.'"[4]

Soon after, Mitchell departed, leaving Culbertson in charge of Fort McKenzie and a garrison of twenty men. The season's trade, while only fair,[5] certainly justified continuation of the post and, while both McKenzie and Mitchell had stressed their faith in Culbertson's abilities, the young trader continued to have doubts.

Mitchell carried to Fort Union yet another apprehensive letter from Culbertson. McKenzie, who had sincerely hoped that Culbertson would have grown into his position, received the letter with annoyance. Nevertheless, he recognized it was foolhardy to leave someone in charge of a post they felt incapable of holding. Therefore, on July 8, 1834, McKenzie notified Culbertson: ". . . in consequence of your mistrust of your powers, I have been compelled to take Mr. [James] Kipp from the Mandan post to assume the charge of Fort McKenzie. . . ."[6] But Kipp would not reach Fort

---

[2]Kenneth McKenzie to Alexander Culbertson, 21 Jan 1834. *Fort Union Letter Books,* MoHS.
[3]Kenneth McKenzie to David Mitchell, 21 Jan 1834. *Fort Union Letter Books,* MoHS.
[4]Kenneth McKenzie to David Mitchell, 8 Mar 1834. *Fort Union Letter Books,* MoHS.
[5]Bradley, *MHSC,* Vol. III, p. 210.
[6]Kenneth McKenzie to Alexander Culbertson, 4 Jul 1834. Chouteau Collection, MoHS. Reprinted in Abel, pp. 371-372.

McKenzie until fall and, by then, Culbertson's impression of his abilities would have changed dramatically.

In mid-June, two sons of Bull's Back Fat, chief of the Buffalo Followers, the pre-eminent band of the Blood tribe,[7] arrived at Fort McKenzie with their sister and her husband.[8] The four had planned a raid against the Crows but abandoned the scheme,[9] perhaps at Culbertson's urging. After receiving gifts of tobacco and ammunition, the four headed north for their winter camp.[10]

A few miles from Fort McKenzie, at the Cracon du Nez, the Crows attacked them. One of Bull's Back Fat's sons and his son-in-law were killed. The other son, though wounded, managed to steal a Crow horse and flee to Fort McKenzie where he told Culbertson what had transpired.[11] The two returned to the scene, collected the bodies of the slain warriors, and brought them back to Fort McKenzie to be "decently interred." Finding no evidence of the woman, Culbertson assumed she had been taken hostage.[12]

Ten days later, as Culbertson sat in front of the fort, he noticed movement in the bushes across the river. Crossing the river in a skiff, he found Bull's Back Fat's daughter huddled in the bushes.[13] The woman was naked, with bunches of sagebrush tied about her, and "in a most wretched and pitiable condition."[14] Her feet had been badly cut by days of walking barefoot across the prairie. Culbertson took the woman, suffering from exhaustion, exposure, and starvation, back to the fort.

The woman told Culbertson that, immediately after the attack, the Crows had headed for their country. At night, they kept her bound to prevent escape. In their village, they forced her to don her husband's bloody shirt and perform the scalp dance with her brother's and husband's scalps tied to her hair.[15] After several days of humiliating captivity, she managed to procure a knife, hiding it under her clothing. The next day, as she worked alongside a Crow woman, the captive bent over and her hidden knife fell to the ground.

---

[7]Dempsey, *Red Crow*, p. 6.  [8]Audubon, Vol. II, p. 178.
[9]Bradley, *MHSC*, Vol. III, p. 211.  [10]Audubon, Vol. II, p. 178.
[11]Bradley, *MHSC*, Vol. III, p. 211; Audubon, Vol. II, p. 178.
[12]Audubon, Vol. II, p. 178.
[13]Bradley, *MHSC*, Vol. III, p. 211.  [14]Audubon, Vol. II, p. 179.
[15]Audubon, Vol. II, p. 179.

Her transgression was immediately reported to the Crow chiefs who ordered her stripped as punishment. That night, believing she would never attempt to escape unclothed, the Crows left her untied. Realizing this might be her only opportunity to escape, she fled, despite her nakedness. For four cold and wet days, she traveled "with *absolutely no covering of any kind*" across the prairie.[16]

The woman also brought Culbertson news of great significance: the Crows planned to attack Fort McKenzie, scare off the traders, and capture the fort's supplies.[17] Several days earlier, all of the fort's horses had been driven off. Culbertson had believed this to be the work of the Crows who had attacked the Blood warriors but, upon hearing the woman's story, he realized at least two bands of Crows must be in the region. Since tribes routinely dispatched scouting parties before an attack, Culbertson immediately recognized the danger represented by two separate parties of Crow warriors.[18]

The loss of the fort's horses had created a critical problem since the men relied almost exclusively on the hunt for food. Without horses, the hunters had been unable to procure rations. Already the personnel had consumed the fresh meat as well as the emergency stores of dried meat. The men had even slaughtered the Company's dogs for food. With nothing left to eat, the men boiled parfleches, the buffalo hide pouches used to store dried meat. The boiled parfleches, softened to the consistency of glue, made disgusting food but provided necessary nutrients. They could not, however, ward off hunger pains.[19]

Upon learning of the Crows' plans, Culbertson began preparing for a possibly long siege. He readied the three pound cannons and established a guard schedule. But no solution existed for the food shortage.

On June 25, four hundred Crows, led by Rotten Belly,[20] set up camp about a quarter mile from the fort. Culbertson waited. Soon, a body of well-armed warriors approached and requested admittance. Culbertson

---

[16]Audubon, Vol. II, p. 179. Emphasis in original. Taylor, "He Hated the Blackfeet." Cf. Bradley, *MHSC*, Vol. III, pp. 211-212, for a slightly different account of the woman's conditions during her captivity. Audubon's version is believed more reliable since it was taken from Culbertson's journal of events at Fort McKenzie kept during 1834. Many years had passed by the time Culbertson told the story to Bradley and it is likely he had forgotten some details.
[17]Denig, p. 172.
[18]Bradley, *MHSC*, Vol. III, p. 212.
[19]Bradley, *MHSC*, Vol. III, p. 214.
[20]Taylor, "He Hated the Blackfeet," gives his Indian name as Arrapooash.

refused, stating that the Crows had declared war by driving off the fort's horses. His fort was only open to friends.

The Crows replied that they had come to discuss the horses and, if Culbertson would admit them, they could clear up the problem. The warriors "used every artifice in their power to persuade [Culbertson] to let in a few of them to smoke the pipe of peace, assuring [him] that their intentions were good, and that they loved the white man."[21] Culbertson still refused, insisting that the Crows return the Company horses. "Then," said Culbertson, "we can believe that the Crows do not come for war."[22] Finally, Culbertson had Bull's Back Fat's daughter show herself. The Crows, believing her dead, realized she must have revealed their plans.

The Crows tried again to gain entry, offering Culbertson their best horses for "the privilege of letting some of them come in," but Culbertson would have none of it, being fully aware "of their treacherous intentions." Culbertson then sent detachments to each bastion, ordering them to shoot any Crow who approached. Informing the Crows of his orders, Culbertson stressed that he "did not wish to strike the first blow, but that if they commenced they would go off with small numbers, and sore hearts."[23]

James Coats, a white trapper who lived among the Crows, was traveling with the war party. Meeting with Culbertson, he confirmed that the warriors were "determined to take the fort." Culbertson told Coats to advise them that "if they thought themselves able [to take the fort], to come and try." Seeing the cannons pointed in their direction, the warriors pulled back but they were not yet ready to abandon their scheme.

The situation inside the fort was becoming desperate due to lack of food. Several of Culbertson's men, led by Alexander Harvey, urged their superior to fire on the recalcitrant Crows, arguing that they were facing slow death by starvation. Culbertson refused, knowing an attack on the Crows would destroy any future hope of trading with them. Although Fort McKenzie was not a Crow post, they frequently visited the area and their enmity would create an untenable situation for the Company.

Culbertson urged patience, arguing that the Indians would grow weary of the siege and depart. Alexander Harvey, however, continued to advocate insurrection and Culbertson learned that some men planned to seize the keelboat and desert.[24]

---

[21]Audubon, Vol. II, p. 179.      [22]Bradley, *MHSC*, Vol. III, p. 213.
[23]Audubon, Vol. II, p. 179.
[24]Bradley, *MHSC*, Vol. III, p. 215, says that this is when Culbertson fired on the Crows.

The next day, the Crows tried anew to capture the fort but once again gave up "after a long and persuasive talk." The warriors then crossed the river and, from a high bank, began firing on the fort. Culbertson, his patience sorely tried by both the intransigent Crows and his mutinous men, "let loose a cannon ball among them," causing the Crows to scatter.[25]

The siege had ended[26] but Culbertson and his men still lacked food and horses to procure it. However, with the Crows dispersed, the hunters could venture slight distances to hunt small game. True relief appeared two days later when a party of Bloods arrived with a large quantity of meat that they willingly shared with the famished traders. The Bloods also presented fifteen horses, captured from the Crows, to Culbertson.[27]

Later, Culbertson learned the full extent of the Crows' plans. They had brought pack horses to carry off the fort's effects,[28] which would only have been possible if the warriors "accomplished the destruction of the building and the massacre of ourselves."[29] Nevertheless, the Crows claimed they did not intend to harm the traders; they simply wanted to shut down the post so that the Blackfeet could not obtain firearms.[30]

Culbertson subsequently blamed David Mitchell for leaving the fort insufficiently supplied; Mitchell, however, accused Culbertson of "keeping back the meat he had salted and preserved with so much care."[31] Although there is no evidence that Culbertson held back food, he may have exacerbated the situation by giving the Crows some dried meat in an attempt to convince them that the fort was well-provisioned.[32]

---

[25]Audubon, Vol. II, p. 180; Bradley, *MHSC*, Vol. III, p. 215.

[26]The length of the siege is variously reported. Bradley, *MHSC*, Vol. III, p. 215, states that "after ten days of starvation, when even the last parfleche had vanished. . . ." A contemporaneous letter from J. Archdale Hamilton to Kenneth McKenzie, written 17 Sep 1834, states that "the Crows have compelled [Culbertson] and people to live on Cords Parfleche for 15 days." Chouteau Collection, MoHS. Also reprinted in Abel, pp. 287-288. Taylor, "He Hated the Blackfeet," and Audubon, Vol. II, pp. 179-180, suggest the actual siege lasted only a couple of days. Both of these accounts were probably taken from Culbertson's contemporaneous journal. Denig, pp. 177-180, gives another version of the story, claiming that the siege ended when the Blackfeet arrived and that the cannon was not fired at all, although Culbertson was prepared to do so. Denig, p. 180, claims the siege lasted "nearly a month." The most likely explanation for these discrepancies is that the men began to run short of food as soon as the horses were run off while the actual siege was relatively short. The story probably became embellished as time went on.

[27]Audubon, Vol. II, p. 180.    [28]Denig, p. 173.
[29]Audubon, Vol. II, p. 180.    [30]Bradley, *MHSC*, Vol. III, p. 215.
[31]James Archdale Hamilton to Alexander Culbertson, 12 Jan 1835. *Fort Union Letter Books*, MoHS.    [32]Denig, p. 178.

In any case, the personnel had withstood the siege and Alexander Culbertson had successfully maintained the American Fur Company's presence in the Blackfeet country.³³ James Archdale Hamilton, commanding Fort Union during Kenneth McKenzie's absence, praised Culbertson for his "conduct when the rascally Crows so annoyed you," assuring him that he had meted out the correct degree of punishment.³⁴ His adept handling of the Crow siege had also convinced Culbertson that he was, indeed, well-suited for command.

Kenneth McKenzie, however, could not forget the young trader's qualms and, in December 1835, he informed Company headquarters that he expected Culbertson to quit the fur trade when his contract expired.³⁵ But McKenzie had seriously underestimated his young employee. That spring, when Culbertson's contract expired, he readily signed on for another term.

For the Crows, the consequences of the siege had not played out. Rotten Belly, leader of the war party, was one of the greatest chiefs the Crows had ever known. Forty-five years old, tall and dignified, his bravery had never been questioned. Rotten Belly held no ill will towards the white man but, like most Indians, he could not stand humiliation.

Rotten Belly had always considered the Fort McKenzie siege ill-conceived; he agreed only to placate his people. After their forced retreat, he angrily told his tribesmen that the ill-begotten enterprise had brought them shame and called for a raid against the Bloods to wash away their disgrace.

With their war party formed, the Crows moved up the Missouri where, unexpectedly, they encountered twelve Gros Ventre warriors. "Now," said Rotten Belly, "we shall see who are brave men. I shall lead the attack though I feel that I am to fall in it." With that, the Crows rushed the Gros Ventres, killing them all.

Despite their ultimate defeat, the Gros Ventres resisted bravely, wounding several including Rotten Belly. With his last breath, Rotten

---

³³Bradley, *MHSC*, Vol. III, pp. 213-215; Holterman, pp. 45-46. For a very different account, see Taylor, "He Hated the Blackfeet," and Denig, pp. 177-180.

³⁴James Archdale Hamilton to Alexander Culbertson, 12 Jan 1835. *Fort Union Letter Books*, MoHS.     ³⁵Abel, pp. 376-378.

Belly addressed his warriors: "Go back to my people with my dying words. Tell them ever hereafter to keep peace with the whites."

The Crows frequently recalled Rotten Belly's words in subsequent years and the Crows never again took up arms against the white men.[36]

In April 1836, for the first time in three years, Alexander Culbertson left the remote Fort McKenzie to take the furs to Fort Pierre. Culbertson, who had survived Indian battles and near-starvation at the hands of the Crows, regarded Fort Pierre as civilization. But, en route back to Fort McKenzie, he encountered a brutal reminder of the ruthless frontier world in which he had chosen to live.

From the earliest years of the fur trade, certain families of mixed-blood Indians lived at or adjacent to the American Fur Company forts. At Fort Union, a family named Deschamps lived nearby and, over the years, they had created numerous problems for the Company. When the AFC steamboat arrived at Fort Union on June 28, 1836, with Alexander Culbertson aboard, the days of the Deschamps family were numbered.

The steamboat's arrival always provided an excuse for excessive drink and the excuse had become a ritual. That day, sixty to seventy Company men began drinking at Fort Union while, at nearby Fort William, the mixed-bloods imbibed. During the peak of the revelry at Fort William, the Deschamps sons killed another mixed-blood trapper named Jack Rem. The men at Fort Union quickly heard of the assault and decided that this would be the last murder committed by a Deschamps.

The Company men, equipped with munitions supplied by Kenneth McKenzie, headed to Fort William where they brutally exterminated the entire Deschamps clan. When Mother Deschamps begged for her life and that of her children, she was shot through the heart.

If the AFC men had any regrets, it was not reflected in the words of Charles Larpenteur, the clerk at Fort Union: "Such was the end of this troublesome family, after which peace and comfort we enjoyed."[37] What role, if any, Alexander Culbertson played in this gruesome affair is not known.

---

[36]Bradley, *MHSC*, Vol. III, p. 216. Taylor, "He Hated the Blackfeet," gives a very different version of Rotten Belly's death as does Denig, pp. 181-184.

[37]Larpenteur, pp. 80-84.

Chapter Five

## *"Nothing but melancholy wrecks of human life"*

When the American Fur Company's steamer, *St. Peters*,[1] pulled away from the St. Louis docks in the spring of 1837, no one knew the devastation it would bring the upper Missouri tribes. In addition to the season's trade goods, the steamboat carried smallpox, a disease for which the tribes had few immunities.

The *St. Peters* departed on schedule with the crew blissfully unaware of the horrors about to unfold. Near Fort Leavenworth, a mulatto employee became ill but Bernard Pratte, the steamboat captain, doubted that he had smallpox. Short-handed, Pratte refused to put the employee ashore at Robidoux's post in the Blacksnake Hills.

By the time the steamboat reached the Indian agency at Council Bluffs, the disease "was fully developed,"[2] having already claimed several lives. At this point, Pratte should have stopped and waited for the disease to run its course. But whether out of ignorance, cupidity, or a belief that he could outrun the disease, he pushed on, arriving at Fort Clark on June 18.

Here, several sources claimed an elderly Indian stole a blanket from a dying man[3] and, despite entreaties from Francis Chardon, head trader at Fort Clark, refused to surrender it.[4] Chardon supposedly promised amnesty for the theft and a new blanket, to no avail. Chardon then allegedly sent messengers to the Indian villages warning them to stay away, but they ignored him, bringing whole villages to the fort to trade.[5] Chardon, however, reported none of this in his journal which first mentions smallpox on July 14 when he perfunctorily recorded the death of a young Mandan "of the Small Pox."[6]

---

[1] Bradley, *MHSC*, Vol. III, p. 221, gives the name of the steamboat as *Trapper* but all other sources give it as *St. Peters*.
[2] Joshua Pilcher to Gen. William Clark, 5 Feb 1838. NAM, M234/884.
[3] Wm. N. Fulkerson, upper Missouri Indian sub-agent, to General William Clark, 20 Sep 1837. NAM, M234/884.
[4] Bradley, *MHSC*, Vol. III, p. 222; Chittenden, *Fur Trade*, Vol. II, p. 614; Holterman, p. 49.
[5] Chittenden, *Fur Trade*, Vol. II, p. 614.   [6] Abel, p. 121.

Although Bernard Pratte should have waited downriver for the disease to run its course, the AFC found itself in a difficult position. The Indians expected the steamboat and its goods and it was too late to send another upriver. If the trade goods had not arrived, the tribes probably would have suspected the Company of stealing their goods. The Company was not acting selfishly since their livelihood depended upon healthy Indians with whom to trade.[7]

In any case, the disease had reached the upper Missouri and the horror was about to begin.

Smallpox, a highly contagious viral disease, can be transmitted before a carrier realizes he is ill. The disease smolders for up to two weeks before overwhelming its victim with chills, high fever, and prostration. Body aches and convulsions often occur before the characteristic scabby rash erupts.[8] Two-thirds of the stricken Indians died before developing the rash.[9]

Three Arikara passengers traveling aboard the *St. Peters* contracted smallpox during the upriver voyage and, although recovered before reaching Fort Clark, they remained infectious. They probably introduced smallpox to the nearby villages.[10] Once it hit the Mandan villages, it "continued as long as there was any one left to attack."[11]

Many died quickly. Seized by pains in the head and back, they succumbed within hours. The corpse then turned black and swelled grotesquely, magnifying the horror for observers.[12] Many of these victims may have died from other than smallpox; cholera, too, may have swept the prairie that year.[13]

Some Mandans vowed revenge, but they had neither the strength nor numbers to effect their plans. When they fell ill and died, the survivors decided the dead had been punished for contemplating reprisals. They charted a new course: beg the white man for help. But, by then, the traders could do nothing. Hundreds died each day and burials became impossible. Bodies were piled in a heap and thrown off cliffs. The stench

---

[7]Chittenden, *Fur Trade*, Vol. II, p. 613.
[8]*Merck Manual of Diagnosis and Therapy*, p. 30.   [9]Denig, p. 71.
[10]Ferch (Winter, 1983), p. 4.
[11]Chittenden, *Fur Trade*, Vol. II, p. 614.   [12]Thwaites, Vol. 23, p. 34.
[13]J. A. Hamilton to Pierre Chouteau, 25 Feb 1838. Chouteau-Papin Collection, MoHS.

permeated the village: "The prairie all around is a vast field of death, covered with unburied corpses, and spreading, for miles, pestilence and infection."[14]

Desperation now swept the villages. Many committed suicide. One chief, not yet stricken, prevailed upon his wife to dig his grave. When she was done, he climbed in and stabbed himself to death.[15] Those who escaped the disease fled, wandering alone across the prairie, finding food and shelter wherever they could. By mid-August, Francis Chardon stopped counting "as they die so fast that it is impossible."[16]

By the end of 1837, the Mandan tribe had been virtually exterminated. Only about thirty tribal members, mostly the very young and the elderly who had been exposed to an 1800 epidemic, remained. Summing up the tragedy, one observer wrote:

> ... the few that are left are as humble as dogs. No language can picture the scene of desolation which the country presents. In whatever direction we go, we see nothing but melancholy wrecks of human life. The tents are still standing on every hill, but no rising smoke announces the presence of human beings, and no sounds but the croaking of the raven and the howling of the wolf interrupt the fearful silence.[17]

From Fort Clark, the *St. Peters* proceeded to Fort Union, arriving in late June. Jacob Halsey, who had taken charge following Kenneth McKenzie's retirement, had the only active case of smallpox when the steamer docked.[18] But that was enough. Following instructions found in *Dr. Thomas' Medical Book*, the employees attempted to vaccinate the men and women at the fort. Without vaccine, they used live smallpox serum from Halsey,[19] a process known as variolation.[20]

Unfortunately, as Charles Larpenteur, AFC clerk, noted, "the operation proved fatal to most of our patients." Within two weeks, smallpox ravaged the fort: "It was awful—the scene in the fort, where some went crazy, and others were half eaten up by maggots before they died.... Many died, and those who recovered were so much disfigured that one could scarcely recognize them."[21]

---

[14]Thwaites, Vol. 23, p. 35.  
[15]Chittenden, *Fur Trade*, Vol. II, p. 614.  
[16]Abel, p. 126.  
[17]Thwaites, Vol. 23, p. 35.  
[18]Larpenteur, p. 109.  
[19]Larpenteur, p. 110.  
[20]Ferch (Spring, 1984), p. 4.  
[21]Larpenteur, p. 110.

At the height of the epidemic, a party of Assiniboines arrived to trade. They demanded entry to the fort which had been locked up to prevent crazed sufferers from fleeing, thereby spreading the disease. The employees tried to explain the dangers to the Assiniboines but failed. In desperation, they showed the visitors a small sick boy. His horribly scabbed face persuaded the Assiniboines to leave, but their brief stop cost them dearly: at least half of the group died.[22] And the disease now spread to their tribe.

Little Dog, an Assiniboine who regularly traded at Fort Union, grew distraught after his favorite child's death. He proposed to his wife that they kill their family before the disease left them so disfigured that they would present "a disgusting appearance in the future world." His wife agreed, but only if Little Dog killed her first; she could not bear to watch her children die. Little Dog concurred and methodically set about his work. First, he killed his horses and dogs. Next, he shot his wife and then cut his children's throats. Finally, he put a gun to his head and pulled the trigger.[23]

Eventually, the staff at Fort Union converted Fort William into a hospital with Indian women ministering to the sick and John Brazeau, an AFC employee, acting as undertaker. Brazeau could do little except dump the bodies in the bushes, a task that numbed his sensibilities. One day, when Larpenteur asked how many had died, Brazeau replied, "Only three, sir; but, according to appearances in the hospital, I think I shall have a full load to-morrow or next day."[24]

❖ ❖ ❖

The Blackfeet did not escape the smallpox epidemic. That spring, Culbertson had sent Alexander Harvey to Fort Union to deliver the winter's returns and pick up new supplies. When Harvey learned that the *St. Peters* carried smallpox, he hastily gathered the supplies and departed. Before he had gotten far, three cases of smallpox erupted on the keelboat: a young girl; a Blood Indian; and, a brawny white trader named LeDouck.

Wisely, Harvey halted the keelboat at the mouth of the Judith River and dispatched a messenger to apprise Culbertson of the situation. Culbertson ordered Harvey to stay put until the disease ran its course and cold weather set in. Meanwhile, some five hundred lodges of Blood and Pie-

---

[22]Larpenteur, p. 111.  [23]Denig, pp. 71-72.
[24]Larpenteur, p. 111.

gan Indians waited at Fort McKenzie for the keelboat. When they learned Culbertson had ordered the keelboat delayed, they threatened to bring it up by force.

Culbertson pleaded with them, explaining his decision and warning of the ravages that could follow if they went down to the boat. But the Bloods and Piegans did not believe the disease could be that deadly. They wanted their trade goods. When Culbertson realized that no exhortations would sway them, he relented and, against his better judgment, ordered the keelboat to proceed. Still, he admonished the tribe to hold the Company blameless if his predictions came to pass.[25]

Not knowing how the keelboat passengers were faring, Culbertson dispatched six employees to assist the crew. But tragedy so infused the upper Missouri that summer that even this mission could not escape. At one of the downstream rapids, a canoe capsized and four men died at what became known as Drowned Man's Rapids.[26]

When the survivors reached the keelboat, they found the girl recovered, the other two still suffering, but no new cases. The newly arrived men conveyed Culbertson's instructions and the keelboat headed for Fort McKenzie, landing toward the end of July. Soon after, the stricken Blood and LeDouck both died, but their deaths did not deter the Indians from demanding that trade begin.

After five days of trading, the Bloods and Piegans dispersed. The traders had little opportunity to consider their fate as smallpox soon enveloped the fort. Within days, fifty-one people at Fort McKenzie fell ill.[27] Culbertson himself contracted the disease but, thanks to previous vaccinations, his illness ran a relatively benign course. Using live virus obtained from some early cases, Culbertson, too, tried to vaccinate the fort inhabitants. Still, some twenty-seven deaths, mostly Indian women, occurred. The traders buried the dead until too few able-bodied men remained. When the epidemic continued to rage, the corpses were thrown into the upper Missouri.[28]

---

[25] Ewers, *Blackfeet*, p. 65.

[26] According to Bradley, *MHSC*, Vol. III, p. 223, the place was originally called Rapids of the Drowned by the French voyageurs but, when it was translated into English, it erroneously became Drowned Man's Rapids, despite the numerous deaths.

[27] J. A. Hamilton to Pierre Chouteau, 25 Feb 1838. Chouteau-Papin Collection, MoHS.

[28] Bradley, *MHSC*, Vol. III, p. 224; J. A. Hamilton to Pierre Chouteau, 25 Feb 1838. Chouteau-Papin Collection, MoHS.

As the disease abated at Fort McKenzie, an eerie quiet descended. For two months, no Indians visited. Finally, around the beginning of October, Alexander Culbertson and Isidoro Sandoval rode out to learn the fate of the Blackfeet. When Culbertson suffered a relapse, the two had to return to Fort McKenzie. As Culbertson recuperated, the fort remained devoid of Indian visitors. Convinced that the disease must have struck the Piegans and Bloods, as soon as he was able, Culbertson and Sandoval again set out, riding toward Three Forks where Culbertson expected to find the Piegans.

After a few days, the traders reached a village of sixty lodges. They saw not a soul. Knowing that the silence was uncharacteristic, they approached warily. As they neared, an overwhelming stench greeted them. The scene, in all its horror, then unfolded: hundreds of decaying forms of humans, dogs, and horses lay amidst the lodges. The only survivors were two old women, too feeble to travel and too disoriented by grief to make sense. Overwhelmed by despair and regret, Culbertson left the two "to chant their wild songs amid the repulsive surroundings" and returned to Fort McKenzie.[29]

Later that year, straggling bands of Piegans and Bloods appeared at Fort McKenzie to tell their story. The disease broke out about ten days after the tribes left the fort. It quickly ravaged even the strongest body, with the victims numbering in the hundreds. As the healthy saw the incredible suffering, terror and despair grew. A great many committed suicide at the first symptoms. At the junction of the Belly and St. Mary's rivers, the death toll was so great that the Bloods christened the place Ah-ki-e-nah-Es-Koo or the Graveyard.[30]

Nonetheless, James Archdale Hamilton praised Culbertson's response in a letter to Pierre Chouteau: "Mr. Culbertson appears to have acted with great energy and judgement" during the epidemic. Hamilton also advised Chouteau that Bull's Back Fat, the Blood chief, had survived and "is as warm a friend to the Company as heretofore."[31]

---

[29]Bradley, *MHSC*, Vol. III, p. 225.

[30]Dempsey, *Red Crow*, p. 14. Holterman, p. 51, offers this spelling: Akai-nuskwi. He further states that "(a)t one time this seems to have been a name for St. Mary River." Dempsey says the name was applied to the confluence of the Oldman and St. Mary rivers. Until 1915, the water below the confluence of the Oldman and Belly rivers was called the Belly; after that date, it was called the Oldman River.

[31]J. A. Hamilton to Pierre Chouteau, Jr., 25 Feb 1838. Chouteau-Papin Collection, MoHS.

# MELANCHOLY WRECKS OF HUMAN LIFE 73

The 1837 smallpox epidemic greatly altered the dynamics on the upper Missouri. Mortality rates alone were staggering: one source put the figure at an astounding 150,000 dead;[32] another estimated 60,000.[33] Only thirty Mandans, from a pre-epidemic population of fifteen hundred, survived. During the disease's peak, between fifty and one hundred Assiniboines died each day. In the end, two-thirds of that tribe, previously estimated at nine thousand, were dead.[34]

The Hidatsas lost seven hundred of their one thousand warriors.[35] About one-half of the Arikara tribe perished, faring better than their neighbors because they had been on a hunt when the disease first appeared.[36] Suicides continued to mount even after the disease waned as survivors chose to end their life rather than face the devastating loss of countless friends and family members.[37]

The death toll among the Bloods, Northern Blackfoot, and Piegans numbered six thousand, approximately two-thirds of their total. Most who survived had been exposed to a 1781 epidemic.[38] The Blood winter count, or calendar, remembers that year with just one word: smallpox.[39] The Gros Ventres, having been exposed through their kinsmen, the Arapaho, only lost about one-fourth of their number.[40] Of all the region's tribes, only the Crows escaped.[41] Joshua Pilcher, the upper Missouri Indian agent, remarked that "the country through which [the smallpox] has passed is literally depopulated and converted into one great graveyard."[42]

In addition to the sheer loss of life, Culbertson noted another tragic consequence: loss of knowledge about familial relationships. In the ensuing years, he claimed that marriages occurred between first cousins and

---

[32]Chittenden, *Fur Trade*, Vol. II, p. 619, attributes this figure to "Audubon, upon the authority of Mitchell."  [33]Thwaites, Vol. 23, p. 36.

[34]Bradley, *MHSC*, Vol. III, p. 226.  [35]Bradley, *MHSC*, Vol. III, p. 222.

[36]Thwaites, Vol. 23, pp. 34-35; J. A. Hamilton to Pierre Chouteau, Jr., 25 Feb 1838. Chouteau-Papin Collection, MoHS.

[37]Joshua Pilcher to General William Clark, 27 Feb 1838. NAM, M234/884.

[38]Bradley, *MHSC*, Vol. III, p. 225.

[39]Hungry Wolf, *Blood People*, p. 197. Holterman, p. 51, claims that 1837 was remembered by the Bloods for the death of Calf Chief and says the winter count records the year as "Onistina Oxitinitahpi." According to Hungry Wolf, this is the entry for 1838, not 1837.

[40]Bradley, *MHSC*, Vol. III, p. 226; J. A. Hamilton to Pierre Chouteau, Jr., 25 Feb 1838. Chouteau-Papin Collection, MoHS.  [41]Bradley, *MHSC*, Vol. III, p. 226.

[42]Joshua Pilcher to General William Clark, 27 Feb 1838. NAM, M234/884.

even brothers and sisters.[43] The traders spent months assessing "the melancholy details of plague, pestilence and devastation, ruined hopes and blasted expectations."[44] But the horrors were most clearly elucidated in a letter to Prince Maximilian:

> The destroying angel has visited the unfortunate sons of the wilderness with terrors never before known, and has converted extensive hunting grounds, as well as the peaceful settlements of those tribes, into desolate and boundless cemeteries. . . . The mighty warriors are now the prey of the greedy wolves of the prairie, and the few survivors, in mute despair, throw themselves on the pity of the Whites, who, however, can do but little to help them. The vast preparations for the protection of the western frontier are superfluous: another arm has undertaken the defence (*sic*) of the white inhabitants of the frontier; and the funeral torch, that lights the red man to his dreary grave, has become the auspicious star of the advancing settler, and of the roving trader of the white race.[45]

The traders, conscious of their responsibility in bringing the disease upriver, worried about retaliation. In November 1837, Jacob Halsey wrote Company headquarters: "The loss to the company by the introduction of this malady will be immense in fact incalculable as our most profitable Indians have died. . . . You are aware that all diseases introduced to the Indians by the whites must have a tendency to make them malicious, we consequently have something to fear."[46]

At Fort Union, James Archdale Hamilton reported that the "Assiniboins are hostile and threaten vengeance."[47] Charles Larpenteur noted: "The winter [of 1837-1838] was spent in great suspense and fear, but, fortunately, nothing serious occurred except some few shots fired at me

---

[43] Ewers, *Blackfeet*, p. 66; Denig, p. 72.

[44] J. A. Hamilton to Pierre Chouteau, Jr., 25 Feb 1838. Chouteau-Papin Collection, MoHS.

[45] An unsigned letter published as an appendix to Maximilian's account in Thwaites, Vol. 23, p. 33 and p. 35. Many have suggested that this letter was possibly written by Edwin Denig. While this is certainly possible, it may also have been written by Alexander Culbertson whose extant writings show a tendency to use very colorful prose. It is also recorded that Culbertson traveled out to the tribes after the smallpox epidemic and, thus, would have been in a position to make this kind of observation while there is no record of Denig having made such a journey. Moreover, Culbertson knew Maximilian better than did Denig.

[46] Abel, p. 395.

[47] J. A. Hamilton to Pierre Chouteau, Jr., 25 Feb 1838. Chouteau-Papin Collection, MoHS.

through the wicket during the night liquor trade; and as this had frequently happened before, it was not attributed to revenge for the smallpox."[48] This sense of defeat extended to the Blackfeet: "They are humbled and very submissive and beg the whites not to desert them in their calamity."[49]

The retribution never materialized. Smallpox had left the Indians decimated, their social structure in tatters. Although the white men had brought this terrible scourge, the Indians knew no way to drive them from the Indian country. The tribes realized that there had been both beneficial and detrimental impacts from the white trade. The traders had brought horses and firearms, tobacco and alcohol, knives and kettles, axes and trade cloth, decorative beads and metal finger rings.[50] While the tribes had survived without these in the past, their lifestyles had changed. By 1837, the Indians had tied their fate to the white traders.

Therefore, once the epidemic subsided, the Indians returned to the forts to trade. To the traders' surprise, they brought an abundance of robes. Charles Larpenteur, amazed by the number of robes being traded, inquired about the supply. The Assiniboines replied "laughingly that they expected to die soon, and wanted to have a frolic till the end came."[51]

At Fort McKenzie, Culbertson received over 10,000 buffalo robes the following year. Some of these, undoubtedly taken from the dead, normally would have been kept for personal use. And while some blamed the entire epidemic on a single infected blanket stolen by an Indian, the wholesale exportation of buffalo robes, many taken from Indian corpses, resulted in no outbreak of the disease back East.[52]

This is probably because, while it is possible for *variola major*, the virus that causes smallpox, to survive in contaminated blankets and clothing, transmission by this method is difficult.[53] Moreover, most of the eastern population had developed immunity through prior exposure or vaccination.

All of which points to the most damning failure of the whites: although white men did not know the etiology of smallpox in 1837, they did know how to prevent it. An effective vaccine had been developed years

---

[48]Larpenteur, p. 112.
[49]J. A. Hamilton to Pierre Chouteau, Jr., 25 Feb 1838. Chouteau-Papin Collection, MoHS.
[50]Ewers, *Blackfeet*, pp. 33-36.   [51]Larpenteur, pp. 111-112.
[52]Bradley, *MHSC*, Vol. III, p. 227.
[53]Ramenofsky, pp. 146-148; *Merck Manual*, p. 30.

earlier. Indeed, Indian delegations visiting Washington, D.C., were routinely vaccinated against smallpox beginning in 1802.

Moreover, five years before the 1837 epidemic, Congress directed the Secretary of War "to take such measures as he shall deem most efficient" to vaccinate the tribes against smallpox. Congress further authorized the hiring of physicians to attend tribes infected or in danger of being infected with the disease. Secretary of War Lewis Cass, however, decided against vaccinating the upper Missouri tribes, perhaps because of the cost, the difficulty in reaching them, or their reputation for hostility to the United States government.[54]

Cass's decision cost the upper Missouri tribes dearly. While they lost at least forty percent of their populations, the Sioux near Fort Pierre lost only about ten percent of their population because the government provided both vaccine and a physician. Similarly, by vaccinating the Indians who traded at their Canadian posts, the Hudson's Bay Company greatly reduced fatalities.[55]

Nevertheless, trade at the American posts continued to increase. In 1841, 21,000 buffalo robes were traded at Fort McKenzie alone.[56] Pierre De Smet, the Jesuit missionary, estimated that 45,000 robes were traded in 1839, 67,000 in 1840, and 90,000 each year thereafter. That number increased to 100,000 annually throughout the 1850s and 1860s.[57]

The wholesale slaughter of buffalo for pecuniary gain had begun.

---

[54]Ferch (Winter, 1983), pp. 3-4.
[56]Bradley, *MHSC*, Vol. III, p. 226.
[55]Ferch (Spring, 1984), p. 7.
[57]Sunder, p. 17.

Chapter Six

## *"Let your heart be liberal"*

In the spring of 1838, Alexander Culbertson sent Alexander Harvey to Fort Union with the larger-than-expected winter returns. On his return trip, Harvey encountered Big Road, a Blood Indian, below Fort McKenzie.[1] Big Road, with several companions, had gone downriver to meet the returning boat. Harvey welcomed the warriors on board.

But Big Road, a large, strong man, was known even among his kinsman as a quarrelsome bully. Once on board, he cursed and insulted the crew and pelted them with stones. Harvey felt inclined to shoot Big Road but restrained himself. Nevertheless, by the time the boat reached Fort McKenzie, everyone on board had had more than enough of Big Road.

Big Road, however, had not yet exhausted his mischievousness. Shortly after arriving at Fort McKenzie, the troublesome Blood burst into Culbertson's room and, without provocation, began cursing him. Culbertson, doubting that Big Road represented any real threat, rose to leave. Big Road suddenly attacked. Although neither was armed, the far larger Big Road quickly gained the upper hand.

Isidoro Sandoval and Alexander Harvey, hearing the struggle, rushed in. They seized Big Road and hustled him outside. Culbertson, aware of both Harvey's short temper and the anger Big Road had already engendered, hurried to prevent harm from coming to the querulous Indian. He was too late: Big Road lay dead, "weltering in his gore."[2]

Culbertson rebuked Harvey and Sandoval. They protested, claiming Culbertson had ordered Big Road's death, a charge Culbertson denied. With several hundred lodges of Bloods camped nearby, Culbertson feared retribution. He ordered Harvey and Sandoval to place the dead body outside the fort's gates. Then the men returned to the confines of Fort McKenzie, closed the gates, and waited.

---

[1]Bradley, *MHSC*, Vol. III, p. 227. His Indian name is given as O-muk-Su-Koo.
[2]Bradley, *MHSC*, Vol. III, pp. 227-228.

The Bloods quickly discovered their slain comrade. Incensed, several young warriors scattered the fort's horses and sought permission from the elders for a broad assault. But the elders counseled patience until Culbertson could explain himself. The next morning they approached Culbertson who invited them inside and patiently explained the events leading to Big Road's death. Somewhat disingenuously, he justified the killing as necessary to save his life. The elders, conscious of Big Road's troublesome nature, accepted the explanation and, after deliberating, quashed further plans to attack the fort.

One chief then offered Culbertson advice: "Here are [Big Road's] two brothers who will expect the recompense usual with us in such cases. Let your heart be liberal and give to them accordingly." Culbertson recognized the wisdom of this counsel but, with the fort's horses driven off, he had little to offer.

Appreciating Culbertson's predicament, the chief ordered the young men to return the horses and Culbertson then presented a fine horse and other goods to Big Road's brothers. They appeared appeased and the council broke up. The fort returned to normal.[3] But bad feelings continued to smolder and Culbertson soon learned that Big Road's brothers planned to avenge his death as soon as an opportunity arose.

That time seemed to arrive two months later when the Bloods were encamped on the Marias River. A delegation invited Culbertson to visit their camp. Harvey argued against this, believing the Bloods meant to isolate and kill Culbertson. Although Culbertson tended to agree, he also recognized that he could not live in fear of the Bloods and still conduct a viable trade. He also realized that to go would show the warriors he possessed the kind of bravery they respected. Since he trusted those issuing the invitation, Culbertson decided to accept.

The next morning, Culbertson set out with the Bloods for their encampment. When he arrived, everyone greeted him courteously except Big Road's brothers. Believing they represented the only threat, Culbertson lowered his guard. Later that evening, the brothers attempted to assault Culbertson but were quickly subdued by their kinsmen. The Bloods kept the brothers under close surveillance until Culbertson left camp the next day, protected by several chiefs.

Although Culbertson had defused another potentially deadly situation, he remained wary of Big Road's brothers until, several years later,

---

[3]Bradley, *MHSC*, Vol. III, pp. 228-229.

they were killed by the Crows. In Culbertson's thirty years of trading with the notoriously warlike Blackfeet, Big Road and his brothers were the only members of that tribe to threaten his life.[4]

The following spring (1839), Alexander Culbertson took the returns to Fort Union where he assembled twenty-four hundred packs of buffalo robes, valued at $100,000, loaded them aboard eight mackinaws, and departed for St. Louis on June 3. One month later, Culbertson arrived in St. Louis with the last commercial mackinaw fleet to descend the upper Missouri.[5]

The journey created controversy. William Laidlaw, a partner in the American Fur Company, complained to Pierre Chouteau that the trip "put us to great inconvenience," necessitating the posting of James Kipp to Fort McKenzie lest the Blackfeet "get discouraged and clear out to the north." Laidlaw charged that Culbertson had left his post "contrary to your instructions[,] to look after his own private affairs." Moreover, Culbertson's scheduled November return would render him useless since all the upper posts would "be established long before that time." Laidlaw further protested that "partners seem to think they are at liberty to go when and where they please. If this kind of work is to be allowed I need not say to you what the Consequence will be."[6]

Chouteau did not share Laidlaw's outrage and did not discipline Culbertson. Moreover, no surviving records reflect Chouteau's instructions that Culbertson not leave his Blackfeet post. It appears that Culbertson took the furs to St. Louis in order to discuss personnel matters at the Blackfeet post.

Kenneth McKenzie and David Mitchell, veterans of the American Fur Company, were both retiring in 1840 and Culbertson had been offered a promotion. But he had reservations, as expressed to Chouteau:

> I feel truly greatful (*sic*) for this mark of confidences but still I beg leave respectfully to decline expecting the terms which Mr. McKenzie stated he was authorized to make. There are many reasons for doing so but let one which is the most ergent (*sic*) suffice. It is simply the fear of having someone placed over me under whom I might be unwilling to act.[7]

---

[4]Bradley, *MHSC*, Vol. III, pp. 228-230.   [5]Larpenteur, p. 136.
[6]William Laidlaw, Mandan Village, to Pierre Chouteau, Jr., 1 Aug 1839. Chouteau-Papin Collection, MoHS.   [7]Holterman, p. 52.

Although Culbertson gave no other clues about the individual under whom he felt reluctant to serve, it was likely William Laidlaw whom Charles Larpenteur referred to as an "old tyrant."[8] In addition to the proffered promotion, Culbertson probably also wished to discuss his concerns about the pugnacious Alexander Harvey.

A rugged, fearless man who stood well over six feet tall, Harvey was born and raised in St. Louis where he apprenticed in the saddlery trade. But his employers disliked his fiery temperament and discharged him.[9] Before turning eighteen, Harvey signed on with the AFC, arriving on the upper Missouri with Alexander Culbertson in the spring of 1833. Both young men were assigned to the remote Fort McKenzie.

Harvey's initial contract expired in 1835 and, that spring, he left Fort McKenzie with James Kipp. Even then, Culbertson apparently had doubts about Harvey's suitability for a position with the AFC. But, on May 5, 1835, James Archdale Hamilton, in charge of the upriver posts, wrote Culbertson: "I have engaged Mr. Harvey for another year having a high opinion of his integrity and bravery (the latter a very desireable (*sic*) quality in this wild country) he professes his willingness to render himself useful in any and every way that you may direct. I hope you will find him a good aid."[10]

Hamilton placed Harvey third in command at Fort McKenzie, behind Culbertson and a trader named Moncravie.[11] When Moncravie was dismissed a few months later,[12] Harvey assumed the second position. Although Culbertson had little choice but to accede to Hamilton's wishes, by 1839, his patience had worn thin. Charles Larpenteur claimed that Harvey was "inclined to do right when sober,"[13] but Harvey either drank too much or Larpenteur's assessment was too generous.

Although Culbertson found Harvey a competent assistant much of the time, his irascible nature often reared its head. During the Crow siege, Harvey nearly succeeded in persuading several employees to desert. His killing of Big Road had almost cost Culbertson his life and jeopardized the Company's position with the Bloods.

In addition, Harvey had had numerous disagreements with Company employees. In 1835, the Bloods had run off some post horses. Culbertson,

---

[8]Larpenteur, p. 137.  [9]Chittenden, *Fur Trade*, Vol. II, p. 683.
[10]Abel, p. 247.
[11]Notes by James Archdale Hamilton, May 1835, *Fort Union Letter Books*, MoHS.
[12]Larpenteur, p. 63.  [13]Larpenteur, p. 143.

Augustin Hamel, and Loretto, a post hunter, rode out to search for the animals. From the bluffs behind the fort, they spotted some Bloods but they had no Company horses. Satisfied that they had had nothing to do with the missing animals, Culbertson prepared to return to Fort McKenzie when Loretto unexpectedly rode after the Bloods.

The Bloods, anticipating no trouble, watched Loretto approach. Suddenly, he opened fire. The warriors returned fire and a bullet ripped through the hunter's right leg and lodged in his groin. Culbertson managed to get Loretto back to the fort but his wounds were fatal. As Loretto lay dying, Culbertson asked why he had attacked the Bloods. The hunter responded pitifully that, had he not, Harvey would have taunted him for cowardice.[14]

In light of these episodes, Culbertson wanted Harvey's contract terminated. He apparently discussed the problem with Laidlaw on his way downriver in 1839 as Laidlaw wrote Chouteau about the "necessity of discharging Harvey."[15] When Culbertson returned to Fort McKenzie that Christmas, he carried with him a letter from Pierre Chouteau requesting Harvey to report to St. Louis as soon as practicable.[16]

Harvey, outraged by his presumed termination, resolved to leave immediately. Everyone believed it foolhardy to risk an overland journey in the dead of winter, but Harvey remained adamant: "I will not let Mr. Chouteau wait long on me. I shall start in the morning; all I want for my journey is my rifle, and my dog to carry bedding."[17] Although convinced he was crazy, no one stood in his way.

The intrepid Harvey reached St. Louis in March 1840, much to Pierre Chouteau's astonishment. Chouteau, impressed by Harvey's exploit, re-engaged him. Everyone, except Harvey, would come to regret deeply this decision.

When Alexander Culbertson returned to Fort McKenzie that Christmas, in addition to Chouteau's letter to Harvey, he brought with him a new employee he hoped would prove a worthy replacement. Malcolm Clarke,[18]

---

[14]Bradley, *MHSC*, Vol. III, p. 217.
[15]William Laidlaw to Pierre Chouteau, 1 Aug 1839. Chouteau-Papin Collection, MoHS.
[16]Larpenteur, p. 143.      [17]Larpenteur, p. 143.
[18]The spelling of Clarke's last name is troublesome. It appears in official documents both with and without a final "e." The author has chosen to spell it with the "e" as this is the spelling used by Malcolm Clarke's daughter, Helen, in *MHSC*, Vol. II, p. 255. See also Bradley, *MHSC*, Vol. III, p. 232n.

a tall, fair-skinned, good-looking man with a broad forehead and intense eyes, sported a full beard and a disposition nearly as fiery as Harvey's. Born in Indiana in 1817, Clarke grew up in a military family and planned to follow in his father's footsteps until his temper got in the way.

Less than a year after entering West Point in 1834, Clarke challenged a classmate to a duel. When the classmate refused, Clarke assaulted him. West Point ordered Clarke dismissed, but President Andrew Jackson overturned the directive. Before Jackson's orders could be implemented, however, Clarke attacked another classmate and, facing court-martial, he quit West Point and headed to Texas.

Clarke spent several years in the Texas Army before returning east. In Cincinnati, he met an old friend of his father's: John Craighead Culbertson, Alexander Culbertson's beloved uncle. Casting about for a new challenge, Clarke listened as John Culbertson suggested a position with the American Fur Company. Clarke was interested and Culbertson agreed to make the introduction.[19]

A letter to Culbertson from his uncle concerning Clarke's pending arrival in St. Louis may have been the personal affairs to which Laidlaw alluded in his letter to Chouteau. Certainly, Culbertson would have wanted to facilitate the employment of anyone coming west under his uncle's sponsorship. Nevertheless, the decision to hire Malcolm Clarke lay with Pierre Chouteau who must have been impressed since Clarke was soon headed upriver.

Charles Larpenteur, the Fort Union clerk who had helped Culbertson bring the mackinaw fleet downriver in 1839, boarded the steamboat *Trapper* on March 30, 1840, to return to the upper Missouri. Alexander Harvey was also on board.

Harvey vowed to Larpenteur that he would get revenge: "I have several settlements to make with those gentlemen who caused me last winter's tramp; I never forget or forgive; it may not be for ten years, but they will have to catch it."[20] Harvey did not wait long.

When the steamer docked at Fort Clark, Harvey beat up one of his

---

[19]Hafen, *Mountain Men*, Vol. VIII, pp. 69-70. Some confusion exists over dates as Hafen says Clarke served four years in Texas which, if true, would make it impossible for Clarke to have arrived on the Upper Missouri in late 1839.

[20]Larpenteur, pp. 143-144.

enemies, telling Larpenteur, "That's number one." The *Trapper* reached Fort Union on June 27 and there, Harvey found more men upon whom to exact vengeance. Harvey was quickly settling the score with those he held accountable for his dismissal.[21] After beating up several others at Fort Union, Harvey returned to Fort McKenzie where he probably continued to mete out frontier justice.

The details of these attacks, however, are not known because, curiously, Alexander Culbertson mentioned neither Harvey's dismissal nor his rehiring in his recollections of affairs on the upper Missouri. Equally interesting, Harvey apparently did not count Culbertson among his enemies. Perhaps he never suspected the role Culbertson played in his termination or, more likely, he deemed it imprudent to attack his well-respected superior. For his part, Culbertson deemed it wise to give Harvey a wide berth.

Pierre Chouteau succeeded in laying to rest whatever qualms Alexander Culbertson harbored about his proffered promotion and, in 1840, Culbertson assumed control of forts Union and McKenzie. After placing Fort Union under command of his friend, Edwin Denig, Culbertson returned to Fort McKenzie.

The next January, Culbertson and Isidoro Sandoval took one hundred horses to Fort Union for the Indian trade. When this number proved insufficient, Culbertson sent Sandoval back to Fort McKenzie for more. Sandoval returned in March with fifty additional horses.

Soon thereafter, Alexander Harvey arrived with the Fort McKenzie returns.[22] Culbertson, intending to spend part of the season at Fort Union, planned to have Sandoval and Harvey oversee operations at Fort McKenzie. Unfortunately, during their years at McKenzie, much bad blood had built up between those two and it was about to spill over. A few years earlier, Sandoval had criticized Harvey for the cruel killing of an Indian at Fort McKenzie and Harvey had sworn to kill him.[23] In recent

---

[21]Larpenteur, p. 144.

[22]Bradley, *MHSC*, Vol. III, p. 231. The actual date of this event is unclear. Bradley gives a date of 1840 but this may be off by a year or more. Larpenteur, p. 144, says that Harvey and Sandoval had taken the returns to St. Louis before this incident occurred. However, Larpenteur was not at Fort Union when the killing happened and other accounts do not seem to confirm a trip to St. Louis by Harvey and Sandoval.

[23]Innis, p. 75.

months, Sandoval had threatened Harvey who considered the Spaniard one of his greatest enemies.

As the Company clerks loaded the keelboat with supplies for Fort McKenzie, Culbertson and Harvey looked for Sandoval. They found him in the retail store. Harvey, having heard of Sandoval's threats, demanded to know his intentions. As Sandoval stood mute, Harvey taunted him: "You are too big a coward to come out and fight me like a man; you want to shoot me behind my back!"[24]

Saying this, Harvey dared Sandoval to follow him outside. Sandoval did not budge. Harvey shouted, "You won't fight me like a man, so take that!" He pulled a gun and shot Sandoval in the head. As the stunned observers stood by nervously, Harvey strolled outside, declaring: "I, Alexander Harvey, have killed the Spaniard. If there are any of his friends who want to take it up, let them come on." No one accepted the challenge.[25]

Sandoval lingered for almost twenty-four hours before dying.[26] Culbertson filed a formal complaint against Harvey for the murder but the Company took no action. Culbertson, having developed a healthy fear of Harvey, did not push the matter.[27]

Culbertson returned to Fort McKenzie that November to learn that Harvey had killed yet again. Kah-ta-Nah, a mixed Gros Ventre and Blood, after committing some infraction, fled. Harvey and Malcolm Clarke pursued, overtook him at the mouth of Shonkin Creek, and killed him.[28] Since neither the Gros Ventres nor the Bloods called for retribution, the killing may have been justified according to frontier standards.

Or the tribes may have let the killing pass because they had seen Harvey act with impunity before. In any case, the murder must have dismayed Alexander Culbertson, especially when he learned Malcolm Clarke had been Harvey's accomplice. Unfortunately for Culbertson, for the American Fur Company, and for the Indians, this would not be the last time that Harvey's ferocious temper would bring death down upon the tribes.

---

[24]Larpenteur, p. 145.
[25]Larpenteur, p. 146.
[26]Bradley, *MHSC*, Vol. III, p. 231.
[27]Holterman, p. 59, citing "Plassman: Forsythe (MT) *Independent.*"
[28]Bradley, *MHSC*, Vol. III, p. 232.

## Chapter Seven

## *"Be without a woman at this moon of next summer"*

After Old Man made Old Woman, the two decided on how the people would be. "I will have the first say," declared Old Man. Old Woman agreed, reserving to herself the final say.

Old Man began: "The people shall have eyes and mouths on their faces and they will be straight up and down." "No," countered Old Woman, "they shall have eyes and mouths set crosswise." It was agreed.

"The people shall have ten fingers on each hand," Old Man decided. "No," said Old Woman. "Ten fingers is too many. There shall be four fingers and one thumb on each hand." It was agreed.[1]

"The people shall beget children," Old Man decided. "The genitals shall be at their navels." "No," declared Old Woman. "That would make child-bearing too easy and then the people would not cherish their children. The genitals shall be at the pubic area." It was agreed.[2]

"The women will tan the hides," Old Man declared. "They will rub brains on them to make them soft and they will scrape them well. It will not be hard work." "No," said Old Woman. "They will tan the hides as you say, but it will be very hard work and it will take a long time. In this way, the good workers will be discovered." It was agreed.

Now, in the beginning, the men and women did not live together. The women, because they could tan hides, had fine lodges, robes, clothes, and moccasins. They dried meat and picked berries to eat during the winter. The men, knowing none of this, lived poorly and wanted to join the women. The women also wanted to live with the men and so it was decided that the women would choose husbands.[3]

---

[1] Wissler, *Mythology*, pp. 19-20; Hungry Wolf, *Ways*, p. 140.

[2] Wissler, *Mythology*, p. 20.

[3] Uhlenbeck, *New Series*, p. 167; Hungry Wolf, *Ways*, p. 141; Wissler, *Mythology*, p. 21. Wissler says that the women approached the men about living together; Uhlenbeck and Hungry Wolf say the men approached the women.

The men donned their best clothes and went to the women's camp. They formed a line so the women could select husbands. The chief of the women chose first. She wore dirty clothes and none of the men recognized her. After reviewing the men, she chose Old Man. But he saw many finely dressed women and refused to go with Old Woman, believing her very common.

Napi's refusal angered her. She returned to her lodge and ordered no one to choose Old Man. Old Woman then changed into her finest clothes. When she emerged, Old Man saw her and said, "There is the chief of the women. I wish to be her husband," not realizing she was the one he had already rejected.

As the chief of the women walked along the line, Old Man repeatedly stepped in front of her, hoping she would notice him. She paid no attention, finally picking another. Soon, all the men had been chosen except Napi. He was very angry. The chief of the women announced, "You will be a tree and you will stand in this place from now on." With that, Old Man became a tree.[4]

During the spring of 1825, the Fish Eaters band of the Bloods encamped near the mouth of Belly River as their chief, Two Suns,[5] and his wife, Red Deer Woman, awaited the birth of their child.[6]

Traditionally, Blood women learned nothing about childbirth until their time was near. But once a woman knew she was pregnant, she cut back on her work and often returned to her mother's lodge where she received advice, support, and counsel.

Her husband, if he had the financial wherewithal, might take another wife to help with the household. Or he might invite his sister or his wife's

---

[4] Wissler, *Mythology*, pp. 21-22; Hungry Wolf, *Ways*, pp. 141-142; de Jong, pp. 31-32; Uhlenbeck, *New Series*, pp. 167-169. Hungry Wolf does not include the element of Old Man becoming a tree but says instead that "He wandered off into the hills, crying, and they say that he became ornery from then on because of his loneliness." Since Old Man shows up in many Blackfeet myths following the union of men and women, this transformation of him into a tree is one of many examples of the transformative cosmology that guided the Blackfeet.

[5] Controversy exists over the identity of Natawista's father. Many sources claim that her father was Menestokos, the Father of Many Children. However, Hugh Dempsey and James Willard Schultz both give her father as Two Suns and the author considers their knowledge of Blood lineage superior to those who list her father as Menestokos.

[6] Steckelberg, p. 53.

sister or a widowed aunt to move into his lodge. This invitation never went to his mother-in-law, however, since Blood tradition forbade him from being in her company.[7]

Throughout her pregnancy, a Blood woman denied herself many pleasures. Eating certain foods was prohibited because of their perceived impacts: hearts or innards would cause her face to become discolored; leg muscles would cause her legs to cramp; brains would cause her child to have a snotty nose. Custom also forbade pregnant women from standing in a doorway and looking out. If something caught her attention, she had to go completely outside or risk a difficult labor.[8] As her time approached, the woman donned old clothes and discarded her bracelets and other metal ornaments.[9]

As Old Woman had decreed, birth was difficult, with only medicinal teas for the pain. In the old days, women never gave birth in a lodge; instead, she delivered in a specially built shade. She avoided the lodge because the Blackfeet believed that men lost their strength if they entered a place where a woman had given birth. In those days, the woman and her child remained in seclusion for nine days before returning to the community.[10]

A father bore responsibility for naming his child, soliciting a respected elder to perform the ceremony. The elder, following a sweat bath, suggested two or three possibilities from which the father chose. Usually, a child received the name of a long deceased individual of distinction. This, the Blackfeet believed, conferred the deceased's power on the child.[11]

Mothers often gave their child a nickname, which the child usually dropped in adulthood.[12] While women rarely changed their names, men frequently did. After his first battle, a youth often received a name tinged with ridicule. When he performed a more worthy deed, he obtained a more dignified name. To ask a man his name was considered rude since it suggested that he was not well-known.[13] Some Blackfeet also believed speaking their own name would bring misfortune.[14]

---

[7]Hungry Wolf, *Ways*, p. 190; Wissler, Social Life, pp. 12-13.
[8]Hungry Wolf, *Ways*, p. 191.     [9]Wissler, *Social Life*, p. 28.
[10]Uhlenbeck, *New Series*, pp. 50-51; Wissler, *Social Life*, p. 28.
[11]Ewers, *Blackfeet*, p. 101; Wissler, *Social Life*, pp. 16-17.
[12]Wissler, *Social Life*, pp. 16-17; Hungry Wolf, *Ways*, pp. 193-194.
[13]Wissler, *Social Life*, pp. 17-18.
[14]Grinnell, *Blackfoot Lodge Tales*, p. 194.

Blackfeet children matured in the embrace of their community. Elders lavished them with attention while also meting out appropriate discipline. Striking a child was considered unacceptable; a dash of cold water or immersion in a chilly stream served as punishment. The elders also invoked bogeymen, often coyotes or wolves, to cow children into proper behavior.[15]

Fathers taught their sons to make miniature bows and arrows and to participate in games designed to build strong bodies and noble characters. Boys learned that, to accomplish anything worthwhile, they must be brave and untiring in battle. It was better to die bravely with their bodies strong, their sight good, their teeth intact, and their hair black and long than to live a long life since the old suffered much discomfort.[16]

Girls played with dolls, miniature tipis, miniature cradleboards, miniature furnishings, and small tanning and cooking tools.[17] They learned to tend their chores without complaint, to respect and serve their elders, to be serious-minded, and to avoid unnecessary giggling. A father taught his daughter not to be frivolous by teasing her. He instructed her: "Look me straight in the eye and, no matter what I do, do not laugh." The father then sang silly songs and shook a rattle. If the girl giggled, her father stopped and waited for her to regain her composure. Then he began again until, finally, she watched him placidly.[18]

Women held positions of great respect among the Blackfeet. In Blackfeet mythology, women often bridged the worlds of the natural and supernatural. Through these contacts, the tribe had learned many of the world's mysteries.[19] Women owned the tipi and its furnishings, the people's food and clothing. She could give of these as she chose. A marriage was effected when a woman invited a man to partake of her food. Moreover, all secular activities in which the men engaged were open to Blackfeet women.[20] Women were also responsible for the daily care of the medicine bundles and only they could unwrap its contents.[21]

Mothers taught their daughters to pick berries, dig roots, gather fire-

---

[15]Wissler, *Social Life*, p. 29.
[16]Ewers, *Blackfeet*, pp. 103-104; Grinnell, *Blackfoot Lodge Tales*, pp. 189-190.
[17]Hungry Wolf, *Ways*, p. 200 and p. 247.
[18]Grinnell, *Blackfoot Lodge Tales*, p. 190; Wissler, *Social Life*, pp. 29-30.
[19]See Chapter Thirteen.
[20]Kehoe, "The Shackles of Tradition," p. 69, in Albers and Medicine.
[21]Kehoe, "The Shackles of Tradition," pp. 67-68, in Albers and Medicine.

wood, haul water, sew clothing, and make lodges and travois. Girls learned to dismantle and re-erect the lodges when the tribe moved camp.[22] Most importantly, they learned how to tan robes. Since the tribe depended heavily on the buffalo robe trade, they often judged a woman by her tanning skills. The complicated, time-consuming task involved stretching and scraping and pounding and rubbing and dousing and stretching and staking and drying and pounding and scraping and rubbing and dousing and stretching and staking and drying and pounding again.[23]

Ironically, as the trade in buffalo hides increased, women's economic independence declined. Although the women prepared the hides, the men conducted the trade, leaving the women more vulnerable to the whims of the males.[24]

Children of both sexes grew up around horses, becoming skilled riders at a young age. Doting mothers or grandmothers sometimes made small saddles for children but most rode bareback. Racing horses was a favored pastime. By age ten, boys often assumed responsibility for the family's herd. Orphaned boys found new homes by helping wealthy families tend their large herds. When he became a teenager, a boy joined the buffalo hunt.[25]

Young men enjoyed remarkable sexual freedom and frequently bragged of their sexual conquests, particularly if they had slept with a married woman.[26] Such braggadocio could have disastrous consequences for the unfaithful wife. A betrayed husband often cut off the tip of his wife's nose, marking her for life as an adulterer. Even if he forgave her, he had to punish her lover to retain the respect of his peers. He might steal his property or kill him.[27]

Because a daughter's marriage could elevate a family's status, marriage decisions were rarely taken lightly. Before a young man could marry, he usually had gone to battle at least once. This not only proved his bravery but also enabled him to secure the horses and property needed to obtain and support a wife.

---

[22]Grinnell, *Blackfoot Lodge Tales*, p. 185; Ewers, *Blackfeet*, p. 102.

[23]Hungry Wolf, *Ways*, p. 234; Steckelberg, p. 54.

[24]Beatrice Medicine, "'Warrior Women' — Sex Role Alternatives for Plains Indian Women," p. 270, in Albers and Medicine.

[25]Ewers, *Blackfeet*, p. 104; Grinnell, *Blackfoot Lodge Tales*, p. 219.

[26]Ewers, *Blackfeet*, p. 98; Wissler, *Social Life*, p. 9.

[27]Ewers, *Blackfeet*, pp. 100-101.

In most cases, parents arranged the marriage. If the bride-to-be came from a well-to-do family, her family provided a new lodge, poles, lining, and backrests as well as an elaborate wedding costume. The bride's family then escorted her, with her new possessions, to the groom's band where they were met by a parade of well-adorned members of her husband's family.

The bride and her mother erected the new lodge in the center of the camp circle. They tied a complement of horses, the bride's dowry, in front of the lodge. The father might also give his soon-to-be son-in-law his war clothing and equipment, signifying respect for the young man. When the groom saw the marriage lodge erected, he sent his father-in-law double the number of horses offered him. The marriage ceremony was complete when the husband took his designated place at the rear of the bride's lodge.[28]

If a family included more than one daughter, the eldest's marriage decision took on great significance since her younger sisters, known as "distant wives," might be offered her husband as additional wives. The husband, however, was under no obligation to accept them. Polygyny, common among the tribes, represented an efficient way to provide for the tribal women who, because of battle losses, always outnumbered males. Men could take as many wives as they could afford, gaining status with each additional wife.

In polygynous households, the husband's favorite wife, usually his first, was the "sits beside him" wife. She accompanied him to feasts and ceremonies and oversaw the household work of the other wives. Jealousy rarely created problems since the wives were often related.[29]

The arrival of white traders altered these customs very little. A white trader who desired an Indian wife also presented gifts, usually including horses, to the would-be wife's parents. The Indians, far from resenting a white man's attention to their daughter, regarded him as an especially fine match since he could offer special privileges to the bride and her family.[30]

[28]Grinnell, *Blackfoot Lodge Tales*, pp. 213-214; Wissler, *Social Life*, pp. 9-10. These were the procedures observed for families of means. According to Grinnell, "Poorer, less important people married more quietly."

[29]Ewers, *Blackfeet*, pp. 99-100; Hungry Wolf, *Ways*, p. 201; Grinnell, *Blackfoot Lodge Tales*, pp. 217-218; Wissler, *Social Life*, pp. 11-12.   [30]Ewers, *Indian Life*, p. 66.

Red Deer Woman gave birth to a beautiful young daughter that spring of 1825. Two Suns took his daughter to Eagle Feather for naming. Daubing the baby's face and wrists with sacred red earth paint, Eagle Feather announced her name: Natoyist-siksina'[31] or Holy Snake.[32]

Later that summer, as the Bloods gathered at the South Saskatchewan River for the annual Sun Dance, Red Deer Woman gave the medicine women gifts and asked them to bless her daughter. The holy women performed a traditional ritual for Natoyist-siksina': facing the setting sun, they chanted prayers and ate the sacred buffalo tongues.[33]

Natoyist-siksina' had been welcomed into her tribe. In European societies, as the daughter of the chief of the Fish Eaters, she might have been called a princess but Indians disdained such titles. Natawista, as she would be known, grew up like all the other girls; she learned necessary life skills from her mother and other tribal women. But Natawista would become very different from the other girls in her tribe. Her name would find its way glowingly into reports of the United States government and, eventually, she would be compared to Sacagawea, the famous Shoshone woman who accompanied the Lewis and Clark expedition.[34]

Alexander Culbertson probably first saw Natawista when she was a child. As she entered her teens, he became attracted to her lithe, graceful figure, beautiful long hair, and flashing dark eyes. Culbertson also noticed the loving adoration showered on the young beauty by her elder brother,

---

[31]This is the spelling given by Hugh Dempsey, *Red Crow*, p. 221, note 2. The author regards his knowledge of the Blood language to be superior and thus has chosen to employ this spelling. In addition, her name is given as Natawistacha-Iksana by both Mildred Walker Schemm and Dabney Taylor; as Natawistacha-Iskana by Jamie Steckelberg; as Nâtowap Tsîs-Tseksîn by James Willard Schultz; as Natúyi-tsíxina in the Canadian Archives; as Natoap-zixina by Jack Holterman; as Natoastsix-in in the Blood Treaty Records; as Natoyestsexinnaw in the Catholic Church records on the Blood Reserve; as No-ta-wis-chick-sa-na by her son, Joseph Culbertson, KP, UCLA; and, as Natawistixina by descendants of her daughter, Julia Culbertson Roberts, in conversations with the author (spelling by the author). Although English translations for Indian names are the norm throughout this book, Natawista will be a prominent exception since she was known by this name throughout her life.

[32]The name has also been translated as Medicine Snake Woman, Sacred Snake Woman, and Holy Snake Woman. Hugh Dempsey, in correspondence with the author, states: "The proper translation of Mrs. Culbertson's name is Holy Snake, not Holy Snake Woman. If it was the latter, it would have '... aki' at the end."

[33]Steckelberg, p. 54.   [34]Ewers, *Indian Life*, p. 62.

Seen From Afar, the far-roaming Blood warrior whom Culbertson had met on his first trip to Fort McKenzie.[35]

Sadly, Natawista's mother, Red Deer Woman, had died during the smallpox epidemic.[36] Shortly after, her aging father turned over leadership of the Fish Eaters to Seen From Afar.[37] This put him into increasingly steady contact with Culbertson who, by then, had become chief trader at Fort McKenzie. And if Culbertson's eye frequently settled on the beautiful Natawista, Seen From Afar surely noticed.

Two versions of the courtship and marriage of Culbertson and Natawista exist. Many years later, Culbertson told the anthropologist, Lewis Henry Morgan, a simple, straightforward account of their marriage: he presented nine horses, nine horses were returned, and the marriage was effected.[38]

A much more romantic version has come down through the Bloods. The Bloods, in their oral tradition, may have exaggerated the romance and splendor of the Culbertsons' courtship and marriage, but the account underscores their deep commitment. And it is certainly possible that Culbertson, who rarely spoke about his family,[39] told Morgan a generic account of how white traders acquired Indian brides.

The Blood version comes from James Willard Schultz, a white man who, after being adopted into the Blackfeet tribe, spent his adult years recording their stories.[40] According to Schultz, Culbertson fell deeply in love with Natawista when she was quite young. However, she was always closely chaperoned and Culbertson could not speak with her directly. Finally finding her alone, Culbertson approached and asked if she could care enough for him to become his wife.

---

[35]Indian genealogy is particularly difficult, especially since Indians frequently do not regard their family members in the same linear method employed by the white world. While nearly all sources agree that Seen From Afar was Natawista's brother, her other siblings are harder to identify. Dempsey, *Red Crow*, pp. 6-7, says that Natawista had an older sister named Sacred Woman as well as a brother named Big Plume (Omuxsapop). Holterman, p. 57, gives her likely brothers as Big Plume, Black Bear, and Scalp Robe with Eagles Ribs, Calf Shirt, Gray Eyes, and Little Dog of the Piegans as close relatives. Taylor, "The Major's Blackfoot Bride," p. 27, lists her brothers as Red Crow, Gray Eyes, and Eagle Ribs. Red Crow, however, was her nephew, according to Hugh Dempsey. In general, the author has opted for Dempsey's genealogical information.

[36]Steckelberg, p. 55. [37]Dempsey, *Red Crow*, p. 3.
[38]Holterman, p. 58; Ewers, *Indian Life*, p. 61.
[39]The account of his life that Culbertson shared with James H. Bradley contains not a single mention of his own family. See Bradley, *MHSC*, Vol. III.
[40]See biographical data in any of the numerous books by Schultz.

Natawista replied that she had long hoped he might ask. "You do, then, really care for me?" asked Culbertson. Natawista "replied only with her eyes, but that was answer enough."[41]

Having received this encouragement, Culbertson asked Two Suns and Seen From Afar for permission to marry. Not so fast, replied Two Suns. First, the trader must prove he was worthy. Culbertson already had a wife, the Piegan woman he had married in 1833.[42] Although polygyny was common, neither Two Suns nor Seen From Afar believed such an arrangement suitable for their dear Natawista since, as a second wife, she would not have occupied the honored position within the household.[43]

Two Suns insisted that if Culbertson wished to marry Natawista, he must divorce his first wife. If he did and was without a woman at "this moon of next summer," Two Suns promised Natawista for his bride.[44] Culbertson protested but his pleas fell on deaf ears. Finally, he accepted the conditions and set about to divorce his Piegan wife. This would not have been difficult as divorce involved little more than public renunciation of the marriage. The woman then returned to her parents who repaid the amount received for her.[45]

Soon after Culbertson agreed to these terms, probably in the summer of 1840, the Bloods left Fort McKenzie. But Seen From Afar kept in touch and was pleased to learn that Culbertson was soon living alone. Convinced that the trader intended to honor his pledge, Natawista's family began to prepare for her marriage.

Her female relatives made gowns of soft buckskin elaborately decorated with porcupine quills, beads, and elk teeth. They prepared brilliantly

---

[41]Schultz, *Signposts*, p. 112.

[42]Schultz, *Signposts*, p. 113.

[43]The "sits besides him" wife was considered more secure from the whims of her husband. Wissler, *Social Life*, p. 11.

[44]Schultz, *Signposts*, p. 113. Schultz's account does not mention Culbertson's Piegan wife, merely saying that Culbertson must be "without a woman" at year's end. The divorce is mentioned by Culbertson's great-granddaughter, Dabney Taylor, in "The Major's Blackfoot Bride." Also, Berglund, SC 414, MtHS, p. 6.

[45]Ewers, *Blackfeet*, p. 100; Grinnell, *Blackfoot Lodge Tales*, p. 218; Wissler, *Social Life*, p. 14. Wissler offers a number of reasons for divorce, none of them applicable in this instance, and goes on to state: "In general, divorce seems not to have been common as it was looked upon as disgraceful under all circumstances and grievously expensive." The expense surely would have been a minimal concern for Culbertson; a more major concern might have been whether his divorce would offend the Piegans. This does not seem to have happened and may not have been a factor since his first marriage had clearly been a business arrangement.

embroidered moccasins and snow white leggings as well as a new lodge with painted lining and willow backrests. Natawista received a beautiful new saddle for herself and one for her husband to use on the white horses she would present him as wedding gifts. Finally, Natawista and her female relatives filled new, brightly painted parfleches with pemmican, dried meats, and berries for the wedding feast.[46]

That winter, business took Culbertson to Fort Union and he was still there when the time arrived for the marriage. This represented only a minor obstacle: Seen From Afar had visited Fort Union before and if that was where his sister's husband-to-be was, that was where he would take her. Other members of the tribe joined the wedding entourage.

Arriving at Fort Union, the Bloods set up camp on the surrounding plain. Culbertson, in keeping with tradition and as evidence of his continuing commitment, sent nine horses to Seen From Afar.[47] Seen From Afar, expecting the gesture, accepted by sending back nine horses. The wedding would go forward.

The Bloods, dressed in ceremonial garb, marched towards the fort. The warriors rode painted, feathered horses and sang a welcoming song to the beat of drums. Behind them came the elaborately dressed Natawista astride a coal black horse. Following her, fourteen white pack horses carried her belongings and, behind them, the rest of the Fish Eaters band.

Flags fluttered and the cannon boomed. Culbertson, dressed in his best attire, stood by the gate awaiting his bride. When all had been welcomed into the courtyard, Culbertson helped Natawista from her horse. He then presented his in-laws with guns, powder and ball, blankets, tobacco, and other goods. Then, while the Company men, their women,

---

[46]Schultz, *Signposts*, p. 114.

[47]In the "white" version of the marriage story, this offering of horses to Seen From Afar (or to her father, in some accounts) is said to be the first statement of Culbertson's desire to marry Natawista. This scenario would seem to have several problems: (1) nine horses is a pretty meager offering for a woman of Natawista's stature. For instance, Grinnell, *Blackfoot Lodge Tales*, p. 213, uses a fifteen horse offering as his example; (2) everyone agrees that the marriage occurred at Fort Union although this was well beyond the normal range of the Blood tribe; and, (3) some have suggested that Culbertson did not divorce his Piegan wife but that she died in the 1837 smallpox epidemic. If that were true, it seems that Janie and Mariah would have gone to live with a relative of their deceased mother since Culbertson could not have assumed primary responsibility for two very young girls. That Janie and Mariah often lived with Culbertson after his marriage to Natawista suggests that their mother was still alive. Since the two stories are not mutually exclusive, and since the romance of Schultz's story is irresistible, the author has combined the two accounts into a plausible version of events.

and the Bloods celebrated, Culbertson escorted his bride to their living quarters where he presented her with beautiful shawls, earrings, bracelets, necklaces, and gowns of silk, wool, and cotton. The Indian wife of a Company man helped Natawista don a gown of red silk while Culbertson waited outside. When his bride reappeared, he proudly escorted her to a feast in their honor.[48]

Only about fifteen years old, Natawista initially must have felt overwhelmed, but she quickly adapted to her role as the sole wife of the chief trader on the upper Missouri. For the next thirty years, she would rarely be separated from her handsome and distinguished husband.[49] If Culbertson's first marriage had been political, his second was suffused with love. The political ramifications, including the elevation of Seen From Afar to one of the most respected man in the Blood tribe, were secondary.

Despite his divorce, Alexander Culbertson did not come into his second marriage unencumbered. Sometime in 1835, he had fathered a daughter named Mariah[50] and a second daughter, Janie, had been born the following year.[51] Very little is known about Mariah and Janie; most likely, their mother was Culbertson's Piegan wife, but even that cannot be said with certainty. What is clear is that these girls lived with Culbertson and Natawista off and on throughout their childhood and youth.

The girls most likely divided their time between their father and Piegan mother. Although Culbertson could have severed his ties to the two girls without opprobrium, he accepted his responsibility for them, assuring that Mariah and Janie learned the ways of the white world and received the best education he could provide them.

---

[48]Schultz, *Signposts,* pp. 115-116.
[49]Berglund, SC 414, MtHS, p. 22.
[50]This name is usually given as Maria. See, for instance, Dabney Taylor and Jack Holterman. In Missouri census records, however, her name is given as Mariah. Quite possibly, she was named after the Marias River, the pronunciation of which is closer to that which is usually associated with the spelling Mariah. An additional consideration in the author's choosing of this spelling is the fact that Mariah eventually had a daughter she named Julia, presumably after her younger half-sister. Julia had a daughter she named Mariah, presumably after her half-sister.
[51]Holterman, pp. 48-49.

Chapter Eight

## *"No one can ask for more politeness"*

By 1843, Alexander Culbertson had spent ten years on the upper Missouri, primarily at Fort McKenzie where he had made the Blackfeet trade one of the most valuable assets of the American Fur Company. Having realized his childhood ambitions, he had made the frontier his home. The Blackfeet considered him an honorable trader and the company had rewarded him by promoting him to chief trader for the upper Missouri forts. He had a beautiful, loving wife and, together, they awaited the birth of their first child.

The society established by the fur trade barons resembled a feudal empire and Alexander Culbertson reigned over the upper Missouri. Wherever he went, he received royal treatment from Company employees. The accoutrements of St. Louis society routinely came upriver on the Company steamboats and Natawista took full advantage, dressing herself in the finest fashions.

Although living far from his childhood home, Culbertson had formed "undying attachments" to those with whom he shared the wilderness, "friends that forsake not in the hour of danger, but cling through all changes; brothers in feeling and action, and 'though there be many, in heart they are one.'" Whenever he left a post, he did so with regret "for amid the common dangers, so well-known, none know when the meeting again will be, and when the hour of meeting comes, the joy is honest and unfeigned that the dangers are safely surmounted."[1]

Culbertson's many duties included entertaining distinguished visitors who came west seeking adventure, scientific knowledge, or personal experience with the Indians. Therefore, in the spring of 1843, Culbertson and his pregnant wife left Fort McKenzie with twenty-one hundred packs of buffalo robes and four packs of beaver pelts[2] to prepare for the arrival at

---

[1] Audubon, Vol. II, p. 195.   [2] Bradley, *MHSC*, Vol. III, p. 233.

Fort Union of the noted ornithologist, John James Audubon, who planned to spend the summer studying upper Missouri wildlife. Pierre Chouteau had rolled out the red carpet for Audubon in St. Louis, selling him supplies at wholesale prices, and guaranteeing him total cooperation upriver.[3] He depended on Culbertson to keep that promise. Expecting to return to Fort McKenzie at summer's end, Culbertson left Alexander Harvey temporarily in command.

Audubon had built a considerable reputation by 1843. Born in Haiti in 1785 and educated in Paris, he began observing and banding birds in 1803. Preoccupied with birds, the mature Audubon was a business failure. To support his family, he painted portraits. His classic folio, *The Birds of America*, published in two parts in 1827 and 1838 finally brought Audubon the recognition he sought. By 1843, he was gathering data for a new book, *The Viviparous Quadrupeds of North America*.[4]

Nearly sixty years old, Audubon traveled with four assistants: a wealthy New Jersey farmer named Edward Harris; Isaac Sprague, a landscape artist and botanical illustrator; John Bell, a taxidermist; and, an enthusiastic young adventurer named Lewis Squires. They would help Audubon collect specimens, sketch species, catalog artifacts, observe the landscape and its inhabitants, and record their experiences.[5]

The *Omega*, after picking up Francis Chardon at Fort Clark, reached Fort Union late in the evening of June 12.[6] She made the journey from St. Louis in forty-eight days, the fastest trip ever. Rounding the final bend, the crew saw "the glorious folds of the starry banner of [their] native land" flying above the fort. The flag welcomed visitors and, according to Culbertson, the "wanderer, as he sees the bright folds from afar, hails them with gladness, as it means for him a place of safety... it protects all, white men or red. Here in the wilderness all fly to it for refuge, and depend on it for security."[7]

As the *Omega* came into view, the men at Fort Union fired the traditional salute. Culbertson mounted his finest horse and led the gentlemen of the fort down to the river. When the steamboat docked, Culbertson introduced himself and his men to Audubon and invited the newcomers to the fort for some "first-rate port wine." Afterwards, exhausted from

---

[3]Sunder, p. 64.
[5]Sunder, p. 64.
[7]Audubon, Vol. II, p. 195.
[4]*New Columbia Encyclopedia*, p. 184.
[6]Audubon, Vol. II, p. 29.

their long journey, Audubon and his entourage returned to the boat to sleep.[8]

Audubon's first full day at Fort Union passed in a whirl of activity. The Company men busied themselves unloading the goods from St. Louis and replacing them with the winter's furs. Culbertson, in between supervising his men, visited with the naturalist, pledging "his services and the command of all the means of the establishment to further the accomplishment" of Audubon's goals.[9] According to Audubon, "no one can ask for more politeness than is shown us."[10]

Culbertson dined on the *Omega* with Audubon and Captain La Barge and, after the meal, outfitted a wagon to take Audubon to the surrounding countryside. But the trek did not sit well with the curmudgeonly old man who complained that it was taken "somewhat at the risk of our necks, for we travelled too fast for the nature of what I was told was the road."[11]

Later that afternoon, with most of the off-loading and re-loading completed, Culbertson enlisted several employees to move Audubon's possession to the fort. Culbertson had reserved the same room for Audubon which Prince Maximilian had occupied ten years earlier. Audubon, however, was less than satisfied. He found it "rather small and low, with only one window, on the west side," although he supposed that he and his men could "manage well enough ... for the few weeks we are to be here."[12]

Audubon, however, spent only one night there. He apparently made little effort to conceal his displeasure and Culbertson promised to find more suitable accommodations. Audubon was duly relieved "as it would have been very difficult to draw, write, or work in" that space, although "it is the very room where the Prince de Neuwied resided for two months, with his secretary and bird-preserver."[13]

The *Omega* departed on Wednesday, June 14. After bidding farewell to the crew, Audubon joined Culbertson for the noon meal. Culbertson took "his seat at the head of the table, [attending] to its honors and [serving] out the luxuries of this wilderness to his visitors and clerks, who [were] seated in their proper order and rank."[14] Audubon mentioned having seen

---

[8] Audubon, Vol. II, p. 29.
[9] Harris, p. 98.
[10] Audubon, Vol. II, pp. 29-30.
[11] Audubon, Vol. II, p. 29.
[12] Audubon, Vol. II, p. 29.
[13] Audubon, Vol. II, p. 34.
[14] *Story of Fort Union*, p. 4.

two wolves and Culbertson promised to give chase to any that might appear and present it, dead or alive, to the naturalist.

That evening, Audubon spied a white wolf. As the naturalist watched from the palisades, fretting that the wolf might escape, Culbertson mounted his horse and, with gun in hand, rode swiftly across the prairie. Tossing off his cap, Culbertson reminded Audubon of "a jockey bent on winning a race." The trader quickly gained on the animal. When the wolf turned into a small ravine, Culbertson followed. He fired one shot and then, without dismounting and "hardly slackening his pace," snatched up the wolf, threw it across his saddle, and headed back.

Riding full speed across the prairie, Culbertson performed "a maneuvre (*sic*) . . . common among the Indians and hunters." Shifting his body weight without employing his reins, Culbertson guided his "beautiful Blackfoot Pied mare" in one direction and then the other in a "gentle curve" along a "serpentine track" toward the fort. The "beautiful exhibition" impressed everyone.[15] Back at the fort, Culbertson presented the dying wolf to a duly appreciative Audubon.[16]

Culbertson, eager to showcase his skills further, proposed a shooting exhibition. A suit of clothes would go to the rider who could load and fire the most shots within a given distance. Riding across the prairie, the participants fired first on one side, then on the other, as if hunting buffalo. The horses were in full gallop and the bridles hung loose.

Culbertson won the contest, most likely the result he anticipated, when he got off eleven shots. He rode a magnificent horse, a five-year-old mare "of the full Blackfoot Indian breed," which Audubon guessed to be worth more than $400.[17] The horse may have been one of Natawista's wedding presents.

The mock hunt went so well that Culbertson staged another a few weeks later. Again, he won. Starting with an empty gun, he fired eleven shots in less than a mile and returned to the fort with his weapon loaded. Audubon thought the feat most impressive: "A more wonderful rider I never saw."[18] Finally, the third and last time Culbertson staged the competition, he lost to Owen McKenzie, Kenneth McKenzie's mixed-blood son, who matched Culbertson's earlier eleven shots while, this time, Cul-

---

[15]Harris, p. 100.
[16]Audubon, Vol. II, pp. 31-32; Harris, p. 100.
[17]Audubon, Vol. II, p. 33.
[18]Audubon, Vol. II, p. 71.

bertson only managed eight. Lewis Squires, Audubon's enthusiastic traveling companion, participated in this last contest, discharging five shots.[19]

On the night the *Omega* departed, Culbertson threw a ball for the employees although he apparently failed to mention it to Audubon. The old man, exhausted by several long walks, the wolf chase, and the mock hunt, had retired early but could not sleep as a "drunken man" above him "roared, laughed like a maniac, and damned himself and the whole creation." As the naturalist waited for the noise to subside, music drifted in from the dining room.

Squires went to see what was happening and returned to report that "all of the beauty and fashion" would be shortly in evidence. Audubon, seeing "no alternative" following an invitation from Culbertson, made his way to the dining room where he found himself "amid the beau monde of these parts," including "several squaws, attired in their best." With Culbertson playing the fiddle "very fairly," Mr. Guèpe on the clarinet, and Mr. Chouteau[20] on the drum, the group danced to cotillions and reels "with much energy and apparent enjoyment" until the early morning.[21] A week later, Culbertson hosted another ball, this one to honor Francis Chardon before his departure for Fort McKenzie.[22]

With Audubon settled in, Culbertson persuaded him to paint his and Natawista's portraits. The assignment caused Audubon many headaches as Culbertson had little time to pose and, when he did, he refused to sit still. Natawista also had difficulty posing but evinced great interest in the work. When Audubon completed the portraits, Culbertson and Natawista were "much pleased." The artist, however, was not, although he had done his best "with a man who is never in the same position for one whole minute."[23]

---

[19]Audubon, Vol. II, p. 73.

[20]Audubon, Vol. II, p. 35, says "Mr. Chouteau" played the drums. Innis, p. 65, identifies the drummer as Pierre Chouteau, Jr., who, according to Innis, came upriver aboard the *Omega*. Harris, p. 101, identifies the drummer as Francis Chardon but states that "Mr. Chouteau" had arrived that afternoon. Francis McDermott, p. 101n, identifies this Chouteau as Auguste Liguest Chouteau, nephew of Pierre Chouteau, Jr. The true identity of the drummer remains a mystery.

[21]Audubon, Vol. II, pp. 34-35. Italics in original. [22]Audubon, Vol. II, p. 42.

[23]Audubon, Vol. II, p. 82 and p. 85. It is not clear whether Audubon did Natawista's portrait or whether that was done by Isaac Sprague. Culbertson's daughter, Julia, owned these paintings and she left them to her son, Alexander Culbertson Roberts. KP, UCLA. They are now housed at the Audubon Memorial Museum in Henderson, KY.

❖   ❖   ❖

During more than two months at Fort Union, Audubon observed lazuli finches, arctic ground finches, cliff swallows, prairie larks, arctic bluebirds, red shafted woodpeckers, Say's flycatchers, sharp-tailed grouse, shore larks, golden eagles, ravens, short-billed marsh wrens, black breasted prairie-bunting flies, sandhill cranes, and numerous others. He studied bighorn sheep, deer, elk, antelope, bears, foxes, otters, beavers, rabbits, badgers, and porcupine. The fort personnel killed numerous wolves and buffalo for Audubon's research or just to entertain the naturalist with the hunt.

While Audubon rarely engaged in the hunt, his assistants participated with enthusiasm. Culbertson praised Harris, the New Jersey farmer, and Bell, the taxidermist, who had "done wonders, for persons who have never shot at Buffaloes from on horseback."[24]

No one expressed much concern for the buffalo slaughter although Audubon noted the "terrible destruction of life, as it were for nothing, or next to it, as the tongues only were brought in, and the flesh of these fine animals was left to beasts and birds of prey, or to rot on the spots where they fell. The prairies are literally *covered* with the skulls of the victims. . . ."[25] But buffalo were plentiful; Audubon remarked that "the roads the Buffalo make in crossing the prairies have all the appearance of heavy wagon tracks."[26]

Audubon did not confine his scientific studies to plants and animals. Soon after arriving, Culbertson and Chardon took the naturalist to an Assiniboine burial site. The Assiniboines, like most Plains Indians, shunned ground burials, instead wrapping the body in skins and placing it in the forked limbs of a tree. Audubon wanted to do more than simply study these practices; he hoped to determine "when it would be best for us to take away the skulls, some six or seven in number. . . ."

Culbertson apparently did not discourage Audubon from this although he cautioned the naturalist about wandering alone so far from the fort. "Even a *single* Indian with a gun and a bow," Culbertson stressed, "might have attacked" the men. They were less likely to assault a group, though, "as that might be construed to mean war."[27]

---

[24]Audubon, Vol. II, p. 107; Harris, p. 35 and pp. 146-150.
[25]Audubon, Vol. II, p. 107. Italics in original.
[26]Audubon, Vol. II, p. 107.  [27]Audubon, Vol. II, p. 38.

Two weeks later, Audubon and Culbertson's old friend, Edwin Denig, himself an amateur anthropologist, "walked off with a bag and instruments, to take off the head of a three-years-dead Indian chief, called the White Cow."[28] White Cow, a famous orator and good friend to the whites, had traded many robes at Fort Union. But he was "consumptive"[29] and, when the end was near, he had thrust an arrow into his own heart. He died soon after and Kenneth McKenzie ordered a coffin for his tree burial.[30]

At the burial site, Denig climbed on Audubon's shoulders to dislodge the coffin. It "tumbled down" and the two men "hammered off" the lid. Inside, they found White Cow wrapped in two buffalo robes and covered with an American flag and a "superb scarlet blanket." The dead Indian's feet, "naked, shrunk and dried up," rested on a pillow.

Audubon went to work. White Cow's head, still covered with hair, "was twisted off in a moment, under jaw and all." The grisly task complete, Audubon and Denig returned to Fort Union, leaving the beheaded White Cow on the ground. Later, Denig enlisted Owen McKenzie and Lewis Squires to try to replace the coffin but "the whole affair fell to the ground, and there it lies." Audubon, ignoring Assiniboine customs, planned to "have it covered with earth" the next day.[31]

While Audubon indulged in scientific grave-robbing, a more humanitarian mission engaged Culbertson and Natawista. The opposition Union Fur Company traders at nearby Fort Mortimer had endured a particularly difficult winter, barely managing to survive on stolen food, wild game, and gifts of food and medicine from their competitors.[32]

That morning, Culbertson, Natawista, Owen McKenzie, and Audubon had traveled to Fort Mortimer to check on the opposition. They found head trader John Collins desperately ill. Culbertson returned to Fort Union, driving the wagon "so fast . . . over this rough ground" that he left Audubon feeling "quite stiff," to gather medicine for Collins. He enlisted Audubon's companion, Edward Harris, who had some medical

---

[28] Audubon, Vol. II, p. 72.
[29] "Consumptive" usually referred to someone suffering from tuberculosis.
[30] Audubon, Vol. II, p. 73. Audubon says that Kenneth McKenzie "ordered" the tree burial but this hardly seems as if it would have been necessary. Most likely, McKenzie ordered the coffin which was unusual. Also, McKenzie left the upper Missouri in 1836. Therefore, if he was present when White Cow died, White Cow had been dead considerably more than three years.
[31] Audubon, Vol. II, p. 73.     [32] Sunder, p. 69.

knowledge,[33] to return with him. As Denig and Audubon headed for White Cow's burial site, Culbertson, Natawista, and Harris, equipped with "a lancet, some calomel and some salts and also an emetic,"[34] went back to Fort Mortimer to minister to Collins.[35]

That Audubon thought little about defiling White Cow's body comports with his scarcely concealed contempt for the Indians. When fourteen Assiniboine warriors, their faces painted black, returned to Fort Union from a raid singing what Culbertson identified as their scalp dance song, Audubon sneered: "They all looked miserably poor, filthy beyond description, and their black and foully smelling Buffalo robes made them appear to me like so many devils."

The group annoyed Audubon as they beat their drum to celebrate their victory over the Blackfeet. "The chief, to show his pride and delight at killing his enemy, has borrowed a drum; and the company have nearly ever since been yelling, singing, and beating that beastly tambour." The next morning, as the celebration continued, Audubon bemoaned "the dirty Indians, who could have washed had they so minded." Instead, they continued "their miserable scalp song" until Culbertson ordered the drum taken away. Nonetheless, Audubon was not satisfied until he saw the "dirty and rascally Indians" leave the fort.[36]

Audubon also questioned the work of George Catlin who painted many Indian portraits during his 1832 visit to the upper Missouri: "When and where Mr. Catlin saw these Indians as he represented them, dressed in magnificent attire, with all sorts of extravagant accoutrements, is more than I can divine, or Mr. Culbertson can tell me."[37]

Culbertson, however, had seen Indians splendidly dressed, as portrayed by Catlin. Most likely, the Indians never displayed their finery for Audubon because he evinced so little interest. Despite Audubon's disparaging comments, he expressed great satisfaction when Culbertson presented him with a "splendid" Indian outfit as well as "a grand pair of

---

[33]Harris, passim.      [34]Harris, p. 123.
[35]Audubon, Vol. II, pp. 72-73.
[36]Audubon, Vol. II, pp. 77-78 and p. 81; Harris, p. 130.
[37]Audubon, Vol. II, p. 108.

leather breeches and a very handsome knife-case, all manufactured by the Blackfeet Indians."[38]

Even mixed-bloods whom Audubon enlisted to gather animal specimens evoked his wrath. After some returned empty-handed, saying they had seen nothing, Audubon remarked: "I fear that all my former opinions of the half-breeds are likely to be realized, and that they are all more au fait at telling lies, than anything else...."[39]

All this made Audubon's reaction to Natawista most remarkable. He described her as "handsome, and really courteous and refined in many ways." However, when she broke open a buffalo skull to partake of the fresh brains, a delicacy among the tribes, he could not "reconcile ... the fact that she partakes of raw animal food with such evident relish."[40]

Audubon frequently referred to Natawista as an "Indian princess—for that is Mrs. Culbertson's rank" and perhaps his sense of her as royalty helped moderate his opinion. But, just as likely, her grace and beauty worked their charms. One afternoon, the ornithologist enjoyed a "curious sight" as Owen McKenzie, the irrepressible Lewis Squires, Culbertson, Natawista, and Natawista's Indian maid all dressed in Indian garb and rode across the prairie.

Although Audubon derided the face painting Natawista had done for Squires and McKenzie, the event pleased him: "The Ladies had their hair loose, and flying in the breeze, and then all mounted on horses with Indian saddles and trappings. Mrs. Culbertson and her maid rode astride like men, and all rode a furious race, under whip the whole way, for more than one mile on the prairie...." Natawista, "a wonderful rider, possessed of both strength and grace in a marked degree," had her "magnificent black hair floating like a banner behind her." The men could not be compared "to anything in the whole creation. They ran like wild creatures of unearthly compound."[41]

Natawista also impressed Audubon as a "most expert and graceful swimmer" when she caught six live mallards in the upper Missouri.[42] She could catch more than mallards. Toward the end of Audubon's visit, he

---

[38] Audubon, Vol. II, p. 71 and p. 87.
[39] Audubon, Vol. II, p. 123. Italics in original.
[40] Audubon, Vol. II, p. 111.
[41] Audubon, Vol. II, pp. 88-89; Harris, p. 134.
[42] Audubon, Vol. II, p. 112.

found her working on a new parfleche, using the feathers of a golden eagle she had killed.[43]

Natawista also practiced her traditional arts, making Audubon a berry necklace.[44] One afternoon, the naturalist watched as Denig and Natawista dyed porcupine quills. First, they boiled the quills to remove the oil. While Natawista washed the quills, Denig boiled vegetable and earth dyes. Then they placed them in the boiling water until they assumed the desired shade.

By the end of the afternoon, Natawista had a fresh supply of red, yellow, green, and black quills. Nonetheless, Audubon could not resist trumpeting his culture's superiority: "Indians are not equal to the whites in the art of dyeing Porcupine quills; their ingredients are altogether too simple and natural to equal the knowledge of chemicals."[45]

Natawista may have used these quills to decorate a new cradleboard for her infant son, Jack, born that summer.[46] She quickly adapted to her new role; when a violent thunderstorm surprised the Culbertsons and Audubon, Natawista "with her child in her arms, made for the willows, and had a shelter for her babe in a few minutes."[47]

In the middle of August, having collected innumerable plant and animal specimens, along with the unlucky White Cow's skull, Audubon prepared to head downriver. Alexander Culbertson, to his regret, would be joining him. Culbertson had received orders to assume control of the Company post on the Platte River in what is now Wyoming at the end of summer.[48]

The American Fur Company had acquired the post, formally Fort John but known to almost everyone as Fort Laramie, five years earlier. The Company conducted no formal trade at this site, but it supplied outposts on White Earth River, the Old Woman's Fork of the Cheyenne, and Horse Creek. Pelts from these outposts were collected at Fort Laramie

---

[43]Audubon, Vol. II, p. 157.      [44]Audubon, Vol. II, p. 154.
[45]Audubon, Vol. II, p. 81.
[46]Berglund, SC 414, MtHS, p. 22. Fannie Culbertson Irvin gives his name as John but he was familiarly known as Jack.
[47]Audubon, Vol. II, p. 163.      [48]Bradley, *MHSC*, Vol. III, p. 233.

each spring and shipped east.[49] For some time, the returns had been disappointing. The Company hoped Culbertson could restore the trade. Meanwhile, Culbertson's superiors wanted Francis Chardon, the Fort Clark trader, to take over at Fort McKenzie.

Culbertson vigorously protested his reassignment: the Blackfeet trade was too volatile to be entrusted to traders inexperienced in their ways. Culbertson had worked long and hard to gain their trust and, he argued, it would not be automatically transferred. But his protestations fell on deaf ears.[50]

On August 16, 1843, Alexander Culbertson, Natawista, and their son, Jack, boarded the mackinaw *Union* to travel downriver with Audubon and his entourage. Meanwhile, William Laidlaw waited impatiently at Fort Pierre. "I am at a loss," he wrote Chouteau, "to account for the delay of Mr. Culbertson [who] was to have been here about the first of August."[51] Even as Laidlaw penned these words, the group neared the post, arriving on September 8. Culbertson, after meeting with Laidlaw, presented Audubon with a parfleche received from a Sioux chief and then bid his new friend farewell.[52]

With twenty ox-drawn wagons and eight horse- and mule-drawn carts, Culbertson, Natawista, and Jack began the more than 300 mile overland trek to Fort Laramie.[53] En route, they saw hundreds of dead buffalo, felled by a severe May snowstorm. The animals, who could survive temperatures of fifty below zero, had sunk in the deep snows and perished by the thousands.[54]

The overland journey took more than a month. When Culbertson had finally settled into his new post, he wrote Pierre Chouteau: "I according

---

[49]Bradley, *MHSC*, Vol. III, p. 235.

[50]Bradley, *MHSC*, Vol. III, pp. 233-234. How exactly Culbertson protested is not clear. Bradley says he protested to Honoré Picotte and someone named "Sierce," whose identity is unknown. If Culbertson wrote letters of protest during his summer at Fort Union, they have apparently been lost.

[51]William Laidlaw to Pierre Chouteau, 8 Sep 1843. Chouteau-Walsh Collection, MoHS.

[52]Audubon, Vol. II, p. 164. The common term "Sioux" is used to designate this tribe because it is often impossible in historical documents to distinguish between the Lakota, Dakota, and Nakota. For more information on the composition of what is loosely called the "Sioux," see Chapter 17, endnote 16.

[53]Hanson, "The Fort Pierre-Fort Laramie Trail," p. 3.

[54]Bradley, *MHSC*, Vol. III, p. 234.

to your request, arrive here a few days since from Fort Union to take charge of Fort John." But Culbertson could not help but remark on his reassignment: "I was somewhat surprised to be removed from the Missouri, a country in which I was well acquainted to a place I knew nothing about." Somewhat disingenuously, he added, "I however cheerfully accord with your desires."[55]

---

[55] Alexander Culbertson to Pierre Chouteau, 16 Oct 1843. Chouteau-Walsh Collection, MoHS.

# Chapter Nine

## *"I am going to kill you"*

Alexander Culbertson had good cause for alarm at the Company's choice of leadership for Fort McKenzie. Neither Alexander Harvey nor Francis Chardon had exhibited the tolerance Culbertson knew was necessary in the Blackfeet trade.

Francis Chardon, born to French parents in Philadelphia,[1] began his career with the American Fur Company in 1817. After several years in the Osage trade, he assumed command of Fort Clark serving the Mandans.[2] When smallpox broke out in 1837, the distraught Mandans kept Chardon under siege for weeks. Although responding with restraint, Chardon evinced little compassion for the tribe.

Judging from his journal, Chardon disliked all Indians but held special contempt for the Mandans. When they undertook a raid against the Sioux, Chardon wished "both parties a severe conflict and heavy losses."[3] He called the Mandans "the meanest, dirtiest, worthless cowardly set of Dogs on the Missouri"[4] and "the Horrid tribe."[5] In their villages, Chardon complained about "Men, Women and Children, bellowing like so many Bedlamites."[6]

Chardon seemed to delight in their suffering: "Fine pleasant weather, Indians all Starveing (*sic*)."[7] When the Mandan chief White Bear died, Chardon claimed the death was "regretted by None" and he was personally "glad of his disappearance."[8] He wrote "What a bande (*sic*) of RASCALS has been used up" after only fourteen Mandans survived the smallpox epidemic.[9]

Chardon held a somewhat more favorable impression of the Sioux,

---

[1] Abel, p. xix, gives his birth name as François Auguste Chardon. His father's name was Anthony or Antoine.
[2] Abel, pp. xxv-xxxiv.
[3] Abel, p. 45.
[4] DeVoto, *Wide Missouri*, p. 243.
[5] Abel, p. 110.
[6] Abel, p. 78.
[7] Abel, p. 110.
[8] Abel, p. 117.
[9] Abel, p. 137. Emphasis in original.

from whom he procured three wives. But his treatment of them was hardly exemplary, giving one "a good whipping" for not mending his moccasins.[10] Chardon did not limit his intemperate outbursts to his wives; in 1843, shortly before his transfer to Fort McKenzie, he was charged with murdering a rival trader. Rather than deal with the allegation, the Company simply relocated him.[11]

Culbertson, then, could hardly have felt complacent about Chardon's command of Fort McKenzie. Even more temperate men had had difficulty reining in Alexander Harvey.

Chardon passed his first months at Fort McKenzie reasonably well. But as the months passed, Chardon, his authority frequently questioned, began to rely heavily on Harvey. Harvey was not the ally Chardon needed since he probably resented Chardon's mere presence. Having spent more than ten years in the Blackfeet trade, Harvey believed himself singularly qualified to sustain Fort McKenzie during Culbertson's absence and felt slighted by Chardon's presence.

In subtle ways, Harvey pushed Chardon into increasingly heavy reliance on his advice. Chardon was probably willing to relinquish his responsibilities if it meant less contact with the Blackfeet. Before long, although Chardon remained titular head of Fort McKenzie, Alexander Harvey held the real power.[12]

It may have been about this time that Harvey committed another in his string of unwarranted murders. A group of Indians with "a spite against the fort" raided it, chased off cattle, and shot a cow. Outraged, Harvey pursued them. When he overcame the offenders, Harvey fired, breaking a warrior's thigh.

With the wounded man lying on the ground, Harvey approached and sat down. Lighting his pipe, Harvey announced his intention to kill him but, first, Harvey offered a smoke. After sharing his pipe, Harvey told the warrior: "I am going to kill you, but I will give you a little time to take a good look at your country." The Indian, admitting his foolishness, begged for his life; Harvey had broken his thigh, surely now they were even.

---

[10]Abel, p. xxi.

[11]Sunder, p. 61. The only apparent reference to this episode found in Abel concerns statements given by Chardon on his deathbed. See Chapter 14.

[12]Bradley, *MHSC,* Vol. III, p. 235.

"No," said Harvey, "look well, for the last time, at all those nice hills—at all those paths which lead to the fort, where you came with your parents to trade, playing with your sweethearts—look at that, will you, for the last time." Harvey then pulled his gun and killed the warrior.[13]

That winter (1843-44), a war party of twenty Bloods,[14] led by Big Snake,[15] stopped at Fort McKenzie and asked to be admitted. Chardon and Harvey refused. To show their annoyance, the Bloods killed some livestock[16] before heading for winter camp. This infuriated Harvey who persuaded Chardon to retaliate. The two, accompanied by half a dozen Company men, pursued the Bloods.

But the warriors had warrior instincts and, realizing they were being followed, set up an ambush in the Teton Valley. The traders sent Reese, a black man, to reconnoiter. As Reese poked his head up over the bluff, a shot rang out, killing Reese instantly. The Bloods rushed forward, scalped their victim, and derisively waved the scalp at the Company men.[17] The traders, shocked by the attack, abandoned their pursuit, collected Reese's body, and returned to Fort McKenzie.

Chardon, who "set great store by [Reese],"[18] was furious. Most likely, he had good reason for this: Chardon owned slaves and Reese probably belonged to him.[19] Livestock could be replaced but slaves could not be easily acquired on the frontier. In addition to outwitting the traders, the Bloods had destroyed some precious personal property. Neither Chardon nor Harvey could let that pass.

---

[13]Larpenteur, p. 190.

[14]Larpenteur, p. 187. Most sources do not identify the band of Blackfeet involved in the initial encounter.          [15]Kane, *Wanderings*, p. 296.

[16]Kane, *Wanderings*, p. 296, says that the Bloods killed thirteen cattle; Bradley, *MHSC*, Vol. III, p. 235, says that they killed a Company pig.

[17]Kane, *Wanderings*, p. 296.          [18]Larpenteur, p. 188.

[19]Chittenden, *Fur Trade*, Vol. II, p. 685, calls Reese "a negro servant of Chardon." For more information about Chardon as slaveowner, see Abel, p. 255, note 228. Chardon acquired a slave named Black Hawk in 1837. Francis Chardon to John B. Sarpy, 27 Jun 1837. Chouteau-Papin Collection, MoHS. Chardon manumitted Black Hawk in his will. Abel, page 268, note 253. The Chouteau family also owned slaves and it is possible that Reese was their slave, assigned to the upper Missouri posts. Supporting this possibility is the fact that a man by the name of "James Reese" appears on the AFC Retail Store Ledgers, 1839-1841, at Fort McKenzie. A "Joseph Reese" also appears on these ledgers and on the ledger for 1842-1845. AFC Fur Trade Ledgers, Volume CC (pp. 328-329, 336-338, 340, 349 and 366) and Volume GG (pp. 31, 32, 55, 242). MoHS. Whether James and Joseph Reese were the same or two different men is unknown. If this is the Reese killed prior to the Fort McKenzie massacre, it argues against his being Chardon's slave since the recorded transactions predate Chardon's presence there.

They soon hatched a despicable scheme for revenge. Most of the Fort McKenzie men remained loyal to Culbertson, who had taught them to act circumspectly, avoiding actions which might be interpreted as needlessly aggressive. This posed a problem for Chardon and Harvey: they worried that if Culbertson loyalists learned of their scheme, they would thwart them or, even worse, alert the tribes.

Therefore, Harvey and Chardon confided in only a select few. The plan was simple. First, they would load the cannon at the fort's gate with half-ounce lead balls. When the next trading party arrived, they would invite the chiefs inside. The balance of the tribe would then gather at the gate. Once they had congregated, the traders would kill the chiefs and then Harvey would fire his pistol, packed with powder, into the cannon's vent. The deadly blast would kill those beyond the gate and the devious traders would acquire, without cost, their victims' horses, robes, and personal possessions.

Since Culbertson had established a thriving trade at Fort McKenzie, the schemers did not have to wait long to launch their plan. Within a few weeks, a band of unsuspecting Northern Blackfoot[20] arrived to trade. The conspirators invited the three chiefs inside while the rest of the tribe gathered at the gate with their pelts. However, yet again, Chardon and Harvey underestimated the heightened senses of nomadic people. The chiefs realized something was wrong, ran from the office, and jumped over the pickets. As they fled, Chardon fired and broke one chief's thigh.[21]

This alerted those at the gate and they, too, began to scatter. Harvey fired into the cannon, as planned, and its discharge killed and wounded several, including women and children.[22] The second half of the wicked

---

[20]Abel, p. 246, note 186. This letter identifies the tribe as Northern Blackfoot.

[21]Larpenteur, p. 188.

[22]The number of those killed varies from Larpenteur, p. 188, who claims only three were killed in the initial attack to Bradley, *MHSC,* Vol. III, p. 237, who, based on Culbertson's account, gives a figure of twenty-one. Kane, *Wanderings,* p. 297, says that ten were killed, "principally women and children." Chittenden, *Fur Trade,* Vol. II, p. 685, says that three were killed and three wounded, including one of the chiefs, in the initial attack and that Harvey then "killed the wounded man." Abel, p. 246, note 186, reprints a letter that appears to be an eyewitness account stating that six were killed with two children taken hostage. Ewers, *Blackfeet,* p. 67, puts the figure at "ten or more." A combined winter count of the Northern Blackfoot and Blood tribes recorded this incident as "American white men attack South Peigan (*sic*) Indian camps near forth (*sic*) Benton with Cannon fire by white man called Running Wolf. Killed thirteen of them." This must have been recorded at least several years later since Fort Benton did not exist at the time of the massacre. The entry suggests that Harvey's Indian name was Running Wolf. Hugh Dempsey to the author.

plot worked better: as the Indians fled, they abandoned guns, bows and arrows, horses, and hundreds of buffalo robes.[23]

A frustrated Harvey, his anger not yet spent, dispatched several wounded Indians with his dagger. Some said that, after stabbing the Indians, Harvey licked the blood from his knife. He then raised their scalps and forced the Indian women of the fort to join the traders in a scalp dance.[24]

This incident was long remembered by the Blackfeet. The Northern Blackfoot winter count recorded that year as "When the Whites first shot the Indians"; the Piegans called it "When the White Man shot at Old Sun";[25] and, the Bloods commemorated it as "The Blackfoot were shot with a cannon by a white man."[26]

The Fort McKenzie traders quickly realized their treachery had made their position untenable. Following the massacre, those few Indians who appeared at Fort McKenzie came not to trade but to cause trouble. Chardon decided that Fort McKenzie, one of the AFC's most profitable posts under Culbertson, would have to be abandoned.

Chardon dispatched a small contingent downriver to the mouth of the Judith River to construct a new fort to be named Fort FAC (Francis A. Chardon). Avoiding the Indians, the group erected a stockade at the chosen site. When the ice on the upper Missouri broke up in early April, Chardon and Harvey loaded Fort McKenzie's effects onto keelboats and headed downriver. As a last act, they burned Fort McKenzie, giving rise to its new name: Fort Brûlé (Burnt Fort).[27]

Hostility followed Chardon and Harvey; the trade at Fort FAC never amounted to much. A few Piegans initially traded there but soon decided against conducting business with the treacherous men. Before long, the only Indians near Fort FAC were hostile Blackfeet who harassed the traders and drove off or killed the stock. After several members of the garrison were slain, it became increasingly dangerous for the men to hunt or gather wood.

---

[23] Abel, p. 246. Cf. Chittenden, *Fur Trade*, Vol. II, p. 686, who says that they "secured very little of the booty which they had expected to obtain."

[24] Larpenteur, p. 189; Bradley, *MHSC*, Vol. III, p. 237; Chittenden, *Fur Trade*, Vol. II, p. 685.

[25] Apparently, the leader of the Northern Blackfoot party was Old Sun who, according to Hugh Dempsey, was a prominent chief.

[26] Hugh Dempsey to the author. Dempsey calls this incident "extremely significant to the Blackfeet nation." [27] Bradley, *MHSC*, Vol. III, p. 238.

Fort FAC existed in a state of siege. The animosity extended to Fort Union where the Blackfeet made several raids, including one in which a band under Big Snake[28] drove off more than forty horses and mules, and another in which they killed two Company men.[29]

In early spring, Alexander Culbertson, who had passed the winter at Fort Laramie, arrived at Fort Pierre with the winter's returns.[30] There, he learned of the Fort McKenzie massacre from Honoré Picotte, the AFC partner in charge of the upper Missouri posts.[31] Culbertson had previously complained to Picotte about his reassignment and warned him that neither Chardon nor Harvey possessed the temperament for command of Fort McKenzie. Now his fears had been realized.

Picotte asked Culbertson to return to the upper Missouri, presumably to Fort FAC, to resume stewardship over the Blackfeet trade. Culbertson declined, but his emotions were complex. Culbertson had come to regard the Blackfeet as "his" Indians and while the actions of Chardon and Harvey outraged him—in later years, he gave exaggerated estimates of the numbers killed[32]—he was also concerned about the welfare of the Blackfeet and the fiscal health of the American Fur Company.

He recognized that he probably was the only one capable of luring the Blackfeet back as trading partners. Nonetheless, Culbertson deemed it prudent to leave Chardon and Harvey at the Blackfeet post for the time being to absorb the wrath for their transgressions. Only after more time had passed did Culbertson believe he might be able to engage the Blackfeet in rational discourse. His supplies replenished, Culbertson returned to Fort Laramie, leaving a frustrated Picotte to travel upriver to confront the murdering traders.[33]

---

[28]Bradley, *MHSC*, Vol. III, p. 238, gives his Indian name as Oh-muck'-see Sin-a-kwan.

[29]Bradley, *MHSC*, Vol. III, p. 238.

[30]Larpenteur, p. 155, suggests that Culbertson was at Fort Union in January 1844 when he allegedly sent Larpenteur and Denig to establish a post at Woody Mountain. However, the date "[1844]" was inserted by Milo Milton Quaife, editor of Larpenteur's journal. This date seems improbable since Larpenteur apparently was at Fort Union when the Fort McKenzie massacre occurred and Culbertson was not around at that time. The author believes that a more likely date for Larpenteur's expedition to Woody Mountain is January 1843 when Culbertson was at Fort Union.

[31]McDonnell, *MHSC*, Vol. X, p. 241, note 2.

[32]Bradley, *MHSC*, Vol. III, p. 237, gives the number killed in the initial blast as twenty-one with more of the wounded killed subsequently. In the next paragraph, this figure grows to thirty, the number of scalps that Culbertson told Bradley were raised by Harvey.

[33]Larpenteur, p. 191. Again, the date given by Quaife is 1845 but this does not square with the historical record since Culbertson returned to the upper Missouri in 1845. Most likely, Larpenteur's account of the arrival of the steamboat with Picotte aboard happened in June 1844.

# I AM GOING TO KILL YOU

Chardon had brought the meager winter returns to Fort Union where Picotte probably met him.[34] Chardon desperately wanted to be relieved of the Blackfeet post but Picotte, having been turned down by Culbertson, had few options. He could leave the post to Alexander Harvey, whom Chardon had left in charge, or send Chardon back. Since nearly everyone believed the ill-tempered Harvey largely responsible for the massacre, it made little sense to reward him, as Harvey surely would have perceived it, with command. No, Chardon would have to return and, this time, exercise better control.

So Chardon packed up the supplies and returned to his besieged fort. The goods turned out to be largely superfluous since the employees conducted virtually no trade. Instead, they "shivered the winter away," near starvation and afraid to gather wood or hunt.[35]

The loss of the Blackfeet trade caused the AFC great consternation. In the fall of 1844, when Pierre Chouteau learned that Culbertson had refused to return to the Blackfeet territory, he ordered Culbertson to meet him in New York the following June. After shipping the Fort Laramie returns down the Platte and dispatching the overland wagon train to Fort Pierre for supplies, Culbertson began the long journey. Natawista probably remained at Fort Laramie with their two-year-old son, Jack, while she awaited the birth of their second child.[36]

Culbertson reached Chouteau's New York headquarters in June 1845. Chouteau appealed to Culbertson to return to the Blackfeet country. So desperate was the Company to re-enlist Culbertson in the Blackfeet trade

---

[34]Sunder, p. 62, note 19. According to Sunder, the *St. Louis New Era* reported on June 24, 1844, that 1,102 packs of buffalo robes and other furs had just landed from Fort McKenzie.

[35]Bradley, *MHSC*, Vol. III, p. 239.

[36]The obituary of Julia Culbertson Roberts in *The Idaho Statesman*, 17 Mar 1929, claims that Julia was born in Chambersburg, Pennsylvania, but gives no year for her birth. This is untrue and it seems clear that Julia, who had married a successful white Civil War veteran and attorney, was trying to obscure her Indian heritage. While the obituary cites Alexander Culbertson as her father, no mention is made of her mother. The obituary further states that Julia "came west as the bride of George H. Roberts." In correspondence with Charles Kessler, Julia Culbertson Roberts states that she was born at Fort Laramie. KP, UCLA. Her sister, Fannie, also says that Julia was born at Fort Laramie. Berglund, SC 414, MtHS, p. 22. Another family story suggests Natawista might have accompanied Culbertson on this journey east. Fannie Culbertson Irvin told Berglund, MtHS, p. 7, that, soon after their marriage, Alexander took Natawista to Chambersburg to meet his family. While this may have happened, the author does not believe it occurred during this 1845 business trip. See Chapter Nineteen, footnote 43.

that Chouteau told him to name his price. But Culbertson did not want money; his refusal stemmed from the injustice of asking him to assume the dangerous posting after the Company had ignored his warnings about Chardon and Harvey. Culbertson argued that the Company wanted him to risk his life to correct a situation he had tried to avoid in the first place.

Chouteau conceded the point and apologized for ignoring Culbertson's advice. However, Chouteau continued, it was precisely because Culbertson saw the potential dangers that the Company now desperately needed his talents. No one else understood the Blackfeet as well. No one else had their trust. No one else had exhibited the skill with them that Culbertson had. Unless Culbertson returned, the Blackfeet trade might be irretrievably lost and the Company forced to withdraw from the area.[37]

Chouteau's blunt concession that the Company had erred and his blatant appeal to Culbertson's ego prevailed. Culbertson agreed to return to the Blackfeet country but eschewed Chouteau's offer of $2,000 as reward.[38] All Culbertson asked before returning to what might be his death was a two week vacation to visit with John James Audubon in New York City.[39]

John James Audubon had purchased thirty acres northwest of present-day Harlem soon after completing *The Birds of America*.[40] Hemlock, pine, hickory, oak, and chestnut trees, many of massive size, dominated the estate where migratory birds, crows, hawks, and owls found homes. Deer

---

[37] Bradley, *MHSC*, Vol. III, pp. 239-240.

[38] An interesting drama was playing itself out in New York City that summer which may have involved Pierre Chouteau and the American Fur Company. As the United States government worked to expand the boundaries of the young nation, they funneled huge sums of money into New York to help those willing and able to advance this cause. Recipients of the government largesse included the adventurer, Lansford W. Hastings, best known for leading the Donner party to their disastrous fate in the Sierra Nevada mountains. During his New York visit that summer, Hastings was also promoting the interests of the Hudson's Bay Company which had helped him on several occasions when he lived in Oregon Territory. The Hudson's Bay Company, of course, stood to reap the benefits if the American Fur Company's trade with the Blackfeet collapsed. But such a collapse would also shrink the influence of the United States on the northern frontier. If Pierre Chouteau learned that the government was investing money that summer to secure and expand its boundaries, it is entirely possible that the shrewd businessman turned to the government for assistance in keeping the AFC position in the Blackfeet territory strong. For additional information about the funneling of money from the United States government to Lansford Hastings, see Bagley, pp. 12-26.

[39] Bradley, *MHSC*, Vol. III, p. 240.   [40] Grinnell, *Audubon Park*, pp. 2-4.

and elk lived there along with a few buffalo, some caged otters, martens, and tame muskrats.[41]

When Culbertson arrived at the grand colonial house with its large colonnaded portico overlooking the Hudson River,[42] Audubon was busy completing *The Viviparous Quadrupeds of North America*. Culbertson thought the mounted specimens brought back from the upper Missouri looked "as natural as life." The trader spent two relaxed weeks working with Audubon, strolling the estate, and fishing with Audubon's sons who were closer in age than the naturalist.[43]

Six years later, Audubon died before completing *The Viviparous Quadrupeds of North America*. His sons completed the work and, when the three volume set was published, they sent Culbertson a copy which remained a valued family possession for generations.[44]

---

[41]Grinnell, *Audubon Park*, pp. 8-9.
[42]Holterman, p. 69.
[43]Bradley, *MHSC*, Vol. III, p. 240.
[44]Taylor, "The Major's Blackfoot Bride," p. 29; correspondence between Julia Culbertson Roberts and Charles Kessler. KP, UCLA.

Chapter Ten

# *"The ground has been made good again"*

Leaving New York, Culbertson faced a journey of more than two thousand miles to the Blackfeet territory. By the time he reached St. Louis, the Company steamboat had already departed, with Honoré Picotte and a large number of new recruits, many destined for the new Blackfeet post, on board.[1] Francis Chardon had earlier been transferred to Fort Clark,[2] leaving Alexander Harvey in charge of Fort FAC until Culbertson's return.[3]

Culbertson first had to settle affairs at Fort Laramie and collect his family, including his new daughter, Julia. En route, Culbertson received more bad news: the previous spring, he had left boats loaded with the Fort Laramie returns to be delivered to St. Louis. But these had been abandoned because of low water, despite Culbertson's instructions to "never think of abandoning" them. After being grounded only six days, his employees had done just that. Culbertson was furious.

He chastised M. J. Bourdeau, "the most experienced hand in the country," whom he had left in charge. "I thought you would know better how to act," Culbertson fumed. Since he had not, Culbertson was replacing him with Joseph Picotte, Honoré's nephew. Meanwhile, Culbertson was sending supplies but, he advised Bourdeau, they would be available for cash sale only. Credit would no longer be extended to the men at Fort Laramie.[4]

The uncharacteristically harsh tenor of Culbertson's letter reflected his growing anxieties. The last thing he needed were reminders of disobedient Company employees. By abandoning the furs, these employees had negated Culbertson's progress in revitalizing the Fort Laramie trade, the very assignment which had taken him away from the Blackfeet post.

Leaving Fort Laramie, Culbertson proceeded overland to Fort Pierre to await Honoré Picotte's return from the upper river. Although the keelboat, loaded with supplies for the Blackfeet country, had already left Fort Union, Culbertson was confident he could catch it.[5] What he did not

---

[1]Larpenteur, p. 191.      [2]Abel, p. 249, note 196.
[3]Larpenteur, p. 192.      [4]Alexander Culbertson to M.J. Bourdeau, 26 Jun 1845. FtLar.

know was that the keelboat left with far fewer employees than anticipated. Many of Picotte's new recruits deserted when they learned their assignment would be the dangerous Blackfeet post. Picotte had assured Charles Larpenteur, temporarily in charge of Fort Union, that "not one" of the "first-rate men" he had brought up would desert.

As Picotte headed downriver, Larpenteur threw a ball to celebrate the birth of his son. The ball proceeded unusually peacefully but, the next morning, Auguste Chouteau reported that twelve men had deserted. Opposition traders from Fort William, while attending the ball, had convinced several new recruits to join them rather than risk their lives among the Blackfeet.[6]

Larpenteur had also heard ominous rumors that some veteran Company men planned to attack Harvey. Chardon himself had enlisted James Lee, who had a reputation as a bully, to teach Harvey a lesson.[7] Larpenteur, rather than meddle in this feud, collected supplies for the new post. Finally, the keelboat, with a "frightened set of men" on board, was ready.

Larpenteur offered each new recruit a jigger of whiskey but this did not allay their fears as the opposition traders, still seeking to bolster their ranks, shouted from shore: "You are going to the butcher shop—goodbye forever!" Even after the keelboat departed, the opposition traders continued their agitation; over the next few days, ten more deserted, causing Larpenteur to notify St. Louis that more men would be needed to man the upper Missouri posts.[8]

Culbertson, meanwhile, waited for Picotte so they could discuss re-establishing the Blackfeet trade. When Picotte arrived at Fort Pierre, the two determined that, first and foremost, Harvey had to be removed from the region. They decided to send him to Fort Pierre.[9] With that, Culbertson hurried off, intent on overtaking the keelboat before it reached Fort FAC. He caught up with it at the mouth of Poplar River, some forty-five miles west of Fort Union.

Culbertson must have heard rumblings that Malcolm Clarke, James Lee, and Jacob Berger, the interpreter who had initially helped establish the Blackfeet trade, planned to punish Harvey for the Fort McKenzie massacre along with his real and perceived sins over the years. The conspirators, however, did not include Culbertson in their scheme.

---

[5]Bradley, *MHSC*, Vol. III, p. 240.   [6]Larpenteur, pp. 191-192.
[7]Sunder, p. 88; Larpenteur, p. 192.   [8]Larpenteur, pp. 192-193.
[9]Honoré Picotte, Fort Pierre, to Jno. B. Sarpy, Esqr., St. Louis, 7 Dec 1845. FtLar.

# THE GROUND HAS BEEN MADE GOOD AGAIN

On August 16, 1845, as the keelboat neared Fort FAC, Alexander Harvey and another employee made the customary overland ride to greet the men. Harvey, boarding the keelboat, extended his hand to Clarke. Clarke refused it, saying "I don't shake hands with such a d——d rascal as you." Clarke then brought his tomahawk down on Harvey's head, cracking open his skull. Berger quickly joined in, striking Harvey with his rifle butt. Harvey reeled and attempted to throw Clarke overboard, but James Lee pounded his pistol on Harvey's grasping hand which withered in response. Eventually, but apparently none too quickly, Culbertson intervened.

Culbertson forced Harvey from the keelboat and, after advising Harvey's companion to take the boat upriver, mounted the second horse to accompany Harvey to Fort FAC. There, Culbertson convinced him to leave the Blackfeet country and report to Fort Pierre. Take a canoe, Culbertson said, and leave tonight. Go in darkness to avoid another confrontation. Since Harvey was badly wounded, Culbertson ordered another man to accompany him. That night, Harvey left the Blackfeet country.[10] But, like a bad penny, he would return.

Culbertson knew Fort FAC had to be abandoned both because of its poor location and the memories it conjured for the Blackfeet. So, after banishing Harvey and several of his confederates from the country, Culbertson loaded Fort FAC's essential effects on a keelboat and, after assigning Malcolm Clarke and five others to protect what little remained, headed upriver to seek a more favorable location. Passing old Fort McKenzie, now burned to the ground, must have been a sad experience but Culbertson could not stop since his mission was cloaked in secrecy.

Culbertson found a good site for his new post on the south side of the Missouri River about fifteen miles upstream from present-day Fort Benton, Montana. He chose the south bank so that the river could protect

---

[10]Bradley, *MHSC*, Vol. III, p. 241. Harvey told a slightly different story of the end of the attack, as reported by Larpenteur, pp. 196-197. Harvey made no mention of Culbertson's intervention and claimed that he returned to Fort FAC alone. Once there, he supposedly closed up the fort and refused admittance to anyone. Eventually, according to Harvey, he allowed Culbertson to enter because Culbertson represented the Company and was not one of his enemies. The story as given by Harvey is repeated in Sunder, p. 88. Yet it seems unlikely that Harvey's version is correct. Would Harvey really not have regarded Culbertson as an enemy if Culbertson had done nothing while Harvey was being beaten by Clarke, Berger, and Lee? Subsequent events on the upper Missouri also suggest that Harvey held some special bond with Culbertson, feelings that may well have grown out of Culbertson's intervening to save Harvey's life.

him from potentially hostile Blackfeet.[11] Hoping to remain undetected until they had a fort erected, Culbertson's men immediately set to work. They eschewed hunting, subsisting on small quantities of dried meat. When they exhausted those, the men slaughtered and ate their dogs.

The work proceeded slowly: the new fort, begun in early September, was not completed until January 1846.[12] Nonetheless, by October 19, Culbertson felt comfortable enough with the progress to inform Honoré Picotte of the post's location. Picotte responded that the site would "no doubt be benificial (*sic*) to the Company as it is more in the center of the Indians for whom it was built."[13]

The new stockade enclosed an area approximately one hundred and fifty feet square. Two bastions, each eighteen feet square and two stories high, guarded opposing corners. The upper stories protruded beyond the walls for greater protection. The interior buildings faced the courtyard; their rear walls composed part of the outer stockade. The only break was a single gate facing the river. Seventy men would be stationed at the post which Culbertson proposed to name Fort Honoré.[14]

But Picotte demurred: "I am flattered and thank you for your good opinion of me in giving my name to your Fort, but, I request you to substitute Lewis in the place of Honoré, which is much more suitable and appropriate."[15] Culbertson acceded, christening the post after Meriwether Lewis, the explorer who, ironically, had initially caused the Piegan distrust of the Americans.

In early 1846, the Crows drove off ten fort horses. Although Culbertson, not wanting to risk hostilities, made no attempt to retrieve them, a Blood war party recaptured them after engaging the Crows in battle. The Bloods then returned the horses to Culbertson.[16]

Most likely, the Bloods and other Blackfeet had been quietly observing the construction of Fort Lewis. They probably also knew who was in charge.[17] That they allowed the work to continue unimpeded suggests they were willing to resume trade, as long as it was conducted by their trusted friend, Alexander Culbertson. It is also likely that Seen From

---

[11]Holterman, p. 72.

[12]Bradley, *MHSC*, Vol. III, pp. 241-242.

[13]Honoré Picotte to Alexander Culbertson, 18 Dec 1845. FtLar and Chouteau Collection, MoHS.

[14]Honoré Picotte to Alexander Culbertson, 18 Dec 1845. FtLar and Chouteau Collection, MoHS.

[15]McDonnell, *MHSC*, Vol. X, p. 239.

[16]Bradley, *MHSC*, Vol. III, p. 242.

[17]Holterman, p. 72.

Afar, Natawista's doting brother, headed the Blood warriors who returned the stolen horses.[18]

Almost certainly, Natawista had accompanied Culbertson on this dangerous mission. She would have lobbied to go and Culbertson would have understood the logic of including her. As Lewis and Clark had discovered, a woman's presence helped convince potentially hostile tribes that the white men meant no harm since Indian women traditionally did not join war parties. But what of their children, Jack and Julia? While Jack may have been left at Fort Union, Julia was still dependent on her mother's milk and would also have gone along.

Early in 1846, a Northern Blackfoot arrived at Fort Lewis, informing Culbertson that his tribe was encamped on Belly River. Culbertson, recognizing his opportunity to re-establish relations with the most aggrieved tribe, gave the warrior gifts of tobacco and asked him to invite the chiefs to a council at the fort. The warrior soon returned; the chiefs had accepted.

The Northern Blackfoot chiefs, led by Big Swan,[19] came to Fort Lewis with fifty warriors. Culbertson met them about a hundred yards from the fort. They shook hands and Culbertson invited them into his new fort. To do otherwise would have been an insult but, recognizing the potential danger, Culbertson had taken special precautions.

The Northern Blackfoot, however, behaved with respect and decorum. They sat quietly and listened as Culbertson explained the Company's reaction to the egregious actions that had taken the lives of their kinsmen. He informed them that the "great chief of the traders" had been very angry over the Fort McKenzie massacre; that he had ordered the perpetrators out of the country; that they would never again be employed by the Company (which was not entirely true); that he, Culbertson, had traveled a great distance to meet with the chief of the traders; and, that he had been sent to re-establish the trade with his good friends, the Blackfeet.

The chiefs considered Culbertson's words for a long, tense moment. Then Big Swan addressed his people: "If there are any present now who have lost friends in the massacre, you must now bury all animosity and take

---

[18]This conclusion is the author's based on the circumstances and the information Culbertson gave to Bradley, *MHSC*, Vol. III, p. 242. It would have been in keeping with Culbertson's reluctance to discuss his immediate family that he did not identify Seen From Afar to Bradley.

[19]Bradley, *MHSC*, Vol. III, p. 242n, gives his Indian name as Ah-KOW-Mah-ki.

a good heart. From this time forward there must be no stealing, no killing of white men nor molestation of the fort, while the perpetrators remain away from it. The ground has been made good again by Major[20] Culbertson's return, and the Blackfeet must not be first to stain it with blood."[21]

The chiefs nodded and then smoked the peace pipe with Culbertson and his aides. Demanding nothing in reparations or atonement, the chiefs agreed to resume trading with the American Fur Company. Culbertson then presented rifles, blankets, and a large quantity of tobacco. Well-satisfied, the chiefs departed to tell their people of the peace that had been struck.[22]

Fort Lewis did a brisk trade during its first four months. By the time Culbertson left for Fort Union the following spring (1846), he had eleven hundred packs of buffalo robes as well as a good quantity of beaver, wolf, and fox pelts. Culbertson had successfully re-established the Blackfeet trade in less than one season.[23] That spring, en route to Fort Union, Culbertson stopped at Fort FAC. After shipping the remaining supplies to Fort Lewis, he burned the fort to further demonstrate the Company's good will.

Alexander Harvey, after being sent from the Blackfeet country, reached Fort Union in early October 1845 where Edwin Denig, recently returned from the States with a new contingent of men, was again in command. As Denig and Larpenteur sat on the porch of the Bourgeois's house, they saw Harvey approach. Stopping a short distance away, Harvey called out, "Am I among friends or enemies here?" Denig and Larpenteur replied that he was in no danger.

Reassured, Harvey joined them on the porch where he announced, "Boys, I came very near being killed . . . [by] Malcolm Clarke, Jim Lee, and old man Berger; but the d———d cowards could not do it." Harvey removed his hat to reveal the gash left by Clarke's tomahawk.[24] Since Larpenteur had heard rumors of the planned attack, Harvey's account did not surprise him. While Denig had never shared a post with Harvey, he had heard numerous stories of Harvey's perfidy from his old friend, Culbertson.

Harvey spent several days recuperating at Fort Union before replenish-

---

[20]This title, totally honorary, was applied to head traders.
[21]Bradley, *MHSC*, Vol. III, pp. 242-243.   [22]Bradley, *MHSC*, Vol. III, p. 244.
[23]Bradley, *MHSC*, Vol. III, p. 244.
[24]Harvey's version of events, in Larpenteur, pp. 195-197, varies slightly from the account given above. See footnote 10.

ing his supplies for the journey to Fort Pierre. Before departing, Harvey told Larpenteur, "Never mind! you will see old Harvey bobbing about here again; they think they have got me out of the country, but they are damnably mistaken. I'll come across Clarke again."[25]

Rage festered in Harvey as he journeyed to Fort Pierre. When he arrived, it erupted. No longer was Harvey the least bit interested in continuing his employment with the AFC; he only wanted the money due him. When Honoré Picotte was slow to authorize payment, Harvey threatened "to pound him."[26]

Harvey told Picotte that Company employees had attempted to assassinate him, fingering Francis Chardon as the ringleader. Harvey, whom Picotte described as "very much dissatisfied," announced his intention to file charges in St. Louis against Clarke, Lee, and Berger.

Although Picotte claimed to know nothing about the attack, he did everything in his power "to keep [Harvey at Fort Pierre] until next spring." But it was for naught as Harvey was "determined to go down." While the Company might have been expected to be pleased to rid itself of this serial troublemaker, Picotte thought differently. He hoped to rehire Harvey for another two years and, in a private letter to John Sarpy, an AFC partner, he implored Sarpy to do whatever he could to induce Harvey to remain with the Company.

Picotte even made a striking suggestion. Harvey had made it clear that only command of the Blackfeet post would satisfy him. Most likely, two facts influenced this decision. First, he had spent his entire career with the Blackfeet. More ominously, he probably sought a position of authority over his enemies. How long Clarke, Lee, and Berger might have survived had Harvey gotten his wish is open to speculation.

Yet this seems either not to have occurred to Picotte or not to have concerned him. Having been assured "possitively (*sic*)" by Harvey, whose word should have been suspect, that Culbertson planned to leave the Blackfeet country the following spring, Picotte suggested that Sarpy offer Harvey the post as "I know of no other as efficient as he. . . ." Picotte exhorted Sarpy to do everything in his power to "keep Harvey quiet (*sic*)" and demanded that

---

[25]Larpenteur, p. 197. Both Larpenteur and Sunder, p. 88, state that Harvey had already been dismissed from the American Fur Company. Sunder claims that Culbertson paid Harvey his back wages while Larpenteur says that Culbertson had given Harvey a draft for those wages which Harvey had to redeem at Fort Pierre. However, the letters of Honoré Picotte, written on 7 Dec 1845, FtLar and MoHS, suggest that Harvey had not been dismissed before he reached Fort Pierre.

[26]Larpenteur, p. 197.

Harvey only discuss his situation with Sarpy, apparently sensing that other Company officials might not share his objectives.[27]

Picotte's intention to keep his plan secret is made clear in another letter written to Company officials that same day where he makes but one reference to Harvey: "I draw on you this day favor of Alen Harvey for 4186.72 Dollars, it being balance due him for serving while you will please pay and charge this outfit."[28]

Ten days later, Picotte wrote Culbertson, never asking about Culbertson's future plans. Instead, the letter suggests Picotte expected Culbertson to remain among the Blackfeet. Picotte, however, did inform Culbertson of Harvey's intention to file charges against Berger, Lee, and Clarke. Picotte also forwarded a list of witnesses whom Harvey wanted to testify in St. Louis. Picotte suggested Culbertson use this situation to the Company's advantage: "as some of these men will not wish to go down [to testify] I think you can take advantage of this circumstance to hire them cheap if you want them...."

Indeed, Picotte knew more about Harvey's plans than he divulged to the AFC partners in St. Louis. He informed Culbertson: "my opinion is that Harvey is going up in the Spring to oppose us at the Blkfeet."[29]

This, in fact, was exactly what Harvey planned. During his stay at Fort Pierre, he had recruited two other dissatisfied Company employees to form an opposition company: Charles Primeau and Joseph Picotte, Honoré's own nephew.[30] Nothing now could dissuade Harvey. Having collected a draft for the more than $4,000 due him, Harvey headed for St. Louis to file assault charges and organize his new company.

---

[27]Honoré Picotte, Fort Pierre, to Jno. B. Sarpy, Esqr, St. Louis, 7 Dec 1845. FtLar.
[28]Honoré Picotte, Fort Pierre, to Messr P. Chouteau Jr & Co., St. Louis, 7 Dec 1845. FtLar.
[29]Honoré Picotte to Messr. Culbertson Esqr, 18 Dec 1845. FtLar.
[30]Larpenteur, p. 198.

Chapter Eleven

## *"When a Nation becomes addicted to drinking"*

Alexander Harvey reached St. Louis in early 1846, with a three-pronged strategy for attacking the American Fur Company. In addition to planning an opposition company and filing assault charges against Berger, Clarke, and Lee, Harvey had one more weapon in his arsenal: he charged Francis Chardon, as an employee of the AFC, with selling alcohol to the Indians.

Before the arrival of white traders, Indians had little experience with intoxicants. Since the fur traders consumed prodigious quantities of alcohol, it did not take long for the Indians to become familiar with the white man's "milk"[1] or to regard its consumption "as an important prerequisite to the conduct of diplomacy with their new Great Father."[2]

Early traders believed the Indians' love of alcohol caused them to be more industrious in order to obtain the coveted item. Duncan M'Gillivray, a clerk at the Hudson's Bay Company's Fort George, claimed in 1794 that "when a Nation becomes addicted to drinking, it affords a strong presumption that they will soon become excellent hunters."[3]

Soon, however, the traders realized that serious consequences often flowed from the tribes' regular consumption of alcohol. In 1810, Alexander Henry, a tough-minded trader at Rocky Mountain House, wrote of the Piegans: "That power for all evil, spiritous liquor, now seems to dominate them, and has taken such hold on them that they are no longer the quiet people they were."[4]

As early as 1802, the United States, with the "Intercourse Laws," prohibited the importation of "spiritous liquors" into Indian territories. Although the law carried no real penalties, that changed in 1822 when amendments authorized government agents to search traders' outfits and,

---

[1]Unrau, p. 16.  [2]Unrau, p. 20.
[3]Ewers, *Blackfeet*, p. 35.  [4]Ewers, *Blackfeet*, p. 35.

if they found alcohol, to confiscate the trade goods. Even more damaging, an errant trader's license could be revoked and his bond put at risk.[5]

Nonetheless, traders were allowed to import a certain quantity of alcohol for personal use. This allowed great amounts of whiskey to enter the country each year. In 1828, Pierre Chouteau received permission to transport 300 gallons of alcohol upriver, based on "one gill [one quarter pint] per day" per employee for a full twelve months. Chouteau had presented fifty names but, as he acknowledged to Kenneth McKenzie, not all those employees would remain upriver all year. Chouteau had "explained the matter" to General William Clark, the ex-explorer who was then Superintendent of Indian Affairs in St. Louis.[6] Although the traders gave much of this alcohol to the Indians, their actions technically did not violate the law since it was not sold.

England had no legislation comparable to the Intercourse Laws and the Hudson's Bay Company traders freely offered alcohol to their Indian customers.[7] The tribes routinely threatened to take their robes to the Canadian traders if the Americans did not supply liquor. As a result, even after the AFC traders recognized "the degrading and demoralizing influence of intoxicating spirits upon the Indian," they felt it imperative to offer alcohol in trade.[8] The best traders offered only reasonable quantities; less experienced traders used prodigious quantities to woo potential clients.[9]

Isolation on the frontier and the long, harsh winters caused many traders to look to the bottle for warmth and companionship. They consumed much purer liquor than what was traded to the Indians. Trade alcohol was diluted with river water and spiced with chewing tobacco, Jamaica ginger, molasses, and pepper.[10]

Charles Larpenteur, one of the few AFC men who abstained, accused nearly all the traders of being drunkards at one time or another. In the winter of 1840-1841, he referred to the Fort Union leadership as a drunken Trinity: "Mr. Laidlaw the Father, Mr. Denig the Son, and Mr. Jacques

---

[5]Abel, p. 204.      [6]Chittenden, *Fur Trade*, Vol. I, p. 26.

[7]Chittenden, *Fur Trade*, Vol. I, p. 21. In 1843, however, the Council of the Hudson's Bay Company passed a resolution stating, in part, "Resolved that . . . the use of spirituous liquor be gradually discontinued in the very few districts in which it is yet indispensable. . . ." The Blackfeet tribes were probably among the last to be cut off. Hugh Dempsey to the author.

[8]Chittenden, *Fur Trade*, Vol. I, p. 23.

[9]Sunder, p. 9.      [10]Sunder, p. 56.

Bruguière the Holy Ghost. . . ." According to Larpenteur, the frequent intoxication of these three led to large losses as Indians traded robes, stole them back, and then traded them once again.[11]

Further complicating the situation, many traders felt the Company neglected their basic needs. Honoré Picotte complained that the Company did not send adequate books, writing paper, and candles.[12] Reading materials were so highly prized that, one year, James Archdale Hamilton sent Alexander Culbertson "all the Newspapers over which I had control to furnish you amusement for the ensuing spring."[13] All things considered, it is hardly surprising that alcohol assumed enormous importance at the forts.

But in Washington, D.C., the government decided in 1832 to crack down further on its importation. The American Fur Company vigorously protested, asserting that additional restrictions might be appropriate and even "beneficial both to the Indians and the traders" where the trade was exclusively in the hands of Americans. Yet where the Company competed with the Hudson's Bay Company "we must either abandon the trade or be permitted to use [alcohol], to a limited extent at least, in order to counteract, in some measure, the influence of our rivals, who can introduce any quantity they please." The Company claimed: "If the Hudson's Bay Company did not employ ardent spirits against us, we would not ask for a single drop."[14]

Their appeal fell on deaf ears and the government banned completely the importation of liquor into Indian territories. The legislation also provided for inspectors at Leavenworth and Council Bluffs to check cargo headed for the upriver posts. In a small nod to the AFC, the government promised to try to persuade the British to enact similar legislation.[15]

The stricter law went into effect on July 9, 1832. Almost immediately, much effort went into circumventing it, with smuggling becoming a fact of life.

The strengthened Intercourse Laws appalled Kenneth McKenzie, the

---

[11]Larpenteur, p. 138.
[12]Honoré Picotte to Jacob Halsey, 24 Feb 1839, as cited in Sunder, p. 33.
[13]J. Archdale Hamilton to Mr. A. Culbertson, 12 Jan 1835. *Fort Union Letterbooks*, MoHS.
[14]Chittenden, *Fur Trade*, Vol. I, pp. 26-27.
[15]Chittenden, *Fur Trade*, Vol. I, pp. 27-28.

venerable Company trader who had built Fort Union and established American trade with the Blackfeet. For years, he had battled competitors on the upper Missouri. These smaller concerns, he believed, would have a much easier time getting liquor past the government inspectors. He felt so strongly about the proposed law's negative impact that he traveled to Washington, D.C., and New York to lobby against it. When that failed, he left Washington "disheartened . . . very much."[16] Although the AFC had cached a fair amount of alcohol before the new law went into effect, they knew it would not last long.

But the shrewd McKenzie soon devised an "ingenious and radical" scheme to circumvent the new law.[17] The law banned importation but said nothing about making alcohol. McKenzie therefore believed nothing prevented him from transporting a still to Fort Union and using the land's bounty to make whiskey. Although McKenzie thought the scheme brilliant, others characterized it as "madness."[18]

When the *Assiniboin* pulled away from the St. Louis levee in the spring of 1833, with Alexander Culbertson and Edwin Denig on board, McKenzie had pieces of a still stashed below deck. The still eluded inspectors and successfully reached Fort Union. But that was the extent of McKenzie's luck. The liquor he attempted to smuggle upriver aboard the *Yellow Stone* was confiscated at Leavenworth.

Even Prince Maximilian, who had a more benign purpose for the illicit liquid, bemoaned the loss: "[T]hey would scarcely permit us to take a small portion to preserve our specimens of natural history."[19] McKenzie complained to Chouteau: "We have been robbed of all our liquors . . . which was in two barrels. They kicked and knocked about everything they could find and even cut through our bales of blankets which had never been undone since they were put up in England."[20]

McKenzie's still now took on added importance. When the steamboat reached the Iowa River, a number of men disembarked to start a corn plantation. McKenzie also picked up a load of corn at Council Bluffs and further augmented supplies with corn purchased from the Mandans.[21]

---

[16]Ramsay Crooks to Pierre Chouteau, 17 Feb 1833, as cited in Chittenden, *Fur Trade*, Vol. I, p. 363. [17]Chittenden, *Fur Trade*, Vol. I, p. 356.
[18]Ramsay Crooks to Pierre Chouteau, 17 Feb 1833, as cited in Chittenden, *Fur Trade*, Vol. I, p. 356. [19]Thwaites, Vol. 22, p. 254.
[20]Chittenden, *Fur Trade*, Vol. I, p. 357.
[21]Chittenden, *Fur Trade*, Vol. I, p. 358.

# WHEN A NATION BECOMES ADDICTED TO DRINKING 131

At Fort McKenzie, the whiskey trade continued as usual, with supplies cached before the 1833 embargo. Maximilian, witnessing a brisk alcohol trade, observed that liquor caused the Indians to become "bad, dissolute, lazy, and, therefore, dangerous." When intoxicated, the Indians sold inferior furs and the Indian women, who did the tanning, had little incentive to do good work since they received little benefit when their men bartered the robes for liquor.

Maximilian lamented the fact that the Indian agents, entrusted with monitoring the liquor trafficking, did not live among the tribes. Instead, the agents, many of whom were related to leading men of the American Fur Company, came out once a year and tolerated most everything "without reprimand." Maximilian believed if they would "carry out their obligations, the harmful consumption of whiskey among the Indians might be effectively controlled."[22]

Although deploring the liquor trade, Maximilian was not above using it to obtain something he desired. One night, after much drinking, "a wizened old Indian... painted grey" appeared with a "very tame female bear" he wished to sell. His asking price, however, was whiskey which Maximilian was loathe to meet. But the Prince watched as the elderly Indian "sat down on the ground with his charge, played with her and kissed her repeatedly. The animal was charming and completely tame." Infatuated, Maximilian relented and, the next day, purchased the bear for liquor.[23]

According to Maximilian, Fort Union had no liquor at all.[24] He was apparently unaware of McKenzie's still which, by the middle of summer, was churning out "as fine a liquor as need be drunk."[25] Indeed, McKenzie felt such pride in his operation that it never occurred to him to be circumspect about with whom he shared it.

On August 24, 1833, Fort Union welcomed two veteran explorers, Nathaniel Wyeth and M. S. Cerré. As was his custom, McKenzie entertained them with flair, sharing his bread, cheese, meat, milk, and wine. Then he took his guests on a grand tour of the fort, showing them everything, including the distillery.[26]

So grateful were Wyeth and Cerré for the hospitality that there might not have been any trouble had McKenzie not been such a shrewd busi-

---

[22]Thomas and Ronnefeldt, p. 107.
[23]Thomas and Ronnefeldt, p. 102.
[24]Thomas and Ronnefeldt, p. 107.
[25]Chittenden, *Fur Trade*, Vol. I, p. 359.
[26]Chittenden, *Fur Trade*, Vol. I, p. 359.

nessman. Wyeth and Cerré needed supplies for their journey downriver. McKenzie outfitted the explorers, but Wyeth considered the bill exorbitant. Although he settled the account, an angry Wyeth may have reported McKenzie's still to the authorities in St. Louis.[27]

Superintendent of Indian Affairs William Clark wrote Pierre Chouteau seeking an explanation. Chouteau, professing innocence, offered an ingenious explanation: "The company, believing that wild pears and berries might be converted into wine (which they did not understand to be prohibited), did authorize experiments to be made, and if, under color of this, ardent spirits have been distilled and vended, it is without the knowledge, authority, or direction of the company. . . ." Nonetheless, Chouteau assured Clark he would order the still dismantled.[28]

When Chouteau wrote McKenzie, McKenzie claimed to have no cognizance of transgressing the law: "If I were conscious of having infringed the laws of the U.S.," McKenzie wrote, "I would at once acknowledge my error and admit the propriety of your censure." Instead, McKenzie cast doubt on the accounts received by Chouteau, suggesting that he had "Lent a willing ear to a marvellous (*sic*) tale of discrepancy in my conduct & proceedings, and admitted as facts, statements which had existence only in the narrator's imagination." McKenzie further asserted that the still belonged to an old friend who would collect his property shortly.

Not content simply to suggest that the still did not belong to him, McKenzie assailed the character of his accusers. He admitted that the still may have been seen "by a person styling himself Capt. Wythe (*sic*), as under that name a stranger introduced himself to me last summer & received the accustomed hospitalities of this place." But McKenzie thought it "exceedingly improbable" that Wyeth and Cerré saw the still. More importantly, McKenzie stressed that it was impossible "for them to prove a single allegation they have made."

McKenzie dismissed the entire event, claiming that the two had been "mortified & displeased" when he refused to sell them whiskey. They had filed their charges because of "the character of the former & the wounded self love of the latter in being deemed unworthy of an engagement with the Am. F. C."[29] Ironically, McKenzie may have blamed the wrong party;

---

[27]Larpenteur, pp. 61-62.    [28]Chittenden, *Fur Trade*, Vol. I, p. 360.
[29]Kenneth McKenzie to Pierre Chouteau, 18 Mar 1834. *Fort Union Letterbooks*, MoHS.

# WHEN A NATION BECOMES ADDICTED TO DRINKING

the damaging information may have come not from Wyeth, but from McKenzie's arch-competitor, William Sublette.³⁰

Although McKenzie's great scheme had come to an end, he made clear his belief that, if the Company could not trade liquor, they would be seriously threatened by their competitors, including Sublette, who had an "abundance of Alcohol in barrels which came up the Missouri independent of what came via the Mountains & down the Y Stone." He bemoaned "the partiality or laxity of the Government officers" that allowed the opposition companies to get great quantities of alcohol upriver while leaving his men not "enough to moisten a hair of our heads."³¹

Without liquor, McKenzie despaired of making a decent trade. He described the Indians as being in "bad humour," disappointed by the goods received and by not knowing whether they could trade for alcohol. "'No liquor, no trade' is prevailing sentiment with the Assiniboines," McKenzie reported.³² "I verily believe if I were destitute of Liquor I should not trade a hundred packs of Robes. . . . nothing but liquor will keep these Indians to us, in fact without it it is a mere waste of time and money to keep up this post."³³

Under the watchful eyes of friendly government employees, the AFC continued to supply their upriver posts with liquor throughout the 1830s and early 1840s. William Clark, who became Superintendent of Indian Affairs in 1807, had long been a friend of the Company. One year after receiving his government position, he joined Pierre and Auguste Chouteau as a partner in an early St. Louis fur company.³⁴ When Clark retired in 1839, Joshua Pilcher assumed the position. Pilcher had entered the fur trade in 1819 and handled AFC affairs at Council Bluffs until the early 1830s.³⁵

Pilcher made few decisions without first clearing them with the AFC. Whenever political forces threatened the Company, Pilcher rose to its defense. Throughout this period, upper Missouri Indian agents knew the consequences of displeasing the American Fur Company. If the AFC cut

---

³⁰Innis, p. 131.
³¹Kenneth McKenzie to Joshua Pilcher, 16 Dec 1833, reprinted in Abel, p. 362.
³²Kenneth McKenzie to J.B. Cabanne, Esqr, 10 Dec 1835, reprinted in Abel, p. 375.
³³Kenneth McKenzie to Messrs Pratte Chouteau & Co., 10 Dec 1835, reprinted in Abel, p. 378.
³⁴Ambrose, p. 444.     ³⁵Chittenden, *Fur Trade*, Vol. I, p. 153.

off an agent, he found himself alone in a hostile environment, literally out in the cold without shelter or supplies. Agents, fearing such a fate, made sure the Company approved of their activities.[36]

In addition, because they operated the only dependable steamboats, the AFC routinely secured the annual government contract to carry treaty goods upriver. If another company bid, the AFC undercut them even if that meant taking a loss on the contract. Any such loss mattered less than the Company's continued monopoly over the river trade. Carrying annuities upriver brought another bonus: the Indians felt indebted to the Company, seeing virtually no distinction between them and the government.[37]

The Company's stranglehold over the St. Louis Office of Indian Affairs was threatened in 1842 with the presidential election of William Henry Harrison, a Whig. The American Fur Company had always been affiliated with the Democratic party and the ascendancy of the Whigs threw the Company into turmoil. The Whigs fired Joshua Pilcher and threatened to remove all Company men from the Office of Indian Affairs. Although Missouri's senator Thomas Hart Benton, a Democrat and long-time friend of the Company, asserted that the AFC was not anti-Harrison, his arguments echoed hollowly.[38]

The Company feared that John Dougherty, a Whig member of the Missouri legislature bitterly opposed to the AFC, would replace Pilcher. But the Company, through Senator Benton, managed to secure the appointment for David Mitchell, the trader who had spent a winter training Alexander Culbertson at Fort McKenzie.[39] Mitchell surfaced as a compromise candidate despite his long association with the AFC because he was believed to be independent.[40]

Having weathered this battle, the Company faced another in its effort to maintain dominion over the upper Missouri: those pesky little competitors. Then Chouteau hit upon a brilliant scheme; he suggested that Superintendent Mitchell appoint a roving agent to curb the liquor traffic.

On its face, this appeared to be against the Company's best interests. But, of course, it was not. A new competitor—Ebbetts, Cutting and Kelsey—had recently entered the upper Missouri trade, with their chief weapon illicit liquor. Ebbetts "opened the firewater floodgates," endan-

---

[36]Sunder, p. 27.
[37]Sunder, p. 28.
[38]Sunder, pp. 26-27.
[39]Sunder, pp. 29-31.
[40]Sunder, p. 30.

gering not only the AFC but the tribes. Pitched intertribal battles erupted, hunting by the warriors fell off, and the AFC predicted whole villages might starve. Superintendent Mitchell reported hundreds of Indians dead from drunken excesses.[41]

Liquor-related violence was nothing new. During Alexander Culbertson's tenure at Fort McKenzie, at least two deaths had occurred during drunken Indian revelries. In 1840, a Piegan named Weasel[42] came to the fort for whiskey. When Andrew Potts opened the wicket through which whiskey was customarily traded, Weasel shot him dead.[43]

A year earlier, the aged Gros Ventre chief, Mo-kwee, arrived at Fort McKenzie with twenty warriors for a drunken celebration. With the carousing at its height, an AFC employee named John Watts went to the river for water. Mo-kwee shot Watts with an arrow. Watts, though severely wounded, survived. Mo-kwee did not. His warriors, fearing retaliation, killed the old man.[44]

Neither of these incidents prompted an AFC crackdown on the illicit whiskey trade. Yet with Ebbetts, Cutting and Kelsey now selling vast quantities of liquor while the AFC had scarcely any, the Company hoped suppressing the whiskey trade might drive their competitors out of business.

In June 1842, the government appointed Andrew Drips as "agent to reside in the Indian Country for the purpose of suppressing the whiskey."[45] Drips, too, had a long history with the AFC, having joined the Company in 1820, marrying an Indian woman, fathering four children, and participating in the early rendezvous system.[46]

After being confirmed in September, Drips inspected Fort Pierre before heading to Fort Clark to winter. Superintendent Mitchell, exhibiting his vaunted independence, suggested that Drips establish camps among the tribes to monitor the liquor trade. Drips demurred, preferring the housing invitation extended by the AFC. This guaranteed the Company advance notice of Drips's schedule, allowing them to cache their liquor prior to his arrival.[47]

Drips planned to begin inspecting the upper Missouri posts in 1843 and word went out to the AFC posts to destroy their liquor supplies. Most

---

[41]Sunder, p. 48.
[42]Indian name given as Ah-pah.
[43]Bradley, *MHSC*, Vol. III, p. 231.
[44]Bradley, *MHSC*, Vol. III, p. 230.
[45]Sunder, p. 49.
[46]Hafen, *Mountain Men*, Vol. VIII, pp. 143-152.
[47]Sunder, pp. 49-50.

was dumped in the river or poured on the ground, resulting in "a very considerable oblation to Mother Earth."[48] At Fort Union, Alexander Culbertson, unable to reconcile himself to destroying thirty barrels of liquor, carried them across the river to a small lake where he intended to sink them for later retrieval.

But the barrels would not sink. No matter how they were weighted, they continued to surface. Finally, Culbertson buried the casks. The plan seemed inspired until Culbertson unearthed his treasure. To his dismay, the iron hoops had rusted and the barrels had burst.[49]

At least some of the alcohol Culbertson lost probably had come upriver aboard the *Omega* which had brought John James Audubon to Fort Union. After the cache escaped detection at Leavenworth, Joseph Sire, the *Omega's* captain, braced for the search at Bellevue, the most difficult checkpoint. The agent, however, was absent when the *Omega* arrived and the steamboat nearly avoided inspection. But four miles upriver, United States troops forced the steamboat to shore for examination.

Now the crew had to act fast to save the precious cargo. Audubon, who had a permit to carry alcohol upriver to preserve his specimens, quickly stepped in. Presenting his permit, Audubon received permission to retain his supply and was "settled comfortably." His permit, though, did not shield the alcohol destined for the upriver trade.

While Audubon used his celebrity status to distract the officers, Sire and his crew rigged up a system to conceal their liquor. The boat's hold contained a tram for moving supplies. The crew loaded the barrels of alcohol on the tram and, as the inspectors searched the hold, the alcohol slowly moved around on the tram, just out of sight. The ploy worked and the alcohol safely reached the upper river posts.[50]

Nevertheless, by 1843, the presence of downriver inspectors had slowed whiskey importation considerably. When a party of Crees at Fort Union demanded liquor, Audubon lamented "there is none for them, and very little for any one." The Crees told Culbertson that if the AFC refused to trade liquor, they would take their business to the Hudson's Bay Company. This caused Audubon to suggest that "the British, who are so anxious about the emancipation of the blacks, might as well take care of the souls and bodies of the redskins."[51]

---

[48]Bradley, *MHSC*, Vol. III, p. 245.    [49]Bradley, *MHSC*, Vol. III, pp. 245-246.
[50]Chittenden, *Fur Trade*, Vol. II, pp. 669-672.

That winter, before the Fort McKenzie massacre, William Laidlaw told Pierre Chouteau that the Blackfeet were "getting more and more troublesome in consequence of certain retrenchment of Liquor." They were "so much dissatisfied that Mr. Chardon says he cannot get out at the gate more than once a week."[52]

There was little hope that the situation would improve once Andrew Drips began his inspections. Yet during his visits to the upper Missouri posts in late 1843, Drips found none of the carefully cached liquor. AFC clerk Larpenteur called Drips "a good, honest old beaver trapper," but noted that he never examined the cellar at Fort Union where much liquor was hidden.[53]

Drips hired Joseph Varnum Hamilton to inspect the Platte River posts where the traders, no doubt acting on Alexander Culbertson's orders, had also cached their supplies. Following his tour, Hamilton informed Drips: "[The Company does] not deny having liquor but defy me to find it." Hamilton, like Drips, found none.[54]

In 1844, the smuggling continued. Before leaving St. Louis, the AFC carefully packed their alcohol inside flour barrels prominently marked for the Company's Bellevue agent. When the *Nimrod* docked at Bellevue, the crew stashed the flour barrels in the warehouse. The inspectors searched the steamboat and found nothing.

The *Nimrod* remained at the dock all afternoon while the crew busied themselves. Then, shortly after midnight, they retrieved the flour barrels with their concealed contents. As the inspectors slept, the barrels were reloaded, the line cut, and the *Nimrod* cast off. In the morning, when the inspectors discovered the flour barrels missing, they realized the deception. The men reported the incident to the St. Louis authorities but, once again, the Company's close political ties quashed the potential threat.[55]

Ironically, the government finally got the ammunition they needed to

---

[51] Audubon, Vol. II, p. 109.

[52] William Laidlaw to Pierre Chouteau, Dec 1843. Chouteau-Walsh Collection, MoHS.

[53] Larpenteur, p. 345. This would seem to contradict the account that Alexander Culbertson gave of burying the casks. Perhaps Larpenteur did not know Culbertson had done this or perhaps Culbertson buried the alcohol on another occasion.

[54] Sunder, p. 70.    [55] Chittenden, *Fur Trade*, Vol. II, pp. 672-673.

charge the AFC with violating the Intercourse Laws from one of the Company's own: the disgruntled Alexander Harvey. In the spring of 1846, Harvey charged his cohort in the Fort McKenzie massacre, Francis Chardon, with selling whiskey to the Indians. Rather than take his charges through the political channels over which the Company held sway, Harvey appealed directly to the United States District Attorney, Thomas Gantt.[56] Pierre Chouteau properly noted: "Mr. Harvey would probably find the revocation of our license, if he could accomplish it, the most profitable speculation in which he ever engaged...."[57]

On June 5, 1846, District Attorney Gantt filed charges against six officials[58] of the American Fur Company for violating the Intercourse Act. Gantt sued for the bonds posted to do business on the upper Missouri in 1842, 1843, 1844, and 1845. In all, the government sought $25,000 for the illegal trade of an estimated forty-three hundred gallons of liquor in Indian country.[59]

Alexander Culbertson, blissfully unaware of the storm about to erupt, left Fort Lewis in the spring of 1846 for Fort Union. There, he boarded the steamboat, *General Brooke*, with Francis Chardon and Honoré Picotte, for St. Louis. When they arrived on August 6, they reported difficult conditions on the upper river with intertribal hostilities wracking the region.[60]

Their attention was soon diverted to more personal concerns: on August 4, District Attorney Gantt had charged Culbertson, Chardon, Picotte, and James Kipp with liquor trafficking. On September 12, Gantt charged Joseph Sire, captain of the *Nimrod*, with transporting "several hundred gallons of alcohol into the Indian Country" using the 1844 flour barrel scheme.[61]

But bringing charges proved easier than prosecuting them. According to Gantt, the Company "endeavored by all means to impeach the credibility of the witnesses." Moreover, many witnesses, employees of the AFC, had been "sent on Distant service. Some of them have since been heard to boast of the Salary they receive for absenting themselves from St. Louis."

---

[56]Sunder, p. 90. Unrau, passim, spells Gantt's surname as "Ganntt." Copies of letters by Gantt in NAM M234/755 show the correct spelling to be Gantt.

[57]Pierre Chouteau to William Medill, 31 May 1848. NAM M234/755.

[58]Pierre Chouteau, Peter Sarpy, Kenneth McKenzie, Benjamin Clapp, Sylvestre Labadie, and Joshua B. Brant.    [59]Sunder, p. 91.

[60]Sunder, p. 86.    [61]Sunder, p. 91.

In one instance, the Company was said to have engaged one witness, who had a claim against the AFC, and "paid off the whole of his demand, the justice of which up to that time they had denied...."[62]

Meanwhile, Chouteau insisted that the government's "laudable" objectives, "namely the breaking up of the liquor trade," had "been the sincere desire of our house for many years."[63] Nevertheless, he charged that "the spirit in which" District Attorney Gantt was pursuing the cases "is unworthy the Office from which it comes." Chouteau believed it "evident" that Gantt "either... expects to ingratiate himself with the authorities at Washington by the manifestation of zeal... or he seeks to injure us for the gratification of feelings of personal hostility."[64]

Gantt fired back that he had "always been well aware that in being the instrument of enforcing against P. Chouteau Jr. & Co. the penalty announced by law... I would incur their sharpest enmity." Moreover, he expected "they would exhibit not much scrupulousness" in their attacks. Nonetheless, he believed the charges of Alexander Harvey against "the character of such exalted persons as P. Chouteau Jr. & Co. (*sic*)"[65]

For three years, the liquor cases dragged on. Company attorneys filed demurrers, the District Attorney amended the declarations of facts, witnesses failed to appear, the court clerk died, the AFC sought and received continuances.[66] Finally, in December 1848, Chouteau wrote Commissioner of Indian Affairs William Medill "to ascertain if it would meet with the views of the Departm$^t$. to receive from us propositions for a compromise...." Citing "conflicting testimony" and the "bad character" of Alexander Harvey, Chouteau assigned most of the blame for the liquor trafficking on the "most obnoxious" trader, Francis Chardon, who, conveniently, had died a month earlier.[67]

Chouteau offered to settle the suits for $5,000 plus court costs.[68] District Attorney Gantt balked, insisting the figure be raised to $7,500. But

---

[62]Thomas Gantt to Hon. R. H. Gillet, Solicitor of the Treasury, 25 Apr 1848. NAM M234/755. Emphasis in original.
[63]Pierre Chouteau to William Medill, 5 Dec 1848. NAM M234/755.
[64]Pierre Chouteau to William Medill, 31 May 1848. NAM M234/755.
[65]Thomas Gantt to R. H. Gillet, 11 Aug 1848. NAM M234/755.
[66]For a recapitulation of the legal technicalities surrounding the lawsuit, see H. R. Gamble to Pierre Chouteau, 29 May 1848, and Thomas Gantt to R. H. Gillet, 25 Apr 1848. NAM M234/755.
[67]Pierre Chouteau to William Medill, 5 Dec 1848. NAM M234/755.
[68]Pierre Chouteau to William Medill, 17 Jan 1849. NAM M234/755.

Superintendent of Indian Affairs Thomas Harvey, with Gantt's reluctant agreement, finally accepted Chouteau's offer.[69]

The Company had survived the most serious threat to its hegemony. On February 15, 1849, the Superintendent of Indian Affairs renewed its trading license on the upper Missouri.[70]

---

[69]"Case of P. Chouteau Jr. & Co." Memorandum signed by William Medill, 27 Jan 1849. NAM M234/755.   [70]Sunder, pp. 115-116.

Chapter Twelve

## *"For the love of God, do not abandon these souls!"*

Alexander Culbertson had succeeded in removing Alexander Harvey from the AFC Blackfeet post but if he hoped this would end the aggravation Harvey had caused, he would be greatly disappointed. When Culbertson arrived in St. Louis in August 1846, two days after District Attorney Gantt had charged him with illegally selling whiskey,[1] Gantt was also investigating the assault on Alexander Harvey. The previous April, a grand jury had indicted Malcolm Clarke, James Lee, and Jacob Berger for the attack.[2]

In July, Superintendent of Indian Affairs Thomas Harvey ordered the three "out of the Indian country forthwith" and "if possible" to be sent to St. Louis "in order that they may be dealt with according to law."[3] Alexander Harvey also requested five additional Company men be questioned about the incident but, to prevent their testimony, the Company transferred them to distant posts, beyond the reach of the Court.[4] Without witnesses, the District Attorney was forced to drop the charges in April 1847.[5]

Shadowed by these legal complications, Culbertson fervently longed to leave St. Louis and return to his fledgling post. But the weeks dragged on; Culbertson finally departed in early October traveling overland, probably with a pack train carrying supplies for the upriver posts.[6] This responsibility further delayed his arrival at the Blackfeet post where, once again, Culbertson confronted Alexander Harvey.

Harvey had formed his opposition company with three disgruntled

---

[1] Sunder, p. 91.     [2] Sunder, p. 89.

[3] T. H. Harvey to Andrew Drips, 13 Mar 1846, reprinted in footnote 2, Chittenden, *Fur Trade*, Vol. II, pp. 687-688.

[4] Honoré Picotte to Alexander Culbertson, undated, and to John B. Sarpy, 1 Dec 1845, *Fort Pierre Letter Book*, 1845-46, MoHS; Sunder, p. 89.

[5] File of *U.S. vs. James Lee, Jacob Berger, and Malcolm Clark*, Case No. 395, Record Book "A," page 349, FRC, KC. Because the case was dismissed, the remaining record consists of only the dismissal. Therefore, it is not known whether Alexander Culbertson was ever questioned about the attack.

[6] Sunder, pp. 110-111.

former AFC employees. Charles Primeau, born in St. Louis, had joined the AFC in 1831 and, during the next fifteen years, gained practical skills in both Indian languages and the mechanics of the fur trade. Anthony Bouis, born into a family of well-respected St. Louis Indian traders, was a "kind hearted, generous" man with a "highly cultivated intellect." The fourth partner was Honoré Picotte's nephew, Joseph.[7]

The new firm, organized as Harvey, Primeau and Company, possessed great experience in the fur trade. The one asset they lacked—sufficient financial backing—came from Pierre Chouteau's long-time rival, Robert Campbell. By 1846, Campbell, who had made his fortune in the fur trade, was active in St. Louis banking, insurance, and land development interests and his business drafts "were as good as gold in the Indian country." Campbell supplied Harvey with nearly fifty thousand dollars in trade goods.[8]

As Culbertson headed to St. Louis, Harvey left for the upper river with forty-five hired hands. En route, he engaged another fifty.[9] The AFC, fearing this new competitor, tried to prevent additional men from signing on. James Kipp, the veteran AFC trader, instructed Malcolm Clarke to hire all available free traders around Fort Lewis before Harvey arrived.[10]

But the Company could do little more. Before winter set in, Harvey had constructed Fort Campbell just south of Fort Lewis. He chose the location in hopes that Culbertson's fort would provide some protection from raids by the Northern Blackfoot who had not forgiven Harvey for the Fort McKenzie massacre. Harvey, who had married a Piegan, planned to trade primarily with that tribe.[11]

Eventually, Harvey, Primeau and Company would compete with the American Fur Company at Fort Lewis, Fort Union, and Fort Pierre.[12]

As the AFC faced their most serious opposition in the Blackfeet country, their leaders were creating needless problems at Fort Lewis. The previous spring, when he left for Fort Union, Alexander Culbertson placed Malcolm Clarke in charge. Perhaps because of the pending charges, Honoré Picotte replaced Clarke with the acquiescent, but relatively hapless, Charles Larpenteur.

Larpenteur had long desired his own post but had never proven him-

---

[7]Sunder, p. 92.  
[8]Sunder, pp. 92-93.  
[9]Sunder, p. 93.  
[10]Larpenteur, p. 209.  
[11]Bradley, *MHSC*, Vol. III, p. 247.  
[12]Sunder, p. 94.

self up to the assignment. He had been easily intimidated by various tribes and could not garner respect from the men under him. An able clerk, Larpenteur lacked the tenacity for a post command.

Nonetheless, Picotte ordered him to assume command at Fort Lewis and, after readying the winter supplies, Larpenteur left Fort Union on July 8, 1846.[13] The trip—a slow, tortuous ordeal—lasted seventy days. When Larpenteur finally arrived, Malcolm Clarke refused to serve under him and left for Fort Union to appeal the command decision.[14] Clarke complained to James Kipp who agreed with Clarke and ordered him to resume command of Fort Lewis until Culbertson returned.[15] A month later, Clarke was back.

Now Larpenteur refused to accept the change in leadership but, when he returned to Fort Union, he received a cold shoulder from James Kipp. Kipp not only refused to reinstate Larpenteur's leadership at Fort Lewis but even declined to re-hire him. Since it was too late to go downriver, Larpenteur spent a miserable winter at Fort Union, unemployed and barely tolerated. He determined to quit the Company the following spring.[16]

Culbertson learned of these leadership squabbles when he reached Fort Union that November. With Harvey poised to challenge the Company's monopoly over the Blackfeet trade, the last thing Culbertson needed was turmoil at Fort Lewis. His swift return became even more imperative. In December 1846, following a six-month absence, Culbertson finally reached Fort Lewis. There, he found a distinguished guest awaiting him.[17]

The Jesuit priest, Nicolas Point, had arrived at Fort Lewis in September 1846 with the highly esteemed missionary, Pierre Jean De Smet. De Smet had left almost immediately, traveling downriver with Malcolm Clarke. Point, however, stayed behind, hoping to establish a Blackfeet mission.[18]

---

[13]Larpenteur, p. 207.   [14]Larpenteur, p. 210.

[15]Larpenteur, p. 210, suggests that Clarke went all the way to Fort Pierre and there received orders to resume command of Fort Lewis. This makes little sense since Honoré Picotte was in charge of Fort Pierre and there is no reason to believe he would have changed his mind about Clarke's command. More significantly, the time frame given by Larpenteur does not provide sufficient time for Clarke to have traveled to Fort Pierre and back. Pierre De Smet, who left Fort Lewis with Clarke, reached Fort Pierre on October 30 which is about when Larpenteur says Clarke returned to Fort Lewis. It is much more likely that James Kipp ordered Clarke back to Fort Lewis.

[16]Larpenteur, pp. 211-213.   [17]Bradley, *MHSC*, Vol. III, pp. 246-247.
[18]Buckley, pp. 306-307.

After years of entreaty from some western tribes, the Jesuits had finally begun to establish western Indian missions about five years earlier.

In the early nineteenth century, free trappers and traders had brought eastern Indians, mostly Iroquois, west to teach those tribes to trap.[19] These Iroquois carried with them tales of the Black Robes[20] they had met back east. In 1825, the Hudson's Bay Company sent several young western Indians to the Anglican mission at Red River, near present-day Winnipeg, Canada. When they returned, the young men spoke English, dressed like whites, and carried Bibles which they said explained the mysteries of the universe.[21]

The Nez Perce, especially, embraced these teachings. In 1831, four Nez Perce warriors traveled to St. Louis to ask the Black Robes to come and live among them.[22] But the St. Louis Jesuits lacked the necessary manpower.[23]

News of the Nez Perce search for Christian teachers spread quickly, exciting eastern religious communities where various denominations began raising funds for missions. Jason Lee, a Methodist missionary, traveled west with a fur trappers' caravan in 1834 to establish a mission in the Willamette Valley. The next year, the American Board of Commissioners for Foreign Missions sent Samuel Parker and Marcus Whitman west. Adjudging the region ripe for missions, Whitman returned east to enlist recruits.

In 1836, Marcus Whitman again headed west, accompanied by his bride, Narcissa, and Henry and Eliza Spalding. The Whitmans established a mission among the Cayuse Indians on the Walla Walla River while the Spaldings ministered to the Nez Perce on Lapwai Creek.[24]

Another tribe which had learned about the teachings of the Black Robes from a transplanted eastern Indian were the Flatheads in the Bitterroot Valley of what is now Montana. The transplanted Indian, Old Ignace, had tried to teach the religious principles he had learned at the Jesuit's Caughnawaga Mission near Montreal but was not satisfied with his efforts. Therefore, in 1835, Old Ignace and his two sons went to St. Louis seeking Black Robes for a Flathead mission.[25]

Meanwhile, a second group of Flatheads attended the Green River

---

[19]Lavender, p. 48.
[20]A term the Indians applied to the Jesuit priests because of their cassocks.
[21]Lavender, p. 62; *Nez Perce Country*, p. 59.
[22]Pfaller, *De Smet*, p. 9.
[23]Chittenden, *De Smet*, Vol. I, p. 28.
[24]*Nez Perce Country*, pp. 63-64.
[25]Ewers, *Blackfeet*, p. 186.

rendezvous looking for missionaries. The Protestant missionaries they met there were disappointing: they did not wear black robes; they did not wear the gold cross; they were married; and, they did not say the "Great Prayer." That December, Old Ignace and his sons met with Bishop Rosati of St. Louis who promised to send missionaries as soon as he received permission from Rome.

Time passed and no missionaries arrived. So, in the spring of 1837, Old Ignace again embarked for St. Louis. Near Fort Laramie, he was attacked by the Sioux and killed. These failed efforts only increased the Flatheads' determination; in 1839, two more Flatheads set out for St. Louis.[26] They followed the Missouri River, eventually reaching the Jesuit mission near Council Bluffs. There, they encountered Pierre Jean De Smet[27] who had established a Potawatomi mission earlier that year.[28]

Born in Belgium around 1800, De Smet came to the United States in 1821. Two years later, he journeyed to the St. Ferdinand Novitiate near St. Louis where he was ordained in 1827.[29] His small stature and pudgy physique belied his great physical and mental strength. A full, frank countenance overflowed with enthusiasm and joy. De Smet's commanding presence had a way of quieting anger and instilling confidence.[30] Throughout his life, he would travel hundreds of thousands of miles, across continents and oceans, founding missions, raising funds, meeting with the tribes, and preaching the gospel.[31]

De Smet wrote of the visiting Flatheads: "I have never seen any savages so fervent in religion"; they "strictly observe Sunday and assemble several times a week to pray and sing canticles."[32] Nevertheless, De Smet could do little but provide letters of recommendation for Bishop Rosati.

Finally, after more than five years of supplication, the Flatheads succeeded. In St. Louis, they received a firm pledge from Bishop Rosati that the Jesuits would send missionaries the following spring.[33] Afterwards, Rosati implored his superiors: "For the love of God, my Very Reverend Father, do not abandon these souls!"[34]

❖   ❖   ❖

---

[26]Pfaller, *De Smet*, p. 10.
[27]Chittenden, *De Smet*, Vol. I, p. 29.
[28]Chittenden, *De Smet*, Vol. I, p. 16.
[29]Chittenden, *De Smet*, Vol. I, pp. 9-12.
[30]Chittenden, *De Smet*, Vol. I, p. 13.
[31]See Chittenden, *De Smet*, passim.
[32]Chittenden, *De Smet*, Vol. I, p. 29.
[33]Chittenden, *De Smet*, Vol. I, p. 30.
[34]Buckley, p. 179.

Not surprisingly, in the spring of 1840, De Smet volunteered to go west to meet the Flatheads. On March 27, he joined Andrew Drips and other AFC employees bound for the annual rendezvous on Green River.[35] There, the missionary found ten Flatheads eagerly awaiting his arrival. De Smet, despite suffering from malaria, was delighted. The following Sunday, he celebrated the first formal mass in the Rocky Mountains north of Mexico.[36]

After the rendezvous, De Smet traveled to the Flathead encampment in Pierre's Hole. The tribe hungrily embraced his teachings and he developed an unshakable faith in the prospects for a mission. After spending most of the summer teaching the Flatheads and baptizing their children,[37] the priest headed to St. Louis to report to his superiors and raise funds for the Flathead mission.

De Smet, accompanied by several Flatheads, followed the Yellowstone and Missouri rivers, being graciously received by the AFC at Forts Alexander, Union, Clark, and Pierre where he baptized numerous mixed-blood children of Company employees.[38] The journey inspired De Smet with a deep love for the wilderness and its perils. He considered the trip between Fort Alexander, in the country of the Crows, and Fort Union, conducted in constant fear, the best "retreat" of his life. De Smet believed that his safe passage showed clearly "the special Providence that protects the poor missionary."[39]

In St. Louis, the fundraising proceeded well and, on April 30, 1841, De Smet, along with two priests and three lay brothers, headed west.[40] In Westport, they joined John Bidwell's caravan, beginning their trek across what would become known as the Oregon Trail on May 19.[41] On August 15, the group reached Fort Hall where some twenty Flatheads awaited. Three days later, the missionaries headed north to establish St. Mary's Mission in the Bitterroot Valley.[42]

One of those accompanying De Smet was the French priest, Nicolas

---

[35]Chittenden, *De Smet*, Vol. I, p. 31.
[36]Chittenden, *De Smet*, Vol. I, p. 32. A marker commemorating this event exists outside Daniel, Wyoming.  [37]Pfaller, *De Smet*, p. 11.
[38]Chittenden, *De Smet*, Vol. I, pp. 33-37.  [39]Pfaller, *De Smet*, pp. 12-13.
[40]Chittenden, *De Smet*, Vol. I, p. 39.  [41]Buckley, p. 196.
[42]Buckley, pp. 200-202.  [43]Buckley, p. ix.

Point. Born in 1799,[43] Point joined the Jesuits, hoping eventually to work among the North American Indians. But the French had only limited Indian missions[44] and Point's superiors expressed concerns about his temperament for such an assignment.[45] Instead, Point's superiors sent him first to Kentucky to serve at St. Mary's College and, in 1836, to Iberville, Louisiana, to establish a new college.[46]

Point's successes did nothing to diminish his yearning to minister to the western Indians. Nor did they lift the priest from his persistent melancholia. Then, in late 1839, Point's superiors agreed to send him west.[47] On the verge of achieving his life's dream, Point still could not find joy. He became obsessed with the thought that, having been judged incompetent, he was being rejected by the Jesuits.[48]

In July 1840, the Jesuits officially removed Point from his Louisiana post and assigned him to work with the Belgian Jesuits, and Pierre De Smet, in establishing the western Indian missions.[49] Thus, on the very day De Smet preached the first mass in the Rocky Mountains, Point left Louisiana for Missouri to prepare for the westward trek.[50]

Point should have been elated as the overland caravan left Westport in 1841 but his inner demons continued to rage. His behavior became so erratic that even the ever optimistic De Smet grew concerned. He appointed Point official trek diarist, hoping thereby "to distract him [from his] sombre (*sic*) and melancholy humor."[51] But Point's brooding personality could not overcome so easily. Throughout his six years on the frontier, depression haunted the priest.

Nevertheless, Point worked tirelessly to minister to the Indians. Between 1841 and 1845, Point helped establish not only St. Mary's Mission among the Flatheads but also the Sacred Heart Mission among the Coeur d'Alenes.[52] Moreover, Point distinguished himself by frequently accompanying the tribes on their buffalo hunts.[53] Yet none of this

---

[44]Although Buckley says that the French had no missions among the North American Indians, Hugh Dempsey, in correspondence with the author, states that the Bishop of Quebec sent Fathers Joseph-Norbert Provencher and Sévèe Dumoulin to Red River (Winnipeg) to work among the Cree and Métis in 1818. Moreover, according to Dempsey, the Oblates (Order of Mary Immaculate) "flooded the British West with missionaries direct from France in 1844 and for years afterward."

[45]Buckley, p. 80.  [46]Buckley, p. 106, 110.
[47]Buckley, pp. 150-151.  [48]Buckley, p. 167.
[49]Buckley, p. 188.  [50]Buckley, p. 178.
[51]Buckley, p. 196.  [52]Buckley, pp. 213-218.
[53]Point, p. viii.

assuaged Point's dissatisfaction. Starting in 1842, he began lobbying De Smet to allow him to establish a mission among the fierce Blackfeet.[54]

The Jesuits at St. Mary's were familiar with the Small Robes, a small Piegan band. The Small Robes hunted in the Three Forks region and had befriended the Flatheads, sworn enemies of the rest of the Blackfeet. The Small Robes occasionally visited the Flatheads in the Bitterroot Valley and, after the missionaries arrived, they noticed many changes: the Flatheads sang songs in a strange language, rested on the seventh day, and made peculiar signs of a cross over their chests. In 1841, while visiting their friends, the Small Robes met the missionaries.[55]

Father De Smet recorded the baptism of "an old chief of the Blackfeet nation . . . with his son and little family, five in all" on Christmas Day 1841.[56] This chief, almost certainly of the Small Robes, received the Christian name, Nicholas. Nicholas carried the missionaries' message to his band and, in February 1842, De Smet noted that "Sunday is religiously observed in the camp where Nicholas resides." More importantly, Nicholas informed De Smet that a Blackfeet chief "with the people of sixty lodges" planned to visit the area to meet with the Black Robes and "attach themselves to the Flatheads."[57]

All this led the missionaries to hope that they might convert the Blackfeet. But the vast majority of the Blackfeet still held a deep hostility for the Flatheads. Moreover, many of the Indians embraced Christianity as simply another piece of powerful "medicine" to add to their pantheon of totems.[58]

De Smet understood tribal factionalism and the complex Indian ideation of religion better than Point. Therefore, when Point sought permission to establish a Blackfeet mission in 1842, De Smet refused, not believing them ready. He did, however, hope that they might receive the word of God "before long."[59] In 1846, De Smet apparently thought that time had come.

---

[54]Chittenden, *De Smet*, Vol. I, p. 391.
[55]Ewers, *Blackfeet*, p. 185.
[56]Chittenden, *De Smet*, Vol. I, p. 338.
[57]Chittenden, *De Smet*, Vol. I, p. 364.
[58]Ewers, *Blackfeet*, pp. 187-188.
[59]Chittenden, *De Smet*, Vol. I, p. 392.

Chapter Thirteen

*lending influence to perpetuate superstitions*

Long before the Jesuits reached the upper Missouri, the Blackfeet shared with them a fundamental belief: religion and daily life were inextricably intertwined. But their views diverged when it came to identifying the source of sacredness.

Although the Blackfeet knew Napi as their creator, they did not worship him. They regarded Napi as very human. In their mythology, he is alternately depicted as powerful and impotent, cruel and compassionate, wise and foolish, sad and joyful.[1] The Blackfeet worshiped the Sun, where they believed Napi went to live after he left the people.[2] Every happiness, every success, every achievement came through the blessings of Sun.[3]

The Sun is chief of the world. The earth is the floor of his lodge and the sky its covering. The Sun, beneficent and generous to all who do right, married Moon.[4] Morning Star was their child.[5] To obtain Sun's good will, the Blackfeet made offerings of clothing, robes, furs, food, flesh, and hair. When they killed a white buffalo, his robe belonged to Sun. Buffalo tongues, the greatest of delicacies, were an especially sacred oblation.[6]

The Blackfeet also worshiped other natural forces: the Above Persons, the Ground Persons, and the Under Water Persons. Thunder, an Under Water Person, was an especially important lesser deity.[7] The Blackfeet rarely crossed a stream without making an offering to the Under Water

---

[1] See the various Napi myths in Grinnell, Wissler, Uhlenbeck, Bullchild, Dempsey, and de Jong.

[2] Grinnell, *Blackfoot Lodge Tales*, p. 258, points out that: "There is some reason to suspect, however, that the Sun and Old Man are one, that Natos is only another name for Napi, for I have been told by two or three old men that 'the Sun is the person whom we call Old Man.'" Wissler, *Mythology*, p. 10, says: "It is of interest to note that the earlier writers are disposed to treat Natos, the Sun, as the home of the Old Man while the later ones make each a character."

[3] Grinnell, *Blackfoot Lodge Tales*, p. 258.

[4] Grinnell, *Blackfoot Lodge Tales*, p. 258, gives the Blackfeet name for Moon as Ko-ko-mik'-e-is.

[5] Grinnell, *Blackfoot Lodge Tales*, p. 258. Grinnell gives the Morning Star's Blackfeet name as A-pi-su'-ahts.

[6] Grinnell, *Blackfoot Lodge Tales*, p. 258.

[7] Grinnell, *Blackfoot Lodge Tales*, p. 259.

Persons.[8] Animals, too, were revered since they possessed special powers from Sun and Old Man.[9]

The Blackfeet knew that things were not necessarily what they appeared. An animal could become a man; a natural force could become an animal or a man. People, too, could be transformed. In legends, women frequently married natural forces, animals, or stars disguised as men. She would return to her people with special wisdom or powers.[10]

Once, two young girls woke before daylight, looked into the sky, and saw Morning Star. "That is a very bright star," said one. "I should like him for a husband."

Several days later, as the girl gathered wood, a handsome young man appeared, blocking her path. When she challenged him to move, the man refused, saying, "You said you wanted me for a husband." The girl replied: "I do not know you."

"I am the Morning Star," the stranger declared. "Now I have come for you." Remembering her wish, the girl agreed to go with him. He placed an eagle feather in her hair, instructed her to close her eyes, and they rose into the sky.

The Sun and Moon welcomed the young girl. Moon gave her a special digging stick but instructed her never to dig up one large turnip. The girl often wondered what made that turnip special.

In time, the girl gave birth. Soon after, she was out digging roots when she could no longer resist the large turnip. She dug it up, creating a big hole in the sky. The wind rushed up through the hole. The girl looked down and saw the camps of her people. Homesick, she started to cry. She cried for a long time before returning to her lodge.

When Morning Star saw her, he asked what had happened. The girl confessed that she had dug up the turnip. He asked if she had seen her people. She said yes. "Do you wish to go home now?" he asked. She did. So Morning Star constructed a long rope[11] to lower the girl and her child back to earth. Before she left, Morning Star cautioned that if her child touched the ground during the first fourteen days he would become a star.

The girl's family welcomed her home and for twelve days she carefully watched her child to assure that he did not touch the ground. On the thir-

---

[8]Wissler, *Mythology*, p. 129.   [9]Grinnell, *Blackfoot Lodge Tales*, pp. 259-260.
[10]See Grinnell, Uhlenbeck, and Wissler, passim.
[11]Wissler, *Mythology*, p. 60, says the rope was made of spiderwebs; de Jong, p. 96, says it was made from buffalo hides.

teenth day, the girl's mother sent her to fetch water. The girl reminded her mother to keep the baby from the ground but the baby managed to crawl away. When the girl returned, she discovered her baby had become a puff-ball. That night, she saw a new star in the sky. This, the Fixed Star, had been her baby.[12]

❖   ❖   ❖

Old Man taught the people: "If you are overcome, you may sleep and get power. Something will come to you in a dream that will help you. Whatever these tell you to do, you must obey and be guided by."[13]

Both old and young Blackfeet men often went alone to fast and dream to gain power. The ritual required him to retreat to an isolated and dangerous spot—a mountain peak, a narrow cliff ledge, an island in a lake, or places where the dead had been buried—where he would be exposed to the power of the Above, Ground, or Under Water People.

Once there, he built a small lodge of moss and brush. After offering prayers and sacred songs, he entered the lodge and began a four day fast. He spent two nights on his right side and two on his left. A pipe lay nearby for any spirit that might come. The man appealed to no particular force but waited and welcomed whatever appeared. By the fourth day, a spirit helper—usually in the form of an animal—appeared to advise the seeker.

Not all men attempted this quest and many who did failed. Sometimes, no spirit appeared. More often, the seeker abandoned the search, unable to endure the fast or frightened by the strange surroundings. There was no disgrace in failure since only a brave man even attempted the search. Moreover, the quest was such an intimate undertaking that few knew where the aspirant had been.[14]

Successful seekers returned with knowledge from their spirit helper. They had learned how to make their personal holy objects, how to care for them, and how to use them. These sacred objects, and the rituals and taboos which accompanied them, comprised their personal medicine bundle. If lost, a medicine bundle could be remade since the objects were symbols of power, not the power itself. The bundle remained a warrior's for life unless he chose to pass it on.[15]

---

[12]Wissler, *Mythology*, pp. 58-61; de Jong, pp. 95-97. Wissler says that "puff-ball" is another term for fungus and adds: "The Blackfoot have a curious belief that certain kinds of fungi are associated with the stars. Sometimes these fungi are spoken of as the 'fallen stars.'" [footnote 1, p. 40]

[13]Grinnell, *Blackfoot Lodge Tales*, p. 141 and p. 263.

[14]Grinnell, *Blackfoot Lodge Tales*, pp. 189-190.    [15]Ewers, *Blackfeet*, p. 163.

Just as animals could confer power, men could transfer power with their medicine bundles. Since powerful medicine brought wealth and good fortune, many desired to possess the medicine bundle of a distinguished warrior. A warrior who wanted to acquire another's medicine offered the owner horses or other property. If the bundle owner agreed to the transfer, an elaborate ceremony ensued.

Transfer ceremonies normally began with a sweat bath. After the heat purification, the owner and purchaser retired to the bundle owner's tipi. There, as sweet grass burned, the bundle owner told the story of his medicine bundle, narrating his vision. Then, the bundle owner, assisted by his wife, slowly and reverently revealed his bundle's contents. As he handled each object, the owner sang its ceremonial song.

The bundle could not be transferred until the recipient understood each item and its rituals. When the purchaser exhibited complete understanding of the bundle's elements, the ceremony concluded with dancing, face-painting, and smoking of sacred tobacco. With a complex medicine bundle, the ceremony might last many hours or days.[16]

Owning a variety of medicine bundles during one's lifetime added to one's prestige and power. Elderly warriors enjoyed recounting all the different bundles they had owned. Everyone knew that attaining a new medicine bundle required not only the sacrifice of considerable personal property but also the exercise of great intellectual abilities.[17]

The most revered Blackfeet medicine bundle was the beaver bundle, the oldest and largest. The beaver man, "those who have power over the waters," kept the tribal calendar or "winter count," played an important role in calling the buffalo and in planting and harvesting the sacred tobacco.[18]

The beaver bundle contained hundreds of bird and animal skins with associated sacred songs learned from the beaver in long-ago times. The beaver had taught these songs to the original bundle owner after he had been kind in raising a child the beaver had fathered with the bundle owner's wife.[19] The owner of the beaver bundle spent years learning the songs, the skins to which they belonged, and their proper sequence in

---

[16] Ewers, *Blackfeet*, pp. 163-165.   [17] Ewers, *Blackfeet*, p. 165.
[18] Ewers, *Blackfeet*, p. 167.
[19] Ewers, *Blackfeet*, pp. 167-169; Uhlenbeck, *New Series*, pp. 93-95; Wissler, *Mythology*, pp. 74-78. Cf., Grinnell, *Blackfoot Lodge Tales*, pp. 117-124.

# TO PERPETUATE SUPERSTITIONS 153

the ritual. Because of its complexity, this bundle was rarely transferred.[20]

The Bloods called Alexander Culbertson Ksîs'tûki Pokah' or "Beaver Child."[21] Culbertson's profession may have influenced the choice of this name but, since beaver pelts represented a minor part of the Blackfeet fur trade, it is more likely that Culbertson received the name, an old and revered one among the Bloods, from a respected tribal member who possessed it.[22] This appellation reflected the Bloods' deep respect for Culbertson as well as their belief that he possessed powerful medicine.

The Jesuit missionaries, Nicolas Point and Pierre De Smet, left St. Mary's Mission on August 16, 1846, for Fort Lewis. In the Yellowstone valley, they encountered an encampment of Flatheads, Nez Perces, and Small Robes planning an attack on the Crows. Although De Smet argued against the raid, he could not prevent it. Fourteen Crows died in the battle while the opposing forces lost just one Nez Perce.[23]

The Blackfeet, attributing the good fortune of the Flatheads and Nez Perces to their Christian prayers and eager to improve their battle fortunes, agreed to De Smet's proposal to meet with their enemies, the Flatheads and Nez Perces. At the mid-September peace council, the Blackfeet listened with interest as the Flathead chief, Victor, attributed his war victories to the protection of "the true God." The Small Robes, the estranged Piegan band which had aligned with the Flatheads, endorsed Victor's tales and interpretations. De Smet then celebrated mass among the more than two thousand Flatheads, Nez Perces, Piegans, Bloods, Gros Ventres, and Northern Blackfoot.[24]

On September 17, two Bloods invited De Smet to their camp, assuring him that there was no reason to "have a shadow of a fear." Three days later, the Jesuits baptized over one hundred children and two old men; two days later, they baptized an elderly former Piegan chief.[25] Finally, on September 24, 1846, Pierre De Smet and Nicolas Point, accompanied by their Indian companions and guides, reached Fort Lewis.[26]

---

[20]Ewers, *Blackfeet*, p. 169.
[21]Schultz, *Signposts*, p. 111; Holterman, p. 66. Holterman spells the name Tsîs'tûki Pokah'.
[22]Hugh Dempsey to the author.   [23]Chittenden, *De Smet*, Vol. I, pp. 54-55.
[24]Chittenden, *De Smet*, Vol. II, p. 593.   [25]Chittenden, *De Smet*, Vol. II, pp. 594-595.
[26]Buckley, p. 306.

Alexander Culbertson had not yet returned from St. Louis when the Jesuits arrived, just as the feud between Malcolm Clarke and Charles Larpenteur was peaking. This resulted in an unexpected bonus for De Smet, who needed to return to St. Louis, when Clarke offered to take him to Fort Union.[27]

Point benefited as well. Although De Smet still harbored concerns about leaving Point, with his erratic emotional nature, among the notoriously hostile Blackfeet, "(a)fter maturely weighing the various plans," De Smet decided to allow him to remain behind to lay the groundwork for a Blackfeet mission.[28] In St. Louis, De Smet would discuss his plans for "a mission and probably a school among the Blackfeet" with the Superintendent of Indian Affairs who believed that "such an establishment will have more control over these wild Indians in that wild country than a half dozen Regts of soldiers."[29]

Six weeks later, on November 6, De Smet reached Fort Lookout, an AFC post near present-day Chamberlain, South Dakota. There, he baptized sixteen mixed-blood children,[30] including eleven-year-old Mariah Culbertson, Alexander Culbertson's eldest daughter.[31] Apparently, Culbertson just happened to be at the post en route back to Fort Lewis. Why Mariah was traveling with her father is unclear; perhaps he had taken her to St. Louis to inquire into schooling possibilities.

This chance meeting between Culbertson and De Smet may have been their first although they may have met in 1839 when Culbertson took the mackinaw fleet downriver or in 1842 when De Smet visited Fort Union. Whether or not they had met before, they certainly knew of one another: the Company had helped De Smet previously and the Indians had often discussed the Black Robes with the traders. De Smet had also visited Fort

---

[27]Exactly how far Malcolm Clarke went is confusing. If Larpenteur's account is believed, then Clarke could not have gone beyond Fort Union. However Point states that Clarke was bound for St. Louis (Buckley, p. 306) and De Smet's journals also suggest that this was the case. (Chittenden, *De Smet*, Vol. II, p. 600ff). But De Smet never identifies his traveling companions. In any case, it is clear that De Smet left Fort Lewis with Malcolm Clarke. Possibly, Clarke disembarked at Fort Union while the Company skiff continued downriver to St. Louis with De Smet on board. This would seem the most likely conclusion since even Point seems to support Larpenteur's version of Clarke's return to Fort Lewis when he states that, by December, Larpenteur was "in disgrace." (Buckley, p. 307.)

[28]Chittenden, *De Smet*, Vol. II, p. 600; Buckley, p. 306.

[29]Thomas Harvey to William Medill, 5 Feb 1847. NAM 234/754.

[30]Chittenden, *De Smet*, Vol. II, p. 609.

[31]McDonnell, *MHSC*, Vol. X, p. 244. McDonnell gives the date as 5 Nov 1846 and the place as Fort Lookout. De Smet's letters give 6 Nov 1846 as the date he baptized children at Fort Lookout.

# TO PERPETUATE SUPERSTITIONS 155

Alexander, the AFC post serving the Crows which Charles Larpenteur had named for Culbertson. Over the next two decades, De Smet and Culbertson would become fast friends, often acting in concert to promote intertribal harmony and peace between the Indians and the whites.

After arriving at Fort Lewis, Nicolas Point, encouraged by Charles Larpenteur, lost no time ministering to the AFC employees stationed at the Blackfeet post. Larpenteur, a French Catholic, also communicated his faith in the Black Robes to the Indians and, initially, they lined up to have their children baptized. But when the Indians learned that the Black Robes disapproved of multiple marriages, their fervent passions cooled.[32] Point nevertheless made inroads during those first weeks.

As was his custom, the priest joined the Piegans on a buffalo hunt shortly after his arrival.[33] Soon after his return, Point traveled to the camp of the Fish Eaters with Natawista's brother, Seen From Afar.[34] Point had been invited to the Fish Eaters camp earlier by the "head chief," probably Two Suns, Seen From Afar and Natawista's father.[35] That invitation could not be accepted because the Company could not spare an interpreter. Later, when Seen From Afar came to Fort Lewis, the missionary asked if he might accompany him to his village. Seen From Afar, displaying little enthusiasm for the visit, replied simply, "Come if you like."[36]

Point characterized Seen From Afar's "brusque arrogance" as his "outstanding mannerism." The Bloods tolerated this, Point believed, because of their great respect for the warrior's courage and generosity. The Fish Eaters fondly told one story about his exemplary bravery: during a battle against the Crows, Seen From Afar, cut off from the main body of warriors, together with a small force of men, managed to slay forty Crow warriors and forced the rest to retreat.

Several years earlier, Seen From Afar had exhibited great generosity when one of his wives took up with another man. Rather than punish

---

[32]Buckley, p. 308.   [33]Buckley, p. 343.

[34]Seen From Afar's name is translated as "Panarkuinimaki" in Buckley, p. 347, and as "Panarquinima" in Point, p. 114. While this seems to give his Indian name extra syllables ("ima" and "imaki"), the identification of Seen From Afar is clear from Point's other statements, including his identification of this Indian as a leader of the Fish Eaters band who was "(i)nflated by his ties to a trader of the American company. . . ." (Buckley, p. 348) That Point did not identify the trader as Alexander Culbertson is understandable since they had not yet met.

[35]Buckley, p. 346.   [36]Buckley, p. 347.

them, as custom dictated, Seen From Afar gave his wife, along with one of his best horses, to his rival. As his own fortunes grew, aided by his status as the brother-in-law of Alexander Culbertson, Seen From Afar frequently gave horses, food, and other essentials to tribal members who had fallen on hard times.

Point, while respecting Seen From Afar, was deeply offended by his superstitious nature. On his head, the warrior wore a small black and yellow stuffed bird which he believed had the power to protect him. Seen From Afar also credited a mysterious piece of iron in the Blackfeet country with the power to produce great horses. Moreover, he insisted that the best cows emerged from a strip of land along the Missouri River known as the Steer's Head.[37] Although Point did not realize it, it was Seen From Afar's belief in the transcendent powers of the supernatural which enabled him to embrace the "medicine" that the Black Robes preached.

Despite Seen From Afar's initially tepid invitation, Point embraced the opportunity to visit the camp of the Fish Eaters. At the village, Seen From Afar welcomed Point into his lodge. As the warrior chief settled himself against the backrests on his "ornamental bed," the missionary surveyed the lodge's ceremonial objects.

In the reserved space between the warrior's seat and the fire pit stood an incense holder shaped like a crescent moon. Nearby, an elegant container held the sacred objects for pipe ceremonies. A large calumet, a scepter with bells, an eagle feather headdress, and various weapons hung on the walls. A dog and a rooster lived in small hidden spaces on the left and right of Seen From Afar's seat.

The distinguished men of the tribe gathered in Seen From Afar's lodge to receive the missionary. Following a traditional pipe ceremony, Point addressed the warriors, explaining the advantages which would accrue were the tribe to enter into a peace agreement with the Flatheads. These benefits would be further enhanced if the Fish Eaters would permit the Black Robes to establish a mission among them. When Point finished, the warriors sat in stony silence.[38]

Finally, one of them, perhaps Seen From Afar, spoke: "But, is what the Black Robe just said really true? How could he speak the truth since nothing but lies comes from the mouths of white men!"[39] The interpreter, while

---

[37] Buckley, p. 348.  [38] Buckley, p. 349.
[39] Buckley, p. 350, identifies the speaker as "the assembly president."

# TO PERPETUATE SUPERSTITIONS 157

acknowledging that many whites told lies, assured the gathering that "not the smallest lie has ever come from the mouths of the Black Robes."

The doubting warrior replied: "If this is so, it is well and good. What you have just told us proves you love the redskins no less than the whites. Therefore you may come on our lands whenever you like." Finally, he vowed to "ever be friends with the Flatheads" and to offer protection to the missionary, should it ever be needed. With that, the other warriors signaled agreement.

The next day, Seen From Afar converted his lodge into a "chapel for true prayer." The women, in numbers far greater than expected, brought their children to be baptized. Before the baptisms could be completed, Point was forced to move outside so that Seen From Afar's wife could dismantle the lodge for an impending move. The missionary baptized the last group of children outside as the cold winter air froze the water on his fingertips.[40]

If Point had hoped to convert Seen From Afar, he failed. The warrior refused to discard his old, faithful medicine and, in February 1847, when the Bloods raised a large war party against the Assiniboines, Seen From Afar performed his traditional rituals, offering Sun clothing, blankets, and fabric.

This traditional medicine appeared to work on the first night when the Bloods stole nearly two hundred horses. But the next night, the Assiniboines reclaimed their horses and forced the Bloods to abandon their robes, pipes, weapons, and medicine bundles. Thoroughly humbled by this defeat, Seen From Afar presented Point with his talisman: the black and yellow bird he had worn in his hair.[41] Although Point interpreted this as Seen From Afar's embrace of Catholicism, there is no record of the warrior ever submitting to baptism.

About the first of December 1846, quite possibly while Father Point was visiting Seen From Afar's camp, Alexander Culbertson finally reached Fort Lewis after his lengthy stay in St. Louis and long return journey. When the priest returned, Culbertson, in keeping with custom, provided him with living quarters as well as a room to hold chapel services and religious classes.

But Point's missionary zeal threatened to suffocate the fort. He repeat-

---

[40]Buckley, p. 350.   [41]Buckley, p. 351.

edly lectured the men about their profanity and sternly rebuked them for living with Indian women without benefit of marriage. He roundly condemned those who kept more than one wife, including Culbertson's old friend, Edwin Denig,[42] who refused to accept Point's criticism, painting his personal situation in more noble terms.

Denig's first wife had developed a chronic illness many years earlier. Under those circumstances, Denig maintained, many white men, both on the frontier and in the States, would have divorced her. Denig, however, refused to cast her out because she was a good woman who did not deserve to be punished for her illness. Nevertheless, Denig argued, God did not give him "strong passions . . . merely to be continually tormented." Therefore, he had taken a second wife both to satisfy his needs and to be a companion for his first wife.

Denig derided Point for conducting sham marriages by joining together Indian women who understood not a word of the ceremony and "dissolute men" who had little intention of honoring their vows. Yet Point accepted their false vows. Denig asked: "Do you not thereby give licentiousness the semblance of your sanction?"[43]

At Fort Lewis, Point conducted daily services as well as Sunday mass. Culbertson, though a Protestant, attended mass as did most of the Company men and their Indian wives. But Culbertson, too, clashed with the dogmatic missionary.

One Sunday, several packs of buffalo robes lay under cover at the boat launch when a storm came up. When a strong wind blew the cover off the robes, Culbertson and his men scrambled to protect them from the rain. Point,[44] seeing the men at work, ran out to chastise the trader: "Major Culbertson, I am amazed. I thought you were a Christian, a reverencer of religion and an observer of the Holy Sabbath; but now I find you, not only violating God's holy day yourself but exacting it of your men. How can my teachings bear fruit when you trample them thus ruthlessly in the dust?"

Culbertson, not wishing to debate the issue, persisted in his chores as Point continued his entreaties. Finally, an exasperated Culbertson asked Point if it was not also a Christian's responsibility to protect his property from destruction. Was it not even more so his responsibility to protect the

---

[42]Bradley, *MHSC,* Vol. III, p. 248.     [43]Kurz, pp. 210-211.

[44]Bradley, *MHSC,* Vol. III, p. 248, attributes this episode to De Smet. However, considering both the context of the anecdote and the character of the two priests, it seems probable that the incident involved Nicolas Point and that the "De Smet" in Bradley's manuscript is an error.

property of his employer? Point could not be persuaded. Losing patience, Culbertson abruptly suggested that the priest take his Bible and go read it in his room rather than watch this great sin be committed.[45]

On another occasion, one of the Culbertson children contracted a bad case of croup. The Blackfeet believed that illness resulted from evil spirits entering the body. The best cure, then, was to expel the spirits.[46] When nothing in the white man's arsenal relieved the child's suffering, Natawista sent for an old Blood woman, well-known for her ability to drive evil spirits from children. The Blood healer arrived and proceeded to purify the child with a steam bath. A low, solemn, monotonous chant accompanied the ceremony.

Father Point had just joined Culbertson for breakfast when the chanting began. When Point inquired about the noise, his host explained that a Blood woman had come to minister to Culbertson's desperately ill child. Point abruptly rushed upstairs to where the treatment was underway. He grabbed the old woman by the neck and pushed her down the stairs. Returning to the dining room, he condemned Culbertson for "lending his influence to perpetuate superstitions."[47] Natawista, deeply resentful of the priest's interference, told him to "mind his own business" and brought the medicine woman back to complete her ministrations.[48] Through whatever medium, the child recovered.

Despite these disagreements, Point praised Culbertson, his temperament, and his influence on the Indians:

> [Culbertson] has made it his rule to act with heroic moderation, and ever since he took charge of dealing with the Indians not a single Blackfoot has tried to do him the slightest harm. And more remarkably still is that during the seventeen years he has lived among the Indians (and he has always dwelt among those hardest to please), not a single Indian has ever killed a white man when it was known that he was in the area.[49]

Despite his disagreements with Point, Culbertson remained committed to assisting the Black Robes in establishing a Blackfeet mission. On Easter Sunday, he suggested that all employees, regardless of religious affiliation, contribute to a mission fund. In short order, they raised nearly $200. Culbertson himself contributed $15 while Malcolm Clarke, Jacob

---

[45]Bradley, *MHSC*, Vol. III, p. 248.  [46]Ewers, *Blackfeet*, p. 184.
[47]Bradley, *MHSC*, Vol. III, p. 249.  [48]Taylor, "The Major's Blackfoot Bride," p. 46.
[49]Buckley, p. 373.

Berger, and James Lee, the men charged with the decidedly un-Christian attack on Alexander Harvey, contributed $5, $7, and $5 respectively. A certificate attesting to their desire to see a Catholic mission among the Blackfeet accompanied the contributions.[50]

During eight months at Fort Lewis, Nicolas Point baptized between 650 and 700 individuals, nearly all of them children.[51] Julia Culbertson, Alexander and Natawista's young daughter and possibly the one whose illness prompted Natawista to turn to traditional Blood medicine, may have been among them. Although Point recorded only four adult male baptisms,[52] he claimed he could have performed a great many more except that he "could not content [himself] with the persuasion generally existing among the savages, that when they have received baptism they can conquer any enemy whatsoever."[53] Point also married a dozen white employees, after first baptizing their Indian spouses.[54]

Father Nicolas Point left the upper Missouri in the spring of 1847, never to return. Twelve long years would pass before the Jesuits finally established a Blackfeet mission.[55] Notwithstanding his occasional disagreements with Alexander Culbertson, Point always remembered his months among the Blackfeet fondly. In an 1862 letter to De Smet, Point begged for information about his old friends, including Culbertson and his family.[56] The priest had even developed fond memories of Natawista, despite what he regarded as her heathen ways. On July 4, 1868, Father Nicolas Point died in Quebec.[57]

---

[50] Buckley, p. 377.
[51] Buckley, p. 377, gives a figure of 700; Ewers, *Blackfeet*, p. 190, suggests 651.
[52] Ewers, *Blackfeet*, p. 190.
[53] Chittenden, *De Smet*, Vol. III, pp. 952-953.
[54] Buckley, p. 377.   [55] Ewers, *Blackfeet*, p. 191.
[56] Buckley, p. 433.   [57] Buckley, p. 435.

Chapter Fourteen

## *"the ball passing a few inches to the right of Culbertson's face"*

Alexander Culbertson left Fort Lewis with Father Point in the early morning of May 21, 1847.[1] Two days earlier, Culbertson had abandoned Fort Lewis, the Blackfeet post he had risked so much to establish just eighteen months earlier.[2] Its site, on the Missouri's south bank, had been chosen to provide protection from the Blackfeet whose attitude toward the returning traders was then unknown. But, while the Blackfeet had welcomed Culbertson and his new post, Fort Lewis's location had proven problematic. Floating ice in spring and fall made it nearly impossible to reach the fort and the Indians were clamoring for a location closer to the Teton River, with its abundant timber supply, where they camped during trading visits.

Culbertson began scouting a new location in early 1847, ultimately choosing a site three miles downstream on the opposite shore. In early April, AFC employees began dismantling Fort Lewis and rafting its timbers downriver where other men began constructing the new post.[3] By mid-May, enough progress had been made for Culbertson to order the goods and pelts transferred.

While the new fort officially retained the name Fort Lewis,[4] it soon began to be called Fort Benton.[5] Fort names usually honored AFC leaders and, while the name "Benton" deviated from that pattern, it made eminently good sense. Few had done as much in recent years to protect the American Fur Company's interests as Missouri's senator, Thomas Hart Benton, whose political intervention in the liquor suits helped ensure the Company's continued ability to operate.[6]

The official renaming occurred on Christmas Day 1850, during a ball

---

[1]Buckley, p. 384.     [2]Buckley, p. 380.
[3]Bradley, *MHSC*, Vol. III, p. 251.     [4]Bradley, *MHSC*, Vol. III, p. 252.
[5]"From the Mountains," 25 Jul 1848, refers to "Fort Benton."
[6]Sunder, p. 114.

Culbertson threw for the fort employees. Natawista, her fingers sparkling with emeralds and rubies,[7] wore a splendid bright red silk dress purchased in St. Louis.[8] At the height of the festivities, Culbertson stilled the fiddles, one of which may have been his own, and proposed the new name. The employees cheered and the Blackfeet post officially became Fort Benton.[9]

The post's new location put it closer to Fort Campbell, Alexander Harvey's opposition fort. In early 1847, floating ice tore an AFC keelboat from its moorings. Although employees rescued it after the river broke up, it was later destroyed by fire. Culbertson blamed his old nemesis, Harvey.[10] His suspicions were confirmed two years later when Joseph Urbin dit Bolduc, a Harvey, Primeau and Company employee, verified in a deposition that he and another Harvey employee, Jean Latour, had been ordered to destroy the "nearly new" keelboat which had been taken from the water and placed on logs "to protect it during the winter."[11]

Culbertson's downriver trip with Point proceeded smoothly. Near old Fort McKenzie, Culbertson killed a bear which seemed intent on attacking the travelers. Later, he presented Point a "white-headed eagle," or "nun," for the priest to paint.[12] At Fort Union, the travelers transferred to the steamboat, *Martha*, which brought them to St. Louis on July 8. The *Martha* carried some fifteen hundred packs of buffalo robes, two hundred and eighty packs of other furs, and almost a hundred sacks of buffalo tongues. In addition, it transported a live menagerie from the upper river: fawns, mountain dogs, birds, bear cubs, and a herd of buffalo calves bound for private collections and the many circuses that performed around St. Louis.[13]

Culbertson, concerned about his newly relocated Blackfeet post, left St. Louis as quickly as possible, to attend to his duties on the upper river and still return to Fort Benton before the river closed. He reached the Blackfeet post in October 1847 and was pleased to find everything in good shape. The reconstruction had been completed and the employees were readying for the winter trade.

Returns from 1847 had been exceptionally good and Culbertson decided to establish three outposts for the 1847-1848 winter trade. He

---

[7]Taylor, "The Major's Blackfoot Bride," p. 45.   [8]Schemm, p. 10.

[9]McDonnell, *MHSC*, Vol. X, p. 240; Bradley, *MHSC*, Vol. III, p. 264; Overholser, p. 19.

[10]Bradley, *MHSC*, Vol. III, p. 251.

[11]Deposition of Joseph Urbin dit Bolduc, 15 May 1849. Chouteau-Maffitt Collection, MoHS. The deposition says the keelboat was burned in February or March 1846 but this must be an error since Harvey, Primeau and Company did not arrive to trade in the Blackfeet country until later in 1846.   [12]Buckley, p. 390.   [13]Sunder, p. 98.

ordered Canadian-born Augustin Hamel,[14] long an interpreter for the Blackfeet, to build an outpost on the Marias River at Willow Rounds.[15] Michel Champaigne, a French-Canadian who began his employment with the AFC in 1829, was dispatched to Milk River.[16] Finally, Culbertson sent Malcolm Clarke some thirty miles up the Marias beyond Hamel's post to a place known as Flatwood.[17] This move, in addition to furthering Culbertson's aims for the Blackfeet trade, kept Clarke away from his sworn enemy, Alexander Harvey.

The three outposts, all built as temporary structures, operated from October to March, the winter trading months. Clarke's Flatwood post was located near the winter camp of the Fish Eaters band and, that winter, Culbertson rode out to visit Clarke and Natawista's family. He found Seen From Afar[18] living in a magnificent lodge of forty skins over thirty-five lodge poles. Two inside fireplaces warmed the interior. The lodge befitted Seen From Afar's status as "the greatest chief" Culbertson had ever known. Eventually, Seen From Afar could boast of having ten wives and one hundred horses.[19]

The 1847-1848 trade at Fort Benton surpassed all previous records and completely exhausted the post's trade goods. When the supplies ran out, provisions intended for Company employees, such as bedding and clothing, were exchanged for furs. By the end of the season, no dispensable supplies remained. In all, twenty thousand buffalo robes as well as a large quantity of other furs had been taken in trade.[20]

Even before the spectacular 1848 Blackfeet returns became known in St. Louis, the AFC partners had voted to reward Culbertson for his faithful and profitable service to the Company. When the Company underwent one of its periodic reorganizations that spring, Culbertson received one share of Company stock in addition to being appointed chief agent for the upper Missouri River posts, replacing Honoré Picotte.[21]

Culbertson left Fort Benton in early April 1848 to take the returns to Fort Union. This mimicked his travel schedule of the previous year, a

---

[14]His name is variously given as Hamelin, Hamell, Hammell, Ammell, and Armell. See McDonnell, *MHSC*, Vol. X, p. 262.

[15]Bradley, *MHSC*, Vol. III, p. 258. Bradley places the establishment of these posts "in the fall of 1848." More likely, they were established in the fall of 1847 and winter of 1848.

[16]Bradley, *MHSC*, Vol. III, p. 258.   [17]Bradley, *MHSC*, Vol. III, p. 258.

[18]Bradley, *MHSC*, Vol. III, p. 258, does not identify him as Seen From Afar which is in keeping with Culbertson's reluctance to discuss his family.   [19]Bradley, *MHSC*, Vol. III, p. 258.

[20]Bradley, *MHSC*, Vol. III, p. 257.   [21]Sunder, pp. 105-106.

schedule to which he would adhere for the rest of his professional life. As early as possible each spring, Culbertson would leave the Blackfeet country, usually with the returns, for Fort Union. From there, he proceeded overland to meet the season's first steamboat, normally encountered near Fort Pierre, with its news from Company headquarters.

Depending on these instructions, Culbertson then spent the late spring and early summer tending to affairs at the various upriver posts. In late summer, he almost always headed to St. Louis to meet with his superiors. Following those meetings, Culbertson headed back upriver on horseback, sometimes escorting the season's last pack train. If all went well, he reached the Blackfeet post some time between October and December. With approximately twenty-five hundred river miles separating Fort Benton and St. Louis, Culbertson averaged more than six thousand travel miles each year.[22]

When Culbertson left Fort Benton in the spring of 1848, one of his primary concerns was ensuring its proper outfitting for the coming season. At Fort Union, he ordered Charles Larpenteur, the long-suffering Company clerk, to take a new seventy-five foot mackinaw to Fort Benton to replace the keelboat destroyed by Harvey's men. Larpenteur also transported trade goods and basic supplies to replace the fort necessities traded out during the previous season.[23]

Since his stormy 1846-1847 dispute with Clarke over Fort Lewis's leadership, Larpenteur's fortunes had been on the wane. After spending the winter of 1847 unemployed and scarcely tolerated at Fort Union, Larpenteur decided to establish himself as a free trader among the Flatheads. When he missed his opportunity to join a westward wagon train, he was forced to sign on with the AFC for another year.[24]

He spent that year opposing Harvey, Primeau and Company near Fort Union but continued to nurture his free trader dreams and convinced James Kipp's nephew, James Bruguière, to join him when their AFC contracts expired. When Culbertson ordered him to take the new mackinaw to Fort Benton, Larpenteur added his own supplies to those for the post and took off.[25] The trip to Benton did not go well, perhaps because the mackinaw was dangerously overloaded. Larpenteur and Bruguière arrived too late to meet up with their guides but Malcolm Clarke, Lar-

---

[22]This understanding of Culbertson's travel schedule comes from the author's own research and is supported by his son, Joseph Culbertson, in his draft manuscript, KP, UCLA, p. 93.
[23]Bradley, *MHSC,* Vol. III, p. 252.  [24]Larpenteur, pp. 212-219.
[25]Larpenteur, pp. 221-225.

penteur's old enemy, offered to provide the luckless trader with horses, wagons, carts, and a guide.[26]

Larpenteur departed in late October but his guide soon deserted. With snow falling, food supplies dwindling, and no sense of where he was going, Larpenteur was forced back to Fort Benton.[27] There, he hired an Indian named Sata who had guided Fathers De Smet and Point from St. Mary's to Fort Lewis in 1846. Three days after returning in ignominy, Larpenteur set off again. A couple of nights later, the men encountered some Blackfeet who informed them that snow had closed the mountain passes. Sata, possessing the sense that Larpenteur lacked, would go no farther. Once again, Larpenteur returned to Fort Benton where he passed another winter in disgrace. This, he stated, caused "a great derangement of my nervous system, from which I never completely recovered." At last, Larpenteur had an excuse for any misadventures that would follow.[28]

Meanwhile, Alexander Culbertson continued downriver to Fort Berthold. Established in the late 1830s, Fort Berthold, serving the Mandans, Hidatsas, and Arikaras, had replaced Fort Clark after the Mandans, decimated by the 1837 smallpox epidemic, moved north to join the Hidatsas.

Francis Chardon, Alexander Harvey's collaborator in the Fort McKenzie massacre, had been posted to Fort Berthold after leaving the Blackfeet country. In the spring of 1848, Chardon became "very ill, with a violent attack of rheumatism."[29] His condition deteriorated until he could do little but lie on his bed and hope for visitors to bring him tales of life outside his room. In late April, the old trader died.

With his dying breath, Chardon denied the charges leveled years earlier that he had killed a rival trader. According to Chardon, the two had gone buffalo hunting and, while passing through a thick grove of willows, his gun accidentally discharged, killing his companion. "As I am going before my God, it was an accident," Chardon declared.[30]

Culbertson, reaching Fort Berthold soon after Chardon's death, decid-

---

[26]Larpenteur, pp. 225-226.     [27]Larpenteur, p. 234.
[28]Larpenteur, pp. 234-238.     [29]Abel, p. 266, fn. 252.
[30]Abel, p. 267, fn. 252. Some confusion exists about the date of Chardon's death since John Palliser, who related the details of it, put the date at the end of May. However, the St. Louis newspapers reported Chardon's death as having occurred on April 20, 1848 (Abel, p. 269, fn. 254) which is consistent with Culbertson's taking the body to Fort Pierre for burial.

ed to take his remains to Fort Pierre for burial.[31] He reached Fort Pierre on May 8, remaining just long enough to bury Chardon.[32] Culbertson continued downriver to meet the steamboat *Martha* and Gideon C. Matlock, the new Indian agent for the upper Missouri. Matlock, a former AFC employee, had argued vigorously for strong regulations against liquor trafficking and was considered to be staunchly pro-Indian.[33]

Culbertson met the *Martha*, which carried annuities for the upriver tribes, near Council Bluffs. Since Matlock had only recently assumed his position, he spent more time than usual among the tribes, introducing himself and getting acquainted.[34] On June 13, the steamboat arrived at the AFC post on Crow Creek in the lands of the Yankton Sioux.

Several hundred warriors gathered on shore for the *Martha*'s arrival. The previous year, Matlock had encountered difficulties with the Yanktons "on account of the promises which was (*sic*) made them by [his] predecessor." According to Matlock, the Yanktons had "been deceived by white men" into believing "that the U.S. is yet indebted to them. . . ." The agent believed he had "succeeded in undeceiving them," but the young warriors remained unhappy. Matlock promised that he "would endeavor to induce their G.F. [Great Father] to give them something next Spring, but could give them no assurance that it would be done."[35]

The warriors, anticipating that the government would again renege on its promises, had formulated a plan to seize the steamboat and its valuable cargo.[36] When the steamer pulled up to the dock, a warrior named Iowa

---

[31]Bradley, *MHSC*, Vol. III, p. 246. Culbertson gave Bradley a date of 1845 but this is clearly in error.

[32]Abel, p. 270, fn. 254. Sunder, p. 106, suggests that Culbertson was on board the *Martha* when it left St. Louis on May 9 but Culbertson arrived at Fort Pierre with James Kipp on May 8. Pierre Garreau to Edwin Denig, 9 May 1848, *Fort Pierre Letter Book*, 1847-1848, MoHS.

[33]Sunder, p. 97.

[34]Chittenden, *Early Steamboat*, Vol. I, p. 178.

[35]Gideon Matlock to Thomas H. Harvey, 29 Jun 1847. NAM, M234/754.

[36]Sunder, p. 107. Sunder's account and the contemporaneous report of Gideon Matlock to Thomas Harvey, 16 Jun 1848, NAM, M884/234, clearly suggest that no goods were distributed to the Indians prior to the attack on the steamboat. But Culbertson (Bradley, *MHSC*, Vol. III, p. 258) and La Barge (Chittenden, *Early Steamboat*, Vol. I, p. 178) both maintained that the Yanktons received some annuities but were unhappy because they believed they had not received all that were due them. The account of the attack in "From the Mountains" states that the Indians expected "to receive ammunition from the Indian Agent. In this they were disappointed." This account is attributed to a "Mr. F. C. Culbertson." This may have been Culbertson's cousin, Ferdinand, or, more likely, was a misprint in referring to Alexander Culbertson. Culbertson and La Barge, in saying that annuities were distributed, might have been referring to the distribution of goods following the attack.

rolled a barrel of flour down to the dock, broke it open, and dumped the contents into the river.

The men aboard the *Martha*, including Culbertson, Matlock, and the two AFC partners, Honoré Picotte and John Sarpy, watched in bemusement, unsure how to interpret Iowa's actions. They did not have to wait long for clarification. Within moments, some thirty warriors rushed the steamer, hustled aside its firemen, and doused the engine fires. With the steamboat now stranded, three young warriors began firing on the boat from shore. One bullet, apparently intended for Captain Finch who was standing next to Culbertson, passed "a few inches to the right of [Culbertson's] face" and continued through two staterooms before killing Charles Smith, a crew member on the far side of the steamer.

The Company men immediately prepared for battle. Then Agent Matlock offered to go ashore to try to "ascertain the State of feeling, the cause of the outrage, etc." Matlock wanted a peaceful resolution, but if that proved impossible, "we would give them the best fight we could." Picotte and Sarpy advised Matlock to adopt "a mild and pacific course" since they had "too much at Stake . . . to engage in a fight if it could possibly be avoided." The families of both Picotte and Captain Joseph La Barge were on board the steamer.

John Sarpy suggested that Matlock offer the Yanktons "large presents to appease the Indians." Matlock refused, insisting that "it was not the policy of the Government to pay the Indians for committing Crime." Matlock disembarked with only his good reputation to offer. Alexander Culbertson, at Matlock's request, accompanied the agent as interpreter.

On shore, Matlock gathered the Yankton leaders. He offered "kind and pacific" language while also "operating on the fears by representing the Strength of their Great Father to crush and destroy them at his pleasure." Matlock instructed Sarpy to prepare a feast for the Indians after which the agent distributed gifts. With the Yanktons appeased, at least temporarily, Sarpy ordered the *Martha* upriver.

The feast over, Matlock sat down with the Yankton chiefs to determine the source of their grievances. Smutty Bear rose to speak. With Culbertson translating, Smutty Bear begged the Indian agent to remove the white traders from their country: "Our Father cannot expect us to do any better so long as he continues to allow bad white men among us."

Smutty Bear explained that traders had advised the Yanktons to steal horses, to rob and murder, and to war against their neighbors. And, said

Smutty Bear, "we have done so." Moreover, the chief continued, "Our trader has advised us to rob & Steal from the other trader. The traders have not only advised us to do these things but in many instances paid us." The Indian concluded his long, impassioned speech: "We will have no peace so long as you permit the traders to remain with us."

Matlock, taken aback, insisted that Smutty Bear tell him which traders had encouraged the tribes to act this way. "Was it this one?" Matlock asked, pointing to Culbertson. Smutty Bear indicated it was not Culbertson, but "the traders of the Country." Again, the Yankton chief demanded that these traders, "a great lot of rascals," be driven out and new ones sent in.

Matlock eventually determined that employees of Harvey, Primeau and Company had incited the attack on the *Martha* by telling the Yanktons that the boat was loaded with annuities which the AFC did not plan to distribute. But Matlock did not find the AFC blameless. He believed Colin Campbell, a mixed-blood Sioux who ran the AFC post at Crow Creek, "a perfect nuisance ... void of principle," helped instigate the troubles.

Respecting the Indians' feelings, Matlock revoked the trading licenses of both the American Fur Company and Harvey, Primeau and Company for that region. He demanded that both companies remove their agents and withdraw their merchandise. Additionally, Matlock forbade the companies from selling "firearms of any description or ammunition" to the Yanktons at any of their trading posts.

Matlock, while "not satisfied as to my authority to revoke licenses," hoped that Superintendent of Indian Affairs Thomas Harvey would sustain his decision. Harvey did. Neither of the affected companies could afford to object too strenuously since, in 1848, the AFC still faced charges of whiskey trafficking and Harvey, Primeau and Company had come under suspicion in the Indian Office due to Harvey's pugnacious reputation. Lacking options, the two companies withdrew from the Yankton country.

But not for long. In September 1848, Matlock returned to the upper river to check conditions. Although still suspicious of Harvey and his outfit, Matlock was willing to allow the AFC "as it now stands under the new organization" to resume trade with the Yankton Sioux. The AFC reorganization which satisfied Matlock was the one that had placed Alexander Culbertson over the upper Missouri posts.[37]

---

[37]Report of Gideon Matlock to Thomas H. Harvey, 16 Jun 1848, NAM, M884/234; Sunder, pp. 108-109; "From the Mountains."

# THE BALL PASSING TO THE RIGHT OF CULBERTSON

Some time later, the Yanktons presented Culbertson with three horses and twenty-five buffalo robes which they asked him to give to the family of Charles Smith, the AFC employee inadvertently killed in their attack on the *Martha*. Although they knew this could not make up for his death, they hoped it would assist Smith's widow and children and show their true remorse for having wrongfully caused his death.[38]

Following the attack on the *Martha*, Culbertson proceeded to St. Louis where he received instructions to accompany the annual supply train from Bellevue to Fort Laramie.[39] With twenty-three ox-drawn wagons, Culbertson followed the Council Bluffs Road along the north side of the Platte River, passing Fort Kearny,[40] then under construction on the river's south bank. Apparently, he did not cross over to visit the outpost.

If he had, Battalion Commander L. E. Powell would have warned him that the Sioux and Pawnees had been battling all summer and that the Pawnees had lost most of their winter's provisions. Powell, preparing to leave for Fort Leavenworth, believed he had negotiated a resolution of the situation[41] and it is doubtful Culbertson would have changed his plans, even had he received the warning.

But, six days west of Fort Kearny, Culbertson fell ill and decided to return to the fort with two companions. As they neared the post, fifteen Pawnee warriors ambushed them, stealing everything except their guns and horses. They probably would have taken those, too, except that their chief intervened, perhaps because he feared angering the military so soon after negotiating a peace agreement.

Culbertson and his men, permitted to pass, rode two hundred yards down the road before Culbertson halted, turned, and fired on the Pawnees. As they dove for cover, Culbertson and his men rode off.

The group reached the north bank of the Platte opposite Fort Kearny after nightfall. With the fort lights as his guide, Culbertson swam across. At the fort, he was courteously received by Captain Stewart Van Vliet and Lieutenant Daniel Woodbury, who must have been a little surprised to find a dangerously ill man swimming the Platte in the dark of night. Cul-

---

[38]Bradley, *MHSC*, Vol. III, p. 258.
[39]Bradley, *MHSC*, Vol. III, p. 259. The dates given by Bradley are confusing but it appears that this occurred in late 1848.
[40]Fort Kearny was spelled without an "e," in contrast to the modern town of Kearney, Nebraska.
[41]Mattes, *Great Platte River Road*, pp. 169-170.

bertson spent ten days at Fort Kearny recuperating before again heading for Fort Laramie.

Within days of taking to the road, Culbertson encountered several hundred Cheyenne warriors. Based on his recent experience with the Pawnees, and now briefed on the Indian troubles along this corridor, Culbertson expected instant death. But the Cheyennes were extremely courteous, giving Culbertson fresh meat and agreeing to carry a letter to Fort Kearny for him. This Cheyenne war party was hunting Pawnees, not white fur traders.

Culbertson overtook his wagon train at the junction of the two Plattes, but his woes had not yet ended. The Pawnees struck again, driving off ten yoke of cattle. Finally, in late October, he reached Fort Laramie where he remained only a few days before setting out for Fort Pierre.[42]

With winter now upon him, Culbertson faced bitter cold and deep snows. At the end of November 1848, he arrived at Fort Pierre where he met with James Kipp and William Laidlaw. Culbertson ordered William Hodgkiss, a New York native who had entered the fur trade in the 1830s,[43] to take command of Fort Pierre. Hodgkiss, believing the post had "not been managed properly" by James Kipp because he had been "too kind," hoped Culbertson would remain for the winter,[44] but the veteran trader continued to Fort Union with Kipp and Laidlaw, arriving in early January 1849.

Culbertson still hoped to return to Fort Benton but, at Poplar River, he once again fell ill and was forced to turn back. Ordering his companions on to Fort Benton, he returned to Fort Union to spend the winter.[45]

Whether or not Natawista accompanied Culbertson on any part of this arduous trek is unknown. If she did, it must have been an especially difficult journey for her as well since, sometime in 1848, she had given birth to their third child, a little girl they named Nancy.[46]

---

[42]Bradley, *MHSC,* Vol. III, pp. 259-260.     [43]Sunder, pp. 111-112.

[44]W. D. Hodgkiss, Ft. Pierre, to Andrew Drips, Ft. John, 30 Jan 1849. Andrew Drips Collection, MoHS.

[45]Bradley, *MHSC,* Vol. III, p. 260.     [46]Holterman, p. 92.

Chapter Fifteen

# *"without a single flower to speak pleasant things to you"*

Poor health plagued Alexander Culbertson throughout 1849; he remained at Fort Union until the spring when he departed for Fort Pierre. He may have journeyed to Fort Laramie in June to represent the American Fur Company during the sale of that outpost to the United States government for a military post to protect the westward emigration.[1] By early fall, he was headed for St. Louis[2] and, from there, back east to meet his half-brother, Thaddeus, who planned to spend the summer of 1850 on the upper Missouri.

Thaddeus Ainsworth Culbertson, the third child of Joseph and Frances Stuart Culbertson,[3] was born in Chambersburg, Pennsylvania, on February 18, 1823, and was only three years old[4] when Alexander left home with their uncle, John Craighead Culbertson. Consequently, the two brothers did not know each other well but Alexander's letters and occasional visits home had sparked Thaddeus's imagination and he longed to see the region that so engaged his brother.

Well-educated, Thaddeus had studied at the Chambersburg Academy before attending the College of New Jersey, forerunner of Princeton University. After receiving his B.A. in 1847, he had taught school in what is now West Virginia where he also pursued his scientific interests on expeditions to the James River. His teaching career ended in 1849 when Thaddeus enrolled at Princeton Theological Seminary. This planned 1850 interlude in his studies would allow Thaddeus to explore the upper

---

[1] In a letter dated 14 Nov 1969, Erwin Thompson suggested to Jim Thompson, Superintendent of Theodore Roosevelt National Park, that Culbertson was "the key man in the selling of Ft. Laramie to the U.S. Army." FtU. However, no mention of Culbertson's participation in the sale and transfer of Fort Laramie on 27 Jun 1849 is found in Hafen, *Fort Laramie*, pp. 141-142. Additionally, Culbertson did not mention any participation to James H. Bradley.

[2] Bradley, *MHSC*, Vol. III, p. 260.  [3] Lewis Culbertson, p. 268.

[4] In the introduction to Thaddeus Culbertson, p. 1, John Francis McDermott states that Thaddeus was ten years old when Alexander Culbertson "traveled first up the Missouri River." While this is correct, Alexander Culbertson had not lived in Chambersburg for any extended period since 1826.

Missouri and the Badlands while pursuing his geological interests.[5]

Thaddeus also hoped the western journey, with its open spaces, fresh air, and vigorous exercise, might improve his health which had been declining in recent years, probably due to tuberculosis. Although he hated to be perceived as sickly, he knew his family worried. In 1848, Thaddeus scribbled a note to his mother: "I am enjoying excellent health and you must always suppose so unless I say that I am sick. I don't intend to mention it every time I write."[6]

To finance the expedition, Thaddeus approached Spencer Baird, an old family friend and professor at nearby Dickinson College in Carlisle,[7] who had heard about Alexander Culbertson's scientific explorations through John James Audubon.[8] Fossil deposits in the Badlands had sparked much recent scientific interest and Baird eagerly embraced the opportunity to acquire specimens from the region. Baird prepared a list of items in which he was especially interested and arranged for a $200 grant to defray some of Thaddeus's expenses.[9] Much of the rest of the expedition's costs would be underwritten by Alexander Culbertson and the AFC.[10]

The Company had undergone a transformation in their attitude towards scientific explorations since Culbertson first arrived on the upper Missouri. In 1833, Prince Maximilian noted that he could report little

---

[5]Thaddeus Culbertson, p. 2.
[6]Thaddeus Culbertson to Frances Stuart Culbertson, 11 Mar 1848. Culbertson Collection, MoHS.
[7]When Thaddeus left for the upper Missouri, Baird was still employed at Dickinson. During Thaddeus's absence, Baird assumed a position at the Smithsonian Institution. Thaddeus Culbertson, p. 3.
[8]Harris, pp. 5-8.
[9]Thaddeus Culbertson, p. 3. McDermott cites the 1850 Report of the Smithsonian Institution in claiming that the money came from the Smithsonian. This report, however, was written after Thaddeus Culbertson's death on 28 Aug 1850 and after Baird had assumed his position at the Smithsonian. Therefore, it is possible that Baird wrote his report to reflect his new position. The conclusion that the Smithsonian partially financed Culbertson's expedition has been challenged by Vince Santucci, a paleontologist at Fossil Butte National Monument near Kemmerer, Wyoming. Santucci has researched the Culbertson fossil collection at the Smithsonian and believes that Baird arranged for the support for Culbertson before Baird accepted his position with the Smithsonian. In support of this, Santucci notes that the fossils which Culbertson shipped to Baird were sent not to the Smithsonian but rather to Dickinson College. There is also an interesting notation in McDermott's introduction which tends to support Santucci's argument. On p. 2, note 4, McDermott notes that on 16 Feb 1850, Baird wrote to Joseph Leidy to announce that he [Baird] had "persuaded Dr. Joseph Culbertson of Chambersburg to present some of his Merycoidodon fossils to the [Philadelphia] Academy [of Natural Sciences]." One wonders why Baird would have been interested in securing these fossils for the Philadelphia Academy if he were, at that same time, arranging for Thaddeus to travel upriver to collect fossils specifically for the Smithsonian. This letter from Baird to Leidy suggests that in Feb 1850, when Baird traveled to Chambersburg to bid farewell to the Culbertson brothers, Baird was not actively soliciting specimens for the Smithsonian but was more interested in ensuring that these unique fossils be properly curated.
[10]Thaddeus Culbertson, p. 55.

about the Blackfeet because "the American Fur Company, who trade with them, and therefore have had the best opportunity of becoming acquainted with them, seldom take any interest in scientific researches."[11]

Since then, the AFC had aided numerous scientific expeditions. In 1835, the renowned geologist, Jean Nicolas Nicollet of the French Academy of Sciences, recorded that the AFC "contributed liberally" towards the expenses of his Mississippi River expedition. Four years later, the Company again assisted Nicollet when he traveled up the Missouri.[12]

The Company's motives were not purely altruistic. Their employees, many of whom fancied themselves amateur naturalists, enjoyed hosting distinguished guests such as Maximilian, Nicollet, and Audubon. And the scientists became great boosters of the AFC when they returned to the States, rarely speaking critically of their benefactors. In addition, the AFC benefited politically since these expeditions helped push back the frontier's boundaries, extending the young nation's influence.[13]

Alexander Culbertson's efforts as an amateur scientist had been widely heralded. Fossils he collected in the Badlands during journeys between Fort Pierre and Fort Laramie found their way into Philadelphia's Academy of Natural Sciences with which his father was affiliated.[14] These included "fossil bones of a new genus of extinct Ruminants, consisting of the cranium and parts of a humerus, ulna, and radius."[15] In 1848, his name became attached to "a new fossil and species of ruminatoid Pachydermata: Merycoidodon Culbertsonii."[16]

Hiram Prout, a St. Louis physician and mineralogist, had described a "fossil maxillary bone of a Paleotherium" from the Badlands in *The American Journal of Science and Arts* in 1846.[17] Prout had received the specimen from "a friend residing at one of the trading posts of the St. Louis Fur Company on the Missouri River," most likely Alexander Culbertson.[18]

---

[11]Thwaites, Vol. 23, p. 97.
[12]"Report to Illustrate a Map of the Hydrological Basin...," House ExDocs (28-2) 52, pp. 41-42, cited in Sunder, p. 24; Chaky, "Fossils." [13]Sunder, p. 25; Chaky, "Fossils," passim.
[14]Sunder, pp. 127-128. [15]Thaddeus Culbertson, p. 1.
[16]Thaddeus Culbertson, p. 1, fn. 3. [17]Prout, p. 248.
[18]Thaddeus Culbertson, p. 1. In notes, editor McDermott suggests, and then discounts, the possibility that Prout meant Harvey, Primeau and Co. when he referred to the "St. Louis Fur Company" since that firm had just been organized. There is no evidence that Harvey ever traveled to the White River Badlands and it seems most likely that the bone came from Culbertson. Prout's identification of this bone as being from a Paleotherium was actually in error. The bone was eventually identified as coming from the family of Brontotheriidae. Prout's misidentification, though, is understandable since this bone was the first to be found from the Brontotheriidae family and, therefore, this family had not been identified at the time of Prout's article. Vince Santucci, paleontologist with the National Park Service, to the author.

This article, documenting the type specimen for an entire family of mammals (Brontotheriidae), represented the first published fossil from west of the Mississippi. The account excited scientists in both the United States and Europe and "was instrumental in the birth of the science of vertebrate paleontology in North America."[19]

Scientific patrons, then, willingly invested $200 in Thaddeus's planned expedition.

Spencer Baird traveled to Chambersburg on February 16, 1850, to bid farewell to the Culbertson brothers as they left for St. Louis.[20] A month later, Thaddeus and Alexander Culbertson boarded the *Mary Blane* for St. Joseph. The two were accompanied by four Company laborers, one "black servant" named Jim who served as their cook,[21] ten horses, and Culbertson's faithful dog, Carlo.

The steamboat, "crowded to overflowing," carried nearly three hundred cabin and two hundred deck passengers. But Culbertson's position entitled the brothers to a berth in the pilot's room. One of their roommates, a Col. Tilton of Polk County, Missouri, knew their uncle James Culbertson of Palmyra,[22] and the two found him "a very agreeable traveling companion."

Nonetheless, the crowded conditions made routine tasks annoyingly difficult. Procuring a meal meant enduring long lines and then sharing a table with the "rough characters on board." To circumvent this, Culbertson assigned Jim to bring the brothers meals in their cabin. Everything about the journey—the cities on shore, the river snags, the other passengers—fascinated Thaddeus. His brother, on the other hand, had seen it all before and preferred to spend his time "enjoying a siesta."[23]

Having been raised in a strict Christian household, Thaddeus was disturbed to find his fellow passengers so often engaged in "card playing, which I dispise (*sic*)." Thaddeus preferred to read *Night of Toil*, a "little book" about early missionaries in Tahiti in which the budding theologian

---

[19] *Park Paleontology*, p. 1.   [20] Thaddeus Culbertson, p. 3.

[21] Although Thaddeus Culbertson never gives a last name, this is almost certainly Jim Hawkins whom Kurz, p. 101, described as "a negro from Fort Union" whom Alexander Culbertson intended to take to Fort Benton in 1851 but left behind at Fort Union "where he was also obliged to serve as cook." Hawkins was probably a slave since he was referred to as a "black servant."

[22] Youngest brother of John Craighead Culbertson. Lewis Culbertson, p. 268.

[23] Thaddeus Culbertson, pp. 15-16.

discovered "some delightful religious thoughts."[24] Unlike his brother, Alexander Culbertson was equally at ease with the Presbyterian teachings of his youth, the Catholic missions of the frontier, and the pantheist traditions of the Indians. His malleable beliefs, although difficult for his devout stepmother to accept, served Culbertson well on the frontier.

On March 25, the *Mary Blane* reached St. Joseph, established by Joseph Robidoux in 1842. Robidoux came to the area, known as the Blacksnake Hills, years earlier to trade with the Indians and, in 1834, purchased the local AFC trading post. By 1850, St. Joseph boasted "a number of fine large brick houses" and a "handsome brick" courthouse. When the brothers disembarked, Culbertson, who knew the river town well, proceeded to the Mansion House where the brothers would bunk during their stay.

Hordes of young men crowded the streets that spring preparing to head for the California gold fields. Among the nascent emigrants, French seemed the dominant language. St. Joseph's primary mission was to outfit the incipient travelers. In great demand, horses, mules, and cattle fetched premium prices. Benefiting from his long ties to the town's traders, Culbertson purchased four horses for the reasonable sum of $245.00.

Culbertson helped outfit Thaddeus, purchasing "a fine saddle, bridle and martingale; a belt and knife, leggins and a few minor articles. . . ." Thaddeus hoped that this "kindness may not go unrewarded."

The next morning, Culbertson took Thaddeus on a short ride to acquaint the younger man with the landscape and the mules they would lead upriver. Thaddeus discovered that the mules "travel quietly, quickly and well together." Afterwards, the brothers returned to the hotel and, despite Thaddeus's feeling "not very well," prepared for a morning departure.[25]

The Culbertsons, accompanied by five Company employees, a growing horse herd, the mules, and at least two dogs, left St. Joseph on Friday, March 29, 1850. Alexander Culbertson knew their route well but did not take the trip lightly. From prior experience, he realized that each trip contained its own surprises and hazards. To grow complacent was to invite trouble.

Nevertheless, his knowledge of the route made the trip infinitely easier. Culbertson knew where and how to cross the streams; where to find lodging and a good meal at the end of a long day; which tribes were most likely

---

[24]Thaddeus Culbertson, p. 18.   [25]Thaddeus Culbertson, pp. 21-22.

to cause trouble; and, how far they had to travel each day to stay on schedule. The schedule was important if Thaddeus were to accomplish all he planned and still get back to Chambersburg before winter set in.

Culbertson added a "carriage"—a small covered wagon—to his usual outfit for his and Thaddeus's sleeping comfort. On the lower river, the brothers rarely used it since Culbertson nearly always found someone—a trader or farm family—to provide them with a modest bed and meal.

Their accommodations included beds with a Mormon ex-soldier who was planning to join his brethren in the Salt Lake valley, a "very reserved" farmer with a "pleasant enough" wife and mother, several old fur traders, a whiskey trader, a Vermonter named Chase and his wife, and a "miserable dirty" hotel in Council Bluffs.[26] In this wilderness setting, Thaddeus's standards changed. Good quarters no longer meant "a fine brick house, or a frame house but a log cabin that has a good roof—a big fire place and plenty of places for air holes." One night, the brothers slept well on a bed which Thaddeus speculated that "at home we would have staid up all night before lying in."[27]

Thaddeus marveled at how his brother handled the rigors and uncertainties of the frontier. Under his guidance, Thaddeus felt no concern for his well-being although he regretted his brother's insistence that they travel on the Sabbath. That first Sunday, Thaddeus lamented that they "had seen no churches to-day and no church going crowd," but consoled himself that the day "had not been violated heedlessly."[28] They averaged twenty-five miles a day although Culbertson shortened the days if he thought either Thaddeus or the horses looked excessively fatigued.[29]

Near Council Bluffs, the travelers encountered the two horse stagecoach, "a new enterprise [that] marks the progress of civilization," which ran twice weekly between the Iowa town and St. Joseph. That night, in a little log cabin with "the old rifle over the door," Thaddeus, "a good distance from home," felt lonely.[30]

On April 4, a severe storm forced the men to halt in late morning. The rain soon turned to snow. The next day, the storm continued to rage with the wind blowing relentlessly. Culbertson secured lodging from a taciturn gentleman and the brothers composed a joint letter home.[31]

The next day, although the storm had not yet abated, Culbertson, tired

---

[26]Thaddeus Culbertson, pp. 25-34.  [27]Thaddeus Culbertson, p. 26.
[28]Thaddeus Culbertson, p. 24.  [29]Thaddeus Culbertson, p. 23.
[30]Thaddeus Culbertson, pp. 25-26.  [31]Thaddeus Culbertson, p. 28.

# WITHOUT A SINGLE FLOWER

of "laying by," decided to push on. Twenty miles later, they reached the "miserable looking village" of Council Bluffs. Thaddeus hoped to visit the nearby Presbyterian mission but, by the time they ferried across the river, it was too late. Instead, the men headed for Peter Sarpy's Bellevue post.[32]

Here, Thaddeus got his first real glimpse of his brother's world. Sarpy lived "in fur trader style" and "had it pretty rough." About ten Indians were in camp, the first Thaddeus had seen in their own country. Struck by their "powerful appearance," Thaddeus found himself pitying the men who felt it "a privilege to get a seat on the floor in such a place, where the very stable boys felt as if they had a right to curse them for 'lousy indians.'"[33]

The next day, Culbertson took his brother to Floyd's Bluff, the burial site for Sgt. Floyd, the only member of the Lewis and Clark expedition to die during the epic journey. They found part of the stake marking the grave. To Thaddeus, the site commanding "a fine extensive view," seemed appropriate "for the repose of a member of so bold a company."[34]

The men finally encountered Indians in their natural habitat as they prepared to cross Floyd's River near what is now Sioux City, Iowa.[35] The canoe Culbertson had hoped to use for the crossing was on the opposite shore when they arrived. Nasselle,[36] a Company employee, volunteered to swim across to retrieve it but then four Sioux women appeared across the river.

Culbertson called out in their language, asking them to bring the canoe to the other side. The women cheerfully agreed and one of them got into the craft. Before her friends could join her, the canoe broke loose and began drifting downstream. The accident, which caused "as much laughing and sport . . . as there would have been amongst as many civilized women," reminded Thaddeus of "the ways of my fair friends at home." The women ultimately delivered the canoe and, after several trips, Culbertson had ferried over all the group's supplies, animals, and personnel.[37]

That night, the brothers stayed with Mr. Bruguière,[38] "a quiet, modest, honest man," at his trading post on Big Sioux River. Bruguière lived "very

---

[32]Thaddeus Culbertson, pp. 28-29.     [33]Thaddeus Culbertson, p. 29.
[34]Thaddeus Culbertson, p. 33.
[35]Thaddeus Culbertson, p. 33, refers to this as "Willow River, marked Floyd's on the maps (the second one of that name). . . ."
[36]The name is alternatively given as Nerselle, Nersalle, Nassel, and Nassell. He was said to have been a Canadian. Thaddeus Culbertson, p. 15.     [37]Thaddeus Culbertson, p. 33.
[38]Thaddeus gives the name as Bruyiere; it is the author's belief that this was Jacques Bruguière.

much as an Indian," with two wives in a large Sioux encampment. After Culbertson purchased more than one hundred robes from the trader, Bruguière and his assistant joined the group to travel to the AFC post at Vermillion.[39]

En route, the Culbertson brothers slept in their carriage while the others braved a "powerful gale . . . with tremendous violence." By morning, temperatures had plummeted. Culbertson, anxious to reach the Vermillion post, rode ahead with Thaddeus. Several hours later, as the brothers sat before a warm fire enjoying a hearty meal, the others arrived after a long fight with nature's fury. Culbertson remained at the post for two days, conducting business. Thaddeus welcomed the hiatus, especially since it allowed him to properly observe the Sabbath.[40]

The group left Vermillion Post, after adding a cart of corn to their cargo. At the Vermillion River, Culbertson complained that "you can't see the river for water." For Thaddeus, the country was beginning to lose its appeal. He did not "experience that elevation of mind so often ascribed to the beholding of these grand prairies." Now he realized:

> it is one thing to be thrown in ecstacies (*sic*) by the description of these magnificent peculiarities of this western country, as one is seated by a warm fire surrounded by all the comforts of home and it is another to travel over them when they are covered by dry grass only, with a regular North Easter blowing in your face and the thermometer below the freezing point.[41]

At the White Earth fork of the Vermillion, the travelers spent the night in an Indian lodge "crowded with children and dogs and . . . well filled with smoke." In the morning, despite high winds and bitter cold, they continued their trek, accompanied by the Indians, "their pack horses and their *pack dogs*, their squalling babes on the backs of their mothers."[42]

To everyone's surprise, the men soon detected buffalo, unusual that far downriver, and the Indians rode off to hunt. When they returned, the traditional feasting began. Culbertson moved from tipi to tipi, sharing buffalo meat in each lodge. Thaddeus went along until he grew quite full. When he tried to retire for the night, his brother explained that that would offend his Indian hosts. The young man resumed the feasting, "although not with much relish."[43]

---

[39]Thaddeus Culbertson, pp. 34-35.
[40]Thaddeus Culbertson, pp. 36-38.
[41]Thaddeus Culbertson, p. 41.
[42]Thaddeus Culbertson, p. 42. Emphasis in original.
[43]Thaddeus Culbertson, p. 44.

Weather again delayed the party at the James River.[44] The winds howled and snow fell, thwarting Culbertson's every effort to cross. They waited for better conditions inside an Indian lodge and, as his brother slept, Thaddeus watched the children play and taught himself to skin birds. Finally, on the evening of April 24, the entourage, in a scene "most picturesque and wild," crossed the river:

> on one side the Indians, their packhorses and children were scattered for about ½ a mile; on the opposite shore were all our horses grazing at their leisure while the canoe was moving swiftly and smoothly in the water and a glorious sun set was gilding the whole scene.[45]

One week later, as the travelers neared the Yankton trading post, some Sioux mistook them for buffalo. Two scouts rode out at full gallop. When they discovered the identity of their intended prey, they greeted Culbertson warmly and escorted his party to their village. After the "men, women, children, dogs, and horses all came out to look," Culbertson sat down with the warriors to engage in "very friendly conversation."

The Company men hoped to reach the Yankton post the next day but "travellers must not calculate too certainly on everything turning out as they desire." After crossing the rolling prairie, the group came upon "probably 200 indian lodges with all that irregularity and those wild appurtenances that well become a scene in the wilderness." But Crow Creek, usually a small rivulet easily crossed, was swollen beyond its banks.

Unable to cross, the group spent another evening with the Sioux, many more of whom swam the cold river to join the encampment. The Indians were all anxious to meet with Culbertson. Some carried receipts from the Yankton trader entitling them to purchase a horse. Thaddeus noted with bemusement their "strange mixture of civilized and savage costumes," including one warrior who wore a "short shirt and a waist coat with the usual indians clout."[46]

Finally, on May 2, the group reached the Yankton trading post. After being shut down in 1848 by Agent Matlock, the post now had new leadership.[47] Nevertheless, Culbertson took special pains to ensure that the

---
[44]Thaddeus Culbertson, p. 44, refers to this as the "River à Jacques."
[45]Thaddeus Culbertson, p. 47.    [46]Thaddeus Culbertson, pp. 50-52.
[47]Thaddeus Culbertson, p. 53, gives the name of the chief trader at Yankton as "Randell," a "Canadien Frenchman and a very common man." His identity is otherwise unknown.

Yanktons were satisfied. He prepared a feast for sixty or seventy warriors, shared his pipe, and then "made quite a long speech."

When he finished, one of the elders rose, shook the trader's hand, and offered a "long and animated" reply. Throughout both speeches, the warriors frequently shouted approval. Although Thaddeus understood none of it, the "earnest manner" of the discussion impressed him. With the speeches concluded and the food consumed, the Indians drifted away and the brothers retired for the night.[48]

Two days later, and forty-five days after leaving St. Louis, the Culbertsons finally reached Fort Pierre. The cannon was fired in welcome and Alexander was soon reunited with Natawista and his three children, following an absence of nearly nine months.[49] Thaddeus settled into his brother's comfortable quarters and Culbertson, wishing to spend time with his long-neglected family, eschewed an invitation to an Indian dog feast. But the Indians, to show their pleasure at having him back among them, cooked the dog anyway and brought it to Culbertson to eat while they sat and talked quietly.[50]

While Culbertson tackled business affairs, Thaddeus prepared for his Badlands excursion. On May 7, equipped with three mules, two weeks' provisions, and a cart, all provided by his brother, Thaddeus set out with Owen McKenzie and another employee named Joe.[51] The journey to White River lasted several days, during which Thaddeus's companions taught him about Indian religious customs, Indian leaders, wildlife, and geology. En route, Thaddeus gathered rock specimens, petrified wood, and plant and animal samples.[52]

Finally catching sight of the Badlands, Thaddeus was overwhelmed. It "resembled a large city," complete with town hall, courthouse, and palaces "arranged upon the grandest scale and adapted for the habitation, not of pigmies (*sic*) such as now inhabit the earth, but of giants such as would be fit to rule over the immense animals whose remains are still found here." In the wind, Thaddeus imagined he heard "the din and bustle of the

---

[48]Thaddeus Culbertson, pp. 52-53.

[49]William D. Hodgkiss, Fort Pierre, to Alexander Culbertson, 14 Feb 1850. Chouteau-Papin Collection, MoHS. Thaddeus, no doubt influenced by the advice of John Evans and his brother, does not mention Alexander's family.  [50]Thaddeus Culbertson, p. 55.

[51]Thaddeus Culbertson, p. 55.  [52]Thaddeus Culbertson, pp. 55-57.

# WITHOUT A SINGLE FLOWER

immense place as these gigantic men with their stentorian voices would jostle each other along the streets...."[53]

Thaddeus's only regret was that he, "a humble pioneer," and not a company of trained scientists, would catalog his findings. His understanding of geological formations, however, proved impressive; he correctly surmised that the highest landforms had been created by the sinking of the surrounding ground rather than by upheaval.[54]

The group quickly found the area with the "petrifactions."[55] Thaddeus found it smaller than expected and containing many broken fossils; nonetheless, he gathered half a bushel of teeth, jawbones, animal heads, and fossilized turtles. The young scientist then filled a bag with clay and crumbs of the petrified turtles.[56] Having accomplished all he could in the inhospitable land, Thaddeus decided to return to Fort Pierre the next day. All that remained was to try to capture in words what his eyes had seen:

> Fancy yourself on the hottest day in summer in the hottest spot of such a place without water—without an animal and scarce an insect astir—without a single flower to speak pleasant things to you and you will have some idea of the utter loneliness of the Bad Lands.[57]

Thaddeus arrived back at Fort Pierre on May 18 with his companions, but without his carefully collected treasures. The cart had proved incapable of hauling the heavy specimens and, much to Thaddeus's dismay, had to be left by the side of the road.[58] Culbertson, assuring his brother they would be safe, promptly sent a Company employee with a heavier cart to retrieve them. Nonetheless, Thaddeus fretted until the samples arrived intact on May 30.[59]

Thaddeus immediately began packing the specimens for shipment back east. His labors were interrupted when a band of Blackfeet Sioux,[60] marching behind an American flag, arrived. As the women erected the lodges, the warriors proceeded to the reception room. Culbertson orga-

---

[53]Thaddeus Culbertson, pp. 60-61.   [54]Thaddeus Culbertson, p. 61.

[55]This area, now known as the Fossil Exhibit Trail, is part of Badlands National Park in South Dakota.   [56]Thaddeus Culbertson, pp. 62-64.

[57]Thaddeus Culbertson, p. 65.   [58]Thaddeus Culbertson, p. 67.

[59]Thaddeus Culbertson, p. 81.

[60]The Blackfeet Sioux are a subtribe of the Sioux nation and should not be confused with the Blackfeet nation that lived higher on the upper Missouri and traded at Fort Benton.

nized a feast and the normal festivities—hand-shaking, pipe-smoking, eating, and speech-making—ensued.

The Blackfeet Sioux had brought a large quantity of robes to trade. They hoped to barter for meat as their hunt had gone poorly and they were near starvation. But Culbertson, not knowing when the steamboat might arrive, had little to spare.[61]

Four days later, the announcement that the *El Paso* had been sighted a few miles below the fort "electrified the whole establishment." With the steamer in sight, the traditional firing of salutes began and Indians and whites alike hurried to the riverbank. Alexander Culbertson spotted Dr. John Evans, geologist for the United States Geological Survey who had explored the Badlands the previous summer, on the hurricane deck and introduced his brother to the experienced surveyor when the steamer docked. The two established an instant rapport, quickly settling in to discuss Thaddeus's recent excursion.[62]

That night, Alexander Culbertson, Natawista, their children, and Thaddeus slept aboard the *El Paso* which continued upriver the next morning. Culbertson's old friend, Honoré Picotte, was also aboard and Picotte engaged Thaddeus in a discussion of the changing patterns of Indian life. On their second day out, the *El Paso* passed six mackinaws belonging to Harvey, Primeau and Company headed downriver with their winter's returns. Culbertson, doing a quick calculation, judged them to be carrying no more than thirteen hundred packs of robes, a fact which delighted him.[63]

Thaddeus, the "only 'distinguished' stranger" aboard the steamboat, found this "the most agreeable traveling," with the air "delightful" and the "shores and trees quite green." Only the mosquitoes, who "made sundry violent attacks . . . with malice aforethought, and intent of blood-drawing," marred the trip. Thaddeus "murdered numbers in pure self defence (*sic*)."[64]

At Fort Clark, several Arikaras invited the Culbertsons and Picotte to their village and, despite some risk, the traders accepted. Two years earlier, an Arikara chief had insisted, over Picotte's objections, on going downriver aboard the steamboat. When he was killed by the Pawnees, the Arikaras blamed the Company.

The next spring, the Arikaras invited Alexander Culbertson to a feast.

---

[61]Thaddeus Culbertson, p. 83.   [62]Thaddeus Culbertson. p. 86.
[63]Thaddeus Culbertson, p. 87.   [64]Thaddeus Culbertson, p. 89.

# WITHOUT A SINGLE FLOWER 183

At their encampment, Culbertson found the warriors "armed to the teeth." Blaming him for their chief's death, the Arikaras threatened Culbertson's life. The unarmed trader, after calmly discussing the situation, offered the tribal elders two horses in compensation. They accepted and Culbertson safely departed. Now, a year later, he returned to their village, without hesitation and with his younger brother in tow.[65]

The brothers' time together was rapidly coming to an end. On June 15, Malcolm Clarke rode out to meet the *El Paso* as she neared Fort Union and Alexander Culbertson disembarked to ride back with him. Thaddeus, feeling "rather sad at the prospect of parting so soon with my brother who has been so kind to me," remained on board the steamer, reaching Fort Union the next day.

There, amid the customary festivities, another familiar face awaited Thaddeus: Ferdinand Culbertson, Alexander and Thaddeus's first cousin,[66] had come upriver several years earlier and had worked for the AFC ever since.[67] Thaddeus also received a collection of stuffed animal skins prepared at Culbertson's request by Ferdinand and Edwin Denig for Thaddeus to give to Spencer Baird.[68]

The next day, while Culbertson tended to business, Thaddeus continued upriver aboard the *El Paso*. This allowed him to see more of the region's wonders, including the fascinating elk horn pyramid. No one, not even the Indian elders, knew when or how the pile began. But passing war parties always added to it.[69] When the steamboat reached Poplar River, Thaddeus noted that he had seen the spot where his uncle, John Craighead Culbertson, had helped negotiate treaties a quarter century earlier with the Atkinson-O'Fallon expedition.[70]

The *El Paso* returned to Fort Union on June 21, after reaching Milk

---

[65] Thaddeus Culbertson, p. 96.

[66] Lewis Culbertson, p. 170. Ferdinand Culbertson (1823-1863) was the son of Samuel Duncan and Nancy Purviance Culbertson. Dr. Samuel Duncan Culbertson was the younger brother of Alexander and Thaddeus's father, Joseph Culbertson.

[67] Various letters from Edwin Denig to Alexander Culbertson, Chouteau Collection, MoHS.

[68] Thaddeus Culbertson, pp. 105-106.   [69] Thaddeus Culbertson, p. 109.

[70] Thaddeus Culbertson, p. 113. Thaddeus referred to the Poplar River as Porcupine River and was actually wrong in placing the Atkinson-O'Fallon expedition this high up on the river. The *El Paso* was about twenty-five miles beyond the highest point reached by the Atkinson-O'Fallon expedition.

River, the highest point on the Missouri River yet attained by a steamboat.[71] In the morning, Thaddeus bid farewell to his brother and boarded the steamer for the journey home. Although "sad at heart to part with my brother," Thaddeus admitted that "nothing could induce [him] to live here."[72]

Thaddeus reached St. Louis on July 6 and immediately set out for Chambersburg where he arrived in mid-August. Two weeks later, on August 28, 1850, Thaddeus Culbertson, aged twenty-seven, died of tuberculosis.[73]

Spencer Baird, who joined the fledgling Smithsonian Institution while Thaddeus was upriver, thanked the American Fur Company for their assistance to Thaddeus Culbertson. A resolution voted by the Board of Regents on March 27, 1851 acknowledged the contributions of the AFC, Edwin Denig, Ferdinand Culbertson, several other traders, and, of course, Alexander Culbertson. Baird encouraged the Company's continued scientific efforts and, throughout the 1850s, Culbertson, Denig, and others sent fossils, bones, stuffed animals, and pelts downriver for museums in St. Louis and throughout the East.[74]

---

[71] Thaddeus Culbertson, p. 114.
[73] Thaddeus Culbertson, p. 2.
[72] Thaddeus Culbertson, p. 116.
[74] Sunder, pp. 129-130.

Chapter Sixteen

## *"a trifling compensation for this right of way"*

Soon after Thaddeus's departure, Alexander Culbertson turned his attention to the Crow trade. The Crows, in the Yellowstone River valley southwest of Fort Union, had long posed special problems for the American Fur Company.

Frequent war parties of Sioux, Blackfeet, and Crows routinely crisscrossed the Yellowstone River valley, making it especially dangerous for both Indians and traders. The river's sandy bogs, rocky ledges, troublesome snags, and swift current made navigation difficult. Over the years, many boats loaded with trade goods and robes had sunk in the Yellowstone; those that made it past the natural obstacles risked attack from Indians hiding in the numerous ravines along its banks.[1]

For years, no trading posts existed in the Crow region. Instead, free traders and trappers bartered in the Crow camps and then brought their returns to Fort Union. After rowdy celebrations and boastful storytelling, the traders and trappers used their profits to purchase supplies for another trading season.

The trappers infuriated other tribes, especially the Blackfeet, because of their perceived wanton killing. Over the years, several trappers had mysteriously vanished. By the late 1830s, with the beaver trapped to near extinction and the eastern market collapsing as silk replaced beaver for fine hats, free trappers, even among the Crows, passed from the scene.[2]

The AFC established their first Crow post, Fort Cass, in 1832 on the Yellowstone two miles below the mouth of the Big Horn River. Fort Van Buren, at the mouth of the Rosebud, replaced it in 1835. Seven years later, Alexander Culbertson dispatched Charles Larpenteur to construct a new Crow fort twenty miles above Fort Van Buren on the north side of the Yellowstone in an area known as Adams Prairie.[3]

---

[1]Sunder, p. 60.   [2]Bradley, *MHSC*, Vol. III, p. 262.
[3]Sunder, pp. 59-60; Larpenteur, pp. 146-148.

Larpenteur, with twenty men, set to work. Despite losing several Company horses to Indian raiding parties, by mid-November 1842, Fort Alexander, named in honor of Culbertson,[4] was operational. Larpenteur enjoyed his new command and his "very comfortably located" quarters. That August, he celebrated the birth of his first child.[5] But his command was about to come to an end.

Whether Culbertson ever intended to leave Larpenteur in charge is doubtful and, in late November, he sent James Murray[6] to take over, ordering Larpenteur back to Fort Union. Larpenteur, a teetotaler who never tired of castigating others for their alcohol consumption, maintained that he was "wanted mighty bad" to handle the Fort Union liquor trade. Larpenteur lamented that "being a sober man was no advantage to me."[7]

Fort Alexander operated profitably for eight years but, by 1850, it had fallen into disrepair. Culbertson decided to build a new post farther upriver, saving a few miles of difficult river passage[8] For several years, Robert Meldrum had been in charge of Fort Alexander.[9] A native of Scotland, Meldrum was a strong man of medium height with dark sandy hair and keen gray eyes. He had come to Kentucky as a small child and studied blacksmithing before succumbing to the lure of the wilderness. In 1832, Meldrum joined Captain Benjamin L. E. Bonneville's expedition to the rendezvous in Pierre's Hole.[10] Afterwards, he worked for the AFC for three years before quitting to become a free trader among the Crows.[11]

Meldrum, whom the Crows called Round Iron,[12] eagerly embraced their lifestyle. He glued long hair to his own to look like his Indian trading partners. He lived in an Indian lodge with his Indian wife and quickly gained the Crows' respect for his intelligence and courage, even being regarded as a tribal chief. When the beaver trade collapsed, Meldrum returned to the service of the AFC.[13]

Although his early years with the Crows gave him an advantage in that trade, it also created problems. Culbertson's friend, Edwin Denig, asserted that the Indians only respected white men who possessed talents they

---

[4]Larpenteur, p. 146.
[5]Larpenteur, p. 148.
[6]McDonnell, *MHSC*, Vol. X, p. 284.
[7]Larpenteur, pp. 148-149.
[8]Bradley, *MHSC*, Vol. III, p. 261.
[9]McDonnell, *MHSC*, Vol. X, p. 284.
[10]Brackett, *MHSC*, Vol. III, pp. 185-187.
[11]Bradley, *MHSC*, Vol. III, p. 255.
[12]McDonnell, *MHSC*, Vol. X, p. 285.

did not, that white men who adopted their lifestyle, went about half-naked, and wore long hair, soon became "the sport of savages."

Denig claimed that Meldrum's influence among the Crows came about not as the result of his considerable hunting skills but rather because of his liberal spending habits. Meldrum, according to Denig, lacked a businessman's skills and, therefore, had become deeply indebted to the Company.[14] Culbertson, however, considered Meldrum the logical choice to head the Crow post.

After bidding farewell to the *El Paso* in 1850, Culbertson and Meldrum departed for the Yellowstone valley with seventeen men and a mackinaw loaded with trade goods. They reached their destination in mid-July and immediately began building a new fort on the Yellowstone's north bank. Culbertson christened the post Fort Sarpy in honor of AFC partner, John Sarpy,[15] but the name did not stick and visitors frequently referred to it as Fort Alexander or thoroughly confused matters by calling it Fort Alexander Sarpy.[16]

Culbertson remained in the Crow country only long enough to see construction begun before returning to Fort Union. There he collected his family and headed for Fort Benton where he had not been for more than two years.[17] In the Blackfeet country, mild autumn weather permitted Culbertson to implement the rebuilding of Fort Benton in adobe, of which he had become enamored while serving at Fort Laramie. The mud bricks offered several advantages over wood: they did not burn or rot; they provided better defense against Indian attacks; and, they moderated the summer's heat and winter's cold.[18]

To his delight, Culbertson discovered that Missouri River bottom soil proved ideal for manufacturing adobe. He set his employees to work and, throughout the fall, mud bricks began replacing Fort Benton's wooden pickets. The reconstruction was completed around Christmas, just as the weather turned cold and the bricks began to freeze. To celebrate, Culbertson and Natawista threw a grand ball. It was during those festivities that Culbertson stilled the fiddles and proposed naming the Blackfeet post Fort Benton.[19]

---

[13]Bradley, *MHSC*, Vol. III, p. 255.
[14]Kurz, p. 205.
[15]Bradley, *MHSC*, Vol. III, p. 261.
[16]Sunder, p. 126.
[17]Bradley, *MHSC*, Vol. III, p. 264.
[18]Sunder, p. 127.
[19]Bradley, *MHSC*, Vol. III, p. 264.

The Culbertsons had another reason to celebrate that Christmas: Natawista was again pregnant. In February 1851, she gave birth to their fourth child and third daughter whom they named Frances, in honor of Culbertson's stepmother.[20]

❖ ❖ ❖

In April 1851, Culbertson and his family took the Fort Benton returns to Fort Union. His family settled in while Culbertson took a horse herd to Fort Pierre. From there, Culbertson and Honoré Picotte headed downriver to meet the steamboat.[21] On June 10, they reached the Bellevue trading post where they found Rudolph Kurz, a young artist, also awaiting the steamboat.[22]

Kurz, a native of Bern, Switzerland, came to the United States when he was twenty-eight. He had planned to continue to Mexico but the Mexican War disrupted those plans. Instead, Kurz settled in St. Joseph. Now, he hoped to obtain passage to the upriver trading posts.[23]

The young artist had long been drawn to primeval landscapes, wild animals, and primitive peoples. His interest in exploring the upper Missouri increased after he discussed the region with Karl Bodmer, the artist who had accompanied Prince Maximilian.[24] Kurz, who wanted to record Indian lifestyles before civilization altered them forever, romanticized about "the human creature, in whom are harmoniously combined lofty intelligence, noble mind, and ardent feeling, represented in corresponding form."[25] Unfortunately, Kurz was already too late: some of the most striking Indians he encountered were dressed in white man's garb.

---

[20] The year of Fannie's birth is problematic. Fannie consistently said she was born in Fort Benton. See Berglund, SC 414, MtHS, p. 22, and her biographical sketch at MtHS. But her obituaries ("Mrs. Frances C. Irvin Dies Here on Sunday Night" and "Funeral Rites for Mrs. Irvin Here Thursday," *Great Falls Tribune*, 5 Feb 1939 and 7 Feb 1939 respectively) give her birth date as 14 Feb 1858. If true, Fannie would have been born in Peoria, Illinois. In the 1860 Peoria Co., IL census, her age is given as eight. Records at the Moravian Seminary for Young Ladies in Bethlehem, Pennsylvania, give two dates for her birth: 14 Feb 1850 and 14 Feb 1851. Only the second date is consistent with her having been born at Fort Benton. The biographical sketch at MtHS further states that she was baptized by Father Pierre Jean De Smet at Fort Union on 20 Jul 1851. Clifford, "Part III," p. 27, gives a "probable" date of 1850 for Fannie's birth. 1850 is also the date which appears on a genealogy chart prepared by Mollie Culbertson Sedgwick, the great-niece of Alexander Culbertson, SC 1386, MtHS. However, it would have had to be late 1850 for her birth to have occurred at Fort Benton but the February 14 date is consistent in all sources giving a specific date. Based on these sources, the author believes that 14 Feb 1851 is the most likely date for her birth.

[21] Bradley, *MHSC*, Vol. III, pp. 264-265.  [22] Kurz, p. 64.
[23] Kurz, pp. vii-ix.   [24] Kurz, p. 3.   [25] Kurz, p. 92.

In the autumn of 1850, St. Louis newspapers had begun carrying stories about a planned treaty conference to negotiate rights of passage through Indian lands for the westward traveling emigrants.[26] Kurz longed to attend the conference; in the meantime, he hoped to go upriver to sketch the Indians and wildlife.

Kurz had previously met both Culbertson and Picotte.[27] Now, in Bellevue, the artist detailed his plans to the traders. They warned him it would not be as easy as he imagined. From the steamboat deck, he would not see much wildlife since the boat's noise scared them from the riverbanks. He also would find it difficult to witness and record the Indians' games, customs, and dress unless he lived at the trading posts for at least a year. Disheartened, Kurz brightened when Culbertson promised to take him to Fort Benton.[28]

Culbertson and Picotte spent one night at Bellevue before leaving for St. Joseph to meet the *St. Ange*.[29] The steamer had left St. Louis with several distinguished passengers on board, including Father Pierre De Smet and Father Christian Hoecken. Hoecken had worked among the Potawatomis for several years. His cheerful disposition, facility for languages, and easy adaptability made him a perfect candidate to serve at the more remote missions.[30]

But Father Hoecken would never make it to the upper river. On June 10, the same day Culbertson and Picotte arrived at Bellevue, a strapping young AFC clerk aboard the *St. Ange* came down with cholera; a few hours later, he was dead. When the disease appeared, De Smet solemnly noted that "a mournful silence took the place of the rude shouts and boisterous conversations...." The steamboat soon "resembled a floating hospital." Within days, thirteen had died.

De Smet, too, took to his bed, struck down by a "bilious attack." Father Hoecken attended the ailing missionary as well as those with cholera. He visited the sick, offered spiritual consolations, heard confessions, performed last rites, and went ashore to bless graves.[31] Little could be done for the victims, although Dr. John Evans, making his third trip upriver for the U.S. Geological Survey, prepared a potion of meal and whiskey for the sick and dying.[32]

With cholera on board, the *St. Ange* did not dock in St. Joseph, leaving

---

[26]Kurz, p. 55.   [27]Kurz, p. 30.   [28]Kurz, p. 65.
[29]Bradley, *MHSC*, Vol. III, p. 265.   [30]Killoren, p. 136.
[31]Chittenden, *De Smet*, Vol. II, p. 640.   [32]Kurz, p. 69.

Culbertson and Picotte standing bewildered on shore. Not knowing why the captain had bypassed the city, Culbertson rode ahead to catch the steamboat while Picotte followed with a wagonload of Company goods. Thirty miles above St. Joseph, the *St. Ange* finally docked to allow the traders to board.[33]

Rudolph Kurz boarded in Bellevue and found the steamboat converted into a "hospital for the sick and the dying." Possessions of the dead filled his cabin.[34] Meanwhile, De Smet's condition had worsened. Fearing he had cholera, De Smet summoned Father Hoecken to hear his confession, but Hoecken was simultaneously called to minister to a dying man. Hoecken told De Smet: "I see no immediate danger for you; to-morrow we will see."

Later that night, De Smet heard Hoecken call out. De Smet dragged himself to his friend's cabin where he found the priest desperately ill. Hoecken, who hours before had been prepared to hear De Smet's confession, now asked De Smet to hear his. De Smet did so as Dr. Evans tried to relieve the missionary's suffering.[35] It was all for naught. Father Christian Hoecken died about four o'clock in the morning of June 19. To Kurz's regret, he had not sketched Father Hoecken for De Smet, as the elder priest had requested.[36]

Father Christian Hoecken, dead at forty-three, was buried that night near the mouth of the Little Sioux River. The next month, as the *St. Ange* headed downriver, the captain retrieved Hoecken's casket for re-internment at the Florissant novitiate near St. Louis.[37]

The cholera slowly abated, finally disappearing after the crew fumigated the steamboat.[38] In all, more than twenty had died,[39] including Picotte's clerk. To fill that position, Picotte turned to Kurz who eagerly accepted.[40] De Smet, recovered, now turned his attention "to the contemplation of the beauties of the wilderness, to reflections on the future of these interesting solitudes—above all, of their poor, despised inhabitants."[41]

---

[33] Bradley, *MHSC*, Vol. III, p 265.
[34] Kurz, p. 69.
[35] Chittenden, *De Smet*, Vol. II, p. 641.
[36] Kurz, p. 70.
[37] Chittenden, *De Smet*, Vol. II, p. 643.
[38] Bradley, *MHSC*, Vol. III, p. 266.
[39] Bradley, *MHSC*, Vol. III, p. 265, says Culbertson estimated the number of victims at thirty while De Smet listed twenty. Bradley notes that De Smet's count would only be valid if he listed all the deaths, something he probably could not do because of his own illness. Kurz gives no estimate of fatalities. Sunder, p. 139, puts the death toll at fourteen or fifteen.
[40] Kurz, p. 70.
[41] Chittenden, *De Smet*, Vol. II, p. 644.

# A TRIFLING COMPENSATION

❖ ❖ ❖

Culbertson, to avoid further exposure to cholera, disembarked the *St. Ange* at Bellevue and proceeded overland to Fort Pierre. En route, he was overtaken by a messenger from David D. Mitchell, Superintendent of Indian Affairs and former AFC employee. Mitchell requested Culbertson to gather a delegation of upper Missouri tribes and bring them to Fort Laramie for a government sponsored treaty conference scheduled to begin September 1.[42]

Such a conference had first been proposed in 1846 by then-Superintendent of Indian Affairs Thomas Harvey. Harvey, having received numerous complaints about wanton destruction of buffalo by emigrants, had recommended that the government hold a "general council inducing the Indians into treaties of peace and friendship." He predicted mounting tensions as more and more whites crossed the Oregon Trail and suggested that "a trifling compensation for this right of way would be calculated to secure [the Indians'] friendship towards the whites. . . ." The government failed to act on Harvey's recommendation but, by 1850, the wisdom of his proposal had become obvious.[43]

Congress authorized a conference of all the "Prairie Tribes of Indians residing South of the Missouri River and North of Texas," declaring its "just and humane" purposes "intended entirely for the benefit and future welfare of the Indians." The treaty they hoped to effect would "promote the safety and interests of the Traders, as well as the Indians themselves" and "be greatly to their advantage for the time to come."

The government promised that the Indians would be "amply compensated for all the depredations of which they complain" and, following the treaty's ratification, would receive "an annual present, in goods, from their Great Father." The circular announcing the conference assured the traders and Indians that a "large military force" would be present to guarantee everyone's safety. The tribes were encouraged to attend "*en masse*, with all their women and children . . . an additional guarantee for the good conduct of the parties present."

"For the permanent good of the Indians," the government hoped to "divide and subdivide the country into various geographical districts, in a

---

[42]Killoren. A copy of the "Circular to Indian Agents, Traders, &C.," dated 4 April 1851 and signed by D.D. Mitchell, appears facing p. 106. Emphasis in original.
[43]Killoren, p. 116.

manner entirely satisfactory to the parties concerned." Such divisions would "go far towards extinguishing the bloody wars which have raged from time immemorable (*sic*)." Other objectives, "too numerous to be stated or commented upon," would be "fully explained around 'our council fires.'" Finally, the circular promised "fair compensation" for the traders and interpreters who accompanied the Indians.[44]

Upon receiving Mitchell's letter, Culbertson immediately headed to Fort Union where he found De Smet, whose assistance had also been solicited.[45] With little time available, Culbertson did not attempt to contact the Gros Ventres or Blackfeet.[46] Instead, he and De Smet concentrated on persuading representatives from the Mandan, Hidatsa, Arikara, and Assiniboine tribes to accompany them.

By the end of July, Culbertson and De Smet had assembled a delegation of some thirty upriver representatives, including Hidatsas headed by Four Bears, Arikaras led by Iron Bear, Mandans under White Wolf, and Assiniboines headed by Fool Bear.[47] The trip "was one of extreme danger,"[48] but De Smet appreciated traveling with Culbertson, "a distinguished man, endowed with a mild, benevolent and charitable temper, though if need be intrepid and courageous."[49]

The party left Fort Union on July 31, 1851, with two carriages[50] and two carts filled with provisions for the eight hundred mile journey. The group followed the Yellowstone River to Fort Sarpy where Culbertson hoped to recruit a Crow delegation.

The travelers took every precaution to avoid hostile tribes but their primary enemies turned out to be mosquitoes. The insects forced Culbertson and De Smet to don gloves and cover their heads with coarse gauze sacks.[51] Finally, the mosquitoes abandoned the travelers in favor of a buffalo herd stretching "as far as the eye could reach." The buffalo tried to escape by rolling on the ground and using their horns to toss earth onto their backs, filling the sky with dust. Throughout the week, the travelers could hear the herd "bellowing like . . . distant thunder, or like the murmurs of the ocean waves beating against the shore."[52]

---

[44]Killoren, facing p. 106. Emphasis in original.

[45]Chittenden, *De Smet*, Vol. II, p. 652.     [46]Bradley, *MHSC*, Vol. III, p. 266.

[47]Bradley, *MHSC*, Vol. III, p. 266; Chittenden, *De Smet*, Vol. II, p. 653. De Smet appears to include Crows in the party that left Fort Union but this is unlikely. Crows arrived at the conference with Robert Meldrum.     [48]Denig, p. 84.

[49]Chittenden, *De Smet*, Vol. II, p. 653.     [50]Bradley, *MHSC*, Vol. III, p. 266.

[51]Chittenden, *De Smet*, Vol. II, p. 655.     [52]Chittenden, *De Smet*, Vol. II, p. 657.

# A TRIFLING COMPENSATION

On August 7, a natural phenomenon severely frightened the Indians. Four circles of azure, deep purple, white, and black surrounded the brightly shining moon. The Indians believed this signaled a hostile band nearby and spent a fitful night, under arms, keeping watch.[53] Nothing untoward occurred, however, and four days later, the group arrived at Fort Sarpy.

Unfortunately, there were no Crows camped at Fort Sarpy. The upper Missouri delegation remained at the post for six days waiting for the Company barge and hoping for the Crows' return. Finally, they could wait no longer and, on August 17, they set out once again, crossing a high plain, and then heading south over the approximate route of what would become known as the "bloody" Bozeman Trail.[54]

The travelers now entered an unknown territory with "not the slightest perceptible vestige of a beaten track."[55] Neither Culbertson nor De Smet knew this region which would be designated "unexplored" on government maps for several more years.[56] For guidance, the two relied on the sun, the stars, and their instincts.

They followed the Rosebud River for several days until it joined the Tongue River. Here Culbertson found Robert Meldrum, the Crow trader, and instructed him to gather a delegation from that tribe and proceed to Fort Laramie while Culbertson and his group continued south.[57] Just north of present-day Buffalo, Wyoming, the upper Missouri contingent camped beside a small lake which Culbertson named in honor of his Jesuit friend.[58]

In the Bighorn basin, the rivers dried up and water grew scarce. The party continued south across the prairie but getting wheeled vehicles through this "very miserable, elevated, sterile plain, covered with wormwood and intersected with countless ravines" proved difficult. After several days of arduous travel, the delegation finally reached Powder River where they found three young Crows who advised Culbertson to follow a small river heading southwest.

The serpentine river, with high perpendicular banks, wound through a tortuously narrow valley. The journey proved "most rugged and difficult"

---

[53]Chittenden, *De Smet*, Vol. II, pp. 662-663.   [54]Chittenden, *De Smet*, Vol. II, p. 664.
[55]Chittenden, *De Smet*, Vol. II, p. 654.
[56]See for instance "Section of Map Compiled in P.R.R. Office, with additions designed to illustrate Lt. Warren's Report of Military Reconnaissances in the Dacota Country, 1855." Copy in Thaddeus Culbertson.
[57]Bradley, *MHSC*, Vol. III, p. 266.   [58]Chittenden, *De Smet*, Vol. II, p. 668.

and the travelers dubbed the area "the valley of a thousand miseries."[59] They abandoned one cart and had to tie a badly battered carriage together with strips of buffalo hide.

On September 1, the day the treaty conference was scheduled to begin, Culbertson, De Smet, and their Indian companions crested a hill. De Smet, who had traveled this route in 1841, recognized the Red Buttes and informed Culbertson they were some one hundred and sixty miles west of Fort Laramie.[60]

The next day they reached the Oregon Trail, which the Indians called "The Great Medicine Road of the Whites." Culbertson had never seen the trail west of Fort Laramie and had not been on it at all since 1848, the year before the California gold rush began. De Smet had not been on the trail for several years either and what they saw astonished them.

In the ten years since the Bidwell-Bartleson party had passed, tens, if not hundreds, of thousands of emigrants had followed the trail to Oregon, Utah, and California. It was this massive wave of emigrants that the government hoped to protect with the upcoming council. While few hostile encounters had occurred so far, the threat loomed as the tribes grew more and more apprehensive. Meanwhile, most emigrants knew little about the Indians, except the sensational and often false stories they had heard, making them prone to strike out at the least provocation.

Now the upper Missouri travelers saw "the broadest, longest and most beautiful road in the whole world" crossing the plains, a highway "as smooth as a barn floor swept by the winds, and not a blade of grass can shoot on it on account of the continual passing." Although late in the season, with most emigrants farther west, evidence of their crossing remained everywhere: cooking utensils, knives, axes, hammers, kettles, pieces of wagons, rotting carcasses of worn-out animals, discarded furniture, old clothing, and bits of earthenware littered the pathway. Hastily dug graves, some with simple inscriptions painted on narrow boards or carved into rocks, testified to the journey's hazards.

The Indians, knowing nothing but "the narrow hunting-paths by which they transport themselves and their lodges," stared in disbelief. Surely, they speculated, the passing of so many whites must have left a terrible void back east. Culbertson and De Smet assured them that the east-

---

[59]Chittenden, *De Smet*, Vol. II, p. 669.     [60]Chittenden, *De Smet*, Vol. II, p. 670.

ern population of whites was so great that the emigrants had scarcely been missed. The Indians could not believe this.[61]

Once the delegation reached the Oregon Trail, the journey proceeded quickly and easily. Hurrying on, for they were now nearly a week overdue, the group reached the environs of Fort Laramie a week later. What they saw, or did not see, alarmed them: no grand encampment, no cluster of tipis, no bustling energy. From a distance, the fort looked deserted; none of the likely explanations comforted Culbertson or De Smet. They approached cautiously until Captain Ketchum, Fort Laramie's commander, rode out to greet them. After a warm welcome, he explained that the conference had been moved east to the mouth of Horse Creek.[62]

The conference was getting off to a rocky start. Commissioner David Mitchell had watched political forces buffet his plans from the beginning. First, Congress only appropriated one-half the requested budget, leaving Mitchell to fear he would have insufficient gifts and rations to offer the tribes. Moreover, he did not know if he would be able to compensate the traders and interpreters. To make matters worse, Congress wanted greater concessions from the tribes than originally proposed. Mitchell doubted he could accomplish more with less.[63]

Then Mitchell learned that cholera had broken out on the *St. Ange*. If the disease struck the upper Missouri tribes, Mitchell knew they might refuse to participate. More frightening was the possibility that they would bring the disease to the council grounds. If they came and were healthy, but learned during the conference that cholera had broken out back home, they might retaliate.

With the problems mounting, Mitchell left St. Louis on July 24, hoping he had received all the bad news. He had not. At Kansas Landing, Mitchell found the twenty-seven wagon supply train contracted to carry the council provisions sitting on the dock, unloaded, when it should have been well on its way. Without gifts to welcome the tribes, Mitchell would be bucking Indian traditions and he had no reason to expect them to be either understanding or forgiving.

---

[61]Chittenden, *De Smet*, Vol. II, pp. 671-673.
[62]"The Encampment at Horse Creek in Indian Territory," *The Wind River Rendezvous*, Vol. XII, Issue 1 (1982). Unpaged. [63]*Wind River Rendezvous*.

Moreover, without supplies, he could not honor the commitment to provide "compensations for the depredations long suffered from the invasion of Indian Territory." A. B. Chambers, senior editor of the *Missouri Republican*, traveling with Mitchell to report on the conference, wrote that the Commissioner "had been put to perplexing and annoying vexations."[64]

Exasperated, Mitchell ordered Robert Campbell, contracted to carry the Indian goods, to proceed as quickly as possible to the treaty grounds. Mitchell then departed for Fort Laramie. En route, he found additional reason for concern: he had counted on buffalo to augment food stocks. But between Fort Kearny and Fort Laramie, his company spotted just one cow. Without the wagon train and without buffalo, how could he possibly feed the thousands of expected Indians?[65]

On August 30, Mitchell reached Fort Laramie where he found thousands of restless Sioux, Arapaho, and Cheyenne Indians gathered. He hastened to find Thomas Fitzpatrick, the renowned mountain man, Indian agent, and conference co-Commissioner. Fitzpatrick had written Mitchell in September 1850 that it was "essentially necessary at this time ... at once, and without further delay, to have some understanding with [the Indians] in regard to the right of way through their country."[66] It had been Fitzpatrick's responsibility to escort the southern tribes to the conference.

Mitchell told Fitzpatrick his bad news. Not only had the appropriations been cut and the supply trains delayed, the requested military escort had been reduced to a nearly imperceptible number. Both commissioners had counted on the military presence to impress the Indians and, frankly, to intimidate them. But instead of the requested one thousand soldiers, Mitchell now expected fewer than three hundred.[67] Reporter Chambers summed up the Commissioners' feelings: "The Government has not acted judiciously in the military escort, and much of the effect that ought to have been given to the treaty will be lost."[68]

Fitzpatrick had his own bad news: only the Cheyenne and Arapaho tribes would be attending. There would be no representatives from the

---

[64]*Missouri Republican*, 6 Oct 1851, as quoted in *Wind River Rendezvous* and Killoren, p. 145.
[65]Killoren, p. 142.
[66]Thomas Fitzpatrick, Indian agent, upper Platte and Arkansas, to D. D. Mitchell, Esq., Superintendent of Indian Affairs, 24 Sep 1850. NAM M234/754.
[67]Killoren, p. 143.
[68]*Missouri Republican*, 26 Sep 1851, quoted in Killoren, p. 143.
[69]Killoren, p. 144.

Comanches, Kiowas, or Apaches; they had insisted the council be held in their own country, a stipulation that could not be met.[69]

Plus, the Shoshones, who had not been invited, had come in force. Mitchell had limited the conference to the Plains tribes under his supervision; the Shoshones, a mountain tribe, fell under the recently established Utah Agency. Further complicating matters, en route the Cheyennes had attacked, killed, and scalped two Shoshone warriors.[70] Mitchell and Fitzpatrick feared retaliation. Mitchell would treat the Shoshones well during the conference, but he refused to reimburse them even for travel expenses.[71]

With the supply wagons not expected until at least September 20, the Commissioners faced a crucial decision: could the conference be held at Fort Laramie, as planned? Fitzpatrick, who had been camped at the site since late July, knew the game was woefully inadequate. Moreover, emigrant trains had exhausted the forage necessary to sustain the Indian horses. And, without a substantial military detachment, Fort Laramie, on a broad open plain, might prove indefensible during a gathering of thousands of normally hostile tribes.

Mitchell and Fitzpatrick decided to move the council to another site, preferably farther east so that the supply train would reach them more quickly. After commandeering the Fort Laramie supplies, Mitchell convened a mini-conference with the assembled chiefs.[72]

After the traditional pipe ceremonies, Mitchell asked the chiefs to choose another conference site, one to the east so that "we will sooner meet the train which has the goods and provisions for you." Speaking frankly, he continued, "I have some beef which I will distribute to the various tribes to eat; this and some tobacco and vermillion is about all I will be able to give you until the train comes up." Terra Blue, a Brulé Sioux chief, suggested the mouth of Horse Creek. The others agreed and Mitchell, having orchestrated a diplomatic coup, breathed a sigh of relief.[73]

The Indians and Commissioners began the move to Horse Creek on September 4, arriving the next day. Surveying the area, Mitchell designated the north bank of the Platte for the tribes and the west side of Horse

---

[70]Chittenden, *De Smet*, Vol. II, p. 679.
[71]Killoren, p. 144.   [72]Killoren, p. 146.
[73]Killoren, p. 147.

Creek for the white traders with the official meeting ground on the east bank of Horse Creek. The topography worked well. The area even offered rich grass and plentiful game. Terra Blue had chosen well.[74]

---

[74] *Wind River Rendezvous.*

# Chapter Seventeen

## *"We do not want your land"*

Alexander Culbertson, Father De Smet, and the upper Missouri Indians spent one night at Fort Laramie. Although all the food had been taken to Horse Creek, after weeks of arduous travel, the fort offered a comfortable rest before continuing east. In the morning, Culbertson and the Indians resumed their overland trek[1] while De Smet rode in a carriage provided by Robert Campbell who had left his employees to transport the trade goods.[2]

Commissioner Mitchell, to buy time, declared Sunday "the White Man's Medicine Day," with no council business. The council would begin on Monday, September 8.[3] Mitchell, counting on the popular De Smet's persuasive abilities to sway the Indians toward the government's position, was delighted when the priest arrived around sunset on Sunday. Co-commissioner Fitzpatrick, who had met De Smet ten years earlier while guiding the Bidwell-Bartleson party, joined Mitchell in enthusiastic greetings.

Jim Bridger, the famous mountain man, also welcomed the missionary. Bridger and De Smet had met previously at the fur trading rendezvous and, recently, the priest had helped Bridger place his children in a St. Louis boarding school.

With old acquaintances renewed, Mitchell introduced De Smet to Colonel Cooper and Major Chilton, commanding respectively the Dragoons and Mounted Rifles, Captains Duncan and Rhett, Lieutenants Hastings and Elliott, Lieutenant Elliott's wife, editor A. B. Chambers, and Mr. B. Gratz Brown, a lawyer and reporter who would act as the council's recording secretary.[4]

---

[1] Bradley, *MHSC*, Vol. III, p. 266.   [2] Chittenden, *De Smet*, Vol. II, p. 674.
[3] Killoren, p. 150.   [4] *Wind River Rendezvous*.

The council officially opened on Monday, September 8, 1851. As the cannon boomed, "the whole plains seemed to be covered with the moving masses of chiefs, warriors, men, women, and children. . . ."[5] Each nation presented itself at the council circle with distinctive song or demonstration after which the chiefs assumed their designated place. In keeping with Indian tradition, the area directly to the east was left open. Commissioners Mitchell and Fitzpatrick, along with Father De Smet, Robert Campbell, and the interpreters, seated themselves under a center arbor.

Mrs. Elliott, the sole white woman present, assumed a prominent place.[6] Mitchell, acknowledging her, said that her presence showed that the white men came in peace. In addition, her attendance demonstrated the faith the Commissioners had in the honesty and good intentions of the Indians.[7] Then, after the traditional pipe-smoking, the council began. Mitchell told the Indians:

> We are but the agents or representatives of your Great Father at Washington, and what we propose is merely what he desires you should do for your own happiness. We do not come to you as traders; we have nothing to sell you, and do not want to buy anything from you. We do not want your land, horses, robes, nor anything you have; but we come to advise with you, and to make a treaty with you for your own good.[8]

He stressed their benevolent Great White Father's concern for his Indian children. The council, Mitchell asserted, was designed not to demand tribal concessions but to offer lasting benefits.

Losses suffered by the tribes would be justly compensated: "The ears of your Great Father are always open to the complaints of his Red Children." In exchange, the Great Father would "expect and will exert the right of free passage for his White Children" over the emigrant trails. Moreover, the Indians must pay for depredations committed against white travelers just as their Great Father would reimburse the Indians for their losses. In the future, military posts would prevent depredations on either side.

Now Mitchell presented the heart of the government's proposal. "In order that justice may be done each nation," the government proposed establishing specific regions for the sole benefit of each tribe. In this way,

---

[5] *Missouri Republican*, 24 Oct 1851, quoted in Killoren, p. 151.
[6] Killoren, pp. 152-153.  [7] Killoren, p. 153.
[8] Killoren, p. 154.

Mitchell explained, responsibility for future attacks could be determined. Then the Great Father could "punish the guilty and reward the good." Mitchell assured the Indians that this division was "not intended to take any of your lands away from you, or to destroy your rights to hunt, or fish, or pass over the country, as heretofore." Boundaries would bring peace not only to the white emigrants but also to the tribes since there would be "no occasion for war parties going into the country of another nation." It would also enable the Great Father "to drive the bad white men out from amongst you."[9]

To ensure the agreement's viability and to indicate tribal unity, Mitchell asked each tribe to designate a "Chief of the whole nation" whom the Great Father would recognize, respect, and revere. The Great Father pledged to distribute annual annuities of $50,000 each year for fifty years to tribes that signed the treaty. Annuities would come in practical goods and provisions, not in cash, to prevent white men from swindling the Indians. As long as the Indians acted honorably, the annuities would be "faithfully delivered."

Mitchell then asked each tribe to select one or two members to travel to Washington, D.C., to meet their Great Father. There they would see for themselves the beneficence of the white man's government. Lastly, Mitchell addressed the thorny issue of the delayed provisions. Promising that "a large train of ox wagons . . . containing a large amount of presents and provisions" would arrive shortly, Mitchell urged the participants to take the intervening time to "think, talk and smoke over" the proposals. Fitzpatrick then assured the leaders that the commissioners would be available to discuss any questions they might have.[10] The commissioners set aside the next two days for tribal discussion and consultation.

That afternoon, Mitchell learned that the Cheyennes had agreed to "cover the bodies" taken in their recent fight with the Shoshones, an act of atonement required before the tribes could share the peace pipe. The principal Cheyenne warriors met with forty Shoshones. Following speeches and a simple feast, the Cheyennes placed tobacco, blankets, knives, and cloth in the center of the circle.

Next they uncovered the scalps they had taken. After swearing they had not performed a scalp dance, they returned the scalps to the victims' brothers. The brothers embraced the offending warriors and distributed

---

[9]Killoren, p. 154.   [10]Killoren, p. 155.

the proffered gifts to their fellow tribesmen. After more speeches, the ceremony concluded. The next night, the Cheyennes and Shoshones sang and danced through the night.[11]

Alexander Culbertson, the Mandans, Hidatsas, Arikaras, and Assiniboines arrived at the treaty grounds on Monday night, too late to hear Mitchell's opening statement. By then, nearly one thousand lodges of Sioux, Cheyennes, Arapahos, and Shoshones dotted the plains.[12] Not to be intimidated, the new arrivals made a great show of entering the treaty grounds. As the opening day concluded, approximately ten thousand Indians, friend and foe alike, peacefully encamped along Horse Creek.[13]

The next day, Mitchell visited the Sioux who were in consultation. He quietly rode off. That afternoon, the Cheyennes displayed their military might to impress not only their White Fathers but their traditional enemies.

Normally such diversions might have struck Mitchell as a frivolous, albeit necessary, waste of time. But wanting to keep the tribes engaged until the supply trains arrived, he received the display with great enthusiasm. As the ceremony ended, Mitchell garnered his first achievement: the Cheyennes had selected Little Chief and Rides on the Clouds to represent them in Washington, D.C.[14]

September 10 brought another welcome delay. Shortly after the cannon boomed, Robert Meldrum arrived with the Crow delegation. Indians from the surrounding camps turned out to witness their entrance. Commissioner Mitchell received them with a short speech and a smoke. The Crow chiefs accepted his pipe, made speeches, and then retired to set up camp.[15]

The council soon reconvened, but the arrival of the delegations under Culbertson and Meldrum required another pipe ceremony and explanation of the proposed treaty provisions. With this completed, Mitchell asked the Indians what they thought of his proposals.

---

[11]Chittenden, *De Smet*, Vol. II, pp. 679-680.

[12]Bradley, *MHSC*, Vol. III, p. 266.

[13]Chittenden, *De Smet*, Vol. II, p. 681.

[14]Killoren, p. 157. Chittenden, *De Smet*, Vol. II, p. 688, gives the names of the three Cheyenne emissaries to Washington, D.C. as: Voki vokammast, or White Antelope; Obalawhsa, or Red Skin; and, Vaive atoish, or Rides on the Clouds. It is likely that Red Skin (Obalawhsa) is the Indian that Killoren, quoting Chambers in the *Missouri Republican*, refers to as Little Chief.

[15]*Missouri Republican*, 2 Nov 1851, quoted in Killoren, p. 158.

Terra Blue of the Brulé Sioux rose to speak. After thanking Mitchell for convening the conference and assuring him that the Brulés wanted peace "with each other and the whites," he explained that the Sioux, by far the largest band of Plains Indians, could never agree on one chief for their tribe. At best, they could appoint one chief per band.[16]

The Cheyennes and Arapahos followed. Their comments were basically favorable. The general outlines of the government proposal had been accepted. The Indians manifested an honest desire to work cooperatively with the white man in settling disputes.[17]

Nevertheless, the delayed supply wagons continued to create problems. Terra Blue announced that his tribe wanted their gifts immediately. Other leaders echoed his demand. Editor Chambers termed these "begging speeches,"[18] failing to recognize the very real problems confronting the tribes. Mitchell had promised compensation for their grievances, motivating many to attend. Yet as the conference proceeded, many bands found themselves "in absolute destitution."[19] How could they believe their past grievances would be compensated when their Great Father did not even feed them at his gathering?

Mitchell and Fitzpatrick could only repeat their assurances that the supply wagons were en route and the gifts would soon be distributed. The Indians, having expressed their displeasure, had no choice but to trust the commissioners.

The gathering lasted "until a late hour" on September 10. By day's end, both the Cheyennes and Arapahos had designated chiefs for their nations whom the commissioners formally presented to the gathering. Henceforth, Mitchell announced, the government would recognize them as their nations' chiefs "and they must be so received, respected and obeyed by all others."[20]

The hard work of defining tribal territories began on September 12

---

[16]The Sioux Nation is divided into three major groups: the Lakota (or Teton), the Dakota (or Santee), and the Nakota (or Yanktonai). Gagnon and White Eyes. These divisions are further divided. For instance, the 1868 Treaty with the Sioux recognized the following bands: Brulé, Oglala, Miniconjou, Yanktonai, Hunkpapa, Blackfeet, Cuthead, Two Kettle, Sans Arc, and Santee. Lazarus, p. 433.   [17]Killoren, p. 159.
[18]*Missouri Republican*, 2 Nov 1851, quoted in Killoren, p. 159.
[19]Chittenden, *De Smet*, Vol. II, p. 682.   [20]Killoren, p. 160.

with the drawing of an accurate map. While Mitchell and Fitzpatrick had a good working knowledge of the plains, no one knew them better than De Smet and Jim Bridger whom Mitchell designated to draw the map.

The map, no matter how accurate, would mean little if the allocations did not respect traditional tribal homelands. This required input from the gathered traders, including Alexander Culbertson who, in the absence of Blackfeet representatives, would protect their interests in this delicate negotiation. A small group of whites worked throughout Friday to demarcate boundaries for the diverse, nomadic peoples. Finally, as twilight loomed, they agreed on a proposal to divide the region into geographic districts. But would the Indians agree?[21]

The council reconvened on Saturday when the commissioners presented the proposed map. The Oglala, through their spokesmen The Snake, The Brave Bear, and Black Hawk, strongly objected. They complained that their traditional hunting grounds extended south of the Platte, designated for the Cheyennes and Arapahos.

Mitchell tried to explain that the territory assigned a tribe would not be held exclusively by them. Rather, "so long as they remained at peace," any tribe could venture into another's territory to hunt or engage in other peaceful activities. The Sioux remained skeptical but, in general, the other tribes agreed.[22] Mitchell suggested that the tribes spend the next day, another "White Man's Medicine Day," debating the boundaries.

Sunday, September 14, marked the Feast of the Exaltation of the Cross. In the camp of the mixed-bloods, a lodge large enough to accommodate vast numbers of communicants was erected where Father De Smet held services "in presence of all the gentlemen assisting at the council, of all the half-bloods and whites and of a great concourse of Indians."[23]

Following mass, the priest baptized twenty-eight children and five adults, mostly mixed-bloods. De Smet took every opportunity during the conference to gain converts. He held "daily conferences on religion" which were received "with great attention." During the council, De Smet baptized 239 Oglalas, 305 Arapahos, 253 Cheyennes, 280 Brulé and "Osage Sioux," and 56 "in the camp of Painted Bear." Nearly all were chil-

---

[21] Killoren, pp. 161-162.    [22] Killoren, p. 163.
[23] Chittenden, *De Smet*, Vol. II, p. 677.

dren. In addition, he baptized 61 mixed-bloods[24] and united Robert Meldrum and his Crow wife in marriage.[25] The Sioux bestowed a new name on the revered, gentle De Smet: Watankanga Waokia, "The Man Who Shows His Love for the Great Spirit."[26]

When the council reconvened on Monday, Mitchell asked if the Indian leaders found acceptable the proposals laid before them. The chiefs raised a few questions and minor difficulties but, all in all, it appeared that the commissioners had their treaty.

The Sioux, however, remained unable to agree on a single chief. Mitchell, his patience wearing thin, announced that if they could not choose a chief, he would do it for them. If they did not like the man he appointed, he would choose another. Mitchell then selected Conquering Bear to represent the Sioux.[27] Conquering Bear was "connected with a large and powerful family, running into several of the bands, and although no chief, he is a brave of the highest reputation."[28]

Initially, Conquering Bear declined this honor. But Mitchell assured him that he had been chosen because of "the character he bore among the whites and Indians, for honesty, intelligence and courage." With noticeable trepidation, Conquering Bear finally agreed, telling those assembled: "If you, Father, and our Great Father, require that I shall be [the Sioux] chief, I will take this office. I will try to do right to the whites, and hope they will do so to my people...."[29]

Mitchell still had to convince the Sioux. Placing Conquering Bear in the center of the council circle, he handed each Sioux warrior a stick. He instructed those who would accept Conquering Bear to hand him their stick. For several nerve-wracking minutes, the Sioux consulted. Finally, a Yankton chief stepped forward and handed Conquering Bear his stick. Another followed until they had all given Conquering Bear their sticks.[30]

---

[24]Chittenden, *De Smet,* Vol. II, pp. 678-679.

[25]*Wind River Rendezvous.*

[26]Killoren, p. 165. In notes, p. 384, Killoren gives the Indian name as Wakánt anka Wawókiya and translates it as "Helper of the Great Spirit."

[28]*Missouri Republican,* 23 Nov 1851, quoted by Killoren, p. 165. Chambers gives his Indian name as Mah-toe-wah-yu-whey and calls him "Frightening Bear." Most historians call him Conquering Bear.

[28]*Missouri Republican,* 23 Nov 1851, quoted in Killoren, pp. 165-166.

[29]*Missouri Republican,* 23 Nov 1851, quoted in Killoren, p. 166.

[30]Killoren, p. 166.

As Mitchell knew, anything less than this unanimous affirmation would have placed the would-be chief in a tenuous position.

The conference had succeeded. On September 17, 1851, everyone gathered to sign and affix their marks to the treaty which contained four primary articles:

Article I: The Indians recognized and admitted the right of the United States to form roads and establish military posts in their territory;

Article II: Solemn obligations agreed upon for the maintenance of peace, and for repairing the damages and losses sustained by the whites on the part of the Indians;

Article III: Indemnity accorded the Indians for the destruction caused in their hunting grounds, forests, pasturages, etc., by travelers from the States who crossed their lands. Additionally, $50,000 was distributed to the tribes and accepted as payment for destruction caused prior to the signing of the treaty; and,

Article IV: A promised annuity of $50,000 for fifty years, to be delivered in such articles as the changing condition of the Indians may, from time to time, require.[31]

Commissioners Mitchell and Fitzpatrick signed first followed by the marks of twenty-one Indian chiefs representing eight tribes. Then, fifteen witnesses, including Alexander Culbertson and five army officers, affixed their signatures.[32] Pierre De Smet did not sign, possibly because he feared that doing so might jeopardize his cherished status as an impartial arbiter.

Commissioner Mitchell, signed treaty in hand, longed to announce success and send the tribes home. But this was impossible: the supply wagons still had not arrived. An "exceedingly annoyed" Mitchell had to wait and hope that the Indians, too, would be patient. It was a dangerous time.

With nothing to occupy the assembled group, a new and controversial issue unexpectedly surfaced. The day after the treaty signing, the traders,

---

[31] *Wind River Rendezvous*; Chittenden, *De Smet*, Vol. II, p. 676. Curiously, Chittenden's volume of De Smet's letters quotes De Smet as saying the annuity period was set at fifteen years rather than fifty. Since Congress later unilaterally reduced the commitment to fifteen years, one wonders whether this is an editing error. [32] Killoren, p. 167; *Wind River Rendezvous*.

most of whom had married Indian women, proposed a special mixed-blood allotment.[33] De Smet noted that such an arrangement would be "the sole means of preserving union among all those wandering and scattered families, which become every year more and more numerous."[34] Editor Chambers noted:

> This application on the part of the parents of the Half Breed children, has many strong claims to consideration. They are, in many respects, estranged from civilized society. The white man who has taken a squaw for a wife, however honestly and virtuously they may have lived, (and in this many of them will compare advantageously with some who claim to be civilized) is, with his wife, for ever debarred admission into society. He has shut himself out, and must reap the consequences which his own course has entailed upon him. Yet, toward the offspring of this alliance, the affections are as warm, and we believe we could with truth say as devoted, as can be found any where in civilized life.[35]

Vigorous debate ensued. The proponents suggested the area around what is now Denver, Colorado, as the designated reserved lands. But these had been included in the Cheyenne and Arapaho country and those tribes vigorously objected. In the end, the commissioners decided to table the proposal, arguing that it fell beyond the scope of their directive.[36] It was never again considered and the mixed-bloods eventually were dispossessed of their land and their heritage.

The supply wagons finally arrived on Saturday, September 20, causing "an occasion of general joy."[37] Mitchell wisely abandoned his habit of suspending business on Sundays and, the next day, the white men unloaded the wagons and prepared to distribute the gifts. The cannon announced the distribution ceremony and the various "men, women and children,— in great confusion, and in their gayest costume, daubed with paints of glaring hues and decorated with all the gewgaws they could boast" hurried to the central gathering place.[38]

Mitchell and Fitzpatrick turned first to the appointed and recognized chiefs, presenting them military uniforms including a gilt sword. Mitchell next enlisted various tribal members to distribute the gifts. Each

---

[33] Killoren, p. 168.  
[34] Chittenden, *De Smet*, Vol. II, p. 676.  
[35] *Missouri Republican*, 30 Nov 1851, quoted in Killoren, p. 169.  
[36] Killoren, p. 170.  
[37] Chittenden, *De Smet*, Vol. II, p. 682.  
[38] Chittenden, *De Smet*, Vol. II, p. 683.

band waited patiently to receive their share. And then, "glad or satisfied, but always quiet," they loaded up their families and lodges and quit the council grounds. All had heard that numerous buffalo roamed on the South Fork of the Platte and they were anxious to return to the hunt.

Thus, the great Horse Creek treaty council of 1851 came to a slow, evolving, and uneventful conclusion. For more than two weeks, traditional enemies had gathered in peace, trading visits, sharing meals, dances, and presents, and telling stories of personal exploits. Old feuds had been set aside and the peace pipe freely shared. Tranquility and cooperation suffused the conference. To Father De Smet, ever the optimist, the tribes "seemed all to form a single nation."[39]

But old enmities would not die. None of the parties represented—not the government, not the white emigrants, and not the Indians—would abide by the terms of the historic document.

---

[39] Chittenden, *De Smet,* Vol. II, p. 681.

Chapter Eighteen

## *"What will become of the aborigines?"*

Alexander Culbertson left Horse Creek to retrace his overland journey with the Assiniboines and their cartful of presents. At Culbertson's request, the Hidatsas, Arikaras, and Mandans had been escorted to Fort Berthold by another interpreter. Also missing was Father De Smet who, feeling confident that the agreement "will be the commencement of a new era for the Indians—an era of peace,"[1] had agreed to lead the Indian delegation to Washington, D.C.

At Fort Sarpy, Culbertson and the Assiniboines boarded a mackinaw for their journey to Fort Union. They sighted one war party of Blackfeet but, although the Assiniboines' sworn enemies, they allowed the party to pass unmolested,[2] perhaps because they recognized Culbertson. The weary contingent finally reached Fort Union on the evening of October 31, 1851.[3]

The upper Missouri Indians were satisfied with their gifts which, for the moment, represented the only tangible results of the council. Culbertson, however, felt much less sanguine. Unlike his missionary friend, Culbertson remained circumspect, conscious of numerous pitfalls in the agreement which he expressed to the artist, Rudolph Kurz.

Culbertson complained that Commissioner Mitchell had often been too drunk to oversee the council effectively. Moreover, he believed Mitchell's promises extravagant and worried that when these were broken, as Culbertson believed inevitable, the result would be massive tribal discontent. Culbertson also considered it a serious mistake for Mitchell to have appointed a chief for the Sioux. Finally, Culbertson voiced regrets that the government had not made a grander display of military might, especially since many Indians had expected it.[4]

After reading the treaty, Kurz agreed with Culbertson's assessment.

---

[1] Killoren, p. 170.  [2] Bradley, *MHSC*, Vol. III, p. 267.
[3] Kurz, p. 220.  [4] Kurz, p. 221.

Kurz opined that the document contained "nothing but hypocritical phrases to impose the belief upon a distant public that Uncle Sam takes the Indians' fate to heart." He also suspected that the cavalier manner in which so-called "supreme chiefs" had been appointed would do little but "engender jealousy among rivals."

Like Culbertson, Kurz questioned the promise of annuities: how long would the commitment be kept? Could future administrations abrogate the treaty? What guarantee did the Indians have that the United States would survive for fifty years? Moreover, both Culbertson and Kurz perceived an enormous loophole in the annuity clause: the government promised to distribute the goods only if the Indians did not wage war against each other or cause harm to white settlers. "What an easy matter," Kurz concluded, "to provoke an affront and then to refuse the annual payment."[5] Culbertson had an additional reason to doubt the government's promises: despite the government's pre-conference assurances, he had not been compensated.[6]

Culbertson's post-conference outlook more closely resembled De Smet's earlier concerns: "What will become of the aborigines, who have possessed [this land] from time immemorial? This is indeed a thorny question, awakening gloomy ideas in the observer's mind, if he has followed the encroaching policy of the States in regard to the Indians."[7]

But for now, the travelers were home and Alexander Culbertson sported a fancy new title. Henceforth, Culbertson would be called Colonel. The discerning Kurz wondered, "Colonel of what? Here we have neither Regular Army nor militia. Oh, the passion for titles among these republican Americans!"[8] In Culbertson's case, that passion grew; as time passed, he would be referred to as Major although he apparently never received any title beyond this honorary designation of Colonel.[9]

To celebrate their return, Culbertson threw a ball for Fort Union's employees. Natawista looked stunning in her gown, "fringed and

---

[5]Kurz, p. 228.     [6]Bradley, *MHSC*, Vol. III, p. 267.
[7]Chittenden, *De Smet*, Vol. II, p. 646.     [8]Kurz, p. 221.
[9]Hanson, "Marking the Grave," p. 127. Hanson suggests that Kurz, as a Swiss native, might have erroneously substituted Colonel for Major but, considering that Mitchell himself only bore the title of Colonel, it seems unlikely that he would have conferred superior titles on the traders and interpreters who attended the conference. The first reference the author found to Culbertson as "Major" is contained in a 19 Oct 1854 report by Alfred Vaughan to the Commissioner of Indian Affairs in Senate ExDocs 1 (33-2) 746, p. 289.

# WHAT WILL BECOME OF THE ABORIGINES?

valanced according to European mode." The attendees consumed more than a little alcohol, leading to "one or more tragicomic intermezzos." Culbertson invited the rival traders, but Joe Picotte, partner in Harvey, Primeau and Company, had to be "put to bed" when he quarreled with Indians loyal to the AFC.[10]

The contradiction between the happy, hoped-for world of the Horse Creek Treaty and the real world became painfully evident with Fool Bear's return.[11] When Culbertson initially approached the Assiniboines about the conference, they refused to attend since they "did not want to risk themselves among the large body of Sioux." Only Fool Bear argued against this. After considering his counsel, the deputation was raised.[12] Fool Bear was recognized for this persuasive contribution by being appointed "supreme chief" of the Assiniboines.

Whatever pride this designation brought was quickly subsumed when he returned. During his absence, three members of his family, including his only wife, had died.[13] His son had been killed in battle with the Blackfeet.[14] Meanwhile, this son's child had also died, probably from cholera. While preparing to bury her grandchild, Fool Bear's wife learned of her son's death. Overcome by grief and fearful for her husband, she hanged herself.[15] Fool Bear's brother brought the bodies of his sister-in-law and her grandchild to Fort Union to be buried next to Fool Bear's daughter who had killed herself earlier after a young man claimed to have taken indecent liberties with her.[16]

To the Indians, suicide carried no shame. As long as an Indian had

---

[10] Kurz, p. 222.

[11] Kurz, p. 218, gives the name as Ours Fou. Denig, p. 84, calls him "The Foolish Bear" and "The Crazy Bear."   [12] Denig, p. 84.

[13] Kurz, p. 221, says that the dead included his only wife, his son, and two grandchildren. Elsewhere in his narrative, Kurz seems to suggest that the dead were his wife, his son, his daughter, and one grandchild. It also appears from some of Kurz's statements that one of these deaths may have occurred at a prior time. Denig, p. 84, says that there were three dead: his son, his "child," and his wife. Denig does not provide as much detail as Kurz about these events but his count suggests that one of the deaths did occur earlier.

[14] Kurz, p. 214.   [15] Kurz, p. 216.

[16] Kurz, p. 218. It is not at all clear that this was the fourth member of Fool Bear's family to die in his absence. This death might have happened at some earlier time and the fourth death could have been that of another grandchild rather than this daughter. Or Kurz may have been confused about the relationship of this girl to the family.

hope for the future, he chose life. But when hope vanished, "doubt, disgust, and weariness set in." Fool Bear's young daughter, being "of good family, blameless reputation, modest manners, and honorable nature," had her future robbed by "one single act of a dissolute boy" and chose suicide. His wife opted for the same when she found herself "far from her husband and he in danger, too soon parted from the dearly beloved children" and longing "to be united" with her loved ones.[17]

Fool Bear, upon hearing the news, "was grieved to the soul. . . ." Had he stayed home, his wife would probably have lived. What a price he had paid to hear his Great Father's words, to have been appointed tribal chief, an honor that now rang hollow since other tribal members refused to recognize the designation.[18] The traders, fearing Fool Bear's pervasive anguish, hid his weapons.[19] In a traditional act of mourning, Fool Bear made small incisions on his body "to allow blood to flow as atonement."[20]

Fool Bear was not the only one to receive dolorous news upon his return. Natawista, who apparently accompanied Culbertson to the conference, also returned to grief.[21] Throughout the fall, the Assiniboines and Blackfeet had battled, with both sides suffering casualties. Among the Blackfeet dead was Natawista's younger brother.[22]

In mourning, Natawista cut short her long black hair. Kurz, who had been searching for the perfect Indian woman to memorialize, believed her to be "one of the most beautiful Indian women . . . an excellent model for a Venus, ideal woman of a primitive race." But, in consequence of her grief, Natawista refused to allow him to paint her portrait.

Instead, Kurz began a portrait of Culbertson. Although Kurz did not chide his subject for an inability to sit quietly, as Audubon had, he did complain about the type and quality of his brushes and paints. Yet the image, once completed, represented such a striking likeness that no sooner had it been hung in the reception room than it was damaged by the probing hands of Indian women and children touching to see if it was

---

[17]Kurz, p. 220.   [18]Kurz, p. 242.
[19]Kurz, p. 221.   [20]Kurz, p. 242.

[21]The assumption that Natawista accompanied Culbertson to Horse Creek is based on the fact that she is not mentioned by Kurz, who found her stunning, until after Culbertson returned. Moreover, it appears that it was then that she learned of her brother's death. Since Mitchell encouraged the tribes to bring women and Natawista frequently traveled with her husband, it seems likely that she accompanied him on this occasion, although she is not mentioned by De Smet.

[22]Kurz, p. 206. The slain brother's name is unknown. Hugh Dempsey to the author.

real.²³ More of Kurz's precious paints had to be used to restore the likeness.²⁴

With winter closing in, Culbertson, his family, and five Company employees left for Fort Benton on Sunday, November 9.²⁵ Ice made river travel impossible and so Culbertson plotted an overland route following the upper Missouri to the mouth of Milk River and then northwest until the Milk could be crossed near what is now Havre, Montana. From there, the group skirted the northwestern edge of the Bear Paw mountains before turning southwest to Fort Benton. For the first time, a wheeled cart had followed this overland route, closely paralleling the present U.S. Highway 2.²⁶

The journey consumed twenty-four days.²⁷ With Fort Benton quiet, and despite his hectic summer and fall schedule, Culbertson embarked on one more trip. Father De Smet had initially planned to visit the Flathead missions that summer but shelved those plans when the government sought his assistance at the treaty conference. The priest, still worried about the missions, prevailed on Culbertson to visit them in his stead.

Culbertson willingly agreed but the "great pioneer," who had never before crossed the Continental Divide, got lost between the headwaters of the Missouri and the Columbia. De Smet, however, found a silver lining, believing that Culbertson's "mishap would greatly improve my great map."²⁸

In the spring, Culbertson took the Fort Benton returns to Fort Union, made a quick trip to St. Louis,²⁹ and then returned to Fort Union.³⁰ When the *Banner State* arrived with the trade goods, Culbertson was dismayed to discover it did not include the annuities promised the upriver

---

²³Kurz, pp. 223-224.

²⁴What became of the original painting is unknown. It may have been destroyed in the Chambersburg, Pennsylvania, buildings owned by the Culbertson family which were burned during the Civil War. Taylor, "The Major's Blackfoot Bride." A reproduction, based on sketches made by Kurz, hangs in the reception room at the reconstructed Fort Union.

²⁵Kurz, p. 225, gives the date as well as the information that Culbertson's family accompanied him. Bradley, *MHSC*, Vol. III, p. 267, mentions the five Company men.

²⁶Bradley, *MHSC*, Vol. III, p. 267.   ²⁷Kurz, p. 274.

²⁸Pierre De Smet to Edwin T. Denig, May 1852. Excerpt in unattributed typescript notes found in the Alexander Culbertson VF, MtHS.

²⁹Kurz, p. 329; Sunder, p. 146.   ³⁰Bradley, *MHSC*, Vol. III, p. 268.

tribes by the Horse Creek treaty. While Culbertson had anticipated treaty violations, he had not expected them this quickly.[31]

The already angry Assiniboines grew even more dissatisfied when no Indian agent appeared to explain the situation. They ridiculed Fool Bear, alleging that he had "come back from the White's country with a lie in his mouth" and accusing him of having "sold their lands for a handful of goods." Fool Bear "maintained the equanimity of his temper," continuing to believe in his Great Father's promises.[32]

Deeply concerned, Culbertson wrote Superintendent Mitchell to complain about the government's failure to deliver the annuities. He also expressed concern that, without a strong upriver Indian agent, the Red River métis, the mixed-blood descendants of French Canadian traders and Indians, would increase their considerable liquor trafficking around Fort Union.[33]

The upper Missouri tribes would remain without an agent for more than a year. The situation had been in flux since 1848 when William S. Hatton had been appointed agent. He immediately complained that his salary was inadequate, his expense account too small, and his character subject to assault by dissatisfied traders. Arguing that prices at the trading posts were unreasonably high, Hatton lobbied for funds to build his own upriver agency.[34]

But his 1849 journey to the upper Missouri did little to inspire confidence. That summer, a massive fire destroyed the St. Louis levee, the fully-loaded AFC steamer, *Martha*, and fifteen blocks of the St. Louis business district. The Company eventually commissioned the *Amelia* to transport the trade goods; Agent Hatton went along to distribute the Indian annuities.

When the *Amelia* tied up below Fort Pierre, the Sioux, fearing their annuities would be turned over to the AFC traders and unfairly distributed, assaulted the crew, boarded the steamboat, and demanded their annuities. Intimidated, Hatton acquiesced.[35] The incident permanently undermined his authority and, in April 1851, he requested another assignment.[36]

James Norwood succeeded Hatton. He spent one winter at Fort Pierre

---

[31]Sunder, p. 147.
[32]Denig, p. 85.
[33]Sunder, p. 148.
[34]Sunder, pp. 111-113.
[35]Sunder, pp. 117-118.
[36]Sunder, p. 148.

# WHAT WILL BECOME OF THE ABORIGINES? 215

and, as had his predecessor, demanded better transportation, additional interpreters, an independent post, and military protection.[37] The Superintendent had little chance to evaluate Norwood's concerns; on September 20, 1852, Norwood was killed at Sergeant's Bluff. Robert B. Lambdin, appointed to replace Norwood, never reported for duty.[38]

That fall (1852), Culbertson traveled to St. Louis where he discussed his concerns with Superintendent Mitchell. With Norwood dead and Lambdin nowhere to be found, Mitchell decided that he and Culbertson should transport the annuities. In early October, with $10,000 worth of goods for the Assiniboines, the two headed upriver.[39] Their arrival at Fort Union occasioned great celebration, especially by Fool Bear who, having been subjected to months of opprobrium, now found himself "flattered" by those same detractors.[40]

Finally, in the spring of 1853, the upper Missouri tribes received a new agent. Born in Virginia in 1801, Alfred J. Vaughan had entered the Indian service in 1842, serving the Osages and then the Iowas, Sacs and Foxes, giving him a good understanding of Indian culture.[41] Even Charles Larpenteur, the acerbic Fort Union clerk, called Vaughan a "jovial old fellow" despite the fact that he "would take almost anything which would make drunk come."[42]

Unlike most agents, Vaughan, who had married an Indian woman,[43] spent most of his time living among the tribes.[44] He tried conscientiously to apply government policies while suggesting practical solutions to solve problems.[45] He worked diligently for the benefit of the tribes, distributing annuities fairly while complaining when they were of inferior quality or benefit.[46] The tribes finally had an honest agent committed to their well-being.

As the 1850s unfolded, few United States citizens or officials exhibited much interest in acquiring the lands inhabited by the plains and

---

[37]James Norwood to Alfred Cumming, 26 Jun 1852. NAM, M234/885; Sunder, pp. 148-149.
[38]NAM, M234/885.    [39]NAM, M234/885; Denig, p. 85.
[40]Denig, p. 85.    [41]McDonnell, *MHSC*, Vol. X, p. 272.
[42]Larpenteur, p. 346.
[43]Larpenteur, p. 346; McDonnell, *MHSC*, Vol. X, p. 272.
[44]Larpenteur, p. 346.    [45]Ewers, *Blackfeet*, pp. 228-229.
[46]Alfred Vaughan to Alfred Cumming, 1 Apr 1854. NAM, M234/885; Richards, p. 233.

intermountain tribes since almost everyone believed them unsuitable for white settlement. What the whites sought, as illustrated by the Horse Creek Treaty, was simply a safe passage corridor for the westward emigrants.

But demands for safe passage rapidly accelerated. For years, politicians had debated a transcontinental railroad and, by 1853, the time seemed ripe. That March, two days before leaving office, President Millard Fillmore signed a law creating Washington territory, a vast territory stretching from the Rocky Mountains west to the Pacific Ocean and north from the Columbia River to the 49th parallel. The next day, as Franklin Pierce waited to be sworn in, Congress authorized surveys for possible transcontinental railroad routes.[47]

In one of his first acts as president, Franklin Pierce appointed his friend and supporter, Isaac Ingalls Stevens, governor of Washington territory.[48] Stevens, born in Andover, Massachusetts in 1818, apparently suffered from a mild form of dwarfism.[49] But the awkward young man grew up to be a good-looking man with dark hazel eyes, thick, curly black hair, a straight nose, and firm chin covered by a well-groomed goatee.[50] After attending Phillips Academy,[51] Stevens entered West Point where he graduated first in the class of 1839.[52] One of his classmates was Michael Simpson Culbertson, Alexander Culbertson's half-brother.[53] Following graduation, Stevens served in the Engineer Corps and the Mexican War before an injury in 1847 ended his military service.[54]

Stevens returned to the Engineer Corps, eventually ending up in Washington, D.C., where he cultivated prominent friends, including soon-to-be-president Franklin Pierce. Stevens, like Alexander Culbertson, believed the West offered the best opportunity for a young man to make his name and he lobbied skillfully for appointment as governor of Washington territory.[55]

But Stevens was not content merely to be governor and Superintendent of Indian Affairs for Washington territory, a position automatically conferred on the governor. Stevens also wanted to lead the northern sur-

---

[47]Richards, p. 96.
[48]Richards, p. 97.
[49]Richards, p. 6.
[50]Richards, p. 30.
[51]Richards, p. 11.
[52]McDonnell, *MHSC*, Vol. X, pp. 267-268.
[53]Lewis Culbertson, p. 293.
[54]Richards, p. 66.
[55]Richards, p. 95.

vey for the proposed transcontinental railroad. He applied to Secretary of War Jefferson Davis, citing three factors which made him uniquely qualified for the job: his prior experience as an engineer and surveyor; his position as governor; and, his personal friendship with Davis. Davis appointed Stevens to head the survey on March 18, 1853.[56]

Facing a congressional deadline of January 1854 for the survey's completion, Stevens threw himself into the project. Through contacts at the Smithsonian, the Coast Survey, and the Engineer Corps, he put together an impressive cadre of assistants: soon-to-be General George McClellan; Andrew Jackson Donelson; civilian engineers Abiel Tinkham and Frederick Lander; Lieutenants Rufus Saxton, Cuvier Grover, Beekman DuBarry, and John Mullan; geologist John Evans; James Doty; and, as artist, John Mix Stanley.[57]

The governor, accompanied by Stanley, left Washington, D.C. in early May, arriving in St. Louis on the 15th.[58] There he met Alexander Culbertson.[59] Stevens recruited the trader to assist the survey since its proposed route passed through the country of the Blackfeet "whose warlike and treacherous character was proverbial."[60] Stevens, who "deemed it highly desirable" to obtain Culbertson's services as special agent, felt little need to justify his choice since the "ascendancy of this gentleman over the Indians, and his important services at the Laramie treaty [of 1851] . . . had already made him very favorably known to the [Indian] department."[61] Culbertson enthusiastically agreed, embracing his new title of special agent to the Blackfeet.

The governor, after signing up Culbertson, headed up the Mississippi River to the survey's starting point in St. Paul. Meanwhile, Lt. Donelson, Lt. Mullan, Dr. Evans, Culbertson, and six sappers headed to Fort Union aboard the *Robert Campbell*.[62] Culbertson, of course, was well-acquainted with Evans who had previously surveyed the Badlands and looked forward to returning to the area as a member of Stevens's party.

But Evans was annoyed to discover that he would have to share the Badlands. Just as the number of westward emigrants had increased, so had the scientific expeditions. Scientists Fielding Bradford Meek and

---

[56]Richards, pp. 98-99.    [57]Richards, pp. 99-101.
[58]Hazard Stevens, Vol. I, p. 302; Richards, p. 103.
[59]Bradley, *MHSC*, Vol. III, p. 268.    [60]Senate ExDocs 1 (33-2) 746, p. 403.
[61]Senate ExDocs 1 (33-2) 746, p. 403.    [62]Hazard Stevens, Vol. I, p. 302; Sunder, p. 154.

Ferdinand Vandeveer Hayden, sponsored by New York paleontologist James Hall and enticed by the Smithsonian's offer to pay for quality fossils, had also planned a Badlands expedition.

Culbertson had met Meek and Hayden in St. Louis and, characteristically, advised them on outfitting their expedition and offered to sell them Company supplies.[63] Although Stevens and Evans attempted to block the rival expedition, Meek and Hayden refused to stay behind. Tensions mounted when Meek and Hayden joined Evans aboard the *Robert Campbell*. Finally, members of the St. Louis scientific community convinced Evans to "share" the Badlands. The rival scientists disembarked at Fort Pierre with their Company-supplied horses, carts, guides, and interpreters and set out separately for the Badlands.[64] Meanwhile, the balance of the survey party continued on to Fort Union to await Stevens's arrival from the east.

Stevens and the eastern survey team reached Fort Union on August 1.[65] There, the governor met up with Culbertson who would escort the group to Fort Benton.[66] Stevens, seeing Culbertson in his natural milieu, was impressed: "He is a man of great energy, intelligence, and fidelity, and possesses the entire confidence of the Indians."

At Fort Union, the governor also met Natawista who, he noted, was "also deservedly held in high esteem." Although Stevens thought she had "made little or no progress in our language," the governor acknowledged her achievements in other areas: "She has acquired the manners and adapted herself to the usages of the white race with singular facility."[67] Furthermore, she "presents the most striking illustration of the high civilization which these tribes of the interior are capable of attaining."[68]

Culbertson, according to Stevens's instructions, had sent presents to the tribes along with the following message:

> I desire to meet you on the way and to assure you of the fatherly care and beneficence of the government. I wish to meet the Blackfoot (*sic*) in a general council at Fort Benton. Do not make war upon your neighbors.

---

[63]Sunder, pp. 151-152.
[64]Sunder, pp. 153-154.
[65]Hazard Stevens, Vol. I, p. 346.
[66]Richards, p. 111.
[67]Hazard Stevens, Vol. I, pp. 347-348.
[68]Senate ExDocs 1 (33-2) 746, p. 403.
[69]Ewers, *Blackfeet*, p. 208; Hazard Stevens, Vol. I, p. 348.

Remain at peace, and the Great Father will see that you do not lose by it.[69]

But, by the time the governor arrived, both Culbertson and Natawista, having observed the survey party, were "full of anxiety" about the anticipated journey. They feared that "some rude or careless act" by the group "towards the jealous and ignorant" Indians "might at any moment be a signal for a declaration of war."[70]

The ever-cautious Culbertson had previously accompanied a wide variety of visitors through the Blackfeet territory without incident, but the Stevens party exhibited a form of arrogant pomposity which Culbertson believed might put them all at risk. To his credit, Stevens acknowledged the attitudes that so disturbed Culbertson and his wife but found it hard to persuade his party of the importance of pursuing a "conciliatory course" toward the Indians.

Many of his men possessed a "contempt for the Indians as an inferior race, and a too confident reliance upon our physical superiority." When one of his cooks complained about serving an Indian, Stevens reminded him that, a few days earlier, the Indians had willingly shared their game with the survey party. Additionally, in the Indian encampments, great feasts had been laid out for their pleasure. "Are you willing," Stevens asked, "that we should be outdone in hospitality by these wild Indians?" The humbled cook promised "more courteous demeanor" in the future.[71]

These reprimands, however, did not allay the misgivings of the Culbertsons. Culbertson knew that the Blackfeet felt increasing anxiety over the number of whites entering their territory. During the last year, he had seen the tribe become more belligerent as they came to believe that the more war-like tribes received the best annuities.[72] The Stevens party, he believed, would present an alluring target.

Culbertson explained to Stevens that young male Indians regarded raids against real or perceived enemies as their best opportunity to attain influence within their tribe, acquire wealth, and impress their female contemporaries.[73] Culbertson was so concerned about the planned journey that, uncharacteristically, he suggested Natawista remain behind. She refused to consider this, telling her husband and Stevens:

---

[70]Senate ExDocs 1 (33-2) 746, p. 403.  [71]Senate ExDocs 1 (33-2) 746, p. 404.
[72]Richards, p. 115.  [73]Hazard Stevens, Vol. I, p. 348.

My people are a good people, but they are jealous and vindictive. I am afraid that they and the whites will not understand each other; but if I go, I may be able to explain things to them, and soothe them if they should be irritated. I know there is great danger; but, my husband, where you go will I go, and where you die will I die.[74]

No one could persuade her otherwise and when the Stevens party left Fort Union on August 10, 1853, Natawista accompanied them.

---
[74] Senate ExDocs 1 (33-2) 746, p. 404.

Chapter Nineteen

## *"these hitherto neglected tribes"*

Any lingering doubts Isaac Stevens harbored about his company's vulnerability vanished when, shortly before their departure from Fort Union, a number of "painted warriors, arrayed in their richest war-dresses" sprang unexpectedly from the bushes.[1] The war party, under White Man's Horses, consisted of one hundred Piegans and Bloods.

Stevens received the warriors, asking them to convey to their tribe "the beneficent policy of our government towards the Indians" as well as "the peaceable character of my own duties and objects." The encounter progressed to "the most friendly interchange of civilities."[2] But the dangers persisted. As the survey party moved west, accompanied by White Man's Horses and his warriors, Stevens reported a "serious difficulty" with another band of Indians.[3] Alexander Culbertson managed to smooth things over while Natawista "was unwearied and efficient in her good offices."[4]

On August 25, the Stevens party met three hundred lodges of Gros Ventres at Milk River. That evening, Culbertson and the governor held a council during which Stevens learned about the types of conflicts which routinely led to intertribal hostilities, even between traditional allies such as the Gros Ventres and Blackfeet. Shortly before, a Blackfeet had killed a Gros Ventre for marrying a Blackfeet woman. The Blackfeet warrior then kidnapped the Gros Ventre's wife, urging her to keep the murder secret. When the woman reported the murder to the Gros Ventres, they planned retaliation.[5]

---

[1] Senate ExDocs 1 (33-2) 746, p. 404.
[2] Hazard Stevens, Vol. I, p. 351.
[3] The location of this event is as shrouded in mystery as the details. Stevens claimed the encounter occurred at Little Muddy as they headed "west" from Ft. Union. Yet, Little Muddy is several miles east of Ft. Union.
[4] Hazard Stevens, Vol. I, p. 352.
[5] Hazard Stevens, Vol. I, pp. 355-356.

At a meeting the next day, with Culbertson interpreting, Stevens exhorted the tribe to abandon their plans, cautioning "how much they would suffer from it and how little was to be gained." Stevens continued: "No idle curiosity brings me here—no mere desire to see the country or the Indians; but I am charged with a great public duty, to deliver to you a message of peace, and to assure you of the kind feelings entertained towards you by your Great Father."[6]

Stevens explained his intention to hold a treaty conference the next year. If successful, the Indians would receive, in the form of annuities, "from the government directly what they now get from other Indians." This would abrogate the need for continuing intertribal raids.[7] The governor urged the tribe to suspend hostilities until after the conference and asked several chiefs to accompany him to Fort Benton. The tribe agreed and Stevens distributed gifts of "blankets, shirts, calico, knives, beads, paint, powder, shot, tobacco, hard bread, etc." which were received "with the greatest satisfaction, and without the slightest manifestation of envy or grumbling."[8]

The Gros Ventres then presented one horse to the governor and two to Culbertson "to whom they seemed to be much attached."[9] The next day, the whites and Gros Ventre delegates set off for Fort Benton.[10] They arrived on Thursday, September 1, greeted by a fifteen gun salute ordered by Malcolm Clarke, who had been left in charge.[11] Stevens spent a week at the fort writing reports for the War and Indian Departments and arranging details for the remainder of the survey.

While laying over, Stevens sent John Mix Stanley north to the Cypress Hills camp of the Piegans to ask them to come to Fort Benton to council with Stevens.[12] Stanley planned to meet Little Dog, the Piegan chief who was Natawista's cousin,[13] considered one of the "bravest and proudest" Indians and a man of "character and probity."[14]

A "fine looking specimen . . . over six feet in height, straight as an arrow,"[15] Little Dog took Stanley into his lodge where the tribal leaders

---

[6]Senate ExDocs 1 (33-2) 746, p. 406.  [7]Hazard Stevens, Vol. I, p. 357.
[8]Senate ExDocs 1 (33-2) 746, p. 407.  [9]Hazard Stevens, Vol. I, p. 355.
[10]Hazard Stevens, Vol. I, p. 358.  [11]Richards, p. 118.
[12]Hazard Stevens, Vol. I, p. 368. Stevens identified this as the "main camp of the Blackfeet." Ewers, *Blackfeet*, p. 209, identifies it as the Piegan camp.
[13]Holterman, p. 57; Taylor, "The Major's Blackfoot Bride," p. 45.
[14]McDonnell, *MHSC*, Vol. X, p. 255  [15]McDonnell, *MHSC*, Vol. X, p. 255.

gathered to hear his message. After smoking the pipe, Stanley asked the Indians to come to Fort Benton "to council with the chief sent by their Great Father." Stanley then spread his invitation from lodge to lodge. By nightfall, his summons had been accepted. The next morning, in "one of the most picturesque scenes," the delegates began their journey south.[16]

The thirty Piegan chiefs, with their families, reached Fort Benton on September 20th. The next day, the governor convened his council. The chiefs, "richly caparisoned [in] dresses of softly prepared skins of deer, elk, or antelope . . . elegantly ornamented with bead-work," had dressed well to meet their Great Father's representative and complained that Stevens had not reciprocated: "[W]hy do you not wear the dress of a chief?"[17] Stevens's feeble excuses did little to assuage the Indians' sense that they were not being accorded due respect.

The governor delivered the same speech that he had given the Gros Ventres. Low Horn, a principal Piegan chief, responded favorably but pointed out the difficulty in restraining the young warriors "who were wild, and ambitious in their turn to be braves and chiefs." Stevens, noting the tribe paid a high price for this, pointed to polygyny. Potential husbands were lost with high battle casualties. "Won't your women," Stevens asked, "prefer husbands to scalps and horses?" The governor then asked the Piegans to attend a regional peace council the next summer. Low Horn, after consulting his warriors, agreed.[18]

Stevens had now secured the agreement of all concerned parties for next summer's conference. Reflecting on his success, he acknowledged Natawista's important contributions. Throughout the journey, the Culbertsons had pitched their tent beyond the sentry line to be more accessible to the tribes. There, Natawista "was in constant intercourse with the Indians, and inspired them with perfect confidence."

After observing her, Stevens realized it was "a great mistake to suppose the Indians to be the silent, unsociable people they are commonly represented to be." Instead, he found them to be "the most talkative, gossipping (*sic*) people I have ever seen." One evening, a group of Indians gathered around Natawista had erupted into "loud shouts of merry laughter." When Stevens inquired about the episode, he learned that Natawista had been entertaining "her simple Indian friends" with stories of the curi-

---

[16]Senate ExDocs 1 (33-2) 746, p. 408.    [17]Hazard Stevens, Vol. I, p. 373.
[18]Hazard Stevens, Vol. I, p. 374.

ous manners of St. Louis's female elite and a fat woman she had seen exhibited there.[19]

In his final report to the Commissioner of Indian Affairs, Stevens thanked Natawista for rendering "the highest service to the expedition, a service which demands public acknowledgement."[20] Sometime later, at a St. Louis dinner for the Culbertsons hosted by the AFC, the governor presented her with a silver loving cup lined with gold and engraved "To the Second Pocahontas."[21]

With the eastern survey completed and the groundwork laid for the proposed council, Isaac Stevens and his party prepared to head west. Stevens praised Alexander Culbertson "for the efficient aid you have rendered to the exploration... and for your services in connection with Indian affairs." The governor found in Culbertson "a spirit of patience and kindness which has never flagged, and an ascendancy over these tribes which could only have been gained by a just and decisive course towards them."[22]

Now Stevens asked Culbertson to travel to Washington, D.C., to lobby for an appropriation for the proposed conference.[23] The two men had frequently discussed the need for a treaty between the Blackfeet and Gros Ventres, "these hitherto neglected tribes," who had not participated in the 1851 Horse Creek Treaty.[24]

Stevens believed that Culbertson, despite his political inexperience, was uniquely qualified to lobby Congress because of his long experience on the upper Missouri. Culbertson could explain the progress the Blackfeet and Gros Ventres had made "from the wild wanderers of the plains to kind and hospitable neighbors." Now, the time was "ripe for a decisive course."[25]

---

[19] Senate ExDocs 1 (33-2) 746, p. 404.   [20] Senate ExDocs 1 (33-2) 746, p. 403.

[21] Berglund, SC 414, MtHS, pp. 51-52. The cup was subsequently destroyed, along with other Indian artifacts owned by the Culbertson family, in a fire. It is not clear when this cup was presented or what fire destroyed it. From Fannie Culbertson's account, it would seem that the cup was destroyed in a fire after it had passed into her possession. However, it may have been destroyed in the fire that destroyed a number of Culbertson properties in Chambersburg, PA, during the Civil War.

[22] Isaac I. Stevens to Alexander Culbertson, 21 Sep 1853, House ExDocs 1 (33-1) 710, p. 463.

[23] Bradley, *MHSC*, Vol. III, p. 269.   [24] House ExDocs 1 (33-1) 710, p. 463.

[25] House ExDocs 1 (33-1) 710, p. 463.

Stevens furnished Culbertson letters of introduction to members of Congress as well as a written request to the Commissioner of Indian Affairs seeking an appropriation of $60,000 including $30,000 for presents, $5,000 for provisions, $10,000 to send a delegation to Washington, and $15,000 for "miscellaneous expenses."

Stevens also recommended the government build a steamboat for the Indian service which, if properly designed, could ascend the river to Fort Benton. Stevens hoped Culbertson could secure the appropriation, purchase supplies, and be back on the upper Missouri in time for a late summer conference.[26]

Culbertson, although reluctant to spend his winter in Washington, D.C., agreed. On September 22, 1853, with cannons booming, he left Fort Benton with Natawista and thirty survey party members whose services were no longer required. The group included Lt. Rufus Saxton whom Stevens had charged with studying the upper Missouri's navigability from Fort Benton to Fort Union.[27]

Culbertson ordered an eighty-foot mackinaw, christened the *Blackfoot*, built for the journey.[28] The trip proved difficult with the season late and the river low. High winds, a frequent feature of fall weather, made it nearly impossible to maneuver the unwieldy mackinaw through the river's crooked channels, waylaying the travelers on several occasions. Passing some AFC employees coming upriver, Saxton marveled at the cordellers' ability "to endure an immense amount of fatigue and exposure" and "toil on uncomplaining." Someday, he hoped steamboats could replace "this uncouth and laborious mode of navigating this magnificent river."[29]

The group reached Fort Union after eleven days. On the surrounding plains, buffalo extended "in every direction as far as the eye could see." The Assiniboines, fresh from a bountiful hunt, invited the travelers to share their table. But Culbertson was anxious to press on and the group spent only one night at Fort Union.[30]

The voyage now became even more difficult. High winds hindered daylight travel while snags and sandbars complicated night travel. On October 8, a snag passed over the mackinaw's bow, breaking three oars.

---

[26]House ExDocs 1 (33-1) 710, p. 464.   [27]House ExDocs 1 (33-1) 129, p. 217.
[28]House ExDocs 1 (33-1) 129, p. 217, 236.
[29]House ExDocs 1 (33-1) 129, pp. 236-237.
[30]House ExDocs 1 (33-1) 129, p. 237.

Another lodged under the *Blackfoot* and threatened to break through the bottom. Stranded in the middle of the river, the crew struggled valiantly, but unsuccessfully, to free the craft. Fearing the mackinaw might sink, the men built a small raft to save themselves if the worst occurred. The next day, they finally managed to lift the boat off the snag, to the relief of Saxton who feared that "a walk from here to St. Louis would be anything but pleasant."[31]

Arriving at Fort Berthold, Saxton and Culbertson visited in the "exceedingly comfortable" Gros Ventre lodges. Saxton believed the tribe "well disposed towards the whites" but was reminded that the plight of the young warriors posed a significant obstacle to peace. To gain status, a young male had to demonstrate bravery, usually by raiding enemy tribes and stealing their horses. If the tribes agreed to forego these raids, how would a young man prove his worth?

After the meeting, the travelers continued downstream where they found themselves shrouded in dense smoke, producing "a very injurious effect upon the eyes." A band of Dakota Sioux had recently visited the Arikara villages to trade. As they left for their buffalo hunt, the Dakotas set fire to the prairie to push the buffalo in front of them. Saxton condemned this "dastardly malignity" since the fires not only kept the buffalo from the Arikara villages but also deprived that tribe of the forage necessary to sustain their horse and cattle herds.[32]

But the Dakotas' hostility threatened more than the Arikaras. As the mackinaw rounded a bend below Fort Clark, the white entourage confronted angry Dakota warriors on both shores, demanding that the *Blackfoot* halt. "Disobedience would have brought down a shower of destructive missiles" and so "pride yielded to prudence, and the *Blackfoot* was brought to shore."

The warriors, in a "somewhat saucy and peremptory" mood, demanded tobacco. Saxton explained they had "not come from a tobacco country" and had little to offer. If true, it is curious that Culbertson, an experienced traveler in Indian country, was caught unprepared since commodities such as tobacco constituted an insurance policy for safe river passage. In any case, Saxton gave the warriors a small amount of tobacco from his personal stash and then, judging the warriors to be "bent on mischief," quickly reboarded the *Blackfoot*.

---

[31]House ExDocs 1 (33-1) 129, p. 238.  [32]House ExDocs 1 (33-1) 129, p. 239.

As the crew pushed off, an arrow struck the boat. Saxton, the trained soldier, craved retaliation. But since no specific offender could be identified, Culbertson argued against a rash response and the *Blackfoot* continued. Before long, the crew spotted an older warrior swimming alongside the mackinaw. He asked to board, offering to escort the group safely through his tribe's lands.

Culbertson agreed. Once aboard the warrior apologized for his tribe's earlier actions, blaming the errant arrow on a young warrior with a "bad heart." He swore the majority had not condoned the action. Culbertson accepted his explanation and the warrior accompanied them until, "soon after sunset," the group reached the main Dakota encampment.

There, on the river's left bank "under a commanding bluff," some three hundred warriors "covered" the cliff. The accompanying chief spoke to his people, assuring them that the white men intended no harm. After distributing a small amount of tobacco, the group was permitted to "proceed without molestation or insult." Culbertson, not wishing to tempt fate, directed the crew to travel through the night to get beyond the Dakota lands.

Meanwhile, Saxton brooded, convinced that the Dakotas held the white men "in a good deal of contempt" and were "sadly in need of a lesson."[33] This opinion was shared by Alfred Vaughan who, the following March, informed Superintendent of Indian Affairs Alfred Cumming that "nothing I fear short of Troops will be of any avail" in calming the Dakotas' hostile attitudes.[34]

At Fort Pierre, Lt. Saxton learned more about how the Sioux regarded the white man's encroachment. Most of the Yanktons who traded at the post were away on a buffalo hunt. Buffalo in the area were "exceedingly scarce," leaving the tribe in "much distress."[35] The remaining warriors requested a council.

A young man confronted Saxton: "We have been told that the Great Father, in sending us all these presents, does it in order that, in time, he can take our lands from us. If that is the case, we do not want presents; we can buy from the traders all we want." The Indian challenged the government's plans: "Some of our warriors have staid (*sic*) at home and raised

---

[33] House ExDocs 1 (33-1) 129, p. 240.
[34] Alfred Vaughan to Alfred Cumming, 6 Mar 1854. NAM, M234/885.
[35] Alfred Vaughan to Alfred Cumming, 6 Mar 1854. NAM, M234/885.

corn and pumpkins, instead of going out to hunt, steal horses, or make war. Their crops have failed; and, in consequence, in the long winters they have been poor and hungry." Although the warrior claimed his tribe wanted to follow the Great Father's advice, he asked: "But what shall we do? The buffalo is our only friend. When they disappear, it is all over with the Dacotahs (*sic*)."

Saxton responded that "it was not the Great Father's object to get away the Indians' land; that he was rich and powerful, and had more land already than he wanted." Saxton insisted that the government sent presents because the Great Father "was anxious that the whites and Indians should be friends" and that "there was room enough for Indians as well as white men." He urged the warriors not to judge white men by the actions of a few since the "great mass" of them, and especially the Great Father, were their friends.

Saxton also denied that the government wanted the Indians to stop hunting. The government simply sought an end to intertribal raids. The lieutenant echoed the themes of Governor Stevens: these battles cost many young lives and, as a consequence, the Indian race was "growing weaker and weaker every year" in contrast to whites who "by pursuing a different policy, were growing stronger and stronger."

The warrior listened attentively before vowing that, while war might come, "I want life for myself and my family." He asked for a document declaring him the white man's friend. Saxton agreed and, after giving the warrior a few additional presents, the two "parted friends."[36]

Saxton's words, translated by Culbertson, were very familiar. In the past few years, Culbertson had heard them so often that he was beginning to feel somewhat uncomfortable about their reliability. It was, of course, true that the white men had plenty of land. But was it true that they did not covet those of the Indians?

From experience, Culbertson knew that Indians and whites could live together in relative peace. But this required a large dose of patience and understanding. These days, the white men Culbertson saw entering the region were men in a hurry, men with little desire to listen and learn from those who had lived on these lands for longer than anyone knew. Culbertson faithfully translated the lieutenant's words but, increasingly, he harbored doubts about their veracity.

---

[36]House ExDocs 1 (33-1) 129, pp. 241-242.

On November 8, after nearly seven weeks on the river, the *Blackfoot* ran aground a few miles below St. Joseph. Fortunately, the steamboat *Honduras* soon appeared and, the next day, the Fort Benton travelers transferred their supplies to the steamer and, with the *Blackfoot* in tow, headed for St. Louis.[37]

Culbertson spent two weeks in St. Louis before heading for Washington, D.C.[38] With Christmas approaching, he only had time for brief meetings. Culbertson presented the introductory letters from Governor Stevens to legislators, offered a brief assessment of their proposal, and promised to return after the holidays.

Culbertson informed Stevens that Senator Donald R. Atchison, "a very worthy Man and Gentleman," offered high praise for their proposal.[39] Atchison lived in Platte City, Missouri, undoubtedly knew many in the American Fur Company hierarchy, and understood the economic importance of peaceful relations among the upriver tribes. As president pro tempore of the Senate and past chairman of the Committee on Indian Affairs,[40] Atchison's support was essential to obtaining the necessary appropriation. Therefore, his pledge to "do every thing in his power to forward" the plan delighted Culbertson. Similar pledges were secured from senators James Shields of Illinois and Augustus C. Dodge of Wisconsin.

The proposal, however, had not been as warmly received by the Commissioner of Indian Affairs. For the moment, Commissioner Manypenny dismissed Culbertson's entreaties, instructing him to return in January when the issue could be more fully examined. Moreover, he held out slim hopes for a government steamboat; utilizing contract agents seemed more economical.[41] This could not have disappointed Culbertson since the American Fur Company was likely to win any contract to transport goods upriver. With nothing more to be accomplished before the holidays, Culbertson headed to Chambersburg where, for the first time in more than twenty years, he spent Christmas with his family.[42]

---

[37] House ExDocs 1 (33-1) 129, p. 243.   [38] Bradley, *MHSC*, Vol. III, p. 270.

[39] Alexander Culbertson, Chambersburg, Pennsylvania, to Governor I.I. Stevens, 26 Dec 1853. SC 586, MtHS.   [40] *Biographical Directory*, p. 552.

[41] Alexander Culbertson, Chambersburg, Pennsylvania, to Gov. I.I. Stevens, 26 Dec 1853. SC 586, MtHS.

[42] Alexander Culbertson, Chambersburg, Pennsylvania, to Gov. I.I. Stevens, 26 Dec 1853. SC 586, MtHS.

Natawista may have accompanied Culbertson to Chambersburg, creating "some flutter and excitement...." "'Alexander is bringing his Indian wife home,' was whispered from one to another. 'What will she be like? What will we do with her, and for her? How will we entertain her? How will she fit into this life of ours?'" These anxieties evaporated when Natawista, with her "pleasing, graceful ways" appeared. "Her confident manner made everything easy and natural" and she was received with "whole-hearted approval." At least that is how her daughter, Fannie, told the story. Whether this was but another of Fannie's romantic ideations will never be known.[43]

While in Chambersburg, Culbertson also visited the Rocky Spring cemetery to pay respects to his mother, grandfather, and dear brother, Thaddeus.[44] Thaddeus's tragic death, only sixteen months earlier, continued to haunt the family. Joseph and Frances Culbertson, knowing how much his western travels had meant to Thaddeus, presented Alexander with the small, dark, leather-bound journal Thaddeus had kept during his journey. The journal became one of Culbertson's most precious possessions which he carried until the day he died.[45]

Following the holidays, Culbertson returned to Washington, D.C. In addition to meeting with President Franklin Pierce[46] and Commissioner Manypenny, Culbertson lobbied both the Senate Committee on Indian Affairs, chaired by Senator William Sebastian of Arkansas, and the House Committee on Indian Affairs, under Representative James Orr of

---

[43]Berglund, SC 414, MtHS, pp. 6-7. Fannie Culbertson implies that this trip happened shortly after Alexander and Natawista were married. However, Culbertson's schedule and the documentary record preclude any such trip prior to this time. Clifford, Section III, p. 26, suggests a date of 1848 for the trip, but this, also, is refuted by the documentary record. The Culbertsons' great-grandson, George Taylor, does not believe Natawista ever visited Chambersburg. (Personal communications with the author.) While it is known that Natawista traveled downriver with Alexander Culbertson, how far she went is a mystery. As so often happens, it is simply impossible to track her movements with certainty. The author remains unconvinced that Natawista ever visited the family in Chambersburg but, if she did, it probably happened at this time.

[44]Although both the graves of Culbertson's mother and grandfather can still be found in Rocky Spring Cemetery, there is no marked grave for Thaddeus Culbertson. KHS confirms that some headstones were lost in the years that the church was abandoned.

[45]This is the author's conclusion based on the fact that the journal ended up in the possession of Culbertson's grandson, Alexander Culbertson Roberts, the son of Julia Culbertson Roberts. It is now in the Culbertson Collection, MoHS.

[46]Bradley, *MHSC*, Vol. III, p. 270.

South Carolina.⁴⁷ In early February, he wrote Stevens that his "feeble" efforts seemed to be bearing fruit: "I believe we can safely state that not the least disapproval of the appropriations has been thus far made."⁴⁸

Commissioner Manypenny, however, was not yet willing to commit to the plan. Culbertson reported that Manypenny "has said nothing for or against my remaining in the position as special agent," but Culbertson claimed "this honour does not matter" since he and Stevens understood their agreement. With or without the title, Culbertson declared himself "determined to render the assistance expected of me in the proposed council."⁴⁹

Culbertson, in appealing to Congress, relied on his experiences among the Blackfeet to dispel their reputation as "predatory and intractable savages."⁵⁰ Unfortunately, his account clashed dramatically with another received that spring from the upper Missouri.

The previous fall, Stevens had ordered Lt. John Mullan to the Bitterroot Valley to collect weather data and to serve as envoy to the Flathead Indians,⁵¹ whom Stevens hoped to include in the upcoming council. On November 18, 1853, Mullan wrote Stevens with disturbing news about relations between the Blackfeet and Flatheads.

The lieutenant bemoaned the "want of attention and care on the part of the government" that the Flatheads received. Moreover, he informed the governor that the Blackfeet had kept their promise to remain at peace "most faithlessly," stealing Flathead horses and then selling them to AFC employees at Fort Benton. Mullan claimed the Company's subterfuge gave "encouragement to [the Blackfeet's] thieving propensities."⁵²

Mullan had concluded that, while the proposed council might bring some benefit, it alone would be ineffectual. The Blackfeet needed to be taught a harsh lesson:

> [O]ur military force should be sent among them, put every man, woman and child to the knife, burn down their villages, and thus teach the nation that, since persuasion will not, force must and shall, effect he (*sic*) ends we have in view.

---

⁴⁷*Biographical Directory*, p. 1786 and p. 1593.
⁴⁸Alexander Culbertson, Washington City, to Isaac I. Stevens, 9 Feb 1854. SC 586, MtHS.
⁴⁹Alexander Culbertson, Washington City, to Isaac I. Stevens, 9 Feb 1854. SC 586, MtHS.
⁵⁰Hazard Stevens, Vol. I, p. 302.   ⁵¹Richards, p. 126.
⁵²Lt. John Mullan, Camp Stevens on the Bitterroot River, to Governor Isaac I. Stevens, 18 Nov 1853. House MiscDocs 59 (33-1) 741, p. 4.

This would not only set a "salutary example," it might secure a lasting peace. The Blackfeet "had better by far be totally exterminated, than thus left to prowl the mountains, murdering, plundering, and carrying everything before them."[53] Branding them "hell-hounds" and "devils," Mullan asserted that "the word 'Blackfoot' has become the by-word of terror and fear among all the tribes of Indians west of the Rocky Mountains."[54]

Whether Culbertson saw this letter is unknown, but Governor Stevens forwarded it to Commissioner Manypenny along with a more temperate cover letter. He suggested that the chiefs probably were honoring their promises, with the problems likely stemming from the young men. Nonetheless, Stevens agreed that "a stringent course" might be required "to compel [the young warriors] to abandon their accustomed depredations."

Although Stevens "would still further try the influence of kindness," he requested a strong military presence for the council and suggested establishing a military post near Fort Benton in the near future. He added that, if "after a fair trial . . . outrages continued to be committed; the force of government should be brought to bear upon them with great weight."[55]

These letters apparently did more to convince Commissioner Manypenny of the need for the peace council than Culbertson's more pacific entreaties. In forwarding them to Secretary of the Interior McClelland, Manypenny firmly backed the council "so that in case any disastrous consequences [resulting from further Blackfeet depredations] follow . . . the responsibility will not rest with this department."[56]

Despite Manypenny's appeals, the wheels of government moved slowly. By spring, Culbertson realized that the necessary appropriation would not be approved in time for a summer conference. The winter's activities had been, for Culbertson, "the most distasteful proceeding" of his life.[57] The unpleasantness had been broken only by an unexpected encounter.

One day, while "walking quietly like an Indian" along the streets of Washington, D.C., Culbertson chanced upon the studio of John Mix

---

[53]Lt. John Mullan, Camp Stevens on the Bitterroot River, to Governor Isaac I. Stevens, 18 Nov 1853. House MiscDocs 59 (33-1) 741, p. 5.

[54]Lt. John Mullan, Camp Stevens on the Bitterroot River, to Governor Isaac I. Stevens, 18 Nov 1853. House MiscDocs 59 (33-1) 741, p. 4.

[55]Governor Isaac I. Stevens, Olympia, Washington Territory, to Commissioner George W. Manypenny, 31 Jan 1854. House MiscDocs 59 (33-1) 741, p. 2.

[56]Commissioner George Manypenny to Secretary of the Interior, R. McClelland, 31 Mar 1854. House MiscDocs 59 (33-1) 741, p. 2.

[57]Bradley, *MHSC*, Vol. III, p. 270.

Stanley, the artist who had accompanied the Stevens railroad survey. Culbertson entered, greeting his old friend warmly. The artist enthusiastically showed the trader a just completed painting of Fort Benton: "Do you remember that?" "Remember?" Culbertson exclaimed happily, "why it is *my own home*—the fort I built myself—the broad plain, the river, the hills, I know every one of them! . . . And those Blackfoot crossing the river, with their horses and their buffalo skin canoes, just as I've seen them a thousand times. The encampment yonder seems almost real to me." But even this bright interlude made Culbertson melancholy: "You make me long to be off over the plains again."[58]

In early May, Culbertson left Washington, D.C., to return to the upper Missouri. Arriving in St. Louis on May 17, 1854, he learned from the newspaper that Stevens had recently arrived in the nation's capital. The two had missed each other by days. Culbertson wrote Stevens that their plans "had been rejected."[59] Although he held out hope that Stevens could "put things through" so that "eventually the Blkfeet Nation will become the Children of the Great Father," for now he only wished to return to his beloved "Children of the mountains."[60]

Alexander Culbertson, who for years had been hailed as a skilled diplomat and trustworthy envoy, was learning the unhappy truth that politics and diplomacy were different endeavors.

---

[58]"John Mix Stanley, 1843-1868, Scrapbook." It was probably durng this winter in Washington, D.C., that Culbertson posed for his portrait by Stanley. (See illustration, p. 234.) That Culbertson is clean-shaven in the Stanley portrait suggests he altered his appearance to present a "more civilized" face in Washington.
[59]Bradley, *MHSC*, Vol. III, p. 270.
[60]Alexander Culbertson, St. Louis, MO, to Gov. Isacc I. Stevens, 17 May 1854. SC 586, MtHS.

ALEXANDER CULBERTSON
Portrait by John Mix Stanley, probably painted in Washington, D.C., circa 1854. Culbertson may be clean-shaven because he was lobbying Congress for funds for the Blackfeet Treaty Council.
Courtesy of Idaho State Historical Society.

NATAWISTA, CIRCA 1859
Natawista appears much heavier in this photograph than in others, perhaps as a result of her recent pregnancy.
Courtesy of George H.R. Taylor, Bethesda, Maryland.

Rocky Spring Presbyterian Church near Chambersburg, Pennsylvania. Culbertson worshipped in this church, built in 1794, when he was a boy. The graves of his mother and maternal grandfather can still be found in the cemetery.
Courtesy of Larry Jansen.

Alexander Culbertson and Natawista, with their son Joe, in a photograph taken in Peoria, Illinois, circa 1863.
Courtesy of Montana Historical Society.

Joseph "Joe" Culbertson,
circa 1863.
Courtesy State Historical Society
of North Dakota. Henry
Boller Collection.

Jane "Janie" Culbertson
An unknown individual wrote on this photo "circa 1866, age 15 or 16." In 1866, Janie would have been closer to thirty years of age.
Courtesy of Montana Historical Society.

Identified as a photo of Janie Culbertson by an unknown individual, others have suggested this is a photograph of Natawista. Note that the book is upside down. Does this indicate a woman with no formal education, such as Natawista? The facial features bear a resemblance both to Natawista and Janie. The hair does not seem to match that of either of them.
Courtesy State Historical Society of North Dakota. Henry Boller Collection.

John "Jack" Culbertson, circa 1863.
Courtesy State Historical Society of North Dakota.
Henry Boller Collection.

Frances "Fannie" Culbertson, circa 1863. The identification of this photograph has long been in doubt. Descendants of Robert Simpson Culbertson identified it as Natawista although clearly this is not a woman in her forties. The discovery of the photographs of the other children in the Henry Boller Collection at North Dakota Historical Society makes it clear that this is a photo of Fannie, the fourth in the series.
Courtesy of John G. Lepley,
Fort Benton, Montana.

Julia Culbertson, circa 1863.
Courtesy State Historical Society of North Dakota.
Henry Boller Collection.

[above] Seen From Afar by John Mix Stanley. This painting, identified as "Cayuse Man," was executed by Stanley as part of his studies for "Barter for a Bride" and "The Last of Their Race." Contemporaneous newspaper accounts establish that Stanley's model for the warrior in those paintings was Seen From Afar, Natawista's brother. How it came to be identified as a Cayuse Indian is unknown. Oil on paper, 23.5 x 32.4.
Courtesy Stark Museum of Art, Orange, Texas.

[top, left] Rev. Pierre Jean De Smet, circa 1863.
Courtesy of Montana Historical Society.

[left] Malcolm Clarke, 1817-1869.
Courtesy of Montana Historical Society.

"Fort Union on the Missouri." 1833, by Karl Bodmer.
Courtesy Joslyn Art Museum, Omaha, Nebraska; Gift of Enron Art Foundation.

"The Travellers meeting with Minatarre Indians near
Fort Clark." 1833, by Karl Bodmer.
Courtesy Joslyn Art Museum, Omaha, Nebraska; Gift of Enron Art Foundation.

"Fort Benton, taken from *Harper's Monthly*, October 1867.
'Rides Through Montana,' by Thomas F. Meagher, p. 570."
Courtesy of Montana Historical Society.

This sketch by Gustavus Sohon, "Indians Gathered to Hear White Speaker," depicts the 1855 Treaty Council held by Issac I. Stevens.
Courtesy of Washington State Historical Society.

"Barter for a Bride," John Mix Stanley. The artist used Natawista and Seen From Afar as models. The painting, originally known as "A Family Group," hangs in the Diplomatic Reception Rooms at the United States Department of State.
Courtesy U.S. Department of State.

"The Last of Their Race" by John Mix Stanley. Oil on canvas. (88.9 x 132.1) Completed circa 1857, this painting was originally owned by Alexander Culbertson and depicts Natawista sitting on a rock next to her brother, Seen From Afar. Originally titled "The Last of His Race," Culbertson changed the title. The painting was sold at auction in Peoria, Illinois, when Culbertson went bankrupt.
Courtesy Stark Museum of Art, Orange, Texas.

[Above] The home in Orleans, Nebraska, previously owned by Julia Culbertson and George Roberts where Alexander Culbertson died in August 1879.
[Right] Culbertson's grave, Orleans, Nebraska. Local citizens spearheaded a drive to mark the grave in 1951 after Charles Hanson discovered that Culbertson was buried there.
All photos on this page ourtesy of Larry Jansen.

Cemetery in Stand-off, Alberta, Canada, where Natawista is buried. Most of the graves are marked only by simple wooden crosses. The exact location of Natwista's grave is unknown.

Chapter Twenty

# *"gradually reclaim the Indians from a nomadic life"*

Political winds buffeted the American Fur Company shortly before Alexander Culbertson reached St. Louis that May. Bids to transport the year's Indian annuities had been opened on April 10 and, to the chagrin of the AFC, Superintendent of Indian Affairs Alfred Cumming awarded the contract to Robert Campbell, long-time rival of the Chouteau family and financial backer of Harvey, Primeau and Company.

After replacing David Mitchell as Superintendent, Cumming had expressed dismay about the 1853 contract. The AFC, Cumming claimed, took advantage of the lack of competition to exact "an exorbitant price" for transportation. Cumming pointed out that the same steamboat "under a previous agreement" had carried Governor Stevens's supplies much more cheaply.[1]

Cumming's scathing attack on the contract and, by inference, the previous superintendent, prompted Mitchell to castigate his successor for his "unfortunate" missive "in which he takes upon himself the gratuitous labor of censuring my conduct." The former superintendent noted that Cumming had added $5,000 worth of "ridiculous" supplies, despite the excessive prices of which he complained. Mitchell suggested that "our zealous Supt" must have been under some "stultifying influence when he purchased 13,392 pounds of white beans." Mitchell pointed out that the Indians "never saw, or heard of such an article of food before! Were it not for the loss to the Govt & the Indians," Mitchell concluded, "the thing would be truly laughable!"[2]

That spring, Cumming used his authority to punish the AFC for their perceived greed in 1853. Alfred Vaughan, agent for the upper Missouri tribes, also expressed his displeasure over awarding the contract to Robert Campbell: "candor forces me to say . . . that for various reasons I regret

---
[1] Alfred Cumming to George Manypenny, 21 May 1853. NAM, M234/885.
[2] David Mitchell to George Manypenny, 29 Jul 1853. Emphasis in original. NAM, M234/885.

that P. Chouteau Jr. & Co. did not prevail over all others." While Vaughan conceded that Campbell was a "highly honorable and responsible Gentleman," the agent doubted that his operation could provide the necessary assistance since Campbell would be hurrying "every foot of the way there and back." By contrast, the AFC routinely supplied Vaughan with "good and secure houses to store the goods ... and furnished me help at all times required to aid me in distributing" the annuities.[3]

Regardless, the contract had been let and the AFC, to the consternation of the St. Louis partners, had lost.[4] Culbertson tried to salvage some of the profitable annuity transportation business by submitting a discounted bid to convey the Crow annuities from Fort Union to Fort Sarpy.[5] When this was accepted, Culbertson agreed to assist Vaughan in distributing annuities near Fort Union.[6]

Culbertson and Vaughan arrived at Fort Union in early July. The two had become good friends and Vaughan frequently relied on Culbertson's long experience to guide his judgments. That summer, they found conditions on the upper river unsettled by "continual warfare" between the Assiniboines and "one or two bands of Sioux."

Hostile bands of Hunkpapa and Blackfeet Sioux had killed several Assiniboines, driving off "the greater portion" of their horses.[7] The Assiniboines believed the 1851 Horse Creek Treaty prevented them from retaliating.[8] Vaughan increasingly worried about the treaty and its designation of chiefs. During the annuity distribution, he observed several Assiniboine chiefs "more intelligent and tractable" than Fool Bear, some of whom "ranked higher as war-chiefs than the *Bear*."[9]

Business interests required Culbertson to remain at Fort Union throughout the summer although he was anxious to meet with the Black-

---

[3] Alfred Vaughan to George Manypenny, 11 Apr 1854. NAM, M234/885.

[4] J. B. Sarpy to Pierre Chouteau, 4 May 1854. Chouteau-Papin Collection, MoHS.

[5] Alexander Culbertson for Pierre Chouteau, Jr. & Co., to Col. A. Vaughan, 7 Jul 1854. NAM, M234/885.

[6] Alfred J. Vaughan, Fort Pierre, to Col. Alfred Cumming, 19 Oct 1854. Senate ExDocs 1 (33-2) 746, p. 289. Vaughan refers to Culbertson as "Major A. Culbertson," the first known reference using this title.

[7] Alexander Culbertson, Fort Union, to Isaac I. Stevens, 1 Jul 1854. MtHS; Alfred J. Vaughan, Fort Pierre, to Col. Alfred Cumming, 19 Oct 1854. Senate ExDocs 1 (33-2) 746, p. 289. Vaughan, not Culbertson, identifies the bands as Hunkpapa and Blackfeet Sioux.

[8] Alfred J. Vaughan, Fort Pierre, to Col. Alfred Cumming, 19 Oct 1854. Senate ExDocs 1 (33-2) 746, p. 289.

[9] Alfred J. Vaughan, Fort Pierre, to Col. Alfred Cumming, 19 Oct 1854. Senate ExDocs 1 (33-2) 746, p. 289. Italics in original.

feet who he feared would react badly when the anticipated treaty conference failed to materialize. He was encouraged, though, by reports that the Blackfeet had behaved "remarkably well" during the winter, in contrast to Lt. Mullan's account. So anxious were the Blackfeet that Little Dog, the Piegan chief, had traveled to Fort Pierre to meet the steamboat, hoping to accompany Governor Stevens to Fort Benton. Upon learning that the council had been delayed, a "disappointed" Little Dog remained with Culbertson at Fort Union.[10]

Finally, at the beginning of September, Culbertson prepared to leave for Fort Benton, hoping "if possible, to make something out of the Blackfeet [trade]." The loss of the annuity contract weighed heavily. Without the government subsidy, the AFC faced greater expenses and Culbertson hoped a good Blackfeet trade might offset those costs.[11]

Culbertson, Natawista, and Little Dog arrived at Fort Benton on September 28. The next day, the Culbertsons threw a ball for the employees, a grand affair "at which two only of the number made a sorry display of their reasons." Little work occurred the next day as "the effects of intemperance [were] a little noticeable."[12]

Even as the Fort Benton employees celebrated, news filtered into Washington, D.C., of an alarming event near Fort Laramie.

Throughout July 1854, the valley east of Fort Laramie filled with Oglala, Miniconjou, Brulé Sioux, and Northern Cheyennes awaiting their annuities. Although the goods had reached Fort Laramie, Indian agent Major J. W. Whitfield had not. Thus, the goods remained in storage while the Indians waited impatiently and their food and forage dwindled.[13]

On the afternoon of August 18, a party of Mormon emigrants entered the valley. A sore-footed, nearly dead cow wandered into the Brulé encampment. High Forehead, a Miniconjou Sioux, killed the animal which the nearly destitute Indians butchered for meat.

Conquering Bear, the Brulé who had reluctantly accepted designation as Sioux chief at Horse Creek, immediately realized the potential consequences of this act and headed to Fort Laramie to offer a horse as compensation for the emigrants' property. This did not satisfy the emigrants.

---

[10] Alexander Culbertson, Fort Union, to Isaac I. Stevens, 1 Jul 1854. SC 586, MtHS.
[11] Alexander Culbertson to Charles Galpin, 6 Sep 1854. Chouteau-Maffitt Collection, MoHS.
[12] "Fort Benton Journal," *MHSC*, Vol. X, p. 1.
[13] McCann, reprint booklet, pp. 5-6.

Lt. Hugh Fleming, in charge at Fort Laramie, considered the incident trivial and did little to effect a compromise.[14]

The next morning, the Indians sent the respected Oglala chief, Man Afraid of His Horses, to Fort Laramie to confer with the military officers. Again, the meeting resolved nothing. Lt. John Grattan, a "rather boisterous, swash-buckling youth, anxious for a notch on his gun," asked to arrest High Forehead. Lt. Fleming acceded, but warned Grattan "to be careful not to hazard an engagement without certainty of success." Grattan recruited thirty-one enthusiastic volunteers and set off.[15]

En route, the soldiers drank freely. One infantryman complained, "They are drunk and we will all get killed...."[16] As the men neared the large Indian encampment late on the afternoon of August 19, Grattan told his men: "When I give the order you may fire as much as you damned please."[17]

At the camp, Grattan asked Conquering Bear to surrender High Forehead. The Brulé chief explained that the Miniconjous were not subject to his authority. High Forehead refused to surrender, saying he preferred to die. The Indians again offered compensation, but Grattan was not interested.[18]

Instead, he ordered a volley fired, mortally wounding Conquering Bear and another warrior. Outraged, the Oglalas and Brulés felled Grattan with arrows. So savage was their attack that army officials had to identify Grattan by his pocket watch. Grattan's command scattered in panic. The Indians quickly overwhelmed and killed Grattan's entire outfit.[19]

For the next two days, the Sioux struck nearby locations. They seized their annuities, knowing they would be denied them under the treaty's provisions. Finally, the Indians departed, leaving the soldiers at Fort Laramie severely shaken.[20]

Repercussions from the attack extended far beyond Fort Laramie. Alfred Vaughan, writing from Fort Pierre on October 19, described the situation in that region as "perilous in the extreme." He exhorted the government to send "a sufficient number of troops of the *proper kind*" to "chastise [the Indians] in such a manner that they will not only respect, but fear the government in future." Otherwise, Vaughan feared, "there is no knowing to what extent they will commit murder and depredations on the whites."

A few days earlier, Vaughan had taken tobacco and other provisions to

---

[14]McCann, reprint booklet, pp. 6-7.
[15]McCann, reprint article, pp. 8-9.
[16]McCann, reprint article, p. 11.
[17]McCann, reprint article, p. 12.
[18]McCann, reprint article, pp. 13-14.
[19]McCann, reprint article, pp. 19-20.
[20]McCann, reprint article, pp. 21-25.

the Yankton village. The Yanktons ripped open the bags and scattered the contents. The Hunkpapa and Blackfeet Sioux at Fort Clark had also refused Vaughan's goods, telling him they "preferred the liberty to take scalps, and commit whatever depredations they pleased, in preference to goods from their Great Father." Vaughan warned that "their Great Father would not only chastise them for their bad conduct, but for the indignity offered to him in not receiving their presents."[21]

By November, the Brulés, Oglalas, and Miniconjous had gathered near Fort Pierre "and their conduct and talk had produced the greatest excitement among the other Bands of Sioux Tribes." Vaughan wrote that those responsible for attacking Grattan were "urging all the others to join with them in defence (*sic*) against any U.S. Troops that may be sent." Even more alarming, Vaughan reported that "they are untiring in procuring ammunition and guns, arrow points, and all implements of war."[22]

In forwarding Vaughan's report to the Senate, Commissioner of Indian Affairs George Manypenny offered an enlightened view. After outlining the "melancholy and heart-rending occurrence" dubbed the Grattan Massacre, Manypenny laid most of the blame on the military, pointing out that the aggrieved emigrants should have been compensated from the Indian annuities. Moreover, the Commissioner concluded, "no officer of the military department was, in my opinion, authorized to arrest or try any Indian for the offence (*sic*) charged against him."

While Manypenny acknowledged that "occasions frequently arise in our intercourse with the Indians requiring the employment of force," he suggested that "the whites may be, and often are, the aggressors." He encouraged the deployment of a "force better adapted to the Indian service," noting that "careful attention and kind and humane treatment will, generally, have more influence upon the savage than bayonets and gunpowder."

Manypenny further suggested that the Indians "be settled in fixed and permanent localities, thereafter not to be disturbed," urging that the "policy of removing Indian tribes from time to time, as the settlements approach their habitations and hunting-grounds ... be abandoned."[23]

Culbertson probably did not learn of these events for several months;

---

[21] Alfred J. Vaughan, Fort Pierre, to Col. Alfred Cumming, 19 Oct 1854. Senate ExDocs 1 (33-2) 746, pp. 296-297. Italics in original.
[22] Alfred Vaughan to Alfred Cumming, 21 Nov 1854. NAM, M234/885.
[23] Senate ExDocs 1 (33-2) 746, pp. 224-225.

his schedule that fall was especially busy as he traveled to inform the tribes of the delay in the treaty conference while also trying to "make something" out of the trade. Within a month of returning to Fort Benton, Culbertson was off again.

During the next six weeks, he traveled twice to the Gros Ventre camp at Milk River.[24] Meanwhile, Natawista took a load of goods to the Bloods.[25] After Culbertson returned on November 27, he and Natawista again headed north to the Blood camps. This trip did not go smoothly. While a number of Indians waited impatiently for Culbertson's return, an express arrived stating that his horses had been stolen and asking that mules be dispatched immediately. The next day, December 8, the Culbertsons reached Fort Benton and settled in for a few weeks.[26]

Their respite was cut short when Culbertson learned that an appropriation had been approved for holding the Blackfeet treaty conference that summer (1855). Governor Stevens asked Culbertson to purchase $1,000 worth of supplies as gifts for the tribes and to inform them of the new schedule.

Since it was the middle of winter, the goods had to come from the AFC's existing stocks. And since Culbertson had succeeded in making a good trade, Company supplies were low. From limited stock, he selected sugar, coffee, rice, flour, and tobacco.[27] Culbertson first met with the Piegans encamped at Fort Benton. Then, the day after Christmas, Culbertson and Natawista left for the Gros Ventre camp on Milk River.[28]

After informing the Gros Ventres of the new plans, Culbertson distributed the food along with instructions for its preparation since the tribe had limited experience with such foodstuffs. The Gros Ventres either did not understand or ignored the guidance. Soon after the Culbertsons departed, members of the tribe, especially the children, came down with severe colic from eating large quantities of wrongly prepared food. A few died. A rival trader claimed that Culbertson had intentionally "poisoned" them, but the elders dismissed this possibility, pointing to Culbertson's long history with the tribe. Contemplated revenge was abandoned.[29]

After leaving Milk River, Culbertson proceeded to Fort Union, arriving on January 25, 1855.[30] Conditions there remained unsettled. An

---

[24]"Fort Benton Journal," *MHSC*, Vol. X, p. 5 and p. 9.
[25]"Fort Benton Journal," *MHSC*, Vol. X, pp. 7-8.
[26]"Fort Benton Journal," *MHSC*, Vol. X, pp. 11-12.
[27]Bradley, *MHSC*, Vol. III, p. 271.   [28]"Fort Benton Journal," *MHSC*, Vol. X, p. 14.
[29]Bradley, *MHSC*, Vol. III, p. 271.   [30]"Fort Benton Journal," *MHSC*, Vol. X, p. 23.

unseasonably warm winter had left the area without snow,[31] forcing the buffalo to the north and leaving the Sioux "near starvation." In response, the Hunkpapa and Blackfeet Sioux had raided the Assiniboines, leading Agent Vaughan to brand them "reckless renegade scamps."[32]

The situation did not improve with the coming of spring. When the river opened, Culbertson headed downriver to purchase conference supplies and meet Superintendent of Indian Affairs Alfred Cumming.[33] En route, Culbertson was held captive for two days by a hostile band of Yanktonai Sioux who threatened to capture or kill any white man who ventured into their territory.[34] The same fate awaited any Indians "who refuse to Join them." They vowed "not in any way shape or manner to have any thing to do with their agent or Government."[35]

While this made the proposed conference even more imperative, both Culbertson and Vaughan worried about the commissioners' security. Vaughan urged Superintendent Cumming "for your safety through the Sioux country whom you are aware are disposed to be refractory" that "one Hundred efficient Troops" accompany the commissioners "to keep in check those who may be disposed to be disorderly during Council." Otherwise, Vaughan warned, "the object of the Government might be unsuccessful."[36] Although Culbertson agreed, the government dismissed their request; no large contingent of troops would accompany the commissioners.

Culbertson arrived in St. Louis on May 18 and met with Superintendent Cumming soon thereafter. Cumming had recently returned from Washington, D.C.,[37] where, much to the consternation of Governor Stevens, he had been appointed senior commissioner for the Blackfeet council. This perceived rebuff angered Stevens, already annoyed that his council had been delayed a year, that the War Department had suspended

---

[31]Charles Galpin to Pierre Chouteau, Feb 1855. NAM, M234/885.
[32]Alfred Vaughan to Alfred Cumming, 17 Feb 1855. NAM, M234/885.
[33]Bradley, *MHSC*, Vol. III, p. 272.
[34]Sunder, p. 165, identifies the band as Yanktons and says they threatened to kill all whites in their region. Alfred Vaughan to Alfred Cumming, 19 May 1855, says that the tribe, identified only as "a portion of the Sioux tribe direct from the hostile party," threatened to capture all whites "who might be found in their country." NAM, M234/885. *Missouri Republican*, 19 May 1855, identifies the tribe as Yanktonai.
[35]Alfred Vaughan to Alfred Cumming, 19 May 1855. NAM, M234/885.
[36]Alfred Vaughan to Alfred Cumming, 19 May 1855. NAM, M234/885.
[37]Alfred Cumming, 11 Apr 1855. NAM, M234/885.

his northern railroad survey, and that the Commissioner of Indian Affairs had flatly rejected his proposed government steamboat.[38]

Instead of building their own steamboat, the government had selected the American Fur Company to transport the supplies. This year, they had had few options. Culbertson's old nemesis, Alexander Harvey, had died on July 20, 1854. The *Daily Missouri Republican*, St. Louis's anti-AFC paper, hailed him as "a brave, an honest, and a kind-hearted man." But Culbertson and the other AFC officials had shed no tears.[39]

Without their driving force, Harvey, Primeau and Company succumbed to disorganization and, in the spring of 1855, opted not to send a steamboat upriver but to carry their supplies overland. Thus, the situation about which Cumming had complained so bitterly in 1854 existed once again: the AFC had no competition. Their "neat and very light draught steamer," *St. Mary*, would carry the goods on her maiden voyage.[40]

Governor Stevens worried that the Company would not start early enough to reach Fort Benton on time since, to do so, would entail extra costs and risks. Moreover, Stevens thought the AFC might have an incentive to undermine the treaty since "civilization" of the Indians went against their best interests.[41] The perceptive Swiss artist, Rudolph Kurz, had reached the same conclusion years earlier, noting that while the fur traders "are no worse than other American tradespeople . . . their traffic with the redskins must inevitably cease when the latter become civilized people."[42]

Stevens had reason to worry. The *St. Mary*, with Culbertson, Superintendent Cumming, and the new Blackfeet agent, Edwin A. C. Hatch, on board, did not leave St. Louis until June 6. Despite a surprisingly uneventful upriver journey, the late start virtually assured a delay in the Blackfeet council. When the steamboat arrived at Fort Union on July 11,[43] the treaty goods were transferred to two large mackinaws. On July 17, the mackinaws, manned by eighty-six men under the leadership of James Kipp, set off for Fort Benton. En route, they stopped to build a third mackinaw to more evenly distribute the load.[44] Meanwhile, Culbertson and Cumming traveled overland to Fort Benton.[45]

---

[38]Sunder, p. 167.
[39]Sunder, p. 164.
[40]Sunder, p. 166.
[41]Hazard Stevens, Vol. II, pp. 96-97.
[42]Kurz, p. 297.
[43]Sunder, p. 166.
[44]Alfred Cumming to George Manypenny, 26 Aug 1855. NAM, M234/30. Some differences as to dates and the number of crew members appear in McDonnell, *MHSC*, Vol. X, p. 270.
[45]McDonnell, *MHSC*, Vol. X, p. 270. McDonnell quotes Hatch's diary which consistently gives the year as 1856, clearly an error.

Throughout the summer of 1855, before heading to Fort Benton, Governor Stevens had held conferences with the western tribes under his jurisdiction. When he finally reached the AFC post on July 26,[46] he discovered that Superintendent Cumming, Culbertson, and the treaty goods had not yet arrived. Fuming, he set off to locate the senior commissioner. On August 15, Stevens found Cumming and Culbertson camped at the mouth of Milk River.[47]

The resentment which Stevens felt towards Cumming boiled over. Cumming, who had been appointed Superintendent of Indian Affairs by President Pierce, had been born into a politically and socially prominent Georgia family fifty-two years earlier. To call him portly would be an understatement; by the time of the Blackfeet council, Cumming weighed at least three hundred pounds.[48] Stevens found him "pompous, and full of his own importance."[49] Nothing would transpire over the next two months to disabuse Stevens of this impression.

In preparing for the conference, Stevens had made several appointments. Most significantly, Stevens designated James Doty, a trusted aid who had spent a year as unofficial agent to the Blackfeet, to serve as commission secretary. Cumming, on the other hand, "had not brought with him a single efficient man." Yet, now, Cumming wanted to appoint all council officers and suggested that Doty be dismissed. While Doty ultimately retained his position, the rancorous tone of the Milk River encounter suggested the difficulties to come.[50]

For his part, Alexander Culbertson found himself in an awkward position. Governor Stevens, although never openly rebuking Culbertson, apparently had lost faith in his abilities after the trader failed to secure council appropriations the previous year. Overlooking Culbertson, Stevens appointed James Bird,[51] a mixed-blood trader, to act as interpreter for the Blackfeet.

No doubt Culbertson felt slighted by this. He was also annoyed by not having been paid for his services with the railroad survey.[52] Moreover,

---

[46]"Fort Benton Journal," *MHSC*, Vol. X, p. 39.  [47]Richards, p. 230.
[48]Bradley, *MHSC* Vol. III, p. 277.  [49]Hazard Stevens, Vol. II, p. 102.
[50]Correspondence from preparations for the Blackfeet treaty conference. NAM, M234/30; Hazard Stevens, Vol. II, p. 102.
[51]The name is spelled as "Byrd" in the official reports of Stevens and Cumming. NAM, M234/30. It appears as "Bird" on the transcribed Blackfeet Treaty of 1855. Kappler, Vol. II, p. 740.
[52]Alexander Culbertson to Charles E. Mix, Esq., 18 Mar 1856. NAM, M234/30.

Culbertson could not afford to offend Superintendent Cumming whose decisions could adversely affect the American Fur Company, as had been amply demonstrated with the 1854 annuity transportation contract.

Culbertson, regardless of his other roles, could not ignore his status as an AFC partner. This also put him at odds with Stevens when the governor proposed that men be sent downriver to secure basic commodities from the mackinaws for immediate delivery to the conference site. Cumming refused to authorize this unless Culbertson assented on behalf of the Company. Culbertson would not do so, apparently fearing that this might be interpreted as an abrogation of the transportation contract.[53] Caught in the middle, Culbertson tried to walk a delicate line between the feuding commissioners.[54]

The meeting at Milk River ended without agreement. The parties headed to Fort Benton, arriving on August 17.[55] As days passed with no word from the mackinaw fleet, Stevens urged Cumming to send men downriver to assist the crew. Cumming refused. Supplies grew precariously low, leaving both whites and Indians short of food. Stevens dispatched hunters, but many of the assembled Indians threatened to depart before the council even began.[56]

Animosity continued to grow between the commissioners. Cumming became outraged when Stevens distributed liquor to his men, leading to a few days of "fighting, cursing, and general uproar."[57] The next day, still in a pique, Stevens made "a fool of himself . . . causing not only remarks of whites but of all the Indians."[58]

Finally, on August 29, Culbertson headed downriver to find the mackinaws.[59] He returned on September 10 with disappointing news.[60] The boats would not arrive for several more days. The situation mirrored that which had occurred four years earlier at Fort Laramie and Culbertson suggested a similar solution: move the council, originally scheduled for

---

[53] Reports of meeting at Milk River, 14 Aug 1855. NAM, M234/30.

[54] This conclusion is primarily the author's, bolstered by clues in the historical record and comments in Bradley, *MHSC*, Vol. III, p. 275. However, nothing in the historical record explains why Stevens's attitude toward Culbertson shifted. Nonetheless, it seems clear that Stevens no longer considered him a partner in the Blackfeet council.

[55] Bradley, *MHSC*, Vol. III, p. 272; "Fort Benton Journal," *MHSC*, Vol. X, p. 41.

[56] Richards, p. 230.   [57] Richards, p. 231; "Fort Benton Journal," *MHSC*, Vol. X, p. 41.

[58] "Fort Benton Journal," *MHSC*, Vol. X, p. 41.

[59] Bradley, *MHSC*, Vol. III, p. 273; "Fort Benton Journal," *MHSC*, Vol. X, p. 42.

[60] "Fort Benton Journal," *MHSC*, Vol. X, p. 44.

Fort Benton, downriver to the mouth of the Judith River.⁶¹ In a rare act of conciliation, Stevens and Cumming agreed.

The dissension between the two commissioners now shifted to more fundamental issues: how the council would be conducted; the character of the Blackfeet; the quality of their territory; and, the proposed treaty terms. The two agreed on nothing. Stevens proposed rules for conducting the council; Cumming dismissed those which threatened his seniority. Stevens objected to Cumming's supercilious attitude, suggesting that "it is more becoming the dignity of a Commission to protect and exercise its own rights than to leave them in the hands of one of its members."⁶²

Most significantly, the two held vastly disparate opinions on how much money should be allocated for the future benefit of the affected tribes. These differences grew out of fundamental disagreements concerning the nature of the Blackfeet and the quality of their lands.

Superintendent Cumming considered the Blackfeet "savages . . . not yet emerged from the darkness of primitive barbarism." Moreover, they inhabited a "remote and sterile wilderness" totally unsuited "for even a limited emigration" and "altogether unfitted for cultivation."⁶³

Stevens completely disagreed and could not "refrain from expressing some degree of astonishment, that opinions so utterly at variance with what the undersigned believes to be the facts of the case, should be so impudently advanced by a gentleman whose acquaintance and observation both of the country and the Indians have been so exceedingly limited." Citing his "large experience both in explorations of the Blackfoot country and in intercourse with the Blackfoot Nation," the governor refuted Cumming's charges.

The Blackfeet were not savages. "For ten years," Stevens pointed out, they "have not killed a white man in their own territory." Moreover, "hospitality in their lodges, kindness to strangers, and great susceptibility to good and generous motives are their marked characteristics."

As for the Blackfeet country, the governor found it "an exceedingly fine grasing (*sic*) country, of great salubrity of climate, much arable land of good quality, with abundant cotton wood on the streams and in many

---

⁶¹Bradley, *MHSC*, Vol. III, p. 274.
⁶²Report of Isaac Stevens, 27 Sep 1855. NAM, M234/30.
⁶³Report of Alfred Cumming, 19 Sep 1855. NAM, M234/30.

localities abounding in pines of the finest quality." Stevens also suggested at least two possible migration routes crossed the territory.[64]

The differing opinions had serious repercussions. Cumming's assessment led him to propose an allocation of $30,000 a year for ten years while Stevens advocated $50,000.[65] Stevens advanced an elaborate ten year plan whereby the annuity money would be spent on food and farm implements for the first two years. Then, as the tribes developed farms, the money could be shifted to schools. This, Stevens declared, would make it possible to "gradually reclaim the Indians from a nomadic life and tend to encourage them to settle on permanent homes."[66] Cumming objected to the farms as "tempting heartless adventurers under the guise of philanthropy."[67]

On this issue, Culbertson agreed with Cumming, although for decidedly different reasons. Culbertson warned Stevens that agriculture "was not to be thought of [by the Indians] as long as Game is abundant." The Indians, Culbertson insisted, "will not work unless their necessities compel them—it is beneath their dignity." To the Indians, the hunt was sport, not work. Thus, as long as sufficient buffalo roamed the plains, "the day is far off when the Blackfeet will turn the Sword into the Ploughshare and make the wilderness bud and blossom like the Rose."[68]

Stevens became angry when Culbertson would not back his position. Frustrated, Culbertson decided not to attend the upcoming council. The governor, knowing the esteem in which he was held, worried that Culbertson's withdrawal would transmit a disastrous message to the Blackfeet. He finally apologized and Culbertson agreed to act as interpreter.[69]

Stevens and Cumming, however, never reconciled and, against this backdrop of competing visions and warring personalities, the Blackfeet council convened on October 16, 1855.

---

[64]Report of Isaac Stevens, 28 Sep 1855. NAM, M234/30.
[65]Report of Isaac Stevens, 18 Sep 1855 and report of Alfred Cumming, 19 Sep 1855. NAM, M234/30.
[66]Report of Isaac Stevens, 18 Sep 1855. NAM, M234/30.
[67]Report of Alfred Cumming, 19 Sep 1855. NAM, M234/30.
[68]Ewers, *Blackfeet*, p. 214.
[69]Bradley, *MHSC*, Vol. III, p. 275. Bradley leaves the impression that Culbertson did not serve as interpreter but his name appears on the treaty. Kappler, Vol. II, p. 740.

# Chapter Twenty-One

# *"the Buffalo will not continue forever"*

Several thousand representatives of the Blood, Piegan, Northern Blackfoot, Gros Ventre, Nez Perce, Flathead, and Pend d'Oreille tribes along with a single Cree chief gathered in a cottonwood grove near the mouth of the Judith River for the Blackfeet treaty conference on Tuesday, October 16, 1855.[1] Twenty-six principal chiefs positioned themselves in semi-circular rows across from Governor Stevens, Superintendent Cumming, secretary James Doty, Alexander Culbertson, and six other interpreters. A canvas-covered arbor provided shelter.

Stevens and Cumming addressed the assembly, stressing the need for peace among the tribes. Stevens, dismissing rumors that the government planned to confiscate the Blackfeet lands and send the tribe north to the British posessions, explained his vision for their future:

> We want to establish you in your country on farms. We want you to have cattle and raise crops. We want your children to be taught.... This country is your home. It will remain your home ... we hoped through the long winters, bye and bye, the Blackfeet would not be obliged to live on poor Buffalo Meat but would have domestic Cattle for food.... You know the Buffalo will not continue forever. Get farms and cattle in time.[2]

To the Blackfeet, a time without buffalo seemed incomprehensible. Indians used buffalo hides for clothing, lodge covers, bedding, hobbles, picket lines, bridles, hackamores, cruppers, whip lashes, and saddles. They carried dried meat and camp equipment in rawhide containers. Rawhide strips bound handles to mauls, arrows, and war clubs. Buffalo horns were turned into spoons, cups, ladles, and flasks. They stuffed saddles and toys with the buffalo's shaggy hair. Buffalo tails became tipi ornaments and fly brushes. Bow strings were made from twisted bull sinew. Paint came from mixing buffalo fat with earth pigments. Rib bones were fashioned into sleds. Cattle might provide food but they could never replace the buffalo.[3]

---

[1]Bradley, *MHSC*, Vol. III, p. 274; Richards, p. 232; Ewers, *Blackfeet*, p. 215. Culbertson estimated the number of Indians present as two thousand while Richards puts the number at thirty-five hundred.    [2]Ewers, *Blackfeet*, p. 216.    [3]Ewers, *Blackfeet*, pp. 73-76.

Stevens continued reading the proposed articles.[4] The first two pledged the tribes to peace among themselves, the surrounding tribes, and the United States government. Article III set forth a "common hunting-ground for ninety-nine years" where all parties "may enjoy equal and uninterrupted privileges of hunting, fishing and gathering fruit, grazing animals, curing meat and dressing robes." No "permanent settlements" would be permitted in this region.[5]

Articles IV and V, illustrated by a map, proposed an exclusive Blackfeet territory. Article VI required the tribes to "remain within their own respective countries" unless traveling to the common hunting ground or visiting other tribes "for the purpose of trade or social intercourse." Article VII guaranteed emigrants safe passage while requiring government protection for the tribes from "depredations and other unlawful acts" by whites. In Article VIII, the Indians agreed to permit "travelling thoroughfares" through their country along with telegraph lines, military posts, agency buildings, missions, schools, farms, shops, and mills, proposals which meant little to the Indians. Furthermore, the tribes agreed to allow whites to "permanently occupy as much land as may be necessary" for these purposes while also granting them permission to gather wood and graze animals. In addition, "the navigation of all lakes and streams shall be forever free to citizens of the United States."[6]

Articles IX and X provided annual annuities of $20,000 for the Bloods, Piegans, Northern Blackfoot, and Gros Ventres for ten years. An additional $15,000 per year would be available to educate the children, "promoting their civilization and Christianization," and to instruct the tribes "in agricultural and mechanical pursuits." The remaining articles provided means for compensating whites victimized by Indian depredations, for withholding annuities for treaty violations, and for excluding liquor from Indian lands.[7]

The Indians said little until the Flathead chief, Alexander, objected to the proposed Blackfeet territory. These boundaries, he argued, would foreclose his tribe from traditional hunting grounds north of the Musselshell River. Although Little Dog, speaking for the Piegans, was willing to allow the Flatheads to hunt there, the commissioners were not. They insisted that the Flatheads use the common hunting ground. Big Canoe, another Flathead chief, added his dissent: "I thought our roads would be

---

[4]Ewers, *Blackfeet*, p. 217.
[5]Kappler, Vol. II, p. 736.
[6]Kappler, Vol. II, p. 737.
[7]Kappler, Vol. II, pp. 738-739.

all over this country. Now you tell us different. . . . Now you tell me not to step over that way. I have a mind to go there."

Lame Bull, a venerated Piegan chief, reminded the disgruntled western chiefs that the "White Chiefs," not the Blackfeet, had proposed these boundaries. The Piegans "shall consider what the White Chiefs wish us to do, and I think we shall do it." Lame Bull expressed his hope that, by council's end, the western Indians "will make friends with us and that it may be shown by a friendly exchange of property."

The Flatheads responded with stony silence. Stevens, recognizing the chiefs' need to confer, recessed the council: "We will try this treaty again tomorrow." In the meantime, he urged the tribes to discuss the proposals, assuring them that the terms were "just and good." Stevens suggested that the Flatheads "talk in friendship with the Blackfeet and see if your hearts cannot be one."[8] The next day, when the council reconvened, Stevens again explained the proposed boundaries. To his delight, the Flatheads now offered no objections.

The Blackfeet, however, raised a new concern. With their traditional enemies—the Assiniboines, Crees, and Crows—absent, Lame Bull wondered how the Blackfeet should respond if these tribes stole horses in the future. The commissioners replied that the Blackfeet could pursue the thieves and, if possible, recover their property and then report the violation to their agent.

Seen From Afar, Natawista's esteemed brother, now expressed apprehensions. The elders, Seen From Afar averred, wanted to end warfare. But without the Crows to "smoke the pipe with us," he feared that "our young men will not be persuaded that they ought not to war against [them]." Seen From Afar explained again the benefits of waging war for the young men. While the elders would "do our best to keep our young men at home," Seen From Afar worried that it might prove impossible.[9]

Cumming reminded the chiefs that their Great Father "wishes all his children to live in peace" and that, if they did not, he "will be ashamed of his children" and withhold their annuities. "Tell your young men to take wives and live happily in their own lodges," Cumming argued, "then the old men will see their sons. Your sons will see their children, and you will all be happy."[10] A skeptical Seen From Afar said nothing.

---

[8]Ewers, *Blackfeet*, pp. 218-219.
[9]Ewers, *Blackfeet*, pp. 220-221; Dempsey, *Red Crow*, p. 49.
[10]Ewers, *Blackfeet*, pp. 220-221.

When the Indians raised no further objections, the assembled tribal leaders, commissioners, and interpreters affixed their marks and signatures to the treaty. Piegan signers included Lame Bull, Mountain Chief, and Little Dog. Two of Natawista's brothers, Seen From Afar[11] and Big Plume,[12] signed for the Bloods. The Three Bulls and Chief Rabbit Runner ratified the treaty on behalf of the Northern Blackfoot while Bear's Shirt, Little Soldier, and Weasel Horse acted for the Gros Ventres. Spotted Eagle and Looking Glass represented the Nez Perces; Victor, Alexander, and Big Canoe, the Flatheads.[13]

No notice was taken of a phrase in Article XI which proclaimed: "The aforesaid tribes acknowledge their dependence on the Government of the United States...."[14]

The 1855 Blackfeet Treaty solidified the power shift within the Bloods which began when Alexander Culbertson married Natawista. Prior to this, the Buffalo Followers led the Bloods while the Fish Eaters, Natawista's family's band, had held no significant role in the tribe's political life.[15] But Seen From Afar was the first Blood to sign the 1855 treaty, signaling his now pre-eminent role within the tribe.[16] Bull's Back Fat, representing the Buffalo Followers, signed third, after The Father of All Children.[17]

The treaty conference ended with a distribution of blankets, fabric, tobacco, and such unfamiliar foodstuffs as sugar, coffee, rice, and flour. The Blackfeet ripped open the flour sacks, tossed them into the air, and laughed as the white dust fell from the sky. They poured the sugar into nearby streams and drank the sweetened water. Disliking the sticky rice, they traded it back to the whites.[18]

With the conference successfully concluded, Cumming and Stevens happily parted. Their feud, however, had not ended. In his last act as Blackfeet conference commissioner, Stevens wrote Commissioner Manypenny to "solemnly [protest] against . . . placing the name of Col. Cumming first on the commission," claiming this had caused "injury to [Stevens's] reputation."[19] The ever-arrogant Cumming responded: "it is

---

[11] Kappler, Vol. II, p. 739. His name appears as Onis-tay-say-nah-que-im.
[12] Big Plume was also known as Big Feather. He signed the treaty as "The Feather." Kappler, Vol. II, p. 739; McDonnell, *MHSC*, Vol. X, p. 265.
[13] Kappler, Vol. II, p. 739. This list represents only the better known signatories.
[14] Kappler, Vol. II, p. 738.   [15] Dempsey, *Red Crow*, p. 3.
[16] Dempsey, *Red Crow*, p. 49.   [17] Kappler, Vol. II, p. 739; Dempsey, *Red Crow*, p. 49.
[18] Ewers, *Blackfeet*, p. 221.
[19] Report of Isaac Stevens, 22 Oct 1855. NAM, M234/30.

to me a matter of perfect indifference what opinions are entertained of my official conduct by Commissioner Stevens."[20]

Nevertheless, Stevens confided to his journal: "We got through the Blackfeet treaty, everything having succeeded to our entire satisfaction, and indeed, beyond our most sanguine expectations." Neither commissioner would ever return to the Blackfeet country.[21]

Culbertson left the council grounds with Superintendent Cumming on October 24, 1855, for St. Louis. Culbertson was once again headed for Washington, D.C., this time to lobby for ratification of the just-completed treaty.[22] The two traveled by mackinaw, leaving others to take a mule pack train overland.[23]

Winter had already arrived and ice slowed the river journey. Near Fort Pierre, the river closed completely and Culbertson and Cumming were forced to abandon the mackinaw and wait for the mules to continue their journey. They waited in vain: a Sioux raiding party had stolen the animals.[24] Agent Vaughan subsequently informed Cumming that the Yanktonai tribe had been responsible, reminding the Superintendent that "those Sioux were represented to you by many to be harmless, inoffensive people, notwithstanding all I could Say to the Contrary."[25]

With the river frozen and the mules stolen, Culbertson turned to General William Harney, who had come upriver to chasten the Sioux following the Grattan Massacre, for assistance.[26] In early September, Harney had attacked an encampment of Brulé, Oglala, Miniconjou Sioux, and Northern Cheyennes at Ash Hollow in present-day western Nebraska,[27] killing eighty-six and taking seventy women and children captive.[28] Afterwards, Harney marched boldly through Sioux country to Fort Pierre.[29]

To billet the growing upriver troops, the army had purchased Fort Pierre from the AFC for $45,000. Considering the dilapidated post conditions, the price was exorbitant[30] and Harney was furious.[31] The appearance of Culbertson, a representative of the AFC, gave the general a

---

[20]Report of Alfred Cumming, 22 Oct 1855. NAM, M234/30.
[21]Ewers, *Blackfeet*, p. 221.   [22]Hazard Stevens, Vol. II, p. 275.
[23]Bradley, *MHSC*, Vol. III, p. 276.   [24]Bradley, *MHSC*, Vol. III, p. 276.
[25]Alfred Vaughan to Alfred Cumming, 15 Feb 1856. NAM, M234/885.
[26]Bradley, *MHSC*, Vol. III, p. 276.   [27]Utley, p. 45.
[28]Mattes, *Great Platte River Road*, pp. 317-321.
[29]Sunder, p. 168.   [30]Sunder, p. 169.   [31]Sunder, pp. 170-171.

convenient target for his wrath. He told Culbertson he had plenty of mules, but "you can't have one." Harney further expressed regret that "when the Indians got your mules they didn't get your scalp also.... All summer I and my men have suffered and boiled to chastise these wretches while you have been patching up another of your sham treaties to be broken tomorrow and give us more work."[32]

Having been so thoroughly dismissed, Culbertson turned to Charles Galpin, an AFC trader operating near Fort Pierre, who provided eight mules.[33] With these, Culbertson and Cumming proceeded to St. Louis where Culbertson, no doubt with some relief, bid farewell to the peevish superintendent.

In Washington, D. C., Culbertson once again appeared before Senate committees considering the Blackfeet Treaty. He lobbied for quick approval so that annuities could be distributed the following summer.[34] The Senate ratified the treaty on April 15, 1856, and President Franklin Pierce signed it into law ten days later. Known to the whites as the "Treaty with the Blackfoot Nation," the Blackfeet called it Lame Bull's Treaty, in honor of the first Piegan to affix his mark.[35]

Ten days after the Blackfeet signed the treaty, the vaticinations of Seen From Afar materialized when some young Bloods set out to steal Crow horses. Other raids followed. In February, Seen From Afar, accompanied by other Blood chiefs, came to the Blackfeet agency in Fort Benton to explain that the young warriors did not believe the treaty applied to the Crows since they had not attended the council.[36] Edwin Hatch, the Blackfeet agent, was disturbed to learn that the Blood warriors had tried to recruit Gros Ventre and Piegan warriors to join their raids. When they refused, the Bloods "ridiculed them for listening to the advice of the whites."[37]

Despite the shaky beginning, tentative peace reigned on the upper Missouri by the spring of 1856. Encouraged by this, white visitors flooded the region. In April, the steamboat, *Clara*, left St. Louis carrying government supplies, AFC freight, military troops, and a "jolly" party of French noblemen and their wives making a "pleasure trip" to the Indian country.[38]

---

[32]Bradley, *MHSC*, Vol. III, p. 276.  [33]Bradley, *MHSC*, Vol. III, p. 276.
[34]Hazard Stevens, Vol. II, p. 275.  [35]Ewers, *Blackfeet*, p. 222.
[36]Ewers, *Blackfeet*, p. 227.
[37]Ewers, *Blackfeet*, p. 227; E.A.C. Hatch Diary, MF 73C, MtHS.
[38]Sunder, p. 179.

On June 7, the *St. Mary* headed upriver carrying Charles Chouteau, Pierre Chouteau's son and successor, agent Alfred Vaughan, and Alexander Culbertson. The previous January, Charles Chouteau, continuing the AFC's patronage of the sciences, had founded the Academy of Science at St. Louis and Dr. Charles Stevens, a St. Louis neurologist, was traveling upriver to collect specimens for the Academy.[39]

The *St. Mary* also transported Lt. Gouverneur K. Warren who, as topographical engineer for General Harney, had been assigned to survey potential sites for military posts.[40] After a year in the Indian country, he filed an extensive report concerning animal and plant life, soil, geology, and geography of the region with seven maps, including one by Alexander Culbertson.[41] Also traveling upriver were Elkanah Mackey, a Presbyterian missionary, and his wife, Sarah Armstrong Mackey.[42] Article X of Lame Bull's Treaty provided for the "civilization and Christianization" of the Indians;[43] Alexander Culbertson had enlisted the Mackeys to further that goal.

In addition to lobbying for passage of the Blackfeet treaty, Culbertson had apparently used his 1855-1856 eastern trip to meet with his half-brother, Michael Simpson Culbertson, Isaac Stevens's classmate at West Point. Unlike most of his classmates, Michael Simpson Culbertson eschewed a military career, preferring to enter the ministry. Simpson, as he was known,[44] received a Doctor of Divinity degree from Princeton Theological Seminary in 1844 and was ordained that May by the Presbytery of Carlisle, Pennsylvania. Soon after, he married Mary Dunlap of Salem, New York, and within a month, they set sail for China to establish a Presbyterian mission in Ningpo.[45]

They traveled with Walter Macon Lowrie, son of Walter Lowrie, United States senator and first secretary of the Presbyterian Board of Missions.[46] Lowrie and Culbertson worked together for six years until the young Lowrie met an untimely death at the hands of Chinese pirates. Simpson Culbertson spent another four years at the Shanghai mission before returning to the United States to visit his family.

---

[39]Sunder, pp. 175-176.   [40]McDonnell, *MHSC*, Vol. X, p. 297.
[41]Sunder, p. 175.
[42]McDonnell, *MHSC*, Vol. X, p. 279. Also traveling with Culbertson was his cousin, John Moodey Culbertson, the son of John Craighead Culbertson. The young Culbertson was making a pleasure trip to see the upper Missouri. John Moodey Culbertson diary.
[43]Kappler, Vol. II, p. 738.
[44]Thaddeus Culbertson, p. 39; Berglund, SC 414, MtHS, p. 27.
[45]Holterman, pp. 69-70.   [46]Holterman, p. 71.

Simpson, his wife, and three young daughters, all born in China, arrived in New York on January 12, 1856. Alexander Culbertson likely awaited them and went along when Simpson reported to the Board of Missions.[47] Alexander Culbertson urged the Presbyterians to establish a Blackfeet mission, telling the Board that he "felt a sincere desire to see [the Indians] brought under the influence of Christian civilization."[48] While he may have hoped the assignment would go to his brother, Simpson chose to return to China.[49]

The Presbyterian Board of Missions, however, agreed to send Rev. Mackey. Mackey was born in Colerain, Pennsylvania, in 1826 and, like Simpson Culbertson, attended Princeton Seminary. He had graduated and married just a few months before heading west.[50] Culbertson joined the newlyweds in St. Louis, extending them "every courtesy and engagement." The trader also met with Pierre De Smet, but only long enough to "shake hands" and receive the missionary's "wish [for] a happy and prosperous journey."[51] Culbertson and the Mackeys then boarded the *St. Mary*. At Fort Pierre, Natawista joined them.[52]

To the relief of Culbertson and Agent Vaughan, the *St. Mary* enjoyed an uneventful voyage. At several locations, Vaughan held brief councils while distributing Indian annuities.[53] On July 10, the *St. Mary* reached Fort Union where the Culbertsons and Mackeys disembarked.[54] Joined by Andrew Dawson, a native of Scotland who had responsibility for Fort Benton during Culbertson's absence,[55] the group set out overland for Fort Benton.[56] As they camped at Milk River on July 29, Edwin Hatch, the Blackfeet agent, arrived to welcome them.[57]

The travelers reached Fort Benton on August 15, 1856.[58] Sarah Mackey, the first white woman ever to visit the Blackfeet territory, created quite a stir. The curious Indians treated her with deference, kindness, and respect.[59] Many of the Company employees and Indians must have been disappointed, though, when the Culbertsons did not throw their customary ball. Possibly Culbertson cancelled the event because he, Natawista,

---

[47]Holterman, p. 123.  [48]Sunder, pp. 179-180.
[49]Holterman, p. 148.  [50]McDonnell, *MHSC*, Vol. X, p. 279.
[51]Pierre De Smet to Edwin Denig, 13 Jun 1856. Transcription found in unattributed typescript notes in the Alexander Culbertson VF, MtHS.
[52]Sunder, p. 180.  [53]Sunder, p. 173.
[54]Sunder, p. 174.  [55]McDonnell, *MHSC*, Vol. X, p. 266.
[56]Sunder, p. 180.  [57]McDonnell, *MHSC*, Vol. X, p. 279.
[58]"Fort Benton Journal," *MHSC*, Vol. X, p. 88.  [59]Ewers, *Blackfeet*, p. 195.

and Sarah Mackey were all ill or perhaps he feared the inevitable drunken rowdiness would offend the missionaries.

As the Mackeys settled in, Agent Hatch reported them "pleased with the place, Indians and country." Nonetheless, based on his own experience, he suspected that they "will probably get enough of it before spring."[60] Two days later, Rev. Mackey held the first Protestant services at Fort Benton. Mackey conducted one service for the employees and another in the "Indian house" for the tribes.[61] Agent Hatch, who attended neither, reported small but attentive audiences.[62]

Culbertson, recovered from his illness, left on September 3 to locate the boats carrying the Blackfeet annuities. Finding them near Cow Island, he returned to Fort Benton.[63] Sarah Mackey, however, continued to feel sick, perhaps as a result of her recently discovered pregnancy. Within days, she began to talk of leaving Fort Benton.

The Rev. Mackey, hoping she would change her mind, preached again on August 31 and then rode out to explore the countryside. But, the next Sunday, there was no preaching.[64] Rev. Mackey realized he could not remain among the Blackfeet with his wife in a "most distressing state of nervous derangement."[65] On September 15, the Mackeys, the Culbertsons, and Agent Hatch left Fort Benton.[66]

At Judith River, they met with Lame Bull and the Piegans to distribute their annuities. Rev. Mackey, still reluctant to abandon his assignment, asked Lame Bull if he might establish a Piegan mission. Lame Bull and his fellow chiefs agreed, but it was too late for Sarah Mackey.

That winter, Rev. Mackey reported favorably to the Board of Missions on the prospects for a Blackfeet mission. He had found the Indians receptive and the climate "one of the most healthy in the world." Mackey praised both Culbertson and his wife. The trader had shown "kindnesses . . . under all circumstances," being especially sympathetic to Mrs. Mackey.[67]

Culbertson had also demonstrated his usual generosity with Company supplies, extending a ten percent discount on freight to Fort Benton and offering to store the Mackeys' goods free of charge until the next spring. Moreover, for their transportation from Fort Union to Fort Benton, "he charge[d] us nothing."[68]

---

[60]McDonnell, *MHSC*, Vol. X, p. 279.
[61]"Fort Benton Journal," *MHSC*, Vol. X, p. 88.
[62]McDonnell, *MHSC*, Vol. X, p. 279.
[63]"Fort Benton Journal," *MHSC*, Vol. X, pp. 88-89.
[64]McDonnell, *MHSC*, Vol. X, p. 279.
[65]Harrod, p. 25.
[66]"Fort Benton Journal," *MHSC*, Vol. X, p. 90.
[67]Sunder, p. 181.
[68]Holterman, p. 128.

As for Natawista, Mackey noted that he and his wife "had an opportunity of seeing her under a variety of circumstances" and found her possessed of "a noble, kind and generous heart, quick to detect the wants of those around her and prompt to relieve them." She had been "a fine and firm friend" to Sarah Mackey[69] and her influence on her husband was "of the most favorable kind."[70]

Mackey suggested that if Natawista's "character may be taken as an index to the character of the nation, our impressions are of the most favorable kind."[71] Mackey urged the Board of Missions to sanction his return to the upper Missouri the following spring, after Mrs. Mackey regained her health. At that time, Mackey hoped to open a school among the Blackfeet. However, the Mission Board demurred, preferring to wait for government appropriations to establish schools and missions.[72]

Rev. Mackey never returned to the upper Missouri. On September 6, 1858, he died suddenly at his Maryland home.[73] The next day, his young son also died. Father and son were buried side by side in the church cemetery.[74]

The Mackeys' historic, yet brief, stay on the upper Missouri created less excitement than that of another 1856 visitor. Sir St. George Gore, a wealthy, Oxford-educated sportsman from northern Ireland,[75] was the eighth baronet of Manor Gore, County Donegal.[76] Born in 1811,[77] Sir George was a stout, balding man with side whiskers. He was a good hiker but a poor horseman.[78] Coming west in 1853 for a pleasure hunt, Gore passed his first year in what is now Colorado before wintering at Fort Laramie.[79] In August 1854, he continued his hunt with an outfit unlike any previously seen.

Sir George left Fort Laramie with forty-one men, three milk cows, four six-mule wagons, two three-yoke ox wagons, and twenty-one bright red horse-drawn carts. Gore filled one wagon with nothing but his firearms. Two other wagons carried fishing tackle. An expert fly-maker was engaged to gather materials and fashion flies.

---

[69]Holterman, p. 127.  
[70]Schemm, p. 7.  
[71]Holterman, p. 127.  
[72]Sunder, p. 181.  
[73]McDonnell, *MHSC*, Vol. X, p. 279.  
[74]Holterman, p. 128.  
[75]Sunder, p. 181.  
[76]Innis, p. 211.  
[77]McDonnell, *MHSC*, Vol. X, p. 296.  
[78]Bradley, "Gore," *MHSC*, Vol. IX, p. 249.  
[79]McDonnell, *MHSC*, Vol. X, p. 296, says that Gore did not leave St. Louis until 1854. Bradley, "Gore," *MHSC*, Vol. IX, p. 246, states that Gore came west in 1853 and spent "the season principally in Colorado" before wintering at Fort Laramie.

A large linen tent sheltered Gore from the blistering sun and vicious winds. He slept on a brass bedstead that unscrewed for packing. Gore's equipage also included a portable writing table and iron washstand. To view the surrounding country, Sir George carried a "splendid telescope" with a six inch lens and tripod.[80]

Guided by Jim Bridger,[81] Gore followed the route north through the Powder River basin blazed by Alexander Culbertson and Pierre De Smet in 1851. He then ascended the Tongue River. Near present-day Miles City, Montana, Gore built a winter fort including stables, storehouses, and living quarters.

When an accidental fire destroyed the grasslands, Gore moved south where his men built a log cabin. Less spacious and comfortable than his original quarters, the cabin sheltered Gore and Steel Trap, his gray Kentucky thoroughbred who fed on cornmeal. Meanwhile, Sir George's men each gathered one hundred and twenty-five pounds of cottonwood bark to feed the livestock.[82]

During the winter, the Piegans ran off twenty-one of Gore's horses. Gore dispatched men to recover them but they lost the trail after a sixty mile chase through a snowstorm. The Bloods, assuming Gore was aligned with their enemies, the Crows, also organized a raiding party. When Gore's cook heard them removing pickets from the corral, he came out shooting. Natawista's brother, Big Plume,[83] was severely wounded in the attack. Gore's men chased the Bloods for thirty miles before their horses became exhausted in the deep snows.[84] Big Plume returned to Fort Benton where Natawista nursed him back to health.[85]

The Bloods, however, had been wrong in believing the Crows welcomed Sir George. Gore's idea of sport entailed killing as many animals as possible. The resulting destruction outraged the Crows who protested to Agent Vaughan. They told Vaughan Sir George could kill for food, but they strenuously objected to the wholesale slaughter, leaving animal carcasses to rot on the prairie.[86]

Around March 1, 1855, Gore broke camp and set off for the Black Hills. As winter approached, the baron returned to Tongue River. The following spring, having grown weary of his "wilderness" experience,

---

[80] Bradley, "Gore," *MHSC*, Vol. IX, pp. 246-247.
[81] Bradley, "Gore," *MHSC*, Vol. IX, p. 278.
[82] Bradley, "Gore," *MHSC*, Vol. IX, pp. 246-247.
[83] Dempsey, *Red Crow*, p. 35.　　[84] Bradley, "Gore," *MHSC*, Vol. IX, p. 248.
[85] Dempsey, *Red Crow*, p. 36.　　[86] Bradley, *MHSC*, Vol. III, p. 279.

Gore ordered two large flatboats built to transport his supplies downriver while he proceeded overland with his wagons and carts.[87]

Four of Gore's men reached the Fort Pierre area, made camp, and waited. A month passed and Sir George did not arrive. Agent Vaughan reported "a rumor afloat" that "Gore and his party of twelve men has (*sic*) been murdered by the Blackfeet and Uncpapa Bands of Sioux." Although Vaughan hoped this was not true, he recognized that Gore's actions in "Killing and Scattering the small quantity of Game which is [the Indians'] only means of Subsistence and the constant Starved conditions they are in, is absolutely enough to drive [the Sioux] to acts of desperation."[88]

In St. Louis, Superintendent Cumming, who had authorized Gore's expedition, passed the rumors along to the Commissioner of Indian Affairs. Cumming observed that Gore had "greatly abused the privilege" granted "by a wanton destruction of the game upon which the Indians rely solely for Support." Considering this, the superintendent would not be "astonished that Such Conduct should have exasperated the Indians nor would I be Surprised if the rumor turned out to be well founded."[89]

But Sir George was safe. Reaching Fort Union, he set up camp to prepare for his journey home. An outraged Vaughan asked Culbertson to accompany him to Gore's encampment. There, Vaughan demanded to know under what authority the baron had entered the region. Gore haughtily replied that it was none of Vaughan's business. When Vaughan demanded Gore produce evidence of his legal passage, Sir George produced the passport issued by Superintendent Cumming.[90] Stymied, Vaughan could only protest the hunting excesses; in all, Gore was believed to have killed two thousand buffalo, sixteen hundred deer and elk, and one hundred and five bears, including forty grizzlies.[91]

Now Gore approached Culbertson to secure downriver transport for himself, his supplies, and game trophies. Culbertson agreed to build a mackinaw for $1 a foot. With the boat nearly complete, Sir George balked at the price. He further accused Culbertson of offering a pitiful amount for the wagons and surplus goods Gore hoped to sell the Company.

---

[87]Bradley, "Gore," *MHSC*, Vol. IX, p. 248.
[88]Alfred Vaughan to Alfred Cumming, 9 Nov 1856. NAM, M234/885.
[89]Alfred Cumming to George Manypenny, 12 Dec 1856. NAM, M234/885.
[90]Bradley, "Gore," *MHSC*, Vol. IX, p. 249.
[91]Bradley, *MHSC*, Vol. III, p. 279; Innis, p. 212. Bradley claims that Vaughan sent these figures to Cumming in a letter written in July 1856. No such letter could be found by the author in NAM, M234/885, although correspondence exists to support Vaughan's irritation with Gore's expedition.

# THE BUFFALO WILL NOT CONTINUE FOREVER 267

Enraged, Sir George gathered together twenty carts, three wagons, and his excess supplies and burned them in front of Fort Union. When the smoldering mass cooled, he ordered his men to gather the remnants and toss them into the river so Culbertson could salvage nothing.

Sir George then sold his livestock, built two rickety flatboats, and floated downriver to Fort Berthold, an opposition post, to pass the winter of 1856-1857.[92] When Fort Berthold personnel also attempted to charge Gore what he considered exorbitant prices, the baron went to live in an Indian earthlodge.[93] Raiding parties of Blackfeet Sioux and Hunkpapas drove off Gore's remaining horses.[94]

The Department of Indian Affairs considered seizing Gore's furs, pelts, and elk horns and selling them to benefit the tribes. In the end, Secretary of Interior McClelland decided that, although warranted, such a forfeiture would probably cost more than it would generate. Instead, McClelland instructed Superintendent Cumming "to be more cautious in future in granting strangers privileges that can be abused."[95]

Sir St. George Gore, after spending half a million dollars on his hunt, returned to Ulster with a large collection of game trophies.[96] Many years later, the famous showman, "Buffalo Bill" Cody, referred to him as a "sportsman among a thousand." But those who lived on the upper river remembered him as the "Irish Butcher" whose excesses presaged the worst of what the white man would bring.[97]

Another white man came to Fort Benton around 1856 to trade with Alexander Culbertson.[98] John Silverthorne, an "old mountaineer," needed to replenish his supplies but had no money. He showed Culbertson a

---

[92]Alfred Vaughan to Alfred Cumming, 25 Dec 1856. NAM, M234/885; Bradley, "Gore," *MHSC*, Vol. IX, p. 249; Bradley, *MHSC*, Vol. III, p. 279; Sunder, p. 182; Thompson, p. 74.

[93]Alfred Vaughan to Alfred Cumming, 25 Dec 1856. NAM, M234/885; Bradley, "Gore," *MHSC*, Vol. IX, p. 249.

[94]Alfred Vaughan to Alfred Cumming, 25 Dec 1856. NAM, M234/885; Bradley, *MHSC*, Vol. III, p. 279.

[95]R. McClelland, 16 Jan 1857. NAM, M234/885.

[96]Innis, p. 213.

[97]Sunder, p. 182.

[98]The exact date is unclear. Alexander Culbertson, in relating the story to James H. Bradley, fixed the date as October 1856. Bradley, *MHSC*, Vol. III, pp. 277-278. McDonnell, *MHSC*, Vol. X, p. 247, supports this or a later date by suggesting that John Silverthorne did not come to Montana until 1856. Nonetheless, an entry in the "Fort Benton Journal," *MHSC*, Vol. X, p. 1, suggests the date might have been October 1854. See also Burlingame, p. 80, and notes, p. 362.

sack of yellow dust which he claimed was gold and offered it for $1,000 worth of goods.[99]

No one at Fort Benton had ever heard of gold in the area, although Father De Smet had noticed it in the Montana mountains as early as 1842. Realizing that a gold rush would severely impact the Indians, De Smet kept his discovery secret.[100]

Culbertson, not knowing what De Smet had seen, doubted Silverthorne's claim. Even if it was gold, he had no way to judge its value. Culbertson refused Silverthorne's request until another employee assured him that the dust was gold and worth every penny Silverthorne sought.[101]

Culbertson finally accepted the dust in exchange for horses, arms, ammunition, blankets, tobacco, and other goods. Still unsure of his trade, Culbertson charged the goods to his own account, rather than the Company's. The prospector, after refusing to divulge his strike's location, quietly returned to the mountains.[102]

The next summer, when Culbertson sent the dust to the St. Louis mint, it was adjudged to be "remarkably pure." For his investment, Culbertson received $1,525.[103] He never saw the mountaineer again and never knew his name. Several years later, a former AFC employee ran into the prospector in one of the now-burgeoning gold camps and learned his identity.[104]

---

[99]McDonnell, *MHSC*, Vol. X, p. 246.

[100]Chittenden, *De Smet*, Vol. I, p. 118.

[101]Bradley, *MHSC*, Vol. III, p. 277, gives his name as "Ray" and says he was a relative of Culbertson's from back east. McDonnell, *MHSC*, Vol. X, p. 246, offers a variant spelling of "Wray." If this man was related to Alexander Culbertson, the author suggests a spelling of "Rhea."

[102]McDonnell, *MHSC*, Vol. X, pp. 246-247; Bradley, *MHSC*, Vol. III, pp. 277-278.

[103]McDonnell, *MHSC*, Vol. X, p. 247; Bradley, *MHSC*, Vol. III, p. 278; Burlingame, p. 80.

[104]McDonnell, *MHSC*, Vol. X, p. 247.

# Chapter Twenty-Two

## *"to help stabilize the family"*

Throughout his more than twenty years with the American Fur Company, Alexander Culbertson had exhibited an indifference bordering on disdain regarding personal financial concerns. In 1845, he agreed to try to restore the Blackfeet trade without additional compensation; in 1850, he used his own funds to further his brother Thaddeus's research; in 1851, he escorted the upper river tribes to the government treaty conference without payment;[1] in 1853, he served as special agent for the railroad survey without pressing for recompense, including expense reimbursement, for three years;[2] in 1856, he paid the travel expenses of missionary Elkanah Mackey; and, when his AFC superiors complained about the terms Culbertson negotiated for transporting annuities to the Blackfeet treaty conference, he personally reimbursed the Company.[3] He had joined the AFC for adventure, not for riches, and he remained steadfast in that devotion. Yet, as Culbertson's desire for adventure became satiated, another motivation began to dominate his actions: securing fair and honest treatment for the Indians.

Pierre Chouteau, on the other hand, was nothing if not a hard-nosed businessman for whom financial concerns always ranked first. As for the Indians, Chouteau cared about them only as business partners; the government could worry about their adjustment to the rapidly encroaching white populace.

Such divergent value systems almost inevitably cause conflict. For Culbertson and Chouteau, common pursuits forestalled this clash until the mid-1850s when everyone could see that the fur trade was nearing its end.

---

[1] Bradley, *MHSC*, Vol. III, p. 267.
[2] Affidavit of Alexander Culbertson submitted to Charles E. Mix, Esq., 18 Mar 1856. NAM, M234/30.
[3] Alexander Culbertson to Pierre Chouteau, 4 Jun 1856. Chouteau Collection, MoHS.

Increasingly, healthy AFC profits depended upon government annuity transportation contracts. True to his nature, Culbertson worried less about the impact of these changes on his employers than about what they meant for the Indians. Chouteau, meanwhile, focused on maximizing profits before time ran out.

Since its inception, the American Fur Company had functioned as a closely held partnership of friends and relatives. Pierre Chouteau owned slightly more than half the Company while John Sanford, John Sarpy, and Joseph Sire held a significant share of the balance. Marriage, as well as business, bound the four primary partners and their interests seldom diverged.[4] Although traders such as Alexander Culbertson got pieces of the Company pie, they received a very small slice.[5]

But in the 1850s, the corporate structure that had served the Company for decades began to crumble. Sanford retired in 1851[6] and Sire died three years later, leaving the Company lacking capital investors.[7] Sarpy, meanwhile, was exhibiting signs of mental illness, causing Chouteau to question his stability and judgment.[8]

At the same time, Culbertson, long the recognized face of the AFC on the upper river, found the Company relying more and more on his influence not only with the Indians and their agents but also with the political powers in Washington, D.C.[9] In April 1855, Pierre Chouteau even hoped "the arrival of Culbertson" would "bring about a change in [Sarpy's] sick mind."[10]

Culbertson's increased responsibilities often led to increased blame without increased compensation. In early 1856, when Culbertson suggested changes in the operation of the upper Missouri posts, Chouteau dismissed the idea: "None of the propositions ... are acceptable to me."[11]

---

[4]Sunder, pp. 4-7.   [5]Sunder, p. 132.
[6]Sunder, p. 132.   [7]Sunder, p. 161.
[8]Pierre Chouteau to Charles Chouteau, 2 Apr 1855. Chouteau Collection, MoHS.
[9]John Sarpy to Pierre Chouteau, 12 Apr 1854. Chouteau-Papin Collection, MoHS.
[10]Pierre Chouteau to Charles Chouteau, 2 Apr 1855. Chouteau Collection, MoHS.
[11]Pierre Chouteau to John Sarpy, 30 Jan 1856. Chouteau Collection, MoHS. The letter does not specify the changes Culbertson advocated, stating only: "I will not go into the details of [the proposition presented by Culbertson], persuaded as I am that you know exactly the kind of affair that is meant." The author could find no further clues in the existing correspondence at the MoHS to clarify what "kind of affair" Culbertson proposed although, based on information in Sunder, pp. 161-162, the author believes that he probably suggested a restructuring of profit distribution for the Upper Missouri Outfit.

# TO HELP STABILIZE THE FAMILY

Two weeks later, Chouteau, belying his long relationship with Culbertson, wrote Sarpy: "Culbertson never darkens my door unless we owe him money. He knows that I will not agree to the propositions of the men of the Missouri, so he stays away." Chouteau concluded characteristically: "Be sure & send me the balance sheet for this month."[12]

None of this, however, prevented Chouteau from turning to Culbertson when it suited him, as it did a few months later when the 1856 transportation contract was due to be let. Chouteau hoped Culbertson could use his influence in Washington, D.C., to secure the contract despite his suggestion that Culbertson might not undertake the trip because "he is afraid that [the competition] has succeeded." Chouteau wistfully recalled the old days: "If Sanford were here, I would send him to Washington, but he is in Philadelphia."[13]

Even as he relied on Culbertson to negotiate the contract, Chouteau demanded that he reimburse the Company for $1600 in expenses which Chouteau believed had not been properly compensated by the 1855 contract. Culbertson agreed, authorizing Chouteau "to charge my account with the same."[14]

Culbertson managed to secure the 1856 transportation contract by underbidding three competitors, including John Shaw, a steamboat captain backed by Chouteau's rival, Robert Campbell. Shaw, in a bold move, had pledged "to use every possible exertion to carry [the Blackfeet annuities] by Steam Boat to Fort Benton," a goal that had long engaged steamboat captains and now greatly interested the government.[15]

Despite obtaining the 1856 contract, the AFC's financial situation worsened in 1857 when John Sarpy, the last original investor outside the Chouteau family, died.[16] Chouteau, hoping to maintain the Company as a family business, tried to recruit his son-in-law, William Maffitt. Chouteau suspected the proposal might not sit well with Culbertson and cautioned that it "would be against Culbertson's interests and he may oppose us secretly. He makes us pay dearly."[17]

---

[12]Pierre Chouteau to John Sarpy, 18 Feb 1856. Chouteau Collection, MoHS.
[13]Pierre Chouteau to John Sarpy, 8 Apr 1856. Chouteau Collection, MoHS.
[14]Alexander Culbertson to Pierre Chouteau, 4 Jun 1856. Chouteau Collection, MoHS.
[15]John Shaw to George Manypenny, 14 Apr 1856. NAM, M234/885; Sunder, p. 173.
[16]Sunder, p. 161.
[17]Pierre Chouteau to William Maffitt and Charles Chouteau, 20 Apr 1857. Chouteau-Papin Collection, MoHS. Again, it is not entirely clear that it was the offer of a partnership to Maffitt that Chouteau believed Culbertson would oppose. This is the author's conclusion.

Chouteau was probably wrong about Culbertson's reaction but, in any case, Maffitt declined. Chouteau then wrote his son, Charles, and Alexander Culbertson informing them that, unless new investors could be found, the AFC should seek a merger with the successors to Harvey, Primeau and Company. Otherwise, Chouteau warned, the Company might be forced to "sell all."[18]

Culbertson probably received this news with equanimity since he had more pressing concerns. Once again, smallpox had appeared,[19] this time striking his children.[20] In any case, Culbertson had grown weary of the business and political machinations. Nearing his fiftieth birthday, Alexander Culbertson decided to retire.

Culbertson began planning his retirement as early as May 1856 when he advised Pierre Chouteau: "I am anxious to have the accounts of Upper Mis. O[21] 1854 entirely closed before my departure."[22] When John Sarpy and the national economy went into decline in 1857,[23] the time seemed auspicious. Culbertson hoped to find a more hospitable environment than the upper Missouri to pass the long, cold winters.

There were also family considerations. The Culbertson family had continued to grow. In addition to Mariah and Janie, Culbertson's daughters from his first marriage, Natawista had given him four children: Jack, born at Fort Union in 1843; Julia, born at Fort Laramie[24] around 1845; Nancy, born at Fort Union in 1848; and, Fannie, born at Fort Benton in 1851.[25]

---

[18]Sunder, p. 161, citing an "uncatalogued" letter dated 28 Apr 1857 from Pierre Chouteau to Charles Chouteau and Alexander Culbertson, MoHS. The author could not locate this document.

[19]Sunder, p. 178.

[20]William Maffitt to Pierre Chouteau, May 1857. Chouteau-Walsh Collection, MoHS.

[21]Upper Missouri Outfit, the legal name of Culbertson's piece of the American Fur Company.

[22]Alexander Culbertson to P. Chouteau Jr. & Co, 10 May 1856 from St. Louis. Chouteau Collection, MoHS; FtLar.

[23]Sunder, p. 187.

[24]In her obituary, Julia Culbertson claimed to have been born in Chambersburg, Pennsylvania, but this is contradicted by her own statements to Charles Kessler. KP, UCLA. Statements in Julia's obituary make it clear that she was attempting to hide her Indian heritage, apparently believing that, if it became known, she would be ostracized by Boise society. "Pioneer of West," *The Idaho Statesman*, 17 March 1929, p. 14, column 3.

[25]Berglund, SC 414, MtHS, p. 22.

Natawista delighted in the children, traveling with them whenever possible.²⁶ She wanted them to know both Indian and white culture and readily consented to their baptism by the Jesuit missionaries. As their father and Pierre De Smet prepared to leave for the Horse Creek treaty conference, Nancy and Fannie were baptized by De Smet at Fort Union on July 20, 1851.²⁷

Two years later, this simple act may have brought some solace to her parents when Nancy drowned in the upper Missouri. Natawista, occupied with young Fannie, had hired an Indian girl to assist with the older children. As the family traveled on the steamboat, five-year-old Nancy wandered away, slipped, and fell overboard. The boat halted but the treacherous current had swept her away. For days, the crew and family searched, but Nancy's body was never recovered.²⁸ Heartbroken, the Culbertsons determined it was too dangerous for the children to continue to live and travel extensively on the river. The best alternative, despite the forlorn consequences, was to send them downriver to be raised in safer surroundings.²⁹

The Culbertsons decided to establish a home in the States where they could live with the children when practicable and entrust them to others when necessary. Therefore, in 1854, Culbertson purchased 160 acres in Limestone Township outside the bustling town of Peoria, Illinois.³⁰ Peoria, founded in 1825, was located on the Illinois River which, with its regular steamboat traffic, provided easy access to the frontier.

Peoria also appealed to Culbertson because of the many Pennsylvanians living there,³¹ including Culbertson's younger brother, William, his wife, Nancy McCulloh, and their three young daughters.³² Culbertson had scant opportunity to enjoy his brother's company, however, since William Culbertson died on June 24, 1857.³³ The Culbertson's first

---

²⁶Berglund, SC 414, MtHS, p. 23.
²⁷Garraghan, Vol. II, p. 479n. Fannie's name is recorded as "Francisca" Culbertson.
²⁸Berglund, SC 414, MtHS, p. 23.
²⁹Schemm, p. 12.
³⁰Notes made by Ernest East of Peoria, Illinois, citing land records of Peoria County Recorder, "GA page 395." PPL.
³¹"Sons of Pennsylvania Attend!" *PDT,* 31 Jan 1860.
³²Lewis Culbertson, p. 268.
³³Lewis Culbertson, p. 268; *PDT,* 26 Jun 1857, page 2, column 4.

Peoria home was a brick house on the site of today's Madison Park.[34] Culbertson's unmarried niece, Anna,[35] cared for the children when Alexander and Natawista were upriver. While Natawista may have spent winters in Peoria beginning in 1854, Culbertson did not join her there until 1857.[36]

Peoria folklore later suggested that the Culbertson home sported a pointed yellow roof reminiscent of a tipi "in an effort to beguile Natawista's sorrow at being separated from her people."[37] Fannie scoffed at this, arguing that had her father "wanted his family to live in tepees he would have left them on the plains."[38]

The family, accustomed to open space, did not live in town long. In 1857, they moved to a spacious "mansion house," named Locust Grove, on the town's outskirts. The estate quickly became a showplace.[39] The nine room home sported sharp gables trimmed with scalloped edges[40] and an ornate picket fence with two handsome gates[41] leading to the driveway and garden.[42] Culbertson hired "Old Jimmy," an English gardener, to landscape and maintain the grounds.[43]

In 1858, Culbertson purchased an additional 160 acres.[44] He imported wildlife from the upper Missouri, including deer, elk, wolves, antelope, foxes, and buffalo, to roam the estate.[45] The grounds also contained stables, playhouses for the children, and a swimming pool.[46] In addition to the gardener, the family employed a cook, stable hands, and other servants.[47]

---

[34]"Ancient Mansion."

[35]Daughter of his brother, James. Lewis Culbertson, p. 271; Schemm, p. 12. Schemm mistakenly calls Anna the "maiden sister" of Culbertson.

[36]*PDT*, 8 May 1857, page 3, column 2, reports that Alexander Culbertson would be traveling upriver with Dr. John Arnold of Peoria. It refers to Culbertson as "also a citizen of Peoria county." Culbertson spent at least part of the winter of 1856-1857 in Washington, D.C., but may have been in Peoria for some of that winter.

[37]Lina Ulrich Belsley to Ernest East, 1 Oct 1936. PPL.

[38]Berglund, SC 414, MtHS, p. 9.     [39]Berglund, SC 414, MtHS, p. 8.

[40]Schemm, p. 12; also photo in "Ancient Mansion."

[41]"Ancient Mansion."

[42]Notes by Ernest East, 31 May 1936. "Drove westwardly seven miles..." PPL.

[43]Berglund, SC 414, MtHS, p. 8.

[44]Notes by Ernest East. PPL. Transaction recorded 16 March 1858 in Peoria County Land Records, Volume XA, page 550.

[45]Berglund, SC 414, MtHS, p. 8.     [46]Berglund, SC 414, MtHS, p. 8.

[47]Schemm, p. 13; Flemming interview, 1 Dec 1937, PPL.

Culbertson kept ponies for the children, a team of beautiful black carriage horses, and several prize thoroughbreds. He exhibited the horses at shows and fairs throughout the region, usually garnering top honors.[48] Then, one year, they came in second in Louisville, Kentucky. "Old Ben," the coachman and groom, was so infuriated by the judges' inability to see their superiority over "any Kentucky-bred animal" that he refused to show them again.[49]

The home's interior reflected the Culbertsons' taste for fine objects. A magnificent pier glass graced the front hall.[50] Elegant rosewood sofas and velvet covered chairs sat on wall-to-wall floral velvet rugs. Imported European wallpaper covered the walls. Several full-length gilt-edged mirrors hung in the drawing room.[51]

But visitors were most struck by the magnificent paintings. Culbertson had purchased from John Mix Stanley, the artist who accompanied the 1853 Stevens railroad expedition, several original oils, including "The Last of Their Race,"[52] considered the artist's masterpiece. The allegorical painting depicted nine Indians, dressed in the style of different tribes, perched on a rocky promontory at ocean's edge. The symbolism conveyed the painter's trepidations about the future of the native people.[53]

The painting held special significance for Culbertson. Natawista had been Stanley's model for the Indian woman seated on a rock closest to the ocean. Standing next to her is Seen From Afar, elegantly dressed with a regal bearing.[54] The spectacular painting, for which Culbertson

---

[48]Berglund, SC 414, MtHS, p. 9; Schemm, p. 13.

[49]Berglund, SC 414, MtHS, p. 9.

[50]Schemm, p. 12.

[51]Taylor, "The Major's Blackfoot Bride," p. 47.

[52]The title of this painting is universally given in the literature on Culbertson at PPL as "Last of the Race"; its correct title is "The Last of Their Race."See illustrations, p. 241.

[53]Interpretation of the painting comes from Sarah E. Boehme, The John S. Bugas Curator, Whitney Gallery of Western Art, Buffalo Bill Historical Center, Cody, Wyoming. Personal correspondence with the author, 17 Jan 1996.

[54]"Works of Art," PDT, 1 Dec 1859, page 4, column 2. The article does not identify Seen From Afar but says simply that it was modeled after Natawista's brother. A comparison of the painting to Gustavus Sohon's previously known sketch of Seen From Afar leaves little doubt that it is he. This identification is further confirmed by the discovery of Stanley's sketch of Seen From Afar in the collection of the Stark Museum, Orange, Texas. How this came to be identified as the portrait of a "Cayuse Man" is unknown. See illustrations, p. 238.

reportedly paid $1,500,[55] arrived on November 30, 1859, and promptly went on display at the Peoria County Fair where visitors paid ten cents to view it.[56]

Culbertson also owned two other Stanley paintings. One depicted Fort Union, the upper Missouri, an Indian encampment, and a mixed party of Indians and whites. "The rugged and romantic character of the landscape" added "additional charm to the figures." The third Stanley painting showed Indian women digging for *pomme blanches* near an Indian village. Although lacking "the delicate finish of the others," it, too, was "a valuable work of art." The two smaller paintings could also be seen, without charge, at the county fair.[57]

---

[55] Frances Culbertson Irvin to Ernest East, 18 Dec 1936. PPL

[56] "Works of Art." When Alexander Culbertson went bankrupt, this painting was bought at auction by William Herron, a pioneer Peoria banker. Mr. Herron subsequently gave it to his son, John W. Herron of Akron, Ohio, who owned it into the 1950s. "(Picture of Indians)," PPL. The author's attempts to locate the painting in the early 1990s proved fruitless. Then, in May 1995, while touring the Whitney Gallery of Western Art at the Buffalo Bill Historical Center in Cody, Wyoming, the author happened upon the painting which she immediately recognized from previously read descriptions, its artist, and title. A follow-up letter from the author to Sarah Boehme, Curator at the Whitney Gallery, established that the Whitney Gallery had purchased the painting from J. N. Bartfield Galleries in New York. Ms. Boehme further informed the author that the Whitney had no further provenance for the painting and the author happily provided the painting's history to Ms. Boehme. At that point, Ms. Boehme informed the author that the Stark Museum of Art in Orange, Texas, possessed another copy of the painting which was virtually identical, with differences only in size and a few details. Research established that the painting owned by the Stark Museum is the one originally owned by the Culbertsons. This painting, done circa 1853, was originally titled, "The Last of His Race" and purchased by Culbertson at auction on December 20, 1858. Later, Culbertson apparently changed the title to "The Last of Their Race." The Stark Museum acquired it through auction in 1955 from Mrs. John W. Herron.

The painting currently owned by the Whitney Gallery was executed by Stanley in 1867 and remained in the Stanley family until it was sold to the Bartfield Galleries which, in 1975, sold it to the Whitney Gallery.

A related painting, "Barter for a Bride," was executed by Stanley between 1854 and 1863. It, too, incorporates images of Natawista and Seen From Afar. (See illustrations.) The painting was recognized in 1965 by Alice Stevens Acheson, the granddaughter of John Mix Stanley and wife of former Secretary of State, Dean Acheson, when it was displayed at the United States Department of State. Mrs. Acheson recognized the painting as the work of her grandfather because of her familiarity with the family group as illustrated in "The Last of Their Race." This painting had been known simply as "A Family Group" throughout the 19th century, acquiring its title "Barter for a Bride" sometime in the 20th century. Mrs. Acheson arranged to have the painting purchased by the Morris and Gwendolyn Cafritz Foundation in 1967 for $20,000 and donated to the State Department. Today, it hangs in the Diplomatic Reception Room at the Department of State.

The author is deeply indebted to John Mix Stanley researcher, Bob Gibson, of Greensboro, North Carolina, for his assistance in sorting out the provenance of these paintings.

Culbertson displayed several other Indian artifacts and "curiosities" at the fair that December. Unfortunately, someone stole a "beautiful horn cup with two silver hands," made in Scotland and given to Culbertson. Culbertson offered a $10 reward for its return, but whether it was recovered is not known.[58]

Culbertson's active participation in the fair reflected his craving to fit in with Peoria society. That desire had been demonstrated the previous September when Culbertson formally married Natawista in a Catholic ceremony at Locust Grove. The marriage license, issued September 9, 1859 by deputy clerk Geo. H. Kettelle, authorized Culbertson to wed "Miss Natowiska of the Blackfoot Tribe of Indians."[59] Later that day, Father Thomas Scanlon of St. Joseph, Missouri, performed the service. Ecumenism triumphed as the Catholic ceremony united the Presbyterian and the pantheist.

The ceremony was reported in the *Peoria Daily Transcript* under the headline, "An Interesting Marriage Ceremony." While acknowledging that the two had been married "according to the Indian ceremony" some "sixteen or seventeen years ago," the reporter noted that Culbertson, "having lately severed his connection with the American Fur Company and settled down to an agricultural life near this city," wished to have the ceremony "performed according to civilized rites."

The *Transcript* noted that the couple's "three very interesting children" witnessed the ceremony.[60] The reporter must not have considered an infant "interesting" because, that January, Natawista had given birth to their fifth child: a son they named Joseph for Alexander's father. Years later, Julia's "gray eyes would gleam with amusement" whenever she recalled her parents' formal wedding.[61] The "large number of invited guests" included "Captain" James Kipp, Culbertson's old AFC friend, who had retired and settled in Parkville, Missouri.[62] Several

---

[57]"Works of Art." The current location of these other two paintings are unknown. Additionally, Culbertson owned a portrait of himself done by Stanley. This portrait is currently owned by George Taylor, the great-grandson of Alexander Culbertson. See illustration.

[58]"Ten Dollars Reward" and "Lost or Stolen," *PDT*, 31 Oct 1859, page 1, column 5, and page 2, column 1.

[59]Marriage Register No. 5000, 9 Sep 1859. PPL.

[60]"An Interesting Marriage Ceremony," *PDT*, 12 Sep 1859, page 4, columns 2 and 3.

[61]Taylor, "The Major's Blackfoot Bride," p. 27.

[62]"An Interesting Marriage."

years earlier, Kipp's son, Samuel, had married Alexander's daughter, Mariah.[63]

The paper noted that Natawista, "a lady of fine native talent," had "rendered great service" to Governor Isaac Stevens and Colonel Alfred Cumming, since appointed governor of Utah, when they negotiated "the treaty of the Judith between this government and the nation to which she belonged."[64]

Frances Stuart Culbertson, Culbertson's stepmother, may also have attended the ceremony but his father, Joseph, had died the year before. [65] Fannie remembered her grandmother, "perhaps [feeling] that it was her mission to help stabilize the family at Peoria," spending nearly a year there. The ever-pious Frances demanded nightly devotions from the family and servants during which she "read long chapters from the scriptures." Young Fannie "couldn't understand a word of it." The servants resented "this self-assumed authority" and found a myriad of excuses to absent themselves. "But for the family there was no escape."[66]

Culbertson, determined that his children be educated, sent Jack to military school[67] and enrolled Janie, Julia, and Fannie at the Academy of the Visitation convent school in St. Louis.[68] Although Culbertson and Natawista tried to visit them frequently, other responsibilities sometimes intervened.

In 1856, Culbertson wrote Julia to apologize for going upriver instead

---

[63]Holterman, p. 137. Mariah and Samuel Kipp had two children: Julia, no doubt named after Mariah's younger half-sister, and Alexander, who died as a child. Following the death of Samuel Kipp, Mariah Culbertson Kipp married Joseph A. Walker, 1 Nov 1865, in the Presbyterian Episcopal Church in Peoria, Illinois. Marriage License #7328. Walker was born in New Jersey in 1836. At some point following their marriage, the Walkers returned to the Kipp farm in Parkville, Missouri, where they apparently managed the farm for James Kipp, who was by then quite elderly. Mariah and Joseph Walker had had two children by 1870: John and James. NAM M593/799.

[64]"An Interesting Marriage."

[65]Lewis Culbertson, p. 268.

[66]Berglund, SC 414, MtHS, p. 10.

[67]Berglund, SC 414, MtHS, p. 22, says that Jack Culbertson "was admitted to West Point, but he could not seem to take the strict discipline of the Military School so he did not return the second year." A search of records at West Point failed to turn up any record of Jack's having attended that school.

[68]Undated letter from Sister Ann Marie Mardoe (last name unclear) to Theresa Berglund. SC 414, MtHS.

of visiting her, as promised. He explained that, in St. Joseph, Agent Vaughan had prevailed on him to "accompany the Expedition" to Fort Benton. Culbertson implored his daughter not to be "disappointed but bear up and endeavour (*sic*) to pass usefully and as pleasantly as circumstances will permit" the time until his return. He encouraged her to "spare no pains . . . to facilitate the Education" and to "keep up a corrispondance (*sic*)" with Janie, who may have been attending school in Pennsylvania. In closing, the dutiful father promised to write frequently and begged his daughter to "accept our affection."[69]

Although Julia adjusted well to school, young Fannie did not, equating the "dark, desolate, solemn world" of the convent school with "a prison." She cried constantly. When the nuns asked what was wrong, Fannie said: "I want my mother." The next day, the nuns summoned her to the parlor to visit "a lady." Fannie expected to find one of her parents' St. Louis friends; instead, Natawista waited to take her home.[70]

Fannie spent the rest of the year in Peoria where she "romped and played and took rides on [her] spotted pony." Still insecure, she sometimes ran inside to confirm that Natawista was still there. Mother and daughter took long walks to talk about Fannie's future. Natawista told Fannie that, eventually, she would have to return to school to "learn to be a fine lady."

The idea "began to take hold" until Fannie decided "it would be a great privilege" to go back to school. The next fall, she returned to the academy. Natawista and one of Fannie's friends accompanied her, remaining in St. Louis until Fannie felt comfortable. After they left, Fannie "didn't cry any more," despite being the youngest girl there.[71]

That same fall, Janie and Julia enrolled at the Moravian Seminary for Young Ladies in Bethlehem, Pennsylvania.[72] The Moravians embraced a communal lifestyle similar to that of the Indian tribes which appealed to Culbertson. He may also have hoped that the girls could enjoy visits from his family in nearby Chambersburg.

But that did not occur. Julia and Janie remained in Bethlehem even during the summer. Trips to Peoria were rare as were visits with their

---

[69]Alexander Culbertson to "My Dear Daughter," 9 Jun 1856. SC 586, MtHS.
[70]Berglund, SC 414, MtHS, pp. 12-13.
[71]Berglund, SC 414, MtHS, pp. 13-14.
[72]Taylor, "The Major's Blackfoot Bride," p. 28.

nearby grandparents and cousins. While Culbertson saw his daughters on his occasional journeys east, Natawista became a vague memory. As a result, Janie and Julia felt "quite strangers" to her, causing Natawista enormous grief. In later years, Julia called Alexander "Father" but referred to her mother as Natty, the family's nickname for Natawista. By contrast, she called Francis Wolle, superintendent of the Moravian Seminary, "Papa Wolle" and his wife "Mama Wolle."[73] Julia's estrangement from Natawista persisted for the rest of their lives.[74]

Meanwhile, the Culbertsons welcomed both Indian and mixed-blood children from the upper Missouri into their Peoria home, helping to facilitate their education.[75] When Culbertson wrote Julia in 1856 from the steamboat *Robert Campbell*, he expressed concern for one of these children, urging Julia to "give [her] every good advice to study" and "be careful of her health as you know she is not over strong." But Culbertson apparently forgot the child's name, leaving a blank where it should have been.

In the same letter, Culbertson asked Julia to remind Janie of Natawista's advice to "keep that Little Girl go (*sic*) constantly to School."[76] Whether Natawista intended this admonition for Janie or another child under their guidance is not clear.[77]

Among those who came to Peoria was an Indian boy named Kisenaw, "from Fort Union." Robert McCulloh, the nephew of Nancy McCulloh

---

[73]Taylor, "The Major's Blackfoot Bride," pp. 28-29. Taylor gives the name as "Sylvester Wohl" but in the filings against Culbertson for unpaid bills in 1869, his name is given as Francis Wolle. PPL.

[74]Records of the Catholic Church on the Blood Reserve in Alberta, Canada, where Natawista lived from 1870 until her death, refer to only two children: Fannie and Joe. At the time of these records, Jack was dead, but Julia was alive and living in Boise, Idaho. Personal correspondence from Hugh Dempsey to the author, April 1996. In Julia's obituary, she makes no mention of her mother. "Pioneer of West," *The Idaho Statesman*.

[75]Holterman, p. 138.

[76]Alexander Culbertson to "My Dear Daughter." SC 586, MtHS.

[77]Information about Janie Culbertson becomes almost non-existent after this. Holterman, p. 137, claims that she died in 1860, but this is incorrect. On 24 Oct 1866, she married William Hunt in Peoria, Illinois. The photograph of Janie which appears in this book and Holterman, p. 164, was probably taken on this occasion. (Holterman, believing she was already deceased, dismissed the identification.) Later, she must have married a man named Wood, as a Mrs. S. G. McCluggage of Peoria later recalled attending a party in 1929 "at which Jane Culbertson, then Mrs. Wood of St. Louis was present." According to Mrs. McCluggage, Janie had a "wonderfully melodious voice and charming manners." Mrs. McCluggage also stated that Janie "died suddenly the next year after attending a dinner party." May J. Belsley to Ernest East, 1 Oct 1936. PPL. Unattributed notes in the Boller Collection, NDHS, dated 20 Nov 1899, say that "Janie Hunt, 2d daughter of Maj. Culbertson . . . is a widow living in Jacksonville, Ill."

Culbertson, Alexander's brother's widow, joined the family at Locust Grove during one of Kisenaw's visits. The "tales of stirring times in the Far West" that Kisenaw and Jack Culbertson told so captivated Robert that he longed to visit the region and see the "picturesque fort" in Stanley's painting. Although Culbertson offered to take him upriver, McCulloh's mother refused. As an adult, McCulloh made his own decisions. He moved to Montana, living there the rest of his life.[78] Kisenaw, too, returned to the frontier where, apparently, he was killed on a trading expedition with Culbertson.[79]

The Peoria newspaper carried frequent mention of the Culbertsons[80] and published Culbertson's articles on Indian lifestyles and Badlands geology.[81] He also shared a copy of the December 10, 1793, issue of the *Chambersburg* (PA) *Gazette* found among his father's possessions. The newspaper, containing the complete text of President George Washington's second inaugural address, carried another item that the retired trader probably found even more intriguing: a listing of the then-known fifty-three Indian nations.[82]

In 1860, a fire destroyed a dwelling house owned by Culbertson and occupied by tenants. A defective flue was blamed for the $1500 loss but there were no injuries.[83] That September, Culbertson reported an early frost with "no material damage"[84] to the apple and fruit trees purchased the previous spring. Culbertson liked the trees so much that he had ordered an additional $100 worth.[85] The next year, Jack Culbertson had a gold watch and $180 in cash stolen while returning to Peoria from Pennsylvania.[86] And when Culbertson's half-brother, Simpson, died in China

---

[78]Robert L. McCulloh to Charles N. Kessler, 12 Feb 1918. KP, UCLA.

[79]Joe Culbertson, p. 1. Joe gives the name as "Kisenar" while McCulloh gives it as "Kisenaw."

[80]*PDT*, 8 May 1857, page 3, column 2; *PDT*, 5 Feb 1859, page 4, column 1; *PDT*, 11 Feb 1859, page 1, column 3; *PDT*, 19 Aug 1859, page 4, column 1; *PDT*, 16 Oct 1862, page 3, column 2; *PDT*, 13 Nov 1862, page 3, column 2.

[81]"A Winter Trip," *PDT*, 9 Feb 1859, page 2, column 2; "The Indians of the Upper Missouri," *PDT*, 10 Mar 1859, page 2, columns 2 and 3 ;and, 11 Mar 1859, page 3, columns 2 and 3.

[82]"An old Newspaper," *PDT*, 25 Apr 1859, page 4, column 2. The total Indian population was estimated to be 352,680, with some 60,000 warriors.

[83]"Fire," *PDT*, 2 Feb 1860, page 4, column 1.

[84]*PDT*, 19 Sep 1860, page 4, column 1.    [85]*PDT*, 23 Oct 1860, page 4, column 2.

[86]*PDT*, 9 Dec 1861, page 1, column 3.

in 1862, the paper carried his obituary, noting that he "had a number of relatives in Peoria."[87]

Culbertson even dabbled in local politics, striking up a friendship with Dr. John Arnold, who served as Peoria's mayor, despite their divergent party alliances. Arnold, a Whig, joined the Republican party after his 1854 election to the Illinois Senate.[88] Two years later, President Abraham Lincoln appointed him American Consul to St. Petersburg, Russia.[89]

Culbertson, a Democrat, took pains in 1860 to announce his disillusionment with "Bob Ingersoll, the candidate of the democratic party" who, he said, had "deceived me and is not worthy of my notice." Culbertson instead threw his support behind "Judge Kellogg,"[90] but did not sever his ties to the Democratic party.

Indeed, that year, Culbertson traveled to Baltimore, apparently to serve as a delegate for Illinois's Senator Stephen Douglas at the Democratic National Convention.[91] Douglas, a candidate for the Democratic nomination for president, authored the Kansas-Nebraska Act allowing settlers in those newly created territories to choose whether or not to allow slavery within their borders.[92] Culbertson had spent his entire adult life aligned with the southerners of the American Fur Company, placing him on the wrong side of history as the Civil War loomed.

Natawista also made her way into the newspapers. During the Civil War, she became involved with two civic organizations and was even elected "Directress" of the Ladies Soldiers Aid Society of the Second Presbyterian Church.[93] This distinction seems most unusual, especially considering her reported inability to speak English. Most likely, Nancy McCulloh Culbertson, also active in the Society, promoted Natawista's election.[94] The women no doubt thought it most unique to have a full-blooded Indian as their leader.

Peoria regarded the entire Culbertson family as an entertaining curiosity. Citizens were fond of driving past Locust Grove while telling stories of the family's latest exploits.[95] Many focused on Jack who once brought

---

[87] *PDT*, 16 Dec 1862, page 3, column 2.
[88] Biography of John D. Arnold. Special Collections, Peoria Historical Society Collection, CDL, BU.   [89] Biography of Dr. John Arnold. CDL, BU.
[90] *PDT*, 31 Aug 1860, page 2, column 3.
[91] "Ancient Mansion."   [92] *Chronicle of America*, p. 346.
[93] *PDT*, 28 Jan 1863, page 3, column 3; *PDT*, 19 Jun 1863, page 3, column 3.
[94] *PDT*, 8 Jan 1863, page 3, column 3.
[95] Schemm, p. 13; Taylor, "The Major's Blackfoot Bride," p. 47.

his pet goat into the house and watched in amusement as it butted its reflection in the beautiful gilt-edged mirrors. And then there was the pinto pony that Jack rode up the steps of the house into the parlor.[96] People claimed Jack even put rubber shoes on the horse so he could ride it into the downtown bars. While Jack drank, the horse allegedly sat on its haunches, its feet up on the bar.[97]

Rumors of the family's excessive drinking were widespread. At least in the case of Jack, they appear to have been well-founded. One newspaper account reported "Jake Culbertson" going on a "bender" and getting picked up by the police. The incident cost Jack, or Jake, $20.[98] Society matrons, usually with raised eyebrows and a barely audible muttering of "Indian," whispered about Natawista's fondness for "firewater."[99]

One anecdote recalled a drunken Natawista, wielding a butcher knife, chasing a young female guest about the house. "If she had not worn a wig," according to the tale, "Natawista would surely have scalped her."[100] The son of the Culbertsons' cook charged that Culbertson "was an awful drunkard" and, indeed, "(t)he whole family was."[101]

How much truth and how much prejudice lay behind these allegations is unclear. The frontier lifestyle certainly lent itself to drinking, often to excess, and there is little reason to doubt that Alexander and Natawista indulged. Nonetheless, Charles Larpenteur, the tee-totaling AFC clerk, lambasted nearly everyone for their drunkenness but mentioned Culbertson's propensity only once.[102] Of course, both Culbertson and Natawista may have imbibed more as their quiet retirement assumed a boring sameness.

Even without the tales of drunkenness, the couple gave the locals plenty to talk about. Natawista continued to dress in the finest, most up-to-date fashions. Expensive jewels adorned each of her fingers. She disdained diamonds, preferring stones of color.[103] During the hot summer, when not upriver, Natawista erected a tipi in the side yard and moved outside to catch the cool river breezes. At those times, she shed her fancy dresses in favor of native garb.[104]

Another story favored by native Peorians concerned the day Natawista stood by, laughing and clapping, as two spirited horses smashed a brand

---

[96]Schemm, p. 13.
[97]Flemming interview, PPL.
[98]*PDT*, 4 Jul 1862, page 1, column 3.
[99]Schemm, p. 13.
[100]Lina Belsley to Ernest East. PPL.
[101]Flemming interview. PPL.
[102]See Larpenteur, p. 150, for his only reference to Culbertson being drunk.
[103]Taylor, "The Major's Blackfoot Bride," p. 45.
[104]Taylor, "The Major's Blackfoot Bride," p. 47; McDonnell, *MHSC*, Vol. X, p. 245.

new carriage recently purchased for $300.[105] As their great-granddaughter later remarked: "Preservation of possessions was never an outstanding Culbertson trait."[106]

Other stories, perhaps influenced by envy or later events, revolved around Culbertson's personal fortune. Peorians whispered that "the Major" kept open casks of gold in the cellar.[107] A variation had "chestfuls of gold coins" lying about, with friends and relatives free to pocket a few. A more modest version placed stacks of gold coins on the lids of the casks.[108] The most extravagant tale claimed Culbertson amused himself by tossing gold coins at turtles in the river.[109]

These stories took on their own vibrancy as rumors began to circulate that the profligate frontiersman was decidedly slow in paying his bills. There was reason for this: Alexander Culbertson was going broke.

---

[105]Lina Belsley to Ernest East, PPL; Schemm, p. 13; McDonnell, *MHSC*, Vol. X, p. 245; Taylor, "The Major's Blackfoot Bride," p. 46.

[106]Taylor, "The Major's Blackfoot Bride," p. 47.

[107]Schemm, p. 13; Flemming interview, PPL; McDonnell, *MHSC*, Vol. X, p. 242.

[108]Taylor, "The Major's Blackfoot Bride," p. 46; East, "Colorful Story," *Peoria Journal*, 24 Feb 1939.

[109]Holterman, p. 137.

Chapter Twenty-Three

## *"the strength and importance of the white man"*

Alexander Culbertson wrote a remarkable article for the *Peoria Daily Transcript* in 1859[1] detailing the changes he had witnessed among the Indian tribes during his quarter-century on the upper Missouri. He divided the tribes into two classes: stationery tribes, such as the Mandans and Arikaras, and "roving" bands, including the Sioux, Crows, Assiniboines, Crees, and Blackfeet. All of them, Culbertson said, remained "as yet in a savage state," having advanced but little "in the path of knowledge." Their "original manners and customs, if not entire (*sic*), are but slightly changed." They maintained their "superstitions" and "Idol-worship" with "art and knowledge . . . yet in their infancy." Nonetheless, Culbertson had witnessed "great and important *changes* . . . brought about by the commerce of trade,"[2] suggesting means for future transformation.

When first encountered, the nomadic tribes "were much more ignorant in every thing, degraded in habits, slovenly in appearance, and barbarous in their actions." With life tenuous, their lives revolved around survival, leading to "frequent and atrocious" crime, "slaughtering their enemies," and generalized murder. "Their women were worse than slaves, the extent of their labors more than they could bear." At that time, the tribes existed in small bands, usually centered around family units, with enmities "arising from the petty jealousies of chiefs or private family annimosities (*sic*)."

With the introduction of firearms, metal cooking utensils, and tools, the Indians increased "their hunting operations, and with them, their domestic comfort." Smaller bands joined together with "unity of purpose

---

[1]"The Indians of the Upper Missouri," *PDT*, 10 Mar 1859, page 3, column 2. Culbertson promised "a general and minute search into all [the Indians'] motions, acts, religion, government and ceremonies, [concluding] with a history of the American Fur Company, embodying many statements of various matters incident to the lives of trappers and traders." Unfortunately, the promise was not kept.    [2]Italics in the original.

and action." This resulted in rudimentary forms of government and "great diminution of family feuds and private quarrels" as the Indians devoted time "to the comfort and welfare of their families, instead of its being spent in bloody contention or domestic idleness and discord."

Culbertson readily acknowledged that the traders were motivated by "personal gain," but considered this "immaterial" in examining the trade's impact. Early traders hired Indians in the Indian camps "to restrain the populace from robbing the trader." The Indians considered this an "honorable station"; to be so relied upon "flattered their pride." These guards used this status to create a "nucleus around which collected a superior and coercive force, which, in the course of time, was applied to their own government, producing order and rendering effective decisions by council."

These positive changes, Culbertson wrote, occurred as a result of the Indians' decision to band together in a more effective, more "civilized" social structure. Culbertson believed that, given the opportunity, the Indians would understand that their lives would improve if they adopted the more settled "white" lifestyle. But his experience convinced the trader that such radical change would take time, perhaps lots of it.[3]

And that time was running out.

Although officially retired, Culbertson and Natawista continued to spend their summers on the upper Missouri.[4] In 1857, they hosted their Peoria friend, Dr. John Arnold, on an upriver adventure. Born in Collins Center, New York, Arnold settled in Peoria in 1849 where he "engaged energetically in the practice of medicine and surgery." His wife had earlier died of tuberculosis[5] which he, too, had apparently contracted.[6] Therefore, when Culbertson offered him an "appointment of surgeon" with the AFC, the doctor embraced the opportunity "to roam in the Western wilds in search of that boon so many have thus obtained—health."[7]

The group left Peoria on May 6[8] and headed for St. Louis where Cul-

---

[3] *PDT*, 10 Mar 1859.

[4] It is clear that Culbertson went upriver every year until 1861 and then continued the pattern until the last years of the Civil War. Natawista probably accompanied him on these trips.

[5] "Biography of John D. Arnold," CDL, BU.

[6] *PDT*, 17 Aug 1860, page 4, column 1; *PDT*, 12 Oct 1861, page 1, column 5.

[7] "Personal," *PDT*, 1 May 1857, page 3, column 2.

[8] "Gone," *PDT*, 8 May 1857, page 3, column 2.

bertson outfitted the doctor for his trip. Arnold sent a daguerreotype back to Peoria showing him with "a gun sitting by his side, a tremendous knife, larger by a hundred times than any he ever used in his profession, a belt and pistol case, with diverse paraphernolia (*sic*) to us unknown."[9]

The uneventful journey took the group to Fort Benton. Although his surgeon's skills were never needed, Arnold "had some fine sport shooting wolves, buffalo, deer and antelope." He judged the "vast" country to be "entirely unfit for any other purpose than that of sustaining the wild animals of the country, and the Indians, who subsist upon them." The buffalo herds, "more numerous than the cattle upon the prairies of Illinois," had "as many as five hundred in one band." When they were encountered swimming across the river, the travelers "shot them, hoisted them on board with the tackle, dressed them, saved the choice pieces and threw the balance overboard."[10]

The *Spread Eagle* returned to St. Louis in July with five thousand packs of furs and fifty mountaineers "attired partly in the Indian garb, with faces almost as dark as that of the Indian."[11] Dr. Arnold, "in good health and spirits," arrived in Peoria that November[12] with an Indian saddle, a large buffalo head, a grizzly hide, a pair of six-foot-long elk horns, and the alleged scalp of a Crow Indian.[13] At Culbertson's urging, he planned to donate the rare white buffalo robe he had obtained to the Smithsonian Institution.[14]

One of Arnold's souvenirs, almost certainly acquired through the Culbertsons' intervention, was more unusual: a "very young" Indian girl named Nataska. Arnold thought she "might be reared in his sister's home and become one of the family," but his plans "worked out only partially well." When Nataska was about twelve, Arnold enrolled her in a "convent in St. Louis," possibly the Academy of the Visitation.[15] Nataska eventually married a white man named I. A. Pascoe. Although she apparently never again lived with the Arnold family, the doctor remembered her in his will.[16]

---

[9]"In Costume," *PDT*, 14 May 1857, page 3, column 2.
[10]"Rocky Mountain Correspondence," *PDT*, 1 Jul 1857, page 2, column 2.
[11]"Head of Navigation," *PDT*, 4 Jul 1857, page 2, column 1.
[12]"Welcome Home," *PDT*, 2 Nov 1857, page 3, column 2. The article makes no reference to Culbertson. [13]*PDT*, 22 Sep 1858, page 4, column 1.
[14]"Scarce Article," *PDT*, 6 Nov 1857, page 3, column 2.
[15]"Biography of Dr. John Arnold," CDL, BU.
[16]Ernest East to Anne McDowell (*sic*), PPL.

❖ ❖ ❖

Even as Arnold enjoyed his quiet trip, forces were converging to disrupt the upper Missouri. In late 1857, a Yankton Sioux delegation traveled to Washington, D.C., where they ceded 640 acres near the mouth of the James River for $1.6 million in annuities over fifty years.[17] Although the treaty remained unratified, speculators began settling on the designated lands the next summer. The Yanktons, while expressing "no regret for having made the Treaty!," were nevertheless "much excited on account of Squatters" and "threatened to use violence" unless the government drove them off.[18]

On a "dismal and dreary" May 15, 1858, the *Spread Eagle* left St. Louis[19] with Culbertson, Natawista, and Alfred Vaughan, recently appointed agent to the Blackfeet, on board.[20] In Yankton territory, hostile warriors fired on the boat. The *Spread Eagle* was not carrying the Indian annuities, making Captain John La Barge and Charles Chouteau, representing the AFC, reluctant to dock. But Natawista prevailed on them to stop and throw the Yanktons a feast. Standing on deck in Indian garb, she signaled the warriors of their peaceful intentions. The feast went well, allowing the *Spread Eagle* to continue upriver.[21]

Between Forts Pierre and Berthold, twenty Mandan and Arikara warriors "stealthily" boarded the steamer and handed Culbertson a letter from the Fort Clark trader. The note, which the Indians could not read, warned that the warriors planned to steal their horses. Culbertson persuaded Chouteau and La Barge to throw another feast and the warriors left happy, without the Company horses. Additional angry and, in some cases, nearly destitute Indians presented themselves above Fort Berthold and again at Fort Union, necessitating more appeasement feasts.[22]

At Fort Union, Alexander Redfield, the new upper Missouri Indian agent, hired Alexander Culbertson to transport two years of Crow annuities to Fort Sarpy. Redfield had hoped the Crows might collect their annuities at Fort Union, but they refused to come, fearing hostile encoun-

---

[17] Alexander H. Redfield to Charles E. Mix, 3 Feb 1858. NAM, M234/885; C. F. Picotte to Charles Mix, 3 Aug 1858. NAM, M234/885; Sunder, p. 200.
[18] Alexander H. Redfield to Charles E. Mix, 5 Jun 1858. NAM, M234/885.
[19] Sunder, p. 189. [20] Ewers, *Blackfeet*, p. 228.
[21] Sunder, pp. 189-190; Berglund, SC 414, MtHS, p. 51; Fannie Culbertson Irvin to Ernest East, 18 Dec 1936. PPL.
[22] Sunder, p. 190.

ters with the Sioux.[23] Redfield offered Culbertson $2,800 to transport the goods.[24] Culbertson delivered the annuities,[25] but when he requested "speedy payment," he learned that Redfield had no funds. Redfield did not even request the appropriation until November.[26] Whether Culbertson ever got paid is not known.[27]

In any case, Culbertson and Natawista soon left for Fort Benton, hoping to cross the Continental Divide, continue to Fort Vancouver, and then catch a ship for New York.[28] Neither had traveled the route before and they looked forward to the adventure. But the era of such pleasure trips had passed.

They easily negotiated the Continental Divide crossing, reaching St. Ignatius mission to find the Flatheads "comfortable and happy, with abundance to live upon." Having embraced the Jesuit teachings, the Flatheads had become "regular worshippers," receiving "salutary Christian instruction, together with instruction in agriculture." The tribe cultivated wheat, oats, potatoes, and other vegetables; in winter, they pursued the buffalo in the common hunting ground designated by Lame Bull's Treaty.[29]

In Washington Territory, the tribes, especially the Yakimas, had been at war for three years. Governor Isaac Stevens had tried councils and martial law to effect peace, without success.[30] West of St. Ignatius, the Culbertsons encountered several Spokane warriors heading east, preferring to take their chances with their traditional enemies, the Blackfeet, than with the military dragoons. They advised Culbertson against continuing and, together, the group returned to Fort Benton. There, Culbertson arranged for the Spokanes' safety before embarking on the long journey back to Peoria.

The Indians the Culbertsons encountered on the downriver trek were

---

[23] Alexander H. Redfield to Charles E. Mix, Jun 1858. NAM, M234/885.

[24] Contract between Alexander H. Redfield and Alexander Culbertson, 26 Jun 1858. NAM, M234/885.

[25] Alexander Redfield to Alfred Greenwood, 25 May 1859. NAM, M234/885; Bradley, *MHSC*, Vol. III, p. 253. The date of 1846 which Culbertson gave Bradley for this event is an error.

[26] Alexander H. Redfield to Alexander Robinson, 4 Nov 1858. NAM, M234/885.

[27] NAM, M234/885. There is no record of payment to Culbertson in these records.

[28] "A Winter Trip," *PDT*, 9 Feb 1859, page 2, column 2. Culbertson never states that Natawista accompanied him; however, that is in keeping with his reluctance to discuss his family. Based on the evidence, the author believes she almost certainly traveled west with Culbertson.

[29] "A Winter Trip."

mostly quiet, although some Arikaras near Fort Clark appeared "rather lukewarm in their friendship to the whites." The weather presented more serious problems. By the time Natawista and Culbertson reached Fort Clark, eighteen inches of snow covered the ground and the temperatures hovered around thirty-five below.[31] The couple apparently decided Natawista should remain at Fort Clark while Culbertson pushed on.[32]

Near Fort Pierre, Culbertson found the Sioux "in deplorable condition—bordering quite on starvation." The buffalo had fled and deep snow prevented them from hunting smaller game. To survive, they had eaten their horses and now "were eking out a miserable existence on the buds of the wild rose." Without prompt assistance, Culbertson feared the "gaunt, wretched and famished" tribe could be "nearly exterminated by spring."

After securing fresh mules, Culbertson continued to Sioux City where he caught the stagecoach, traveling in "comparative ease and comfort" until he reached Peoria on February 3, 1859. There he announced that he had "determined upon giving up further expeditions to the Indian country."[33] The promise lasted four months.

In May, Culbertson and his son, Jack, took the steamboat upriver, meeting Natawista at Fort Clark. As usual, she elicited much comment from the visiting whites. A St. Louis physician, Elias Marsh, observed that she "dressed like a white woman and is said to be a very fine woman," but "as she cannot speak English, I can say nothing to her."[34]

Many, including Isaac Stevens, believed Natawista could not speak English.[35] The evidence, however, suggests otherwise. Her daughter, Fannie, recalled Natawista bargaining with St. Louis shopkeepers over the price of a doll's hat.[36] And both John James Audubon and George Roberts, Natawista's son-in-law, recorded conversations with her in English.[37] Moreover, a mixed-blood Piegan, Caroline Connoyer, who worked for the Culbertsons at Fort Benton, remembered Natawista teaching her both English and the traders' patois French.[38]

Most likely, Natawista simply pretended not to speak English. This allowed her to remain aloof when she desired while also offering her hus-

---

[30] Richards, p. 235ff.    [31] "A Winter Trip."
[32] Marsh, MoHS. Unpaged. Marsh says that they met Natawista at Fort Clark in the summer of 1859. The suggestion that she wintered there is the author's.
[33] "A Winter Trip."    [34] Marsh, MoHS.
[35] McDonnell, *MHSC*, Vol. X, p. 244.    [36] Berglund, SC 414, MtHS, pp. 9-10.
[37] Audubon, Vol. II, p. 112; Taylor, "The Major's Blackfoot Bride," p. 47.
[38] Hugh Welch, great-grandson of Caroline Connoyer, to the author.

band significant advantages. White men, believing her ignorant of their language, would speak freely around her. She could then eavesdrop and report these conversations to her husband.

Although she did not speak to Dr. Marsh, Natawista did present him with "two very pretty pair of moccasins."[39]

1860 marked a turning point in steamboat navigation. Three steamers, the most ever,[40] headed upriver that spring and two, the *Chippewa* and the *Key West*, "in great commotion," finally attained the long-anticipated destination of Fort Benton.[41] Alexander Culbertson, no doubt beaming, arrived aboard the *Chippewa*.[42]

The steamers carried Company employees, the increasingly common retinue of eastern tourists, fur trade supplies, Indian annuities, three hundred Army officers, soldiers, and a "due allowance of laundresses." The military disembarked at Fort Benton to march west over the nearly completed military road constructed under the supervision of Lt. John Mullan linking Fort Benton to Fort Walla Walla in Washington Territory.[43]

Agent Vaughan cheered the unprecedented display of military might. The Blackfeet had remained so isolated that Vaughan found it difficult to convince them of the white man's numbers. When he tried, the Blackfeet scoffed: "If the whites are so numerous, why is it the same ones come back to this country year after year, with rarely an exception?" Vaughan's proposals to take Blackfeet delegations to Washington, D.C., "to impress the Indian with a proper view of the strength and importance of the white man,"[44] had fallen on deaf ears.[45] Thus, he hoped the military detachment would cause the tribe to "respect and fear the government accordingly."[46]

Generally, Vaughan felt optimistic about Blackfeet progress under Lame Bull's Treaty. In 1859, the Jesuits had established a mission on the Teton River under Father Adrian Hoecken and Brother Vincent Magri.[47]

---

[39]Marsh, MoHS.
[40]Sunder, p. 211.
[41]Sunder, pp. 212-213.
[42]Bradley, *MHSC*, Vol. III, p. 280.
[43]Sunder, p. 204 and p. 211; Burlingame, p. 108 and p. 128; Overholser, p. 25.
[44]Ewers, *Blackfeet*, p. 233; 1858 Report to the Commissioner of Indian Affairs.
[45]Ewers, *Blackfeet*, p. 234.
[46]Ewers, *Blackfeet*, p. 234; 1860 Report to the Commissioner of Indian Affairs, p. 83.
[47]Harrod, p. 53; Ewers, *Blackfeet*, p. 234; Killoren, p. 239. Killoren seems to suggest the mission was established in 1858. Culbertson, however, places Hoecken in charge at St. Ignatius in late 1858. De Smet visited the mission on 29 Jul 1859.

Moreover, Little Dog, the Piegan chief, had taken up a small farm near the agency on Sun River.[48] If Little Dog succeeded, Vaughan hoped the rest of the tribe would follow his example.

While the Blackfeet were relatively quiet in 1860, to the east, the Sioux presented a different picture. They complained bitterly that the government was cheating them and, that summer, they undertook several bloody raids against rival tribes.[49] Then, on August 22, 1860, as the watchman opened the Fort Union gate, two hundred and fifty mounted Hunkpapa and Blackfeet Sioux warriors "well mounted and all caparisoned in their war costumes,"[50] raced toward the fort. The watchman slammed the gates and raised the alarm. Company men rushed to the bastions.

Culbertson's friend, Edwin Denig, had retired several years earlier,[51] leaving Robert Meldrum, the former Crow trader, and Malcolm Clarke, Culbertson's former subaltern at Fort Benton, in charge of Union. With only fifteen men to defend the fort, Meldrum and Clarke decided to hold their fire to see if the relatively new agent, Bernard Schoonover, who was also present, could reason with the warriors.

Schoonover, through an interpreter, made "an ineffectual effort" to counsel with the warriors, "but they were so intent on mischief that it was impossible to command their attention."[52] The warriors began slaughtering Company cattle and setting fire to haystacks, woodpiles, wagons, mackinaws, and outbuildings while others ransacked the garden. Within hours, the Sioux had destroyed all Company property beyond the gates. Their rage not yet spent, a dozen warriors advanced on Fort Union with firebrands and hatchets. Meldrum and Clarke finally ordered their men to open fire. They killed one and wounded others before the Sioux retreated.[53]

While the physical attack ended, its psychological impacts lingered. For days, the Fort Union traders refused to venture outside: "The panic among the men employed is so great that it is almost impossible to get any

---

[48] Ewers, *Blackfeet*, p. 232; 1860 Report to the Commissioner of Indian Affairs, p. 83.
[49] Sunder, p. 212.
[50] Bernard Schoonover to A. M. Robinson, 23 Aug 1860. NAM, M234/885.
[51] Thompson, p. 74.
[52] Bernard Schoonover to A. M. Robinson, 23 Aug 1860. NAM, M234/885.
[53] B.S. Schoonover to A. M. Robinson, 23 Aug 1860 and Pierre Chouteau, Jr., and Company to A.M. Robinson, 2 Jan 1861. NAM, M234/885; Pierre Chouteau, Jr., and Company to Charles Primeau, 6 Feb 1861, Chouteau Collection, MoHS; Sunder, p. 215; Utley, p. 47.

of the employees outside of the pickets."[54] The even smaller garrison at nearby Fort Berthold feared they would be next.[55]

1860 ended with unsettled conditions on the upper Missouri. Then, in December, following the presidential election of Abraham Lincoln, South Carolina seceded.

Repercussions from the Civil War quickly spread west. Missouri, home of the American Fur Company, was a slave state and the Chouteaus slaveowners. Most steamboat owners supported the Union, but the captains frequently sympathized with the South. Federal officials viewed them with suspicion and Confederate guerrillas targeted them for attack.

The threat of ambush deterred traffic on the lower river just as the war created more demand to service increased numbers of upriver troops protecting telegraph lines and trying to keep the Indians peaceful. Meanwhile, the frontier beckoned draft-dodgers and deserters from both sides.[56] Even as more and more expatriates poured into the region, the most experienced government agents and military men were recalled to the States.[57]

Abraham Lincoln's election also brought new Indian agents, most of whom viewed the American Fur Company with suspicion. Samuel Latta, Bernard Schoonover's replacement, vehemently denounced the AFC: "This old American Fur Company (so called) is the most corrupt institution ever tolerated in our country."[58] Latta charged the Company with hiding annuities and then trading them to the Indians for robes.[59]

With unrest enveloping the country in 1861, Culbertson forewent his annual upriver journey. But his reputation in Indian affairs led fellow Peorian,[60] Thomas McCulloh, to recommend him as special government agent to the upriver tribes.[61]

---

[54] Bernard Schoonover to A. M. Robinson, 23 Aug 1860. NAM, M234/885.

[55] Sunder, p. 215.

[56] Sunder, p. 220; Chittenden, *Early Steamboat*, Vol. II, pp. 249-250; Burlingame, p. 110.

[57] Ewers, *Blackfeet*, p. 236.

[58] Sunder, p. 223; S.N. Latta to W.P. Dole, 27 Aug 1862, House ExDocs 1 (37-3), pp. 340-341.

[59] Sunder, p. 223; House ExDocs 1 (37-3).

[60] Robert McCulloh to Charles Kessler, 12 Feb 1918. KP, UCLA. McCulloh is said to be a "distant relative" of Culbertson's. The exact relationship is unclear but Thomas McCulloh may have been the brother of Nancy McCulloh Culbertson, the widow of Dr. William Culbertson.

[61] T.H. McCulloh to Caleb Smith, 5 Sep 1861, Letters Received, Office of Indian Affairs, Record Group 75, National Archives, as cited by Sunder, p. 221. The author could not find this letter.

Jack Culbertson did go upriver in 1861, traveling under the supervision of Andrew Dawson, Culbertson's replacement as chief AFC trader for the upper Missouri.[62] En route, Jack and a young New York artist named William de la Montagne Cary decided to go hunting. Climbing a bluff, they encountered several Sioux warriors.

The warriors "recognized Jack" and invited him and Cary to their village for "a hearty welcome." The chief spread a table and asked after Jack's family. Jack, speaking Sioux, replied to his inquiry before turning the conversation to his companion, Cary, who fancied himself "something of an athlete." Jack suggested Cary "turn some handsprings and somersaults." Cary demurred, claiming fatigue, but Jack persisted: "It will please them, I know, and it will do you no harm."

Cary finally agreed and a crowd of several hundred gathered to watch the young acrobat. When Cary had exhausted his repertoire, the chief presented his visitors with "some beautiful moccasins." Late in the afternoon, Jack and Cary departed. En route back to the steamboat, Jack told Cary that the Indians belonged to a hostile band of Sioux. Had they not been together, Jack said, anything might have happened.[63]

Years later, Cary met Sitting Bull, the Hunkpapa medicine man, following a performance of Buffalo Bill Cody's Wild West Show. Sitting Bull immediately "made a circle with his arms three or four times." Cary looked puzzled until Sitting Bull exclaimed, "Jack! Jack Culbertson." The Hunkpapa chief had been present in the village in 1861 when Cary performed his gymnastic feats. When Cary inquired about Jack, the medicine man informed him that Jack had been killed several years earlier.[64]

By 1862, river conditions had degenerated so much that steamboat passengers regularly engaged in military drills as a precaution against attacks by either Indians or Southern guerrillas.[65] Nonetheless, the *Spread Eagle* and *Key West* left St. Louis that May crowded with prospectors eager to try their luck in the recently discovered intermountain goldfields.[66] Many believed they could simply "go over the ground and pick up the big chunks." The AFC did nothing to discourage them,

---

[62]Ladner, p. 30.
[63]Ladner, pp. 36-37.
[64]Ladner, p. 162, 164.
[65]Sunder, p. 224.
[66]Burlingame, p. 84; Ewers, *Blackfeet*, p. 236.

promising that all necessary horses, mules, wagons, and equipment could be purchased in Fort Benton.[67]

The steamboat passengers included upper Missouri agent Samuel Latta, the new Blackfeet agent, Rev. Henry H. Reed, Father Pierre De Smet, Alexander Culbertson, Natawista, Fannie, and Joe.[68] As the *Spread Eagle* approached Fort Pierre, hundreds of angry Sioux lined the shores. The warriors accused the AFC of stealing annuities and arming their enemies. The Indians also complained that the soldiers who were to protect their interests had never arrived. They denounced their Great Father, refused to accept their annuities, and threatened to disrupt river commerce.[69]

Bear's Rib, designated Hunkpapa chief, led the only Sioux band to accept their annuities.[70] He informed Latta that doing so might endanger his life.[71] Soon after the steamer departed, one hundred and fifty Miniconjou and Sans Arc warriors rode into Fort Pierre, vowing to kill all the false chiefs appointed by the government. Bear's Rib confronted them. Mouse, a Sans Arc warrior, shot him. Bear's Rib returned fire. When it was over, Bear's Rib, Mouse, and another Sans Arc warrior lay dead. The dissidents then composed a letter to Agent Latta:

> We notified the Bear's Rib yearly not to receive your goods; he had no ears, and we gave him ears by killing him. We now say to you, bring us no more goods.... If you have no ears we will give you ears....
>
> We also say to you that we wish you to stop the whites from travelling through our country, and if you do not stop them, we will. If your whites have no ears we will give them ears.[72]

The passengers aboard the *Spread Eagle*, unaware of Bear's Rib's fate, continued to Fort Benton, arriving on June 20, 1862.[73] Sixty Blackfeet tipis surrounded the fort. Since many of the passengers had never been to the region, Father De Smet, Natawista, and Jack led a sight-seeing party to the Great Falls on June 30.[74]

---

[67] Sunder, p. 230.

[68] Sunder, pp. 230-231. Sunder calls this "one of the most extensively documented voyages to the Upper Missouri" and references De Smet's journal, Lewis Henry Morgan's journal, and the diary of John O'Fallon Delany.

[69] Sunder, p. 232; Utley, p. 48.   [70] Killoren, p. 238.

[71] John Pattee to Brigadier General Blunt, 21 Jul 1862. NAM, M234/885; Utley, p. 48.

[72] Utley, p. 49.   [73] Killoren, pp. 238-239.

[74] Sunder, p. 239; Killoren, p. 239; Harkness, *MHSC*, Vol. II, p. 350. The group included Margaret Harkness and Madame La Barge, the first white women to view this natural wonder.

Following the pleasure trip, De Smet traveled to the new Blackfeet mission.[75] The mission was in "a rather bad way, lacking, in fact, almost everything, even necessaries . . . ." De Smet brought with him "a fine assortment of church ornaments and sacred vessels, victuals for nearly a year, garments and bed coverings, . . . agricultural and carpenters' tools, several plows, some picks and shovels, an ambulance and a wagon."[76]

The Culbertsons, meanwhile, passed the summer at the Blackfeet agency on Sun River.[77] Agent Reed gave them an agency house and, throughout the summer, they traveled extensively, visiting Fort Benton and the nearby Indian encampments. Natawista enchanted Electa Bryan who also spent the summer at Sun River. The young white woman found Natawista "a romantic figure," "so spirited, so proudly reserved."[78] For days she made Natawista "the subject of her sentimental imaginings."[79]

Reed appreciated Culbertson's calming influence on the Blackfeet who had begun complaining about the whites in their territory. Five to six hundred prospectors had passed through Fort Benton that summer[80] and Reed knew the Blackfeet peace could easily evaporate.

When word reached Culbertson that a band of Indians were preparing to attack the region's whites, he asked Caroline Connoyer, a mixed-blood Piegan who had worked for him at Fort Benton, to ride out to warn the settlers. Connoyer knew the region and Culbertson hoped that, as an Indian girl, she could make the journey unmolested. Moreover, her ability to speak the Indian dialects, English, and patois French would enable her to communicate the warning properly.

Culbertson instructed her to leave at dark and travel north to the home of her mother, Black Bear Woman,[81] who lived with Joe Cobell, an old AFC trader, about fifty miles north of Fort Benton on Shonkin Creek. Caroline left at sunset, riding along the Missouri's north bank, stopping at five homesteads. Near midnight, within sight of Cobell's home, her horse gave out, forcing Caroline to walk the rest of the way.

After warning Cobell, Caroline mounted a new horse for the return

---

[75]Chittenden, *De Smet*, Vol. II, p. 786; Killoren, p. 239.
[76]Chittenden, *De Smet*, Vol. II, p. 786.
[77]Bradley, *MHSC*, Vol. III, p. 281.       [78]Clifford, "Part II," p. 17.
[79]Clifford, "Part II," p. 8.       [80]Utley, p. 51.
[81]Black Bear Woman was the sister of Mountain Chief. Hugh Welch to the author. She would later marry Cobell and adopt the white name, "Mary." Ege, p. 40.

ride. On her way back, Caroline followed the south bank, warning settlers on that side. Near sunrise, Caroline walked into the fort, leading Cobell's horse. It, too, had played out and Caroline had led it the last few miles. Culbertson rewarded Caroline with her own horse and a replacement for Cobell's. The rumored attack, to Culbertson's relief, never materialized.[82]

In his annual report, Agent Reed expressed surprise that so few hostilities had broken out since "not a few" of these whites would scarcely "be tolerated in any civilized society."[83] With a gold strike on Grasshopper Creek that July, Reed expected even more miners the following summer.[84] He suggested at least one company of soldiers be stationed at Fort Benton. Moreover, the farm experiment appeared to be turning sour, just as Alexander Culbertson had predicted in 1855. Not long before, Little Dog had abandoned his efforts, returning to the nomadic lifestyle.[85]

In early September, Culbertson purchased a mackinaw and headed downriver with twenty Missouri "rebels." Near the mouth of Milk River, fifty Assiniboines appeared, intent on plunder. Recognizing Culbertson, they let his party pass unmolested.

Another group a few hours behind did not fare as well. The Assiniboines left them "scarcely enough clothing to hide their nakedness and nothing beside." Traveling throughout the night, they managed to catch Culbertson's party. He agreed to provide them passage as long as they helped row, a decision he soon regretted.

The group included a woman, "a virago of the first order," who could not control her fury. She berated the Indians, the West, the river, and most of all, her "unfortunate husband." Culbertson mentioned that Big Head had led the Assiniboine raiders; the woman never forgot the name. Several years later, when Culbertson accompanied a delegation of Teton Sioux to Washington, D.C., they encountered the victimized woman in

---

[82]Hugh Welch to the author. No certain date can be fixed for this event, although Caroline Connoyer stated that it happened "a few years" after she arrived in Fort Benton. Connoyer arrived in Fort Benton about the same time as the first steamboat (1859), the arrival of which she witnessed. Connoyer also told her descendants that, after this event, she was more accepted at the fort.

[83]Ewers, *Blackfeet*, p. 237.

[84]Burlingame, p. 84.

[85]Ewers, *Blackfeet*, p. 237; 1863 Annual Report to the Commissioner of Indian Affairs, p. 179.

St. Louis. When she learned that one of the Sioux was named Big Head, she accused him of being the "dirty rascal" who had orchestrated the attack.

Culbertson tried valiantly to explain that this man was a Sioux, not an Assiniboine. Although both were named Big Head, they were different men. To Culbertson's relief, the woman finally lapsed into silence.[86] At times like these, Culbertson did not regret his decision to live among the so-called savages.

---

[86]Bradley, *MHSC*, Vol. III, pp. 282-283.

Chapter Twenty-Four

## *"provoked by numerous injustices and misdeeds"*

Whatever hopes existed for a peaceful transition by the Indians to an agrarian society exploded on August 17, 1862, when four Santee Sioux killed five white settlers in Acton Township, Minnesota.[1] After adopting an agricultural lifestyle, the Santees suffered total crop failure in 1861. Nonetheless, their agent, Thomas Galbraith, callously ignored requests for food.

Little Crow, a Santee chief, had farmed for several years and worshipped regularly at the Episcopal church. The chief initially condemned the young warriors but, after conferring with other elders, concluded that the entire tribe would be blamed. Therefore, the Santee chiefs decided on an aggressive response.[2]

Over the next month, the Santees attacked white settlements, killed settlers, took prisoners, and destroyed property. Altogether, they murdered between four hundred and one thousand[3] settlers before General Henry Sibley crushed the rebellion on September 22.[4] A military court ordered three hundred warriors hanged, but President Lincoln, after an impassioned appeal from Father De Smet, reduced that number to thirty-eight who were hanged in Mankato, Minnesota, on December 26.

Two months later, the government dispossessed the Santees of their land and treaty rights and banished them from Minnesota.[5] Most fled west, joining their kinsmen on the upper Missouri. Emotions among the river tribes became so inflamed that one-fourth of the white settlers aban-

---

[1] *Encyclopedia of American Facts & Dates*, p. 279
[2] Killoren, p. 242.
[3] Estimates vary from 400 from a 26 Dec 1862 St. Paul, MN, newspaper cited in *Chronicle of America*, p. 371, to 1,000 cited in *Encyclopedia of American Facts & Dates,* p. 279. Chittenden, *Early Steamboat*, Vol. II, p. 370, puts the figure at 1,000.
[4] Utley, p. 52.
[5] Killoren, pp. 242-244.

doned their homesteads out of fear.⁶ Meanwhile, the army made plans to punish the Indians.

❖   ❖   ❖

On May 13, 1863, the *Robert Campbell* left St. Louis carrying annuities for the Sioux, Crows, Blackfeet, and Assiniboines.⁷ Also on board were Blackfeet agent Henry Reed, upper Missouri agent Samuel Latta, Henry Boller, a young Philadelphian who had entered the fur trade in 1858,⁸ Alexander Culbertson, Natawista, Jack, and Joe, and an assortment of mountaineers and prospectors.⁹

Everyone expected trouble. The previous year, the Sioux had warned Latta not to return.¹⁰ Despite the tension, five-year-old Joe Culbertson entertained the passengers with "some fine dancing" near Sioux City.¹¹ But fear escalated when the *Robert Campbell* encountered the *Spread Eagle* heading downriver "riddled to pieces with bullets."¹²

At Fort Pierre, Agent Latta met with the Two Kettles band of Sioux who "were greatly exasperated" by the killing of eight warriors by soldiers.¹³ When Latta tried to discuss the situation, the warriors sat "in silent groups that brooks evil to the white man."¹⁴ The agent "gave the relatives of the deceased a Special present to reconcile them as far as possible"¹⁵ and then distributed about two-thirds of the annuities due. The shortages so enraged the tribe that they followed the steamboat for hundreds of miles, firing repeatedly on the boat, and attacking every time the crew stopped to gather wood.¹⁶

Near present-day Bismarck, North Dakota, the *Robert Campbell* met the *Shreveport* and the two steamers traveled upriver in tandem.¹⁷ On July 5, as the *Shreveport* stopped to take on wood, the Sioux fired on it. Can-

---

⁶Utley, p. 52.     ⁷Chittenden, *Early Steamboat*, Vol. II, p. 299; Sunder, p. 246.
⁸Boller, pp. xvii-xviii.
⁹Chittenden, *Early Steamboat*, Vol. II, p. 300; Sunder, p. 246; Boller, p. 358.
¹⁰Sunder, p. 246.     ¹¹"Log of Steamer *Robert Campbell*," p. 272.
¹²"Log of Steamer *Robert Campbell*," p. 269.
¹³Samuel Latta to William P. Dole, 27 Aug 1863. NAM, M234/885; Chittenden, *Early Steamboat*, Vol. II, p. 301; Boller, p. 359.
¹⁴"Log of Steamer *Robert Campbell*," p. 275.
¹⁵Samuel Latta to William P. Dole, 27 Aug 1863. NAM, M234/885.
¹⁶Chittenden, *Early Steamboat*, Vol. II, p. 301; Sunder, p. 246.
¹⁷Chittenden, *Early Steamboat*, Vol. II, p. 302; Sunder, p. 246; Boller, p. 360; "Log of Steamer *Robert Campbell*," p. 277.

non fire from the *Robert Campbell* allowed the *Shreveport* to escape.[18] A heavy rain the next day kept the peace, but the crew and passengers remained wary with Indians "on all sides" and "some rare sport... expected soon."[19] In the early morning of July 7, as the *Shreveport* and *Robert Campbell* approached Tobacco Garden landing about halfway between Fort Berthold and Fort Union, a hunter from the *Shreveport* warned that "at least fifteen hundred" Indians were massing "to capture the boat."[20] The *Robert Campbell* crew piled flour sacks on the boiler deck as breastworks.

Around mid-morning, Natawista, with her "eagle eye,"[21] noticed something crossing a distant ridge. Whether animals or mounted Indians, the sighting raised anxiety. The suspense turned to fear when more than two hundred Hunkpapa, Miniconjou, and Blackfeet Sioux appeared on shore.[22] The steamers dropped anchor in the middle of the channel so that Agent Latta, the crew, and Indians could converse.

The Indians announced they did not intend to cause trouble, but wanted the rest of their annuities. To demonstrate their peaceful intentions, they threw down their tomahawks and covered them with dirt.[23] Latta denied their claims but asked Joseph La Barge, captain of the *Robert Campbell*, to send a yawl out to bring several chiefs back to the steamboat to receive additional presents. The Indians insisted that Agent Latta accompany the yawl.

Alexander Culbertson and Natawista, understanding Sioux, became convinced that the Indians were laying a trap.[24] Natawista told La Barge and Latta that "if you pull into the shore we will all be killed as the brush must be full of Indians and the few on the bank are only a decoy...."[25]

---

[18]Sunder, p. 246; "Log of Steamer *Robert Campbell*," p. 277.
[19]"Log of Steamer *Robert Campbell*," p. 277.
[20]Chittenden, *Early Steamboat*, Vol. II, p. 304; Sunder, pp. 246-247; Boller, p. 367.
[21]Boller, p. 368.
[22]Samuel Latta to William Dole, 27 Aug 1863, NAM, M234/885, says that the Indians "informed us they were of the Uncpapa, Miniconjou, and Blackfeet tribes." Blackfeet, in this context, refers to Blackfeet Sioux. Boller, pp. 367-368.    [23]Innis, p. 147.
[24]Boller, p. 369, claims that the Indians were calling out for the "whites to come ashore and be killed; that they wanted provisions, arms, and ammunition; that the whites were dogs and only fit to be killed." No other chronicler suggests that the Indians used this kind of inflammatory language. Possibly the Culbertsons heard the Indians saying these things among themselves and later shared this with Boller. Also Innis, p. 148.
[25]Joseph Culbertson draft manuscript, KP, UCLA, pp. 92-93.

Latta replied haughtily, "Why, I'll go; I'm not afraid."[26] La Barge finally agreed to send the yawl if Latta could raise a volunteer crew.

One deckhand and six roustabouts[27] soon enlisted, although witnesses later disagreed about whether they were willing volunteers.[28] La Barge then summoned Latta who had "disappeared upstairs."[29] The agent, apparently thinking better of his boast, sent back word that he felt ill and could not go. Despite this, La Barge ordered the seven men to shore as the passengers hid behind the crude breastworks.

The yawl landed and four warriors approached. As the steamboat passengers watched, the Indians killed three crew members and seriously injured a fourth. The steamboats responded with small arms and cannon fire as the survivors scrambled to escape.

For three hours, the two sides exchanged gunfire. It may have been during this time that the Indians challenged the whites to "come ashore and be killed"[30] because "the whites were dogs and only fit to be killed." One warrior, "hideously painted with a white stripe down the middle of his breast and transverse stripes like ribs extending from it," held up a lance containing several scalps. The whites fired and the warrior fell dead.

Three howitzers aboard the steamboats were brought into play. As Indian casualties rose, the warriors finally withdrew, leaving behind at least eighteen dead and numerous others seriously wounded.[31] Except for the three crew members sent ashore, no whites died. In late afternoon, the two steamboats continued upriver.[32] At the mouth of the Little Muddy River, the boats halted and the crew carried the three dead to the top of the highest bluff to be buried.[33]

The attack at Tobacco Garden apparently convinced the Culbertsons to forego any further travels that summer. They passed the season within Fort Union's protective walls where their well-deserved reputations as peacemakers helped calm the less experienced traders. During the evenings, as the breeze blew in off the river, the aging trader and his still-

---

[26]Chittenden, *Early Steamboat*, Vol. II, p. 306.    [27]Innis, p. 148.

[28]Boller, p. 371; Larpenteur, p. 297. Cf. Chittenden, *Early Steamboat*, Vol. II, p. 307, who claims the men were all volunteers.    [29]Chittenden, *Early Steamboat*, Vol. II, p. 306.

[30]Boller, p. 369, claims that this exchange occurred prior to the yawl being sent ashore but he is the only one to suggest the Indians were this brazen.

[31]Innis, p. 149. Other accounts estimate as many as thirty warriors died.

[32]Numerous accounts of the Tobacco Garden incident exist. See especially: Chittenden, *Early Steamboat*, Vol. II, pp. 305-311; Boller, pp. 367-374; "Log of the Steamer *Robert Campbell*," pp. 278-279; Larpenteur, pp. 296-297; Sunder, pp. 246-247.    [33]Innis, p. 150.

beautiful Indian wife joined a "social circle" on the second floor balcony of the Bourgeois House to tell about their "wild adventures."

In addition to Culbertson, Natawista, and their sons, the gatherings included Henry Boller, W. D. Hodgkiss, a New Yorker then in charge of Fort Union, Hodgkiss's mixed-blood son, William, an AFC clerk, and former agent Alfred Vaughan who, while no longer a government employee, continued to return upriver.[34] When the stories ran out, Vaughan entertained with song while Culbertson played his fiddle.[35]

Despite these pleasant interludes, the fort remained on alert against possible Indian attacks. Culbertson and Boller often went hunting with their weapons at the ready. Once, they came perilously close to an unexpected encounter with a war party before safely retreating to Fort Union.[36] Jack Culbertson, Boller, and John Wallace, an AFC hunter, made plans to travel to Fort Benton at the end of summer. From there, they hoped to head to the coast. Throughout the summer, they groomed their horses for the journey. Then, in September, a hostile band of Sioux stole their horses, forcing the trio to abandon their plans.[37]

The next morning, Alexander Culbertson[38] took his "customary walk out on the prairie" with young Joe. Boller had taken up a position in the bastion; as he cleaned his gun, the young man watched the mixed-blood children playing. Suddenly, he heard them cry "most lustily in chorus."

Stepping out on the gallery, Boller saw a nearby sandbar "literally alive with naked savages, who with bounding strides were making directly for the fort!" To his dismay, Boller also saw the cook, his Indian wife, and small child near the river. Boller fired his weapon, wounding one raider.[39] The shot roused the men inside the fort and they, too, began firing. With the element of surprise lost, the Indians retreated. Boller's quick action probably saved those beyond the gates that morning, including several wood cutters, the cook and his family, and Alexander Culbertson and Joe.[40]

As the small contingent of traders, employees, and visitors spent a wary summer at Fort Union, the army stepped up their campaign against the

---

[34]McDonnell, *MHSC*, Vol. X, pp. 272-273.
[35]Boller, p. 377.
[36]Boller, pp. 380-381.
[37]Boller, pp. 382-384.
[38]Interestingly, Boller here refers to Culbertson as "Col."
[39]Innis, p. 79, identifies the Sioux as "Dakota."
[40]Boller, pp. 385-390.

upper Missouri Sioux. General Sibley marched northwest from Minnesota while General Alfred Sully came upriver. The troops were primarily raw, untested recruits, most of whom had signed up to fight in the Civil War.[41]

During five days in late July, Sibley's troops engaged the Sioux in battle at Big Mound, Dead Buffalo Lake, and Stony Lake. Defeated, the Sioux fled west and Sibley retreated, leaving the pursuit to General Sully.[42] Meanwhile, Sully moved north. In early September, he killed one hundred Sioux, captured one hundred and fifty-six, and destroyed most of the tribe's food supplies and camp equipment at Whitestone Hill.[43] Afterwards, Sully built Fort Sully, his winter quarters, north of Fort Pierre.[44]

In early February 1864, Alfred Vaughan, Alexander Culbertson, Natawista, and five-year-old Joe began the long downriver trek.[45] Why they waited until the dead of winter to begin the rigorous journey is unclear. Perhaps they hoped to calm the passions of the increasingly angry Indians. The Indian elders, respecting both men, would have been inclined to listen to their representations. But the young warriors, with the army engaged against them, resented all whites.

More likely, Culbertson and Vaughan stayed at Fort Union until they knew the Indians had moved to winter camp. From their long experience, the two knew where those camps would be located. This winter, their goal was to avoid them. The journey took six weeks as "they were compelled to take a very circuitous route in order to avoid Indians."

Stopping at Fort Sully, Culbertson and Vaughan predicted "very troublesome" times the next summer; the Indians "will, as far as possible, prevent steamers from ascending the Missouri and emigrants going to Idaho." They warned that only "very large parties" should "venture on the plains."[46]

As the military prepared for their 1864 campaign, they made one last effort to secure peace by soliciting Pierre De Smet's intervention. General Sully believed that "with certain bands of Indians Father De Smet

---

[41]Utley, p. 52.
[42]Chittenden, *Early Steamboat*, Vol. II, p. 372; Utley, p. 52.
[43]Chittenden, *Early Steamboat*, Vol. II, p. 373; Utley, p. 53.
[44]Chittenden, *Early Steamboat*, Vol. II, p. 373; Utley, p. 54.
[45]Notes of 31 Mar 1864, A 85/32/12, Orin C. Libby Papers, NDHS.
[46]Notes of 31 Mar 1864, A 85/32/12, Orin C. Libby Papers, NDHS; Larpenteur, p. 300. The assumption that Culbertson and Vaughan stopped to discuss their concerns with Sully is based on the presence of these notes in the Libby collection.

can possibly do much to prevent a hostile collision with the whites." Nonetheless, he warned, "as regards most of the bands of Sioux above Fort Randall, I fear nothing but force will bring them to a state of peace."[47]

De Smet worried that presenting himself "as the bearer of the word of the Big Chief of the Big Knives in Washington, no longer their Great Father but now their greatest and bitterest enemy... would place [him] in rather an awkward situation." Thus, he agreed to meet with the tribes only "on [his] own hook, without pay or remuneration."[48]

The missionary met first with the still-friendly bands of Sioux, inducing them to accompany him to the hostile bands.[49] After listening to the hostile Indians' grievances, De Smet concluded that the seeds of this "unhappy war" had been "provoked by numerous injustices and misdeeds on the part of the whites, and even of agents of the Government" who had for years "deceived the Indians with impunity in the sale of their holdings of land" and "the open theft of immense sums paid them by the Government in exchange therefor."[50]

On July 9, 1864, De Smet presented his findings to General Sully who evinced little interest, informing De Smet ominously that "circumstances obliged him to punish by force of arms all the Sioux tribes that harbored in their camps any murderers of white men." According to Sully, "all the Indian camps harbor some of these desperate ruffians."[51]

The military had decided against negotiation. In July, Sully battled the Sioux at Killdeer Mountain,[52] killing more than a hundred. The troops then scattered the survivors and destroyed their village.[53] The Indians regrouped and, in early September, attacked a party of emigrants heading to the Montana goldfields. They harassed the wagon train for three days, cutting down the whites "with arrows, tomahawks, and knives," before the emigrants, having lost at least ten people, constructed defensive ramparts. A few days later, the Indians grew bored and drifted off. The shaken emigrants remained barricaded until a military contingent arrived to rescue them.[54]

---

[47] Alfred Sully to William P. Dole, 30 Mar 1864. NAM, M234/885.
[48] Killoren, p. 251.   [49] Killoren, p. 256.
[50] Killoren, p. 253.   [51] Killoren, p. 257.
[52] Chittenden, *Early Steamboat*, Vol. II, p. 374, gives the Sioux name for this battle as Tahkahokuty.
[53] Utley, pp. 55-57; Sunder, p. 254; Chittenden, *Early Steamboat*, Vol. II, p. 374.
[54] Utley, pp. 59-62; Chaky, "Bad Bread."

The war against the Sioux continued throughout 1865, providing employment for thousands of soldiers freed up following the end of the Civil War.

The hostilities raging among the Sioux inevitably spilled over into the Blackfeet country. In addition to thousands of prospectors pouring into their region following gold strikes at Bannack in 1862 and Virginia City in 1863,[55] the Blackfeet were angry at the government's failure to deliver their annuities.

In 1861, the steamboat *Chippewa*, carrying the Blackfeet annuities, exploded below Poplar River. The fire broke out when deckhands, trying to siphon off whiskey from barrels of alcohol cached below, dropped a candle into the alcohol.[56] As smoke billowed forth, "panic ensued." Fearing fire might reach the stored gunpowder, the chief engineer landed the steamer as terrified passengers rushed ashore. With the steamboat emptied, the captain ordered the hawser cut and the *Chippewa* floated downstream. Soon, "she was burnt to the waters edge and then blew into ten thousand atoms the whole sinking in about twenty feet of water." The next day, passengers and Indians alike scrambled to recover singed blankets, scorched cloth, and canisters of food thrown ashore by the blast.[57]

Although insurance claims were filed and honored for the lost annuities,[58] the Blackfeet only knew their 1861 goods did not arrive. Nor did they in 1863. That year, the Tobacco Garden incident left Agent Reed too shaken to venture west with the annuities.[59] Instead, he stashed them at Fort Union and sent a letter to "his children" with men more courageous than he.[60]

Later that summer, a party of Gros Ventres arrived at Fort Union, causing a flurry of concern until the Culbertsons recognized them. Invited inside, the chiefs announced they had come to collect their annuities. Without Agent Reed present, the men at Fort Union had no legal authority to distribute the goods. Nonetheless, the Gros Ventres "had come a long distance through a dangerous country" to receive what was rightfully

---

[55] Burlingame, pp. 85-87.
[56] Overholser, p. 40; Sunder, p. 228.
[57] Sunder, pp. 226-227; Overholser, p. 40.
[58] Sunder, p. 228.
[59] Ewers, *Blackfeet*, p. 237; Chittenden, *Early Steamboat*, Vol. II, p. 318; Boller, p. 391.
[60] Ewers, *Blackfeet*, p. 237; Chittenden, *Early Steamboat*, Vol. II, p. 318.

theirs and they decided to act. Former agent Vaughan drew up a formal declaration for the Interior Department detailing the circumstances and had Alexander Culbertson and Henry Boller sign it. Then, William Hodgkiss, in charge of Fort Union, distributed the annuities.[61] Latta later complained that the annuities were "delivered to the Indians in the absence of any instructions to that effect from me."[62]

In December 1864, the government appointed Gad Upson to succeed Henry Reed as agent to the Blackfeet and Gros Ventres. By then, no agent had visited them for eighteen months. Not surprisingly, when Upson arrived, he found the agency "in a deplorable condition" with the farm buildings dilapidated, implements missing, and no seed for a new crop. Moreover, alcohol was routinely being sold to the Indians. The tribes were also ignoring key provisions of Lame Bull's Treaty, with the Piegans warring against the Gros Ventres and young warriors stealing white men's horses.[63]

A strong, sympathetic agent such as Alfred Vaughan might have ameliorated the situation but Gad Upson was not such a man. According to one trader, Upson, who branded the Blackfeet "degraded savages,"[64] "knew as much about an Indian as I did about the inhabitants of Jupiter."[65] With their minds clouded by cheap liquor, restless Blackfeet youth decided it was time to protect their way of life.

The United States carved Montana Territory out of Idaho Territory on May 26, 1864. By then, nearly $8 million in placer gold had been mined in Bannack and Virginia City with new strikes being reported almost weekly. During 1864, nearly thirty steamboats headed upriver, with eight landing at or near Fort Benton.[66] Fort Benton had become the recognized outfitting post for both civilian prospectors and military expeditions to the region;[67] visitors paid $4 a day for lodging at the fort. They provided their own blankets, but received "corn bread, bad bacon and coffee" for their outlay.[68]

---

[61]Boller, pp. 390-392.
[62]Samuel Latta to William P. Dole, 2 Mar 1864. NAM, M234/885. Latta refers to the "Crow Goods stored a (*sic*) Forte (*sic*) Union" being distributed but Boller makes no mention of any annuities being distributed except to the Gros Ventres.
[63]Ewers, *Blackfeet*, p. 238; 1863 Report of the Commissioner of Indian Affairs, p. 179.
[64]Ewers, *Blackfeet*, p. 238.  [65]Ewers, *Blackfeet*, p. 236.
[66]Overholser, pp. 45-49.  [67]Sunder, p. 216.  [68]Overholser, p. 248.

Although the fort still offered the only accommodations, a town had begun to sprout. Clement Cornoyer built the first log building outside the fort in 1862 or 1863.[69] By early September 1864, the town boasted a large mercantile store, a blacksmith shop, and six saloons.[70] Knowledgeable whites expected "some hundreds of inhabitants" to soon be "settled there."[71]

On July 4, 1864, Fort Benton residents turned out en masse to celebrate the nation's birthday. "There were 1500 men in Benton at that time and I saw such desperate characters as the James brothers among them," recorded William Gladstone, a former Hudson's Bay Company carpenter. "It was hell upon earth for a time."[72] Gladstone recalled that "shooting and stabbing and rows of all kinds were a daily occurrence."[73]

Fort Benton ceased to be a Company town the following summer when Charles Chouteau sold the old fort to James Hubbell and Alpheus Hawley, owners of a new operation known as North West Fur. North West Fur invested a little in the traditional Indian trade while focusing primarily on outfitting white prospectors. The company conducted their Indian trade at outlying posts, including one on the Marias River run by John Riplinger which served the Piegans, Bloods, and Northern Blackfoot.[74]

But nature's vicissitudes restrained the growth of Fort Benton. Low water frequently forced steamboats to stop short of Benton. A group of prominent men proposed building a new river port several miles downriver at the confluence of the Marias and Missouri rivers. The backers began constructing the town of Ophir in the spring of 1865. Field manager N. W. Burris laid out four hundred lots and hired woodcutters to fell enough cottonwoods to build three hundred cabins. By late May, several cabins had been erected.[75]

That spring, a measles epidemic swept the Blackfeet camps, causing scores of deaths. The Indians, already angered by the throngs of whites entering their lands, blamed the intruders. On April 23, 1865, a Blood war party stole some forty horses from Fort Benton's residents. The victimized included Charley Carson, nephew of the noted frontiersman, Kit

---

[69]Overholser, p. 46. The name is also given as Clement Corneille.
[70]Overholser, p. 248.
[71]Henry Reed to William P. Dole, received 22 Aug 1864. NAM, M234/885.
[72]Overholser, p. 46.   [73]Overholser, p. 248.
[74]Overholser, pp. 28-29.   [75]Overholser, pp. 50-51.

Carson.[76] Events rapidly escalated. Outraged townsmen vowed to kill the next Indian who ventured into Fort Benton. A month later, when three Bloods came to town, the citizens killed them and dumped their bodies into the Missouri River.[77]

Two days later, Calf Shirt, a Blood who signed Lame Bull's Treaty, raised a war party of two hundred from the Fish Eaters, Fat Horses, and Black Elk bands.[78] At Ophir, the warriors surrounded and killed ten woodcutters.[79] The warriors later claimed they had planned to attack Fort Benton, but when the woodcutters fired on them, they struck back.[80] The killings ended plans for Ophir. When news of the deaths reached the territorial capital, Governor Sidney Edgerton called for volunteers to avenge the deaths. But the Bloods had fled north across the border and the proposed campaign had to be called off.[81]

Soon after, Agent Upson returned to the Blackfeet country with instructions from the Commissioner of Indian Affairs to hold another treaty conference. The government hoped to persuade the Blackfeet and Gros Ventres to relinquish their lands south of the Teton River, thereby opening up new territory for white settlement.

Upson convened the council in mid-November. The principal chiefs of the Piegans and Gros Ventres attended, along with a few minor Blood representatives and one Northern Blackfoot, Fish Child.[82] Upson offered $250 in individual annual payments "so long as they and their respective tribes remain faithful to their treaty obligations." The tribes would also receive $50,000 worth of annuities each year for twenty years in compensation for their lands south of the Teton.

Little Dog, the Piegan chief, affixed his mark to the treaty and

---

[76]Dempsey, *Red Crow*, p. 57; Burlingame, p. 40; Ewers, *Blackfeet*, p. 238; Chittenden, *Early Steamboat*, Vol. II, p. 279. Burlingame says the raid occurred on a "party of trappers near Fort Benton." Everyone else agrees it happened in the town itself.

[77]Ewers, *Blackfeet*, p. 238; Burlingame, p. 40; Chittenden, *Early Steamboat*, Vol. II, p. 279. Cf. Dempsey, *Red Crow*, p. 57, who says only that a Blood chief was killed and Overholser, p. 51, who offers two slightly different versions of events.

[78]Dempsey, *Red Crow*, p. 57.

[79]Overholser, p. 51; Dempsey, *Red Crow*, p. 57; Burlingame, pp. 40-41; Ewers, *Blackfeet*, p. 238; Chittenden, *Early Steamboat*, Vol. II, p. 281. The dead included nine whites and one black: Franklin Friend, George W. Friend, Abraham Lotts, John Alley, John Andrews, N.W. Burris, Frank Angevine, Henry Martin, Henry Lyons, and James Berry.

[80]Dempsey, *Red Crow*, p. 57; Bradley, "Blackfoot War," *MHSC*, Vol. IX, p. 255.

[81]Ewers, *Blackfeet*, p. 239.  [82]Dempsey, *Red Crow*, p. 60.

declared: "We are pleased with what we have heard today . . . .The land here belongs to us, we were raised upon it; we are glad to give a portion to the United States; for we get something for it." The white settlers were also satisfied. The *Montana Post* rejoiced that Upson had made the "concessions on our part as few and light as possible."[83] The Bloods and Northern Blackfoot, however, considered the treaty a farce.[84] Many whites doubted the Indians would live up to the treaty's terms. They were right. Two months later, after the Piegans and Bloods killed several white miners and traders, the Commissioner of Indian Affairs refused to recommend ratification of the just negotiated treaty.[85]

Had Alexander Culbertson been around Fort Benton during the tumultuous year of 1865, he might have been able to calm the raging passions. But Culbertson, one of the few white men still trusted by the Blackfeet, had not been to their land since 1862.

Precious little information exists to explain how Culbertson spent the years from 1864 to 1868. Whereas the local press frequently reported his early activities in Peoria, Culbertson's name vanishes from the newspaper after 1863. Moreover, it appears that Culbertson's eventful 1863-1864 journey to the upper river was his last for several years.

Most likely, the explanation lay in Culbertson's growing financial difficulties. With his financial situation precarious and his unpaid bills multiplying, Culbertson probably adopted a low profile in Peoria. When the AFC sold most of their upriver holdings, travel costs may have become prohibitive.

By 1866, Culbertson recognized his financial trouble. That spring, he sold one of his Stanley paintings,[86] but when the proceeds could not cover his debts, he executed a trust deed on Locust Grove to Thomas McCulloh, the man who had recommended his appointment as special Indian agent. In exchange for $1, Culbertson granted McCulloh the right to operate his estate. The deed directed that McCulloh pay Culbertson the proceeds for as long as he lived. After that, the income would go to

---

[83]Ewers, *Blackfeet*, pp. 239-240.   [84]Dempsey, *Red Crow*, p. 60.
[85]Ewers, *Blackfeet*, p. 240; Dempsey, *Red Crow*, p. 60.
[86]Albert D. Richardson, 9 May 1866, to Col. Geo. H. Roberts, Jr. SC 586, MtHS; letter from Julia Culbertson Roberts to Charles Kessler. Date illegible. KP, UCLA.

Natawista and, when she died, to Fannie and Joe, as tenants in common. The deed made no provision for Mariah, Janie, Jack, or Julia.[87]

A year later, Culbertson's financial situation had deteriorated further and he borrowed $1,050 from McCulloh.[88] Culbertson defaulted on his note for this debt. In addition to McCulloh, Culbertson owed a variety of Peoria merchants, including teachers, daguerreotype artists, livery operators, jewelers, harness makers, milliners, gunsmiths, furriers, carriage makers, dry goods dealers, clothiers, booksellers, and shoemakers. The claimants also included his former employer, Charles Chouteau.[89]

Culbertson's house of cards finally collapsed in February 1869 when Francis Wolle, superintendent of the Moravian Seminary, filed suit to recover $514.59 in expenses incurred for Fannie's education. Culbertson had sent her to the Moravian Seminary for a "finishing touch," but Fannie hated it, especially after she overheard students talking about "that Indian girl" in less than flattering terms.[90] Despite this and his darkening financial clouds, Culbertson spared no expense to provide Fannie the most complete educational and social experience.

Her unpaid bills included expenses ranging from music and language lessons to corsets, gloves, and velvet hats. She had been treated to sleigh rides and horse rentals, concerts and railroad trips. In all, Fannie's expenses between December 21, 1865, and July 12, 1866, totaled $604.59. But Culbertson had paid only $90, forcing Wolle to sue for the rest, including his travel expenses to Peoria. At the trial in late February 1869, Henry Grove, representing Culbertson, waived his client's right to a jury. The judge, finding Culbertson "justly indebted," ordered him to pay up.

But Culbertson had no money and thirty-three additional creditors soon surfaced. That July, Culbertson's land and other possessions were sold at sheriff's auction. By then, Culbertson had left the county.[91]

Many years later, Fannie accused Thomas McCulloh, "a very great ras-

---

[87]Trust Deed, 19 Sep 1866, Peoria County, Illinois, Land Records, Vol. 18, p. 559; notes by Ernest East, PPL.

[88]Note dated 30 Apr 1867. T.G. McCulloh vs. Alexander Culbertson, November term, 1869, Circuit Court, Peoria County, IL, document file, box 230; notes by Ernest East, PPL.

[89]Peoria County, IL, Index to Deed Books, Index Book 3, p. 35. Sheriff's sale of Culbertson's lands in favor of his creditors; notes by Ernest East, PPL.

[90]Berglund, SC 414, MtHS, p. 26.

[91]Circuit Court, Peoria County, IL, document file, box 230. Moravian Seminary for Young Ladies vs. Alexander Culbertson; notes by Ernest East, PPL.

cal and utterly devoid of honesty and principle," of cheating her father.[92] Others pointed to bad investments Culbertson made in projects "promoted by his close friend Thomas Hart Benton."[93] But the Missouri senator had died a decade before Culbertson's bankruptcy. Descendants also blamed Culbertson's "many relatives and friends" who took "advantage of his inexhaustible generosity."[94]

The truth of how Culbertson lost the estimated $300,000 he had when he retired is probably not terribly complicated.[95] The family's lifestyle, with their servants, extravagant furnishings, and frequent travels, was very costly. Moreover, during his years with the Company, Culbertson rarely paid cash for lodging, food, or transportation. Money was added and subtracted from a Company ledger and, with little to buy, the money accumulated. All that changed when he retired. Additionally, he had become accustomed to the Indian tradition in which a gift given today is reciprocated at some future date. However, in white society, gifts given were often accepted with no sense of future obligation. In all likelihood, Culbertson was deeply in debt before he even realized a problem existed.

With bankruptcy looming, the trader took Natawista, Fannie, and Joe and headed back to the upper Missouri.

---

[92]Fannie Culbertson Irvin to Earnest (*sic*) E. East, 18 Dec 1936. PPL.
[93]Taylor, "The Major's Blackfoot Bride," p. 47; McDonnell, *MHSC*, Vol. X, p. 242.
[94]Taylor, "The Major's Blackfoot Bride," p. 47.
[95]Taylor, "The Major's Blackfoot Bride," p. 46; Schemm, p. 12; Bradley, *MHSC*, Vol. III, p. 280. This figure may well have been exaggerated as it probably originated with Culbertson.

Chapter Twenty-Five

## *"a fresh and furious war has broken out"*

It is impossible to know how Alexander Culbertson's presence on the upper Missouri in the mid-1860s might have altered events. Most likely, had he been around, Seen From Afar, the respected Blood chief, would not have stayed away from Fort Benton. And perhaps he could have influenced his tribe's angry young warriors. But with the Culbertsons gone, Seen From Afar opted to trade with the British north of the border at Fort Edmonton.[1]

Meanwhile, attitudes hardened in the now rough-and-tumble frontier town of Fort Benton. The new governor, Sidney Edgerton, told the Montana territorial legislature in December 1864: "While I shall endeavor to punish with promptness and severity any Indian aggression upon our settlements, I shall at the same time, hold to a strict accountability any who may trespass upon the rights of the Indian." Edgerton then declared: "I trust that the Government will, at an early day, take steps for the extinguishment of the Indian title in this territory, in order that our lands may be brought into market."[2] The Indians, of course, strongly disagreed about to whom the land belonged.

In late 1865, a well-known prospector, John McClellan, decided to spend the winter "in repose" in the Sun River valley. Eager prospectors soon began whispering about McClellan's big strike. Although it was the dead of winter, miners headed for the Sun River valley. They set forth with no food, flimsy clothing, and inadequate shelter. Approximately five hundred had arrived by the beginning of 1866; several hundred more turned back before reaching their destination.[3]

About the time the greedy prospectors realized there was no gold, a huge snowstorm hit. Many ended up stranded at the Sun River mission where they might have starved had not Little Dog, Natawista's cousin,

---
[1]Dempsey, *Red Crow*, p. 61.
[2]"Governor Edgerton's Message," *MHSC*, Vol. III, p. 344.
[3]Bradley, "Sun River Stampede," *MHSC*, Vol. IX, p. 251.

come to their rescue. The chief, a "faithful friend to the whites," brought almost daily supplies of antelope to the men, saving many from near-certain death.[4]

That same winter, four friendly Piegans stopped to visit John Morgan, a white man with a small cabin on Sun River. The previous summer, Morgan had attempted to negotiate a peace with the Bloods after the killing of the Ophir woodcutters. Morgan enlisted former AFC trader, Malcolm Clarke, to translate. In keeping with Indian customs, the Bloods offered horses as compensation for the deaths. An agreement was struck but Clarke intentionally misinterpreted the Bloods' action, claiming the horses had been given to him rather than as reparations for the dead.[5]

At first, Morgan received his Piegan visitors cordially. But he soon grew tired of their presence and recruited some prospectors to help rid him of his guests. The prospectors, who had boasted that they would get even with the Indians, ambushed the Piegans, shot one, and hanged the others. Unbeknownst to the vigilantes, five Piegans witnessed the incident. The tribe decided to retaliate. In April, a Piegan war party attacked the Blackfeet agency at Sun River, killing an employee and setting fire to the buildings.[6]

Two weeks later the warriors targeted Morgan. When they reached his cabin, they found it empty. A clear track led to the nearby Jesuit mission where the prospector had fled for protection. At the mission, the Piegans killed the herder, Fitzpatrick, and several head of cattle.[7] The frightened Jesuits abandoned the mission and retreated to the Flathead valley. When Father De Smet reached Fort Benton that summer, he reported: "A fresh and furious war has broken out between the whites and the Blackfeet, in which again the whites have given the first provocation."[8]

De Smet believed that the Indians, "often wronged, insulted and outraged beyond measure by the whites," could find no justice except to "dig up the war hatchet and utter the cry of vengeance against the pale-faces."[9] The missionary left the Blackfeet country soon after, never to return. On May 23, 1873, he died in St. Louis, greatly mourned by both whites and Indians.[10]

---

[4] Ewers, *Blackfeet*, p. 241; Bradley, "Sun River Stampede," *MHSC*, Vol. IX, p. 252.
[5] Bradley, "Blackfoot War," *MHSC*, Vol. IX, p. 253.
[6] Bradley, "Blackfoot War," *MHSC*, Vol. IX, pp. 253-254; Ewers, *Blackfeet*, p. 241.
[7] Bradley, "Blackfoot War," *MHSC*, Vol. IX, p. 255.
[8] Chittenden, *De Smet*, Vol. III, p. 858; Ewers, *Blackfeet*, pp. 241-242; Killoren, p. 277.
[9] Chittenden, *De Smet*, Vol. II, p. 785.
[10] Chittenden, *De Smet*, Vol. II, p. 782; Killoren, p. 360.

# A FRESH AND FURIOUS WAR HAS BROKEN OUT    315

Scattered assaults occurred throughout the spring and early summer of 1866. After Indians killed two freighters near Fort Benton, the whites retaliated by killing a Blood. They shoved his body through the ice of the upper Missouri and his feet could be seen protruding for days. A week later, the Blackfeet killed Kit Carson's nephew, Charley. In Fort Benton, Indians scalps were accepted as legal tender in the bars.[11]

As rage spread through the Indian camps, Little Dog sought peace. In May, he brought twelve stolen horses to Fort Benton and turned them over to acting agent Hiram Upham. As the chief headed for home, a party of drunken Piegans led by Three Suns attacked and killed him and his son, Fringe. Upham reported that the two had been killed "because they were suspected of being too friendly with the whites."[12]

Raids against the whites did not end intertribal warfare. Throughout 1866, the Northern Blackfoot and Bloods battled the Crees[13] while the Piegans battled the Gros Ventres and Crows.[14] Seen From Afar intervened to protect some mixed-blood Cree traders from the Northern Blackfoot and Sarcees.[15] But the whites paid little attention to this, concerned only with what they dubbed the "Blackfeet War" against the whites.

The so-called "Blackfeet War" amounted to little more than guerrilla attacks on both sides. Augustus Chapman, the Flathead Indian agent, called it "the biggest humbug of the age" and accused acting governor Thomas Meagher of using it "to advance his political interests, and to enable a lot of bummers who surround and hang on to him to make a big raid on the United States Treasury." Chapman believed the large number of whites traveling between Helena and Fort Benton each day were in no more danger "from hostile Indians than they would [be] in Washington [D.C.]."[16] But when Meagher called for federal troops, the army sent a

---

[11] Overholser, p. 309. Dempsey, *Red Crow*, p. 60, says Carson was killed in 1865, but Overholser is probably more reliable on this.
[12] Ewers, *Blackfeet*, p. 242; Overholser, p. 307; McDonnell, *MHSC*, Vol. X, p. 255.
[13] Dempsey, *Red Crow*, p. 63. Joseph Culbertson, pp. 34-35, gives an account of a battle between these tribes which sounds remarkably similar. Joe gives a date of 1869, but his dates are notoriously unreliable. If, in fact, Joe Culbertson witnessed this event, it suggests that Culbertson and Natawista may have been on the upper river during the tumultuous summer of 1866.
[14] Ewers, *Blackfeet*, p. 243.
[15] Dempsey, *Red Crow*, pp. 61-62.
[16] Ewers, *Blackfeet*, p. 244; Report of the Commissioner of Indian Affairs, 1867, p. 259.

battalion of the Thirteenth Infantry to establish Camp Cooke at the mouth of the Judith River, site of the 1855 Blackfeet treaty conference.

Meagher was still not satisfied. In April 1867, the Piegans killed John Bozeman, a pioneer settler who had established the Bozeman Trail from the Oregon Trail to the Montana goldfields along the route followed by Alexander Culbertson and Father De Smet in 1851.[17] Mountain Chief, leader of the Piegans, was believed to have headed the war party.[18] Bozeman had written Meagher a month earlier to advise that "we are in imminent danger of hostile Indians, and if there is not something done to protect this valley soon, there will be but few men and no families left in the Gallatin Valley."[19]

Meagher seized on Bozeman's killing to ask General William Tecumseh Sherman, who, as General of the Army,[20] had command of all western troops, for authority to raise and equip six hundred volunteer soldiers. Sherman, urging moderation, assured Meagher he was sending reinforcements as rapidly as possible. But if "the danger was as great as represented," the general authorized Meagher's plan.[21] A few months later, four hundred additional troops established Fort Shaw on Sun River.[22]

Despite this increased military presence, the Blackfeet continued their hit-and-run attacks throughout the winter of 1867-1868, killing several ranchers. Among other complaints, the Blackfeet pointed to the government's failure to provide the annuities promised by the 1865 treaty. That Congress had never ratified the treaty meant nothing to the Blackfeet who simply saw another broken promise.[23]

Alexander Culbertson, Natawista, Fannie, and Joe returned to the upper Missouri in the summer of 1868. The government once again solicited Culbertson's assistance in negotiating a treaty, this time between the Gros Ventres and their new allies, the River Crows. The negotiations were to be held at Fort Hawley above the Musselshell River, with Culbertson and the venerable Alfred Vaughan as interpreters.[24]

---

[17]Ewers, *Blackfeet*, p. 244.
[18]Overholser, p. 309.
[19]Burlingame, p. 122.
[20]Ewers, *Blackfeet*, p. 247.
[21]Burlingame, p. 122.
[22]Burlingame, p. 126.
[23]Ewers, *Blackfeet*, pp. 244-245.
[24]Joseph Culbertson, p. 11, gives the name as "Col. Von," almost certainly a reference to Alfred Vaughan.

Young Joe Culbertson, aged ten, accompanied his father and almost brought the council to a ruinous conclusion. While the government officials, interpreters, and chiefs gathered in the council room, Joe sat outside with two elderly Indians not much interested in the proceedings. Joe, eager to emulate his father, decided to play "making treaty."

Joe knew the first step: pipe-smoking. He borrowed his father's meerschaum pipe, possibly the one given Culbertson by Prince Maximilian in the 1830s, and filled it with gun powder topped by tobacco. Returning to his new Indian friends, he shook hands, and "made peace." Then Joe handed them "the pipe of trouble."

One of the Indians brought the pipe to his mouth as Joe simultaneously struck a match and prepared to run. The Indian touched the match to the pipe which exploded, burning the Indian's eyebrows and lashes and pushing the pipestem into his throat. As Joe ran to his father, the Indian pursued him. The prank nearly caused the council to collapse, but Culbertson smoothed things over by making proper recompense to the wounded Indian. The next day, when the steamboat arrived, Culbertson prudently sent Joe to Fort Benton.[25]

When the council had been successfully concluded, Culbertson headed to Fort Benton, the now-booming town he had founded twenty-two years earlier as a remote fur trading post. Having been absent for four long, eventful years, Culbertson encountered astonishing changes. "[M]erchants, thieves and blackguards" now dominated the town[26] which boasted twenty saloons and two billiard halls.[27] Few of the people the Culbertsons had known, either traders or Indians, remained.

Nevertheless, the family quickly assumed new positions in the changed environment. Fannie, now eighteen, taught in the brand new log-and-adobe schoolhouse on Main Street. Her students were mostly mixed-bloods, white children still being rare in Fort Benton.[28]

Culbertson's nephew, Robert Simpson Culbertson,[29] joined the family later that year.[30] Though only twenty-five, Robert, like many young men of

---

[25]Joseph Culbertson, p. 12.

[26]Ewers, *Blackfeet*, p. 246; Report of the Commissioner of Indian Affairs, 1868, pp. 206-207.

[27]Overholser, p. 174.

[28]Holterman, p. 172; Overholser, p. 261. Overholser identifies the teacher as Mariah Culbertson, Alexander's oldest daughter. This is an error. By this time, Mariah was married to Samuel Kipp and living in Parkville, Missouri.     [29]Lewis Culbertson, p. 271.

[30]NAM, M593/827. Chouteau County, Montana Territory. Robert S., age 27, occupation, clerk in store, is enumerated in the household of Alexander Culbertson.

that era, had attained maturity fighting in the Civil War.[31] He worked with his uncle for a time[32] before assuming a clerk's position with a Fort Benton outfitter. Eventually, he managed the Centennial Hotel[33] and kept the Culbertson name alive in Fort Benton, raising nine children there.[34]

For Alexander Culbertson, Fort Benton, despite its changes, meant returning to a relatively familiar lifestyle. One of his first jobs that fall was translating at another Blackfeet treaty council. This time, in contrast to the 1865 council, Culbertson's presence ensured the meaningful participation of both the Bloods and Piegans.

The council convened on September 1, 1868, with William J. Cullen acting for the government. Mountain Chief represented the Piegans; Three Bulls, the Northern Blackfoot; and, Seen From Afar, Calf Shirt, and Big Plume appeared for the Bloods. The treaty virtually mirrored the unratified 1865 agreement: the Blackfeet agreed to surrender their territory south of the Teton River while the government agreed to establish a new agency in the north. This treaty, however, did not provide for individual payments to chiefs, as the 1865 agreement had.

After all present solemnly affixed their marks and signatures, Commissioner Cullen forwarded the treaty to Washington, D.C. There, like its predecessor, it languished without ratification. Once again, the Indians had negotiated in good faith only to discover that what white men on the frontier said meant little in the long run.[35]

Even without ratification, everyone agreed that the Indian agency should be moved out of Fort Benton where relations between whites and Indians had grown increasingly hostile. Innumerable Blackfeet had ended up dead in the town's streets or bars during the years the agency had been located there. Moreover, soon after signing the 1868 treaty, Mountain Chief had been badly abused by townspeople after requesting, in

---

[31] Holterman, p. 172.

[32] Clifford, Section III, p. 36. Cites "Robert Culbertson, 'Interview.'" This is presumed to have been an interview Ms. Clifford personally conducted with Robert Simpson Culbertson's son, Robert. The author's search of the collections at MtHS did not uncover this interview.

[33] Overholser, p. 115 and p. 240. The hotel was originally known as the Culbertson Hotel but its name was changed in 1876 in honor of the nation's centennial celebration.

[34] Personal communication to the author from Wayne York of Houston, Texas. Mr. York's wife is the former Helen Fay Johnson, Robert Simpson Culbertson's great-granddaughter.

[35] Ewers, *Blackfeet*, p. 245; Dempsey, *Red Crow*, p. 62; Burlingame, p. 43. Burlingame erroneously gives the date as 1869.

accordance with the treaty, that some especially hostile whites be expelled from the region.[36]

The previous spring, another Piegan chief, Heavy Runner, echoing Seen From Afar's 1855 concerns, had warned that he might not be able to keep his young warriors in line.[37] The government discounted this, preferring to trust Calf Shirt, a Blood chief, who had declared: "We will force our young men to keep this [1868] treaty and keep them from stealing.... The past is buried."[38]

Thus, in 1869, the government moved the Indian agency seventy-five miles northwest to a site near present-day Choteau, Montana. As the agency moved north, so did Alexander Culbertson, re-entering the fur trade among the Bloods with his nephew. Gray Eyes, an influential Blood chief who was either Natawista's brother or cousin,[39] helped Culbertson build a post across the international border and brought old and new friends to trade.[40] Culbertson apparently sold the acquired robes to John Riplinger of the North West Fur Company.[41]

But the peace Culbertson hoped might result from the 1868 treaty never materialized. In January 1869, an Indian war party attacked a party of hunters near the Dearborn River. Three months later, the Blackfeet wounded a freighter near Fort Benton. That night, the whites in Fort Benton killed two Indians in retaliation.

Then, in July, a group of passing Crows attacked a wagon train near Fort Benton and killed two herders.[42] Fort Benton's residents vowed vengeance and, ignorant of or indifferent to the nationality of the killers, seized and hanged three Blackfeet, leaving a note which read: "These are three good

---

[36]Ewers, *Blackfeet*, p. 246; Overholser, p. 310.

[37]Overholser, p. 174.

[38]Overholser, p. 310.

[39]Clifford, Section III, p. 36. Clifford calls Gray Eyes Natawista's cousin while Holterman, p. 57, calls him a "close relative," and Taylor, "The Major's Blackfoot Bride," calls him her brother.

[40]Clifford, Section III, p. 36.

[41]No records of North West Fur employees have been located. Culbertson's apparent connection to the North West Fur Company comes from Ege, pp. 91-92. Ege quotes a report by Brigadier General Philippe de Trobriand regarding "a trader of the Northwest Fur Company, named Cobetson or Coveson..." This is almost certainly a reference to Alexander Culbertson. Additionally, the records of T. C. Powers Company (MC55, MtHS) show that North West Fur frequently settled Culbertson's account with the Fort Benton outfitters.

[42]Burlingame, pp. 222-223; Overholser, p. 310; Joseph Culbertson, p. 3; Holterman, p. 172; Ewers, *Blackfeet*, p. 246. Overholser calls the dead "freighters" while all others identify them as "herders."

Indians."⁴³ Joe Culbertson later remembered that "Benton was not a very healthy place for any Indian to visit after the killing of these two herders."⁴⁴

Alexander Culbertson, in the northern camps when the hangings occurred and unaware of the worsening situation, sent Mountain Chief's brother and a young Blood warrior to town several days later. The two, Bear Child and Rock Old Man,⁴⁵ were shot down on Fort Benton's main street in broad daylight.⁴⁶

Nearly everyone knew that Henry Kennerly and Peter Lukins had been among the killers.⁴⁷ Nevertheless, General Alfred Sully, newly appointed Superintendent of Indian Affairs for Montana, told his superiors that he could arrest the murderers, but he doubted they could be convicted. "Nothing can be done to insure peace and order," Sully asserted, "till there is a military force here strong enough to clear out the roughs and whisky-sellers in the country." He added, "I fear we will have to consider the Blackfeet in a state of war."⁴⁸

The Piegans escalated the tactics perfected during years of intertribal raids. They attacked freighters on the road between Fort Benton and Helena and raided outlying ranches, running off horses and killing isolated settlers.⁴⁹ But the biggest shock of that tumultuous year came on

---

⁴³Joseph Culbertson to Charles Kessler. KP, UCLA. No other source mentions this.

⁴⁴Joseph Culbertson, p. 3. Joe tells another story in his book and in correspondence with Charles Kessler, KP, UCLA, which is of interest but could not be dated: "A few days later, according to Joe Culbertson, a Blood Indian came into Fort Benton to visit with the Culbertsons who were then in town. During the visit, a white man named George stormed into the Culbertson's house, dragged the Indian out into the street and shot him. The body was then dumped down a well where it was finally discovered after the water began to taste funny." Joe suggests this happened in 1869 but that would not seem to be possible considering Alexander Culbertson's letter to General Alfred Sully written in September 1869, in which Culbertson says he has "recently arrived from the interior where I have been since last winter with the Bloods and Blackfoot Indians." The author believes it may have occurred during the early months of 1870.

⁴⁵Schultz, *Blackfeet and Buffalo*, p. 299.

⁴⁶Ewers, *Blackfeet*, p. 246; Burlingame, p. 223; Overholser, p. 310; Holterman, p. 173. Why Culbertson would have sent these men into Fort Benton, given the state of hostilities, is something of a mystery. The answer may have something to do with the fact that Caroline Connoyer, the daughter of Mountain Chief's sister and a former employee of the Culbertsons, was still living in Fort Benton at this time. Perhaps Natawista wanted Caroline to come north and join the Culbertsons in the Indian camps. Or perhaps Mountain Chief himself had a message which he wanted conveyed to Caroline. Unfortunately, Hugh Welch, Connoyer's great-grandson, does not recall Caroline ever discussing this event. Hugh Welch to the author.

⁴⁷Schultz, *Blackfeet and Buffalo*, p. 299.

⁴⁸"Piegan Indians," House ExDocs 269 (41-2) 1426; Ewers, *Blackfeet*, p. 246.

⁴⁹Ewers, *Blackfeet*, p. 246.

# A FRESH AND FURIOUS WAR HAS BROKEN OUT

August 17 when Piegan warriors murdered Malcolm Clarke at his ranch in Prickly Pear Canyon near Helena.

Clarke, the rugged West Point-educated frontiersman, first came upriver with Culbertson in 1839. "Shrewd, tough, stubborn and eloquent,"[50] Clarke flourished as a trader. He married Cutting off Head Woman, daughter of a Piegan chief, and together, they had four children.[51] Later Clarke took the mixed-blood daughter of Isidoro Sandoval, the AFC clerk killed by Alexander Harvey, for his second wife and she bore him another child.[52] Like his mentor Culbertson, Clarke sent his children downriver to be educated.[53]

From the beginning, Clarke had a curious relationship with the Blackfeet. Calf Shirt, the Blood chief, once told him: "My friend, you are continually acting in a manner displeasing to the Nation." Culbertson, Calf Shirt explained, always gave the chiefs "magnificent presents" and paid "richly" for their robes whereas Clarke, with only his smile, got them to part with their robes for almost nothing. "There is something about you which steals away our hearts against our inclinations," the chief said, adding, "I hate the white man, but I hate you less than any white man I ever knew."[54]

Clarke, however, made his share of enemies. In 1863, for reasons that remain obscure, he killed Owen McKenzie, the well-respected mixed-blood son of Kenneth McKenzie. Clarke always claimed he acted in self-defense, but the death so angered McKenzie's friends that Clarke had to flee to avoid retribution.[55]

In the 1850s, Clarke briefly joined an opposition trading company. He returned to the AFC a few years later, retiring in 1864 and settling on a ranch in the Little Prickly Pear Valley not far from Fort Benton. There, he raised horses and cattle[56] and operated a way-station on the stage route between Helena and Fort Benton. His fellow Montanans considered him one of the territory's outstanding citizens.[57]

But his relationship with the Piegans had begun to sour. In the summer

---

[50]Ege, p. 5.
[51]Ege, p. 5, gives her Indian name as Kahkokima; Holterman, p. 173, gives it as Kakokima.
[52]Holterman, p. 173.   [53]Clarke, *MHSC*, Vol. II, p. 259.
[54]Clarke, *MHSC*, Vol. II, p. 256.
[55]Sunder, pp. 250-251; Larpenteur, p. 298; Clarke, *MHSC*, Vol. II, p. 258; Ege, p. 7. Joseph Culbertson, draft ms., p. 92, KP, UCLA, says that the killing of McKenzie occurred in Alexander Culbertson's office.   [56]Ege, p. 6; Clarke, *MHSC*, Vol. II, p. 255.   [57]Ege, p. 7.

of 1867, some of Clarke's Piegan relatives spent several days at his ranch. During their visit, someone stole horses belonging to Pete Owl Child, Mrs. Clarke's cousin.[58] The tracks indicated white settlers were to blame. Clarke's daughter, Helen, claimed her father was "indignant" and felt "honor bound" to return the horses. Despite his bold reputation, Clarke failed to recover the animals although the "whereabouts of some were discovered." Owl Child could not forgive this insult and, before leaving, he stole some of Clarke's horses and his spyglass.[59] At least, that is how Helen Clarke remembered events.

The Piegans told a different story. According to them, Clarke made unwanted advances toward Owl Child's wife, causing Owl Child to steal Clarke's horses and spyglass. Whatever led to the theft, what happened next is clear: Clarke rode out to the Piegan village and publicly berated Owl Child, calling him an "old woman." Clarke's son, Horace, struck Owl Child in the face with a quirt. Clarke, his property recovered, forgot the incident. But Pete Owl Child, insulted in front of his tribe, could not.[60]

On August 17, 1869, Malcolm Clarke awoke concerned about cattle which had been missing for several days. He sent his hired hand, a young Piegan named Jackson, to look for the stock while Clarke and his oldest son, Horace, tended to chores. The day passed quietly. That evening, as the Clarkes finished supper, they heard the lowing of cattle. Jackson had found the stock grazing far to the south. Malcolm Clark checked the livestock and then returned to the ranch house where he challenged his daughter to a game of backgammon. They had played a few games when they heard the dogs barking outside. Four Piegans, including Pete Owl Child, had come to visit. It was about 9:00 P.M.

The Clarkes and Owl Child exchanged warm greetings and all their earlier disputes seemed forgotten. The women prepared food and everyone enjoyed the repast. Afterwards, Owl Child informed Clarke that Black Weasel, Mountain Chief's son, was outside, too shy to enter. Clarke, remarking that Black Weasel was "one of the finest Indians [he] had ever known," went out to invite the young warrior inside. The Indians and Clarke shared a pipe and then Owl Child announced that the Piegans had brought back several of Clarke's horses, stolen earlier by some Bloods. They had also brought an invitation from Mountain Chief for Clarke to come to their village to trade. The announcements delighted Clarke who

---

[58]Clarke, *MHSC*, Vol. II, p. 259, gives his Indian name as Ne-tus-che-o.
[59]Clarke, *MHSC*, Vol. II, p. 259.
[60]Ege, p. 9; Clarke, *MHSC*, Vol. II, p. 260; Welch, p. 27.

had worried that Mountain Chief, following the recent killing of his brother in Fort Benton, would react precipitately. Only the year before, Mountain Chief had told Clarke:

> I despise all whites; they have encroached on our territory; they are killing our buffalo, which will soon pass away; they have treated my nation like dogs; and hereafter I shall no longer be responsible for the depredations committed by my young men; for we, the Piegan, have been made to suffer for the bad deeds of other tribes.[61]

Around midnight, the Piegans prepared to leave. Owl Child suggested that Horace Clarke accompany Bear Chief to Clarke's stolen horses. Horace agreed and looked around for his pistol. When he could not find it, Helen teased her brother: "What is the use of a firearm? You are with a friend." Horace nodded and headed outside with Bear Chief.

Bear Chief, complimenting Horace on his fine horse, suggested he ride ahead. Horace agreed but, as he rode along, he heard a pistol being cocked. He turned to face Bear Chief who laughed: "My friend, you are a brave, you have a great heart." Since Indian warriors frequently challenged each other with feigned acts of violence, Horace let the matter pass.

Then he heard the eerie sound of Bear Chief singing a Crow war song. Horace recognized this as a presage to death. Before he could react, a bullet ripped through his right nostril, coursed through his cheek, and exited in front of his left ear. The shot knocked Horace from his horse and he became tangled in his lariat. The horse dragged the badly wounded youth for several yards before he freed himself. Blood poured from Horace's wounds. Believing him dead, Bear Chief left Horace lying on the ground.

As Horace lay there, his father, unaware of what had transpired, stepped outside with Owl Child and another warrior named Eagle's Rib. Suddenly, Eagle's Rib pulled his gun and shot Malcolm Clarke in the heart.[62] As Clarke staggered and fell, Owl Child slashed at his forehead

---

[61]Clarke, *MHSC*, Vol. II, p. 260.

[62]Ege, p. 16, names the killer as Eagle's Rib. Clarke, *MHSC*, Vol. II, p. 265, says the killer was Crowfoot. These may be two names for the same man. Holterman, p. 57, says that an Indian named Eagles Ribs may have been one of Natawista's relatives. This is confirmed by correspondence between William Pocklington, Indian Agent for the Blood Reserve, and the agent for the Fort Peck reservation, in 1890. This Eagles Rib is designated as a "minor chief." (See Chapter Twenty-Eight) Holterman also says that Crowfoot, who would become a chief of the Northern Blackfoot, was the brother-in-law of Natawista's nephew, Red Crow. Hugh Dempsey in a letter to the author, 25 Mar 1996, says that the Eagles Ribs who killed Malcolm Clarke was a Piegan. The name is also common in the Blood tribe and, according to Dempsey, if Natawista was related to an Eagles Ribs, it was almost certainly the Blood of that name, not the Piegan.

with an axe. Malcolm Clarke was dead. The Piegans had placed their blows carefully: the shot to Horace Clarke's face and the gash to Malcolm Clarke's forehead symbolically avenged Horace's earlier intemperate attack on Pete Owl Child.

Inside, the stunned Clarke women looked out and saw a large group of Indians riding wildly around the house, chanting war songs. Helen Clarke thought "the demons in hell had broken loose."[63] Then they saw Malcolm Clarke's lifeless body. As they tried to fathom the ghastly sight, Helen heard Horace, who had dragged himself back to the house, crying weakly for help. Helen and her aunt pulled Horace inside and tried to stanch his bleeding.

The warriors eventually departed, leaving the family huddled inside with the horribly wounded Horace and Malcolm Clarke laying lifeless in the front room. When the Piegans returned to ransack the house, Malcolm Clarke's elderly Indian sister-in-law confronted them: "The man you murdered here tonight was your best friend. You have committed a deed so dark that the trees will whisper it, and before the sun reddens these mountains, a hundred horsemen will be here to avenge his death."[64]

The killing of Malcolm Clarke outraged Montana's settlers who demanded justice. Before this, none of those who claimed to have been victimized by Indian raids could identify the perpetrators. That changed with the Clarke killing. Both Helen and Horace Clarke, who survived his horrendous wounds, could name their father's killers. In October 1869, the newly appointed marshal for Montana territory sought indictments against Malcolm Clarke's murderers.

Marshal Wheeler estimated that fifty-six whites had been killed and more than a thousand horses stolen in 1869 alone.[65] The grand jury indicted Pete Owl Child, Eagle's Rib, Bear Chief, Black Weasel, and Black Bear, all of whom were affiliated with the Piegan leader, Mountain Chief,[66] declaring: "Ours is a contest between civilization and barbarism . . . ." In conclusion, the grand jurors sought government protection, citing the fact that they had "left homes of comfort in the East to plant civilization in the wilderness."[67]

---

[63]Clarke, *MHSC*, Vol. II, p. 264.
[64]Ege, pp. 10-19; Clarke, *MHSC*, Vol. II, pp. 261-266.
[65]Ewers, *Blackfeet*, p. 247.     [66]Ege, p. 24.     [67]Ege, p. 23.

Not everyone believed the situation beyond redemption. On September 2, 1869, Alexander Culbertson wrote General Alfred Sully from the new Blackfeet agency on Teton River, thinking it "not... unwise" to convey his thoughts. Culbertson, only recently returned from "the interior," had spent the spring and summer with the Bloods and Northern Blackfoot.

Shaken by the murder of his friend, Culbertson assured Sully that the Bloods and Northern Blackfoot "are perfectly friendly to the Whites" and "evinced no disposition as to be otherwise." He reminded the general that the Piegans, too, "have allways (*sic*) professed to be the friend and protectors of the Whites—living as they have in allmost (*sic*) constant communication with Benton."

Admitting that he had not recently been in the Piegan camps "to know for what reason they are now committing these depredations," Culbertson nonetheless asserted that his "knowledge of their character will not permit me to think that there exists a general hostile feeling amongst them." He insisted that "these depredations have been committed by a portion of the young rabble over whom the chiefs have no controal (*sic*)."

Even while conceding that "nothing but the strong arm of the government" might be capable of containing the angry youth, Culbertson refused to put all the blame on the Indians, young or old. He reminded Sully that the "non-ratification of treaties made with these Indians has had any thing else but a tendency to keep them quiet." Without effective treaty stipulations to the contrary, Culbertson contended that the warriors "think they have a perfect right to help themselves to any Horses falling in their way." He urged the government to deal more fairly and equitably with the Indians in the distribution of their annuities, believing this alone might "well go a long way to keeping them quiet." Considering the "fast decreasing herds of buffalo," they would soon be "wholly dependent on the Govt for support."

Fearing retribution, Culbertson pointedly reminded Sully that the Bloods and Northern Blackfoot were "distinct" from the Piegans, that they lived "remote from each other," and most importantly, that the two northern bands "have no sympathy with the Peigans (*sic*) and of course will take no part with them in any way." Expecting that the Bloods and Northern Blackfoot would soon be visiting the agency, Culbertson suggested to Sully that "a little straight formal talk will convince them that the Govt is determined on making them keep the peace."

In conclusion, Culbertson informed Sully that he planned to spend the winter at the Blackfeet agency and hoped that the two might meet there so that he could provide the general "all the reliable information [he] might want" about the Blackfeet nation.[68]

Sully believed Culbertson's insights important enough to pass along to the Commissioner of Indian Affairs. Sully, acknowledging that he had known Culbertson "for a long time" and that the trader had lived with the Blackfeet "for a great many years," assured the Commissioner that the "information given in his letter can be relied upon."[69] But the government paid little attention to the overall tone of Culbertson's letter, focusing instead on his contention that "nothing but the strong arm of the Government can control" the young radicals.

In late October, having read Culbertson's letter, Lieutenant General Philip H. Sheridan, then in charge of the Military Division of the Missouri[70] including Montana Territory, wrote Brevet Major General E. D. Townsend, the Adjutant General of the U.S. Army, recommending that the "best plan" would be to ascertain where the Indians planned to winter and "about the time of a good heavy snow I will send out a party and try and strike them." Sheridan predicted that, by mid-January, the Indians should be "very helpless," enabling the military "to give them a good hard blow."[71]

Two weeks later, Adjutant General Townsend had the "honor" to inform Sheridan that his plan "for the punishment of these marauders" had been approved by General of the Army, William Tecumseh Sherman.[72]

---

[68]Alex. Culbertson to Genl. A. Sully, 2 Sep 1869, SC 1280, MtHS; "Piegan Indians," House ExDocs 269 (41-2) 1426.

[69]Alf. Sully, U.S. Army, Supt. Indians from Helena, Montana Terr. to Hon. Commissioner of Indian Affairs, Washington, D.C., 28 Sep 1869. SC 1280, MtHS.

[70]Ewers, *Blackfeet*, p. 247.

[71]"Piegan Indians," House ExDocs 269 (41-2) 1426, p. 52.

[72]"Piegan Indians," House ExDocs 269 (41-2) 1426, p. 53.

Chapter Twenty-Six

## *"Tell Baker to strike them <u>Hard</u>"*

General Alfred Sully still hoped a peaceful resolution of the "Blackfeet War" might be possible. When Marshal Wheeler, indictments in hand, demanded Sully, as Superintendent of Indian Affairs, arrest the Indians charged with Clarke's murder, the general asked Commissioner of Indian Affairs Ely Parker how to proceed. Parker instructed Sully to council with the Blackfeet chiefs and charge them with bringing in the offenders. Parker also told Sully to inform them that, if they were not surrendered, army troops would be sent to punish the tribe.

Thus, on January 1, 1870, Sully and Wheeler traveled to the Blackfeet agency. Couriers, probably including Alexander Culbertson, had been dispatched to bring the Blackfeet chiefs to the agency. But when Sully and Wheeler arrived, only Piegan chiefs Heavy Runner, Little Wolf, and Big Leg[1] along with Gray Eyes from the Bloods waited. The messengers reported the others too drunk to travel.

Sully told the four chiefs that the government was "tired out with the repeated aggressions of their people" and, to protect the lives and property of white settlers, "was determined to make war against them." Sully even threatened to chase the Blackfeet beyond the international boundary, an empty threat which Sully nonetheless believed impressed the chiefs.[2]

The chiefs, while disavowing responsibility for the depredations, promised to turn the offenders over to Sully. They also vowed to return all horses stolen from white settlers. Sully gave them two weeks to accomplish these tasks, but simultaneously recommended the army "be ready to strike if necessary."[3] He then returned to Fort Shaw to wait.

General Philippe Regis de Trobriand commanded the troops at Fort Shaw. Born in France, de Trobriand compiled an impressive Civil War record. Afterward, while stationed at Forts Totten, Rice, and Stevenson

---

[1]Also referred to as Big Lake.
[2]Ewers, *Blackfeet,* p. 248. Welch and Steckler, p. 30, says that Sully told the chiefs to "capture, kill, and bring back the bodies of Owl Child and the others in his war party...."
[3]Ewers, *Blackfeet,* p. 248; Bennett, p. 83.

in present-day North Dakota, he fought against the Sioux. Initially reluctant to use force against the Blackfeet, de Trobriand changed his mind after Malcolm Clarke's murder.

De Trobriand wrote General Sheridan on December 13, 1869: "No better time or opportunity can present itself to punish the parties guilty of the murders and depredations committed last summer." The offenders, encamped with Mountain Chief, were "within easy reach" and de Trobriand detailed a plan "to strike [Mountain Chief's camp] first, by surprise, killing or capturing those who may be found there...."[4]

Although he acknowledged "no state of war actually exists," de Trobriand stressed that an attack would serve "not only to chastise the culprits, but as a warning to prevent others."[5] To prepare for the strike, he ordered four cavalry companies, under Major Eugene M. Baker, to Fort Shaw. They arrived on January 14.

Meanwhile, General Sully suggested another option if the Blackfeet failed to surrender the wanted men: capture Mountain Chief and hold him hostage until the tribe turned over the offenders. Faced with conflicting recommendations, General Sheridan dispatched his assistant, James Allen Hardie, to assess the situation.

Hardie reached Fort Shaw on January 7, 1870. There, he met with de Trobriand, Sully, Marshal Wheeler, Joe Kipp, and Joe Cobell. Kipp, born at Fort Union in 1847, was the mixed-blood son of AFC trader James Kipp and his Mandan wife, Earth Woman.[6] After his father retired, Joe remained on the upper river where Alexander Culbertson and Natawista helped raise him.[7] Kipp spoke both English and Blackfeet fluently.

Joe Cobell, born in Italy, came to the United States with an uncle and joined the American Fur Company as a hunter and herder. Cobell had married the sister of Little Dog, making him a cousin to Natawista. When the AFC quit the fur trade, Cobell bought a small ranch near Fort Benton but, as civilization encroached, moved north to live among the Blackfeet. After his first wife died, Cobell married Mountain Chief's younger sister.[8]

Hardie asked Joe Kipp to go to the Indian camps, learn the mood of the Indians, and report back. Hardie then interviewed local officials, including the Blackfeet agent and the head of the North West Fur Company, to gather information regarding the recent depredations. Sully recommend-

---

[4]Ege, pp. 31-32.     [5]Bennett, p. 92.
[6]Ege, p. 40, gives her Indian name as Sah-kwi-ah-ki.
[7]Holterman, p. 138.     [8]Ege, p. 40.

ed that Hardie also contact Alexander Culbertson but Culbertson "had left for Belly River."[9]

After listening to the various opinions, Hardie notified Sheridan that de Trobriand "thinks impunity encourages Indians and recommends prompt chastisement." Moreover, de Trobriand believed Mountain Chief's camp could be hit "without molesting friends, either Piegans or Bloods." If Sheridan authorized the strike, the mission would fall to Major Baker. Although Hardie admitted to being "quite unprepared" for Sully's hostage-taking suggestion, he noted that the "experience and character of General Sully, as well as his official position, lent to his recommendation due weight."[10]

Although Hardie suspected that "to surprise an Indian band and capture prisoners without bloodshed would be ordinarily to attempt an impracticability,"[11] he deferred to Sheridan: "Question is, whether chastisement or capture for hostages should be the principal design."[12]

Sheridan cabled his decision: "If the lives and property of citizens of Montana can best be protected by striking Mountain Chief's band, I want them struck. Tell Baker to strike them Hard."[13]

With his plan approved, de Trobriand hired Joe Kipp and Joe Cobell as scouts. Kipp, having just returned from the Indian camps, believed he knew the location of Mountain Chief's band. Moreover, he could distinguish the hostile camps from the friendly ones.[14] In addition to Kipp and Cobell, Horace and Nathan Clarke, anxious to avenge their father's murder, would accompany the troops.

By January 19 more than two weeks had passed since the Piegan and Blood chiefs had met with Sully. With no progress, it was decided to proceed with military action. That morning, Baker's units moved north with orders to strike Mountain Chief's band. The somewhat muddled instructions also directed Baker to leave "unmolested" the "uniformly... friendly" bands of Heavy Runner and Big Leg.[15]

---

[9]"Piegan Indians," House ExDocs 269 (41-2) 1426, p. 26.
[10]"Piegan Indians," House ExDocs 269 (41-2) 1426, p. 28.
[11]"Piegan Indians," House ExDocs 269 (41-2), 1426, p. 29.
[12]"Piegan Indians," House ExDocs 269 (41-2) 1426, p. 47.
[13]Ege, pp. 32-33; Ewers, *Blackfeet*, p. 249; Burlingame, p. 224; Bennett, p. 101. Photocopy of telegram in possession of author. [14]Bennett, p. 94.
[15]"Piegan Indians," House ExDocs 269 (41-2) 1426, p. 33.

De Trobriand, fearing detection, instructed Baker to travel only at night. As the men left Fort Shaw, temperatures hovered around thirty below. The soldiers wore blankets and buffalo robes over their woolen coats and stopped frequently to prevent frostbite. During the day, Baker's men bivouacked while Kipp and Cobell scouted the route for that night's march.[16]

At daylight on January 22, the troops halted near the Dry Fork of the Marias. That night, they continued northeast. Eleven miles later, the scouts spotted a small Piegan encampment. The soldiers surrounded the village of Gray Wolf, a friendly chief, and rousted the inhabitants. The frightened Gray Wolf told the soldiers that the hostile Piegans were camped six or seven miles downstream.[17]

Baker dispatched troops to protect Riplinger's North West Fur Company post near Willow Rounds, ordered a small contingent to remain at Gray Wolf's village, and then proceeded to the camp of the hostile Piegans. At the Big Bend of the Marias, the troops found a village of more than thirty lodges. Baker ordered his troops to form a skirmish line on the bluffs above the encampment. The soldiers, shielded by the dark, took up their formation and aimed their .50 caliber rifles and carbines at the village. As dawn neared, the Piegans slept.

Suddenly, an agitated Joe Kipp approached Major Baker. In the early morning light, Kipp recognized the painted lodge at the center of the village. This was the village of Heavy Runner, he announced, one of the friendly chiefs whom Baker had been instructed to hold harmless.[18] An irritated Baker shoved Kipp aside, declaring: "That makes no difference, one band or another of them; they are all Piegans and we will attack them."[19] Baker then placed the mixed-blood scout under guard. If necessary, Baker instructed his men to shoot Kipp to prevent another outburst which might alert the village.

But the village was already coming to life. A lone male exited the lodge identified by Kipp as belonging to Heavy Runner. The chief, waving a piece of paper over his head, ran toward the bluffs. "I am the Heavy Runner," he shouted. "I am friend to the whites. Do not shoot my people. We wish only peace with the whites."[20] As Heavy Runner brandished the

---

[16]Ege, p. 41.  [17]Ege, p. 42.
[18]Ewers, *Blackfeet*, p. 249; Ege, p. 49, disputes this and makes much of the presence in this camp of Big Horn and Red Horn.
[19]Welch and Steckler, p. 31.  [20]Bennett, p. 116.

paper received from General Sully attesting to his friendly status, a single shot rang out. Heavy Runner fell dead.[21]

The soldiers began to fire. Volley after volley rained down on the village. Panicked Indians ran in every direction as the soldiers shot indiscriminately. Some villagers may have initially returned fire, but soon the only volleys came from the military. The barrage lasted nearly an hour.[22]

When the only sounds emanating from the village were the low moans and screams of the wounded and terrified, the soldiers, sabers drawn, charged down from the bluffs. Riding through the encampment, they tore down lodges and rounded up survivors. Lodges collapsed on still-burning interior fires. As dense smoke curled up from the toppled tipis, many women and children, hiding inside, suffocated or burned to death. Private Walter McKay, peering into a lodge, was shot by a wounded warrior, becoming the only military casualty.

By 11 A.M. the village had been totally destroyed. At least one hundred and seventy-three men, women, and children lay dead,[23] with another one hundred and forty captured. The troops also seized more than three hundred horses. After interviewing some of the hostages, Kipp and Cobell informed Major Baker that his intended target, the camp of Mountain Chief, was located several miles downstream.

Baker, after instructing Lieutenant Gus Doane to complete the destruction of Heavy Runner's village, proceeded to Mountain Chief's camp.[24] When Baker reached the village, he found it deserted. The inhabitants had been alerted by a Piegan who had escaped from Heavy Runner's village. Thwarted, Baker ordered his troops to set up camp to rest.

Back at Heavy Runner's village, Lt. Doane counted the dead. Along with Heavy Runner, Kipp and Cobell identified Big Horn and Red Horn, two hostile chiefs. Doane then gathered the village's food and supplies and ordered them burned. After posting a guard around the captives, Doane went to sleep. That night, Wolf Tail, another friendly chief, was killed when he allegedly tried to escape.

---

[21] Ewers, *Blackfeet,* p. 250.   [22] Ege, p. 44.
[23] One hundred and seventy-three dead is the commonly accepted number. Joe Kipp later said he counted two hundred and seventeen dead; de Trobriand put the number at two hundred and twenty; the Piegans claimed that "upwards of three hundred" were killed. Al Hamilton affidavit, Blackfeet Claims Commission, 16 Jan 1915. Also Gibson, "Missing Parts," p. 2.
[24] Ege, p. 44-45.

In the morning, Doane noticed smallpox among the captives. The disease had struck several weeks earlier and, by the time of the attack, about three Piegans were dying every day with more and more falling ill.[25] When Baker returned later that day, Doane informed him of the situation. Considering the widespread illness, Baker "allowed [the prisoners] to go free,"[26] abandoning them on the frozen prairie without shelter or food, except some bacon and hardtack the troops left behind. Many who survived the initial attack died in the days that followed from exposure or smallpox.[27]

But smallpox may have been a convenient excuse for Baker's callous treatment of the captured Indians. Early accounts of the engagement do not mention the disease; instead, the officers insisted they turned the captives loose because of insufficient rations and a lack of means to transport them to Fort Shaw, despite the availability of the seized Piegan horses.

Three weeks later, de Trobriand advanced smallpox to explain why the prisoners had been abandoned in the bitter cold.[28] Yet the army may never have intended to bring the prisoners to Fort Shaw. In an earlier journal entry, de Trobriand had discussed military tactics in fighting Indians. He advocated "[surprising] the permanent villages where the tribes keep their women and children" with the "confessed aim" being "to exterminate everyone." Otherwise, he warned, "just another burden would be added—prisoners."[29]

Many survivors walked for days through sub-zero temperatures to reach assistance.[30] Among these was Heavy Runner's five-year-old daughter, Double Strike Woman. With her mother and three siblings, she walked more than ninety miles to Fort Benton. Several years later, she married Joe Kipp, Major Baker's mixed-blood scout.[31]

The repercussions from Baker's strike extended far beyond the Montana frontier. In his report, submitted two months after the incident, Baker asserted that all but fifty-three dead had been able-bodied males.[32] Indian agent William Pease, himself an army lieutenant, disagreed,

---

[25]Bennett, p. 113.     [26]"Piegan Indians," House ExDocs 269 (41-2) 1426, p. 17.
[27]Bennett, p. 163.
[28]"Piegan Indians," House ExDocs 269 (41-2) 1426; Gibson, "Missing Parts," p. 17.
[29]Kane, *Military Life*, p. 64.
[30]Ege, pp. 37-46; Ewers, *Blackfeet*, pp. 247-250; Burlingame, p. 225.
[31]Ege, p. 62.     [32]"Piegan Indians," House ExDocs 269 (41-2) 1426, p. 73.

reporting that the dead included just fifteen men between the ages of twelve and thirty-seven. The rest of the victims, Pease asserted, were women and children under the age of twelve.[33]

Condemnation came from many quarters. Lt. Doane called the massacre the "greatest slaughter of Indians ever made by U.S. troops."[34] Horace Clarke, so grievously wounded by the Piegans, lauded Heavy Runner as "a good Indian and friend of the white people" and accused Baker of being so drunk that he "did not know what he was doing." Joe Kipp claimed that "(a)ll of the able-bodied Indians were out hunting, and those who were killed were the Chief and such Indians as could not hunt, being old men and women and children." But de Trobriand, in a letter to his daughter, remained unruffled: "Sustained by the testimonials which I received in Helena on this matter, my attitude remains serenely amused and unmoved."[35]

Initial press reports applauded Baker's actions. The *Rocky Mountain News* proclaimed, "Most of the murderers and marauders of last summer were killed. The expedition was a complete success."[36] The *Chicago Tribune* claimed that the Indians "fought desperately [with] men, women, and children joining in the battle. It is feared some of the women and children were killed in the melee, but it is hoped not many. In Indian attacks, where all fight, the killing of a few women and children is always unavoidable." [37]

Yet, as more facts became known, the press changed its tune. The *New York Times* called "the slaughter of the Piegans in Montana . . . a more serious and a more shocking affair than the sacking of Black Kettle's camp on the Washita." They asked: "Can we call the killing of 173 people, of whom 140 were women and children, anything but a sickening slaughter?"[38]

The Montana press felt no such ambivalence. The *New North-West*, published in Deer Lodge, warned its readers that "all the namby-pamby, sniffling old maid sentimentalists of both sexes who leave most of their brains on their handkerchiefs when under excitement, will join the jargon of discontent."[39]

Politicians soon joined the critics. Representative Daniel Voorhees of Indiana, recalling that when the Indians were "a power," the nation

---

[33]Ewers, *Blackfeet*, pp. 250-251; Ege, p. 144; Bennett, p. 131.
[34]Bonney, p. 22.   [35]Bennett, pp. 151-152.
[36]"Miscellaneous," *Rocky Mountain News*, 29 Jan 1890.
[37]"The Indian Country," *Chicago Tribune*, 3 Feb 1870.
[38]"The Slaughter of the Piegans," *New York Times*, 24 Feb 1870.
[39]*The New North-West*, 4 Feb 1870.

engaged them in "manly battle," deplored the fact that now that the Indians were "poor, broken and miserable remnants; corrupted and demoralized," the army chose not only to fight the warriors but also "the woman and the babe in her arms."[40]

Representative John Logan of Illinois, a former major general from the Civil War, said the incident "made my blood run cold in my veins." [41] Congressman Aaron Sargent of California rebuked Baker's assault as an "act of cruelty," adding that "civilization shudders at horrors like this." Charles Eldridge, representative from Wisconsin, charged: "If [the Indians] are the wards of the Government, then we who are taking care of them are the most barbarous people on earth."[42]

The outrage did not trouble General Sherman: "It is of Course to be expected that Some of our People prefer to believe the story of the Piegan Massacre as trumped up by interested parties." Unconcerned with facts, Sherman continued: "I prefer to believe that the majority of those killed at Mountain Chief's camp were warriors," apparently also preferring to ignore the fact that it was Heavy Runner's, not Mountain Chief's, camp which Baker had struck.

As for the hostages so cruelly abandoned, Sherman declared that "a hundred women & children were allowed to go free to join the other Bands of the Indian tribe known to be camped nearby." The massacre was entirely justified, Sherman insisted, since "the army cannot resist the tide of emigration that is flowing towards these Indian Lands." Therefore, "when called on we must to the extent of our power, protect the Settlers."[43]

The massacre had tangible effects. For several years, politicians had recommended moving the Bureau of Indian Affairs from the Interior to the War Department. Baker's actions ended those discussions. After 1870, the Interior Department no longer even sanctioned the appointment of army officers, such as William Pease, as Indian agents.[44]

The impact of what came to be called the Baker Massacre was even more immediate in Montana Territory. The Blackfeet, ravaged by smallpox and cowed by the massacre, abandoned all thoughts of retaliation. When Jesuit missionary John Imoda met with Mountain Chief and seven other Piegan chiefs soon after, they unanimously expressed their desire for a lasting peace.[45]

---

[40]Ege, p. 51.     [41]Ege, p. 52.     [42]Bennett, pp. 132-133.
[43]W. T. Sherman to General P. A. Sheridan, 24 Mar 1870. Copy in the author's possession.
[44]Ewers, *Blackfeet*, pp. 251-252; Ege, p. 52.     [45]Ewers, *Blackfeet*, p. 252; Bennett, p. 161.

News of the massacre on the Marias devastated an already grief-stricken Natawista. Several months earlier, her beloved brother, Seen From Afar, had died from smallpox. The noble chief, in Fort Benton when smallpox broke out in the Indian camps, became concerned about his daughter, Otter Woman, who was camped on Belly River with the Bloods and, probably, the Culbertsons.[46] Despite four consecutive dreams warning him that he could only escape the plague by remaining south of Milk River, Seen From Afar decided to return to his people. Before leaving, he rode through camp:

> My people! My children! The Sun looks down upon me. I am going away. My dreams have told me not to cross the Milk River Ridge; four times I have been told. But I have no power to stay here. I must go to my daughter. My people! I will not see you again. Live good lives and do the best you can.

When Seen From Afar and his wife reached Belly River, they found Otter Woman safe and well. Together, the family turned south. But that night, on Milk River Ridge, Seen From Afar complained of back pain. "I have the sickness," he told his family. "I will die today." The great chief of the Fish Eaters was dead. At the confluence of the Belly and St. Mary's rivers, his wife and daughter placed his body on a burial scaffold.[47]

To Natawista, the world appeared to be devolving into chaos. Not long before, she had been ensconced on a lavish estate, enjoying her position as the local curiosity capable of raising the eyebrows of Peoria's stuffier society matrons. Prior to that, she had reigned over the upper Missouri. For most of her life, the world had been hers for the asking. Wherever she went, she was welcomed and fêted. If she wanted to visit her family, Company employees provisioned a wagon and off she went. Her appetite for fancy clothes and colorful jewels was easily satisfied with finery from the best shops in St. Louis.

But now there was no money, no home, and no social stature. While Culbertson knew how to be a successful trader in the old fur trade world, a new one had arrived and its ways perplexed him. After just one season, he was considering abandoning his trading post.[48] The situation for Natawista was even worse. Not only was she no longer queen of the realm but, as

---

[46] Alex. Culbertson to General A. Sully, 2 Sep 1869, SC 1280, MtHS.
[47] Dempsey, *Red Crow*, pp. 68-69.
[48] Robert Culbertson, "Interview," cited in Clifford, Part III.

a full-blooded Indian, she was treated as less than a full person in the town she and her husband had founded. Natawista might have adjusted to a less ruthless frontier. But since their return, horror after horror had piled up, subjecting her to a continuous round of sorrows.

Her own people had killed her cousin, Little Dog, because they believed him too friendly with the whites. Close friends sent to Fort Benton by her husband had been shot down in broad daylight simply because they were Indians. Seen From Afar had died from the dreaded smallpox. And now, the military, having rejected her husband's advice, had slaughtered nearly two hundred of her people,[49] mostly peaceful women and children in the village of an avowedly friendly chief.

Natawista had returned to Fort Benton with her husband in late 1869. When the federal census was taken the following spring, her name appeared along with two hundred and seventy-two white males and some eighty individuals admitting to some Indian blood.[50] But the situation continued to deteriorate. By spring, Natawista had reached a difficult decision. Feeling she no longer belonged in the white man's world, she announced her intention to return to her people.[51]

Why Natawista chose to return to the Bloods is perhaps easier to understand than why Culbertson did not go with her. He certainly would have been welcome and that lifestyle was at least as familiar as the rough-and-tumble world of Fort Benton. But what would he have done in the Indian camps? Despite his sixty-one years, Culbertson remained vital. The idea of living without a job, without a tangible purpose for his exis-

---

[49] According to the affidavit of Bear Head, given to the Blackfeet Indian Claims Commission on 18 Jan 1915, several members of the Blood tribe were present in the village of Heavy Runner when Baker struck.

[50] NAM, M593/827; Overholser, p. 75.

[51] Exactly when and how Natawista left is unclear. On May 28, 1870, she is recorded as having purchased "3 Bottles Eau D Cologne" from T. C. Powers in Fort Benton. Ledger Books, T. C. Powers, Account of Major A. Culbertson, MtHS, MC 55, Vol 61, p. 265. This appears to be the last record of her in Fort Benton. Broomfield says that she went north with Culbertson in the fall of 1870 and then decided to remain with her people. This information would have come from Joe Culbertson but, in other accounts, Joe said that Natawista went north with other traders. Joe also told Charles Kessler that part of the reason for Culbertson's journey north in the fall of 1870 was to attempt to persuade Natawista to return to Fort Benton. KP, UCLA. This directly contradicts the information given Broomfield. George Taylor, the Culbertson's great–grandson suggests that Natawista and Culbertson were at their daughter Julia's home in Orleans, Nebraska, when Natawista announced her intention to return to the Bloods. GTOH. This is not true. All the evidence suggests that Natawista left in 1870. Julia Culbertson and George Roberts did not move to Orleans until several years later and there is no evidence that Natawista ever visited Orleans.

tence, would have been incomprehensible. In the white man's world, Culbertson could always find work as an interpreter or minor trader.

Nonetheless, the realization that the society he had worked so hard to foster, a society in which whites and Indians could live together, had failed to materialize caused Culbertson great sadness. While he may have felt more at home with the Indians now, in his heart, he knew he was an American and always would be. His grandfather had fought in the Revolutionary War to establish the country and Culbertson could not now abandon it. Moreover, he had Joe to consider. While he wanted his children to know, understand, and respect their Indian heritage, he also wished them to be educated and that could not happen in the Indian camps.

Culbertson could not reinvent his life, although he surely understood Natawista's decision. Throughout their marriage, she had been his full partner; she had willingly accompanied him into many dangerous situations, including those frightening early months when he had reestablished the Blackfeet trade following the Fort McKenzie massacre and the potentially hazardous Stevens railroad survey. Never timid, she had always known her own mind. Now, that independent spirit mandated that she return to her people while he stayed with his.[52]

Heartbroken, the Culbertsons parted. Years later, Joe ascribed "the downfall of my dear old father" to Natawista's departure.[53] The rapid influx of white settlers had permanently rent the carefully knit community of Indians and whites established through years of mutually beneficial commerce. And now, it had torn apart the first family of that fragile, integrated society.

---

[52]There is very little in the historical record to explain why Natawista decided to return to the Bloods. Their daughter, Fannie, had left Fort Benton by the time Natawista made her decision, leaving only twelve-year-old Joe to interpret events. His mother's decision was so traumatic for the young boy that he never spoke about it until shortly before his death when he wrote a letter to Charles Kessler about Natawista's departure. Even then, Joe was so concerned about divulging the information that he felt compelled to write Kessler "in [his] own handwriting" rather than using a typist, as had been his custom. KP, UCLA. According to Hugh Dempsey, Blood oral tradition maintains that Natawista returned to her people because she was "homesick." Hugh Dempsey to the author, 25 Mar 1996. Many of the conclusions presented are the author's own, based on the existing evidence.

[53]Joe Culbertson to Charles Kessler, KP, UCLA: "After my father had done everything in the world for my mother and took her east and marrie (*sic*) her as a white lady and raized (*sic*) a big family she left him and went off with a man by the name of John Ripinger (*sic*) he use (*sic*) to trade for T. C. Powers." There is no evidence that Natawista was involved with John Riplinger although it is possible that, out of convenience, she traveled north with him to the Blood camps.

In the fall of 1870, just seven months after the Baker massacre, Culbertson set off on another trading expedition to the Blood country. That he felt safe undertaking this trip suggests the strength of his ties to the tribe. In addition to making money for the winter, Culbertson had another motive: he hoped to convince Natawista to return to Fort Benton.[54]

The controversial Jean L'Heureux, who claimed to be a Jesuit priest, joined Culbertson on the trek. Although not ordained, L'Heureux conducted mass and performed marriages and baptisms.[55] Also accompanying Culbertson were his son, Joe, and two teamsters.[56] Whiskey trafficking in the northern Indian camps had accelerated at an alarming rate, but Culbertson carried only "a keg of very palatable wine" made from local serviceberries. Perhaps because the Piegans had fled their normal winter camps, Culbertson followed an unknown course, "travelling altogether by our slight knowledge of locality."[57]

At Milk River, the group encountered a vast buffalo herd. It was rutting season and "the thunder-like bellowing of the bulls could be heard for miles." From far away, Culbertson watched the animals "pawing and throwing up the earth which raises like smoke in the air." The abundant game and water made this "a favorite wintering quarters for Indians," but it was August and Culbertson found no Indian encampment. He pushed on, hoping to find the Piegans "in the vicinity of a spur of the Cypress Mountains, called the Buffalo's Head."

Water grew scarce. Basins which had previously contained water "were now perfectly dry." With humans and animals feeling "the want of water," the traders camped for the night. In the morning, "trusting to Luck and a kind providence," they continued on. When they encountered a small buffalo herd, Culbertson knew water would be nearby. At a cool spring, the party rested.[58]

---

[54]Joe Culbertson to Charles Kessler. KP, UCLA.

[55]Dempsey, "Journey to Bow River," p. 11. Dempsey corrected numerous spelling errors and the author has used the corrected spellings. Original journal in Culbertson Collection, MoHS. A typescript copy is in SC 586, MtHS. A copy can also be found in KP, UCLA.

[56]Joe Culbertson to Charles Kessler, KP, UCLA. Joseph Culbertson, p. 1, suggests that Natawista may have been with this group. However, in his letter to Kessler, Joe says that she had already returned to the Blood camps and the trip was designed, in part, to visit her and attempt to convince her to return. It seems likely that Joe's reference to his "mother" on p. 1 of his book is a typographical error and should read "father," especially since the manuscript copy, KP, UCLA, says father, not mother. [57]Dempsey, "Journey to Bow River," p. 11.

[58]Dempsey, "Journey to Bow River," pp. 12-13.

From a hill, Culbertson saw "dust flying and the Buffalo running," suggesting the animals were being pursued, and that the Piegans might be camped nearby. When Culbertson sent Joe[59] out to scout, he reported seeing smoke from Indian lodges. Culbertson was "elated" at finding the Piegan encampment "after being so long in doubt whether we should find either the Indians or water for ourselves or animals."

The next day, a Piegan hunter "politely" agreed to lead the traders to the encampment.[60] Before long, additional Piegans, all expressing "the most friendly feeling," appeared. At their village, the chief received Culbertson "with hospitality and kindness," even offering him his lodge. Culbertson traded with the Piegans for three days. He estimated the total population at only two thousand, greatly decreased by "this most awful of all diseases, the smallpox" and "the attack upon them by the United States troops." Culbertson suspected these forces had hastened "[the Piegans'] inevitable extinction from the face of the earth," but took solace in "their ignorance and unconcern for what the future may have in store for them."

He marveled that, despite the "trying scenes" these "once-happy" people had endured, they "evince no hostile nor unfriendly feeling toward the whites, whom they know are the whole cause of their misfortune." Culbertson wished there could be a "Grand Council" during which the white men could convey their pacific intentions to the Indians, "humble and peaceable as they are now." Such a proceeding might clear "the sky from that black and threatening cloud which [the Piegans] are afraid is still hovering around them."[61]

The traders then left to find the Blood camp. Unsure of their route, the traders, "Trusting to Luck," pressed on. The group followed Belly River to the Little Bow.[62] After resting a few days, the group proceeded down the Little Bow into familiar country. Culbertson was anxious to reach the Blood village, but the weather refused to cooperate. On August 10, the traders awoke to find the ground "beautifully covered with three inches of snow." In the afternoon, a ferocious wind forced them to lay over again.

---

[59] Culbertson identifies him only as the "Indian boy" who was "more anxious than the rest." It is the author's assumption that this was Joe. However, this may have been Kisenaw, the Indian boy who lived with the Culbertsons in Peoria. Although Culbertson never mentions Kisenaw, Joseph Culbertson, p. 1, says that Kisenaw was killed on this trip.

[60] Dempsey, "Journey to Bow River," pp. 13-14.

[61] Dempsey, "Journey to Bow River," pp. 14-15.

[62] Dempsey, "Journey to Bow River," p. 17. Culbertson calls it Nam-ich-ty.

The next day, the group reached Blackfoot Crossing[63] where Culbertson "had slight hopes of finding the Blood Indians." Once again, he sent Joe[64] "ahead for reconnoitering"; Joe returned to report that he had seen lodges "on the opposite side of the river at the exact place [Culbertson] expected [he] might find them." As news spread of Culbertson's arrival, the river filled with Indians eager to greet him. The Bloods, including Natawista, had not seen Culbertson "for near six months" and they welcomed him with open hearts. Culbertson remained with the tribe for several days. The trade went well but, when it came time to leave, he could not convince Natawista to return. Saddened, he began the long trek back to Fort Benton.

Culbertson continued to ponder what might have been. If only the Indians could have missions, farms, and schools "where they could be taught industry and economy," they might "eventually save the remnant of this tribe from ultimate extinction." But this now seemed unlikely. Most Montanans regarded the Blackfeet "only as a blood thirsty savage people," which was "a vague idea formed upon an ignorance of the actual characters of the Indians." Those "who are acquainted with them and received their hospitality and kindness will give them a more enviable reputation" which Culbertson wished could be "reciprocated by the settlers of Montana for all time to come."[65]

The wistfulness Culbertson felt remains palpable more than a hundred years later.

---

[63]Dempsey, "Journey to Bow River," p. 18. Culbertson calls it Soh-yo-pah-ith-coo-yat. Dempsey, in his notes, gives the Indian name as Soyo-pow-ahko.
[64]Identified by Culbertson only as "the boy."
[65]Dempsey, "Journey to Bow River," pp. 15-20.

Chapter Twenty-Seven

# "We will remain and see the whole affair through"

After spending the winter in Fort Benton, Culbertson and Joe went north again the next spring to trade and visit Natawista.[1] The situation in the Indian camps had deteriorated dramatically. Years later, Joe recalled that it was not unusual "to see the whole Black Foot and Blood Indians drunk day in and day out," with several dying each day in drunken brawls.[2]

For generations, the Blackfeet, especially the Bloods and Northern Blackfoot, had traveled freely across the forty-ninth parallel without regard for its status on maps as an international boundary. In the 1860s, they began to exploit this so-called "medicine line." Raiding parties stole horses in Montana Territory and drove them north, beyond the reach of American authorities, selling many to the Hudson's Bay Company.[3]

In late 1869, John Healy and Alfred Hamilton, two white traders from Sun River, realized they, too, could benefit from the international boundary. Although the Intercourse Laws banning liquor sales to the Indians had rarely been enforced, in 1868 some whiskey traders had been arrested, tried, convicted, and imprisoned. In another blow to whiskey traders, the government restricted the Fort Benton Blackfeet trade to two licensed dealers: the North West Fur Company and I.G. Baker and Company.[4]

The future looked bleak for the freelance whiskey traders until the Hudson's Bay Company ceded their lands to Canada. Healy and Hamilton, members of the Montana Territorial Legislature,[5] realized trading posts in this new territory would not be subject to American liquor laws. With $25,000 worth of trade goods, an ample stock of Henry repeating rifles, and fifty gallons of liquor, the two headed north in late 1869, osten-

---

[1] Joseph Culbertson, p. 2. Joe says that they spent "the winter of 1871" at Fort Whoop-Up before returning to Fort Benton. While Joe's dates are not always reliable, this would seem to be accurate since Culbertson's own journal of the trip north in 1870 has them returning to Fort Benton in late 1870 and he never mentions going to Fort Whoop-Up during that trip. However, subsequent events convince the author that this stay at Fort Whoop-Up did not last all winter.

[2] Joseph Culbertson, p. 2.　　　　　　　　[3] Ewers, *Blackfeet*, p. 255.
[4] Ewers, *Blackfeet*, pp. 255-256.　　　　[5] Ege, p. 25.

sibly to prospect. They established a trading post at the junction of Oldman and St. Mary's rivers, forty miles north of the border.[6]

Experienced traders, such as Culbertson, knew that selling too much liquor to Indians adversely affected the trade because, when inebriated, Indians refused to hunt. The new generation of whiskey-traders, however, relied on liquor to generate profits. They did not care if their customers hunted or stole horses from white settlers to pay for their addiction, as long as the profits rolled in.

Their first winter, Healy and Hamilton netted $50,000. But, after they returned to Fort Benton, angry Indians burned their post. Undaunted, the partners rebuilt their post, christening it Fort Whoop-Up. The appellation, extending to the trail north, arose from Healy's announcement: "We'll whoop things up for the Johnny Bulls when we get this place finished."[7] Joe Culbertson suggested the name should have been "'Hell on Earth' as it was certainly hell."[8] Within four years, more than a dozen stockaded posts flew the American flag in Canada, including Fort Standoff, run by Joe Kipp. For all, liquor constituted the primary commodity.[9]

Through dilution, the traders transformed a hogshead of whiskey (approximately sixty-three gallons) into two hundred gallons of trade liquor. To ensure a fiery taste, traders added molasses, red ink, castile soap, bluestone, peppers, and tobacco. The drink itself, especially the dregs, could be lethal in large quantities.[10]

Even worse, many traders did not begin with whiskey; they diluted pure alcohol and colored it with burnt sugar and oil of bourbon. They added water depending on the purchaser's condition: a sober Indian got four parts water to one part alcohol; a somewhat inebriated Indian got six parts water; a drunken Indian got eight or ten parts water.[11]

A prime head-and-tail buffalo robe bought three pints of trade alcohol. A good horse sold for a gallon or two. More than one Indian sold his wife for liquor.[12] The area around Fort Whoop-Up soon became known as "the toughest camp now existing in the Rocky Mountains."[13]

The devastating impact of this unbridled whiskey trade came at a most inopportune time for the Bloods. The 1869 smallpox epidemic had reduced their population by nearly a third. Moreover, it had robbed them

---

[6]Ewers, *Blackfeet*, p. 256; Dempsey, *Red Crow*, pp. 67-68.
[7]Joseph Culbertson, p. 80.   [8]Joseph Culbertson, p. 2.
[9]Ewers, *Blackfeet*, pp. 256-257; Dempsey, *Red Crow*, p. 72.
[10]Ege, p. 26; Dempsey, *Red Crow*, p. 74.
[11]Dempsey, *Red Crow*, p. 74.   [12]Ege, p. 26.   [13]Overholser, p. 81.

of their respected chief, Seen From Afar. Leadership had passed to his brother, Black Bear, but he, too, died of the smallpox after which his son, Red Crow, became chief of the Fish Eaters.[14]

Red Crow, Natawista's nephew, was forty years old when he assumed tribal leadership.[15] To his dismay, he found leading an almost impossible task, thanks to the whiskey traders. As the whiskey forts multiplied, whiskey became the coin of the realm. Father Constantine Scollen noted that the "fiery water flowed as freely . . . as the streams running from the Rocky Mountains." The Indians "sold their robes and their horses by the hundreds" for liquor.[16]

With whiskey polluting the country, most Indians fell victim to its spell and hazards, with unknown numbers dying. The crudely mixed brew poisoned many. Others, heavily intoxicated, froze to death. The Indians, displaying a macabre sense of humor, sometimes propped a frozen, dead comrade against the fort gates so the corpse would fall on the traders when they opened up in the morning.[17] When the traders felt threatened, as they frequently did, they shot freely, hitting many of their targets. The Indians also killed many of their own in drunken brawls.[18]

One visitor to the whiskey forts claimed that seventy Bloods had died from liquor in one winter.[19] An 1871 report listed eighty-eight Northern Blackfoot dead from intoxicated mêlées.[20] The Blackfeet agent, after an exhaustive study in 1873, concluded that one-fourth of the 1867 Blackfeet population had died from whiskey.[21]

In addition to killing Indians, liquor undermined the native social structure. As the Indians killed each other, previously cooperative bands split apart. The Fish Eaters succumbed to this fate in 1872. After the rupture, two brothers, Many Shot and Young Sun, headed one family group. When they had nothing to trade for liquor, the brothers waylaid other Indians, stealing their whiskey or anything they could trade for the deadly brew.

Red Crow also drank heavily, remaining drunk for days and then sobering up for a few weeks before beginning the cycle again. Natawista's brother, Big Plume, also imbibed freely as did Red Crow's brothers, Kit

---

[14]Dempsey, *Red Crow*, pp. 69-70  
[15]Dempsey, *Red Crow*, p. 1.  
[16]Dempsey, *Red Crow*, p. 73.  
[17]Ewers, *Blackfeet*, p. 258.  
[18]Dempsey, *Red Crow*, pp. 73-74; Ege, p. 26.  
[19]Dempsey, *Red Crow*, p. 73.  
[20]Ewers, *Blackfeet*, p. 258.  
[21]Ege, p. 26; Ewers, *Blackfeet*, p. 259; Report of the Commissioner of Indian Affairs, 1873, p. 252.

Fox and Sheep Old Man. Almost certainly, Natawista, too, was frequently drunk. The possibility that she became seduced by alcohol remains one of the saddest possible explanations for her return to the Blood camps.

The violence of the whiskey trade soon invaded Red Crow's family. Red Crow was drunk when two inebriated brothers stopped to visit. They took seats on either side of the chief who offered them his pipe. The first brother refused; the other then drunkenly fired at his host. Missing the chief, he mortally wounded Red Crow's wife, Water Bird. Red Crow killed the young man as his brother fled into the night.[22]

Then, in 1872, Big Plume died when several Northern Blackfoot came to his camp looking for whiskey. Big Plume tried to force them from the camp, resulting in a brawl in which Big Plume was shot and killed. Natawista had lost her third brother in two years.

That same year, Red Crow became convinced that his youngest brother, Kit Fox, had taken up with one of his wives. When both were drunk, the two argued about Red Crow's suspicions. As Kit Fox reached across to strike his brother, Red Crow grabbed him by the hair and slammed him to the ground. Red Crow pulled a stone from the fireplace and smashed Kit Fox with it repeatedly until he lay dead. The killing created a long-lasting rift.[23]

The devastation wreaked on the Bloods by the whiskey traffickers dismayed Alexander Culbertson, but he could do little. After a winter near Fort Whoop-up, Culbertson left the Blood country for good, returning to Fort Benton in the spring of 1871.[24]

---

[22]Dempsey, *Red Crow*, pp. 75; Liddell.   [23]Dempsey, *Red Crow*, pp. 75-76.

[24]Joseph Culbertson, p. 2; Overholser, p. 75. Another factor contributing to Culbertson's decision to leave the fur trade may well have been the fact that, apparently, in March 1871, he was indicted for trading whiskey to the Indians. House ExDocs 1 (42-2) 1505, p. 826. According to the report by Jasper Viall, Montana Superintendent of Indian Affairs, to the Commissioner of Indian Affairs, Culbertson "was cleared entirely by superior skill on the part of his counsel which the money of his backers had procured for him." No further information regarding this could be found. It is not mentioned at all in the letters sent by the Montana Superintendency, 1871. NAM M833/3. Newspaper accounts of court actions that spring do not mention Culbertson's indictment. However, there is mention of a number of traders being indicted for trading with the Indians without the proper licenses. See, for example, *Helena Herald*, 18 March 1871. Records of Culbertson's purchases from T. C. Powers (MC55, MtHS) would not seem to support sizable liquor purchases of the type that would be expected for someone trafficking in liquor. Thus, it seems more likely that Culbertson's indictment, if it occurred, was the result of his trading without the proper license. Moreover, Culbertson could not have been employed by the government, as he soon was, without the approval of Viall. Thus, the outrage in Viall's report would seem to be exaggerated.

Conditions there were little better. The town had become increasingly lawless as residents and elected officials alike headed north to profit from the whiskey trade. Following one saloon killing, the citizens learned that their sheriff, constable, coroner, and justice of the peace were all up north, trading at Fort Whoop-Up.[25] Joe Culbertson called Fort Benton "one of the toughest places, outside of the Whoop Up country . . . in the territory of Montana." Barroom brawls regularly culminated in death.[26]

The fur trade had been supplanted by the whiskey trade. Needing work, Culbertson turned to the government which had recently established Fort Browning on Milk River to serve the Assiniboines, River Crows, and Gros Ventres. The region was also home to several bands of hostile Sioux led by Sitting Bull, the charismatic Hunkpapa chief.

These bands, including some of the refugees from the 1862 Minnesota uprising, regarded all whites as enemies. For years, they had attacked white settlers and the military. They even refused to trade with the whites, preferring to obtain their ammunition and supplies from mixed-bloods and friendly Indians. But, with the game herds dwindling, the Sioux needed more reliable arrangements.[27]

Thus, after nightfall on September 8, 1871, Sitting Bull and a small band of followers appeared at Fort Peck, a trading post established in the late 1860s by Durfee and Peck. Sitting Bull, calling out his name, announced that he had come in peace. The traders, who for years had attempted to induce the Sioux to trade at their post, received them hopefully. Following a truce, small bands of hostile Sioux began trading at Fort Peck.

On October 12, Sitting Bull asked to meet with Andrew "Jack" Simmons,[28] the Fort Browning agent. Since Superintendent of Indian Affairs Jasper A. Viall had previously tried to open negotiations with Sitting Bull, the government enthusiastically embraced the opportunity.[29] Viall wrote the Commissioner of Indian Affairs: "justice, humanity, and economy alike demand that our best efforts should be put forth to aid and assist these people, who now desire peace with the Government, that a savage and a bloody warfare may be prevented."

Viall authorized Simmons to organize a party "of good and reliable men"

---

[25]Overholser, p. 177.   [26]Joseph Culbertson, p. 2.
[27]"Appropriations," House ExDocs 102 (42-2) 1511, p. 5.
[28]Simmons signs his own correspondence, A. J. Simmons. See, for example, House ExDocs 102 (42-2) 1511, p. 9, while Joseph Culbertson, p. 4, refers to him as "Jack Simmons."
[29]House ExDocs 102 (42-2) 1511, p. 4; Utley, p. 93.

to negotiate with Sitting Bull.[30] Simmons, having previously met Alexander Culbertson, now offered him a position as interpreter for the Milk River agency.[31] Culbertson accepted and, with his son, Joe, moved east.[32]

The Simmons delegation arrived at Fort Peck on November 4, 1871. Believing it imprudent to enter the Indian camps without military escort, Simmons sent runners to the camps to ask the leaders to come to the fort for a council. Ten days later, the conclave convened with Black Moon,[33] Iron Dog, Long Dog, Little Wound, Sitting Eagle, and Bear's Rib representing the nearly two hundred lodges of hostile Sioux. Sitting Bull, not trusting the government's safety guarantees, declined to attend.

For ten days, Simmons conferred with the Indians. He urged them to abandon warfare and live in peace, claiming that the tribes which had done so no longer feared the soldiers and were demonstrably better off than the Teton Sioux.[34] While Simmons had no authority to negotiate a treaty, he hoped to raise a Sioux delegation to journey to Washington, D.C., to visit with their Great Father.

In response, Black Moon presented the demands of his tribe, primarily involving the removal of whites from their territory. Simmons tried to explain that this was impossible. The Sioux had to understand, Simmons argued, that the Great Father "was strong and powerful," that his "white children were as numerous as the trees in the mountains," that he could easily "exterminate the Tetons if he so desired." But, Simmons continued, their Great Father "took pity upon [the Indians] because they were weak and inferior."

Simmons urged the Tetons to abandon the warpath, to tell their young men "who would rather throw their lives away fighting than accept peace and its benefits" that if they "were brave men they would think of their women and children, and not subject them to the sacrifice of war and starvation." If they would do this, "there would probably be no occasion for soldiers coming into their country."

---

[30] House ExDocs 102 (42-2) 1511, pp. 4-5.

[31] Joseph Culbertson draft manuscript, KP, UCLA.

[32] Broomfield; Joseph Culbertson, p. 3. Joe puts the date as 1872 but his dates are not reliable. Simmons and Viall, House ExDocs 102 (42-2) 1511, do not give the names of the white men hired to assist with this peace council but it seems probable, based on known circumstances, that Culbertson was among the "eight white men" present at the council with Black Moon.

[33] House ExDocs 102 (42-2) 1511, p. 5. Simmons gives his Indian name as We Sapa.

[34] The Teton Sioux or Teton Lakota comprise the Blackfeet Sioux, the Hunkpapa, and the Santee Sioux refugees from the 1862 Minnesota uprising.

Black Moon "declared himself emphatically in favor of peace," adding that "Sitting Bull agreed," as did "most of their headmen and men of sense." He promised to "talk and counsel for peace with his people" and, if they refused to listen, to move those who wanted peace to the north bank of the Missouri. He also pledged to raise a delegation to visit Washington, D.C.

Simmons distributed "a small amount of flour, sugar, and coffee" to the assembly, sending additional supplies to Sitting Bull's camp. Following the council, he reported to Superintendent Viall that "a portion of the Teton Sioux are not only willing, but anxious to make peace," that they "have a wholesome fear of the power of the Government and its military," and that it was important for the government to render "prompt and substantial aid" to keep them from returning to their warring ways.[35]

But governments rarely act expeditiously and the Indians found it difficult to abandon their old lifestyle. Soon after the conference, Standing Buffalo, a Santee Sioux chief, came to Fort Browning to see his old friend, Alexander Culbertson. The two had known each other for years. After his wife, Secret, had died, Standing Buffalo had sent his seven-year-old daughter, Mary, to live with the Culbertsons.[36] Now, Standing Buffalo sought Culbertson's advice about a planned horse-stealing raid against the Gros Ventres.

Culbertson, weary of the incessant warfare, urged Standing Buffalo to abandon the plan. It was time to try to find a path to peaceful coexistence. Culbertson, worried that Standing Buffalo might be killed, feared the Santees might lose a strong leader. Standing Buffalo listened carefully and then consulted his warriors. Afterwards, he returned to Culbertson's room and announced: "My friend, my men want me to go, so I will try my luck."

Two days out, the Santees attacked and killed a Gros Ventre and his wife at the foot of Bear Mountain. Three hundred Gros Ventre warriors soon appeared and Standing Buffalo was shot. When his son and two other warriors tried to assist the old chief, Standing Buffalo advised them to leave him and save themselves. Standing Buffalo, along with ten of his men, died, just as Culbertson had feared.[37]

Later that year,[38] Culbertson took Joe to visit the Assiniboine camp of Red Stone, another old friend. While in camp, a war party of Yankton Sioux, who were preparing to attack the Gros Ventres, arrived. The young

---

[35]House ExDocs 102 (42-2) 1511, pp. 5-9.   [36]"Julia Schultz," MF 159, MtHS.
[37]Joseph Culbertson, pp. 58-59.
[38]Dates come from Joe Culbertson and there is no way to verify them independently.

Assiniboines, anxious to recapture some of the old glory, decided to join the raiders. After a feast and council, the war party, including several women, rode west.

The Sioux and Assiniboines found the Gros Ventres on Beaver Creek. After running off one hundred horses, they attacked. The battle ended with ten Sioux and Assiniboine warriors and one Gros Ventre dead. The Culbertsons were still in Red Stone's camp when the surviving warriors returned. Joe Culbertson remembered the "pitiful sight" for the rest of his life. Spouses and mothers, upon learning of their loved ones' deaths, wept and wailed, cut off their hair, and chopped off the first joint of their little fingers. Dogs howled as the old chiefs sang war songs.

Anxious and scared, Joe asked his father if they could return to Fort Browning. "No, my boy," Culbertson replied, "they won't bother us. We will remain and see the whole affair through." The Culbertsons spent the night in Red Stone's grief-stricken camp.[39]

In May 1872, the government finally authorized $500,000 for the Teton Lakota near Fort Peck. With this lure, Assistant Secretary of the Interior Benjamin R. Cowen traveled to Fort Peck to assemble a delegation of Sitting Bull's followers to visit Washington, D.C. That August, a handful of minor chiefs met with Cowen. Although more than eight hundred Lakota tipis would dot the nearby landscape when winter set in, abundant buffalo had lured most of the tribe south to hunt.[40]

Nonetheless, Cowen and Agent Simmons assembled a small delegation, headed by Medicine Bear and Black Fish, to travel to Washington, D.C. Alexander Culbertson and William Benwire accompanied the group as interpreters.[41] Thirteen-year-old Joe Culbertson also went along. The group traveled to St. Louis and then took a train to the capital city, staying at the Capitol Hotel.[42]

---

[39]Joseph Culbertson, p. 60; "Joseph Culbertson Was Son," 12 Feb 1934, newspaper article from unnoted source. FtU and "Alexander Culbertson," VF, MtHS.

[40]Utley, pp. 95-96.

[41]Bradley, *MHSC*, Vol. III, p. 282; Joseph Culbertson, draft manuscript, KP, UCLA; 1873 Annual Report of the Commissioner of Indian Affairs. Culbertson's name does not appear in Simmons's report on this delegation which may be an oversight. There is little doubt that Culbertson and Joe went since both provided extensive details about the journey.

[42]Joseph Culbertson, p. 4, and draft manuscript, KP, UCLA. In his draft, Joe says they took a steamer to Sioux City, Iowa. Bradley, *MHSC*, Vol. III, p. 282, also makes reference to the group traveling through St. Louis.

After a brief conference with the Commissioner of Indian Affairs, the Sioux chiefs met with President Ulysses S. Grant at the White House. Shaking hands with Grant, Medicine Bear turned to the assembled warriors and declared, "His hand feels the same as any other man's hand." Grant then presented the chiefs with small gifts and promised each a suit of clothing, a hat, and a valise. In addition, when they returned, their agent would provide them a horse, saddle, and bridle.[43]

Now it was time for the Indians to offer their Great Father gifts. For Medicine Bear, this meant literally giving Grant the shirt off his back. Dressed in full regalia, Medicine Bear placed his calumet on the mantle and removed his eagle-feather headdress. He then took off his war shirt, adorned with the scalp locks of his fallen enemies, and attempted to place it on President Grant. The President's military aides quickly intervened, laying the shirt on a nearby chair, assuring Medicine Bear that the President "would accept it as proof of Medicine Bear's good will."[44] Medicine Bear then told Grant: "You have many white people. They are like flies and there is no use of my people trying to fight the white people."[45]

Before leaving Washington, D.C., Agent Simmons helped the chiefs purchase suits, hats, and suitcases. Most opted for swallowtail coats and black or white stovepipe hats around which they tied red ribbons.[46] The delegation then returned to the upper Missouri via "all the main cities" of the East. From Salt Lake City, they followed the bustling Mullan Road to Fort Benton and Fort Peck.[47] At Sun River Crossing, Simmons purchased the authorized horses and saddles for the delegation.[48]

After returning from Washington, D.C., Alexander Culbertson was transferred from Fort Browning, abandoned the previous December, to Fort Peck.[49] James Stuart, who operated the Fort Browning trading post, deeply regretted the reassignment: "Col. Culbertson and son to go to Peck, rough on me for the colonel was the only companion I had." Concurring with nearly everyone who had ever worked with Culbertson, Stuart concluded: "The colonel is an agreeable companion and a man of great common sense and general information. I will miss him sadly."[50]

---

[43]Joseph Culbertson, draft manuscript, KP, UCLA.
[44]Viola, pp. 108-109; Joseph Culbertson, draft manuscript, KP, UCLA.
[45]Joseph Culbertson, draft manuscript, KP, UCLA.
[46]Joseph Culbertson, draft manuscript, KP, UCLA.
[47]Joseph Culbertson, p. 4.          [48]Joseph Culbertson, draft manuscript, KP, UCLA.
[49]Utley, p. 97.
[50]Journal entry of James Stuart, 12 Jun 1872. Unattributed typescript notes, p. 6, "Alexander Culbertson" VF, MtHS.

The following July (1873), the government established Fort Belknap to serve the Assiniboines, Gros Ventres, and River Crows, and Culbertson again relocated.[51] Despite his sixty-four years, he maintained a vigorous work and travel schedule, journeying regularly to Fort Benton, the surrounding Indian camps, and the growing number of white ranches in the region. Even the bitter cold could not curtail his travels; during the winter of 1873-1874, Culbertson made at least eleven trips to the Indian camps as well as three to Fort Benton, often traveling with Major W. H. Fanton, the Fort Belknap agent.[52] Only slippery ice derailed his journeys.[53] While officially employed as an interpreter earning $400 a year,[54] Culbertson also handled other functions. He frequently issued the ration tickets Indians needed to collect their subsidies. He also hosted feasts for the tribes, conducted census counts,[55] and journeyed to the Indian camps "on peace business."[56]

But he was never too busy to perform humanitarian missions. In early January 1874, Long Hair, the Assiniboine chief, fell ill. It had been Long Hair who, in 1833, decided against killing Culbertson when the trader had blocked his entry to Fort McKenzie during the Assiniboine attack on the Piegans in Culbertson's first days on the upper Missouri. Now, Culbertson took "some delicacys (*sic*)" to the old chief,[57] who died soon after.[58]

Joe Culbertson, still too young to care for himself, lived with his father at the agencies until the winter of 1873-1874 when he went to live with his half-sister, Mariah, at the Kipp farm in Parkville, Missouri.[59] When Joe returned to the upper river the following spring, he joined his father at Fort Belknap, working as a post hunter and courier.[60] Jack Culbertson

---

[51]"Fort Belknap Journal," SC 251, MtHS. The first reference to Culbertson in the Fort Belknap journal appears on 4 Nov 1873, shortly after the surviving post journal was begun.

[52]"Fort Belknap Journal," SC 251, MtHS.

[53]3 Feb 1874. "Fort Belknap Journal," SC 251, MtHS.

[54]House ExDocs 5 (44-1) 1605, p. 92. Cf. Broomfield, who states that his yearly salary was $300.

[55]22 Jan 1874. "Fort Belknap Journal," SC 251, MtHS.

[56]5 May 1874. "Fort Belknap Journal," SC 251, MtHS.

[57]5 Jan 1874. "Fort Belknap Journal," SC 251, MtHS.

[58]Joseph Culbertson, "Joseph Culbertson, Son of A 'King of the Upper Missouri,'" undated. "Alexander Culbertson" VF, MtHS.

[59]Joseph Culbertson, p. 47. Joe gives the date as the winter of 1874 but the Fort Belknap journal makes clear that he was on the upper river during the winter of 1874-1875. "Fort Belknap Journal," SC 251, MtHS. The author believes his sojourn in Parkville happened during the winter of 1873-1874. By then, Samuel Kipp had died and Mariah had married Joseph Walker but they lived on the Kipp farm.

[60]February 1875. "Fort Belknap Journal," SC 251, MtHS.

also frequented the fort in the summer of 1875, traveling to the Indian camps with his father and helping with the haying.[61] Together, father and sons took advantage of the mild fall weather that year to go hunting.[62]

At Fort Belknap, Culbertson also met James Bradley, an army lieutenant and burgeoning historian. The old trader, who spent more and more time living with his memories of the long-gone days when the frontier really was the frontier, found the young soldier an enthusiastic audience for his stories. Relying on his journal for details,[63] Culbertson told Bradley many tales of those by-gone days which the lieutenant faithfully transcribed.[64] Unfortunately, Bradley, who had been among the first to see the carnage following the battle of the Little Bighorn, died in August 1877 at the battle of the Big Hole before completing his record of Culbertson's life.[65]

Reliving his past adventures brought Culbertson much pleasure, but it also brought sadness. During one trip across the plains, he confided to Joe that "it makes me feel bad to see those mountains and to travel over this country." When Joe asked why, Culbertson replied: "Joe, long before you were born or ever thought of, I traveled from old Fort Union to Fort Benton with your mother when there was no sign of a trail and the country was black with buffaloes." Asked if he was scared, Culbertson laughed: "The whole Sioux tribe knew me by the name of Red Coat and all the Blackfeet and Piegans knew me by the name of Beaver Child and wherever I met any of them—either on the war path or in a buffalo hunt— they treated me as one of their tribe."[66]

But more frequently now, Culbertson felt like the old man he had become. All his fur company friends had long since left the upper river and most of the Indians he had known were dead. People listened with interest to his stories, but the world he described was as far removed from

---

[61] Summer entries, 1875. "Fort Belknap Journal," SC 251, MtHS.

[62] 15 Sep 1875. "Fort Belknap Journal," SC 251, MtHS.

[63] The existence of a journal kept by Alexander Culbertson is confirmed by Audubon, Vol. II, pp. 133-134, and by Joe Culbertson in communications with Charles Kessler. KP, UCLA. The details of Culbertson's early experiences, especially the remarkably accurate recall of obscure names, reflected in Bradley, *MHSC*, Vol. III, indicates that Culbertson referred to this journal in discussing his experiences with Bradley. Nonetheless, the dates given by Bradley are not always accurate, suggesting that Culbertson's journal was not kept on a regular basis but was a compilation of significant events.

[64] See the ten volume set of *MHSC* for the numerous pieces written by Bradley. See especially, *MHSC*, Vol. III.

[65] Bradley, *March of the Montana Column*, pp. 3-4.

[66] Joseph Culbertson, draft manuscript, p. 88, KP, UCLA.

their daily lives as he had been from the tales of Indian warfare in colonial Pennsylvania which had so enthralled him as a child.

By 1875, Culbertson, while not yet feeling "to any great extent . . . the infirmities of old age," had grown conscious "of being on the down hill of Life."[67] He had probably already decided that, when the time came, he would spend his last days with his beloved daughter, Julia, who had married George Roberts, a Civil War soldier wounded at Gettysburg,[68] in Peoria in 1865.[69] Following their marriage, the two had tried their luck in the then-booming town of Bannack.[70]

The newlyweds had traveled upriver on the steamboat *Benton*. Many years had passed since Julia had been on the upper river and the reception she received was less than cordial. Her fellow passengers disparaged the couple, referring to Julia as the "halfbreed daughter of Alexander Culbertson" and to her husband as "a white man who called himself 'Gen. Roberts.'"

When the Sioux attacked the *Benton*, Roberts handed his rifle to the steward and went to his cabin "to look after his wife." One of the white women passengers reported that Julia "was marching up and down with a butcher knife in her hand determined to give any Sioux a warm reception."[71] The inherent racism seared Julia who considered herself cultured and well-educated.

After one year in Bannack, Julia and George Roberts returned to more civilized society. By the mid-1870s, they had settled in the small town of Orleans, Nebraska, while George Roberts served as the first elected attorney general of that state.[72] Culbertson longed "to have that pleasure of being" with his daughter, her husband, and their young daughter, "Maggie," "to help Dear Julia to make Guarden (*sic*)" since there was none at Fort Belknap. "We plant plenty but the Grass Hoppers Reap." Neverthe-

---

[67]Alexander Culbertson, Fort Belknap, M.T., to Genl George H. Roberts, 4 Sep 1875. SC 586, MtHS.

[68]Taylor, "First Attorney General," *The Idaho Sunday Statesman*, 8 Dec 1963, page 9C.

[69]McDonnell, *MHSC*, Vol. X, p. 245.

[70]In 1995, Lonny and Joey Wheeler owned the Orleans, Nebraska, home previously owned by Julia and George Roberts. The house had been converted to apartments in the 1960s and, when the Wheelers purchased it in the 1980s, they began restoring it to its nineteenth-century condition. During renovations, Mrs. Wheeler discovered in the walls an old letter, written 29 Sep 1865, from E. M. Thompson in "Diamond City, Confederate Gulch" to Julia Culbertson Roberts in Bannack City. The author has reviewed this letter which remains in Ms. Wheeler's possession.

[71]"Log of the Steamer *Benton*," p. 308, note 3.

[72]"General Roberts, Pioneer Idahoan," *The Idaho Statesman*, 17 Jun 1922, p. 3.

less, Culbertson felt "held" to the upper river by his sons who were "both doing as well as I could expect—but not very anxious I should leave them." Therefore, plans for his visit would have to be "indefinant (*sic*)."

Culbertson assured his daughter and her husband that, while they might "hear a great deal about Indians and their depredations . . . most of the rumors of that kind is (*sic*) as a general—falsehoods upon the Indians." The tribes near Fort Belknap "are . . . perfectly peaceable and quiet" with "greater reason of complaint than we have."[73]

The old trader also worried about his youngest daughter, Fannie, who had returned to live in the East.[74] At twenty-five, Fannie enjoyed an active social life which put her into conflict with her older sister. While living with Julia in Nebraska, Fannie had met a young lawyer named Louis Irvin. Irvin vigorously courted Fannie who was also seeing Silas McCormick of the wealthy Chicago McCormicks. Although Fannie enjoyed the attentions of both men, Julia, who "didn't trust [her sister] quite so much," disapproved of Irvin because "his background did not come up to her measure of refinement." Rebelling, Fannie "began to encourage" the young lawyer[75] and the two eventually married, creating a permanent rift between the sisters.[76]

Alexander and Joe Culbertson moved back to Fort Peck in the late spring of 1876. There, they met Charlie Reynolds and Frank Gruard[77] who were heading for Fort Abraham Lincoln to sign on as scouts for General George Armstrong Custer.[78] Joe offered them one of his best horses. Six weeks later, the Culbertsons learned that Reynolds, and Joe's horse, had been killed at the battle of the Little Bighorn.[79]

---

[73]Alexander Culbertson, Fort Belknap, M.T., to Genl George H. Roberts, 4 Sep 1875. SC 586, MtHS.

[74]Alexander Culbertson, Fort Belknap, M.T., to Genl. George H. Roberts, 4 Sep 1875. SC 586, MtHS.

[75]Berglund, SC 414, MtHS, pp. 27-31.    [76]Berglund, SC 414, MtHS, passim.

[77]Joseph Culbertson, draft manuscript, KP, UCLA, gives the name as "Gruard," although his published manuscript gives the name as "Guard."

[78]Joseph Culbertson, p. 49. Joe's reference to "Frank Gruard" is curious. Frank Grouard did participate in—and survive—the battle of the Little Bighorn, but he apparently signed on with General George Crook and marched north from Wyoming, not west from Fort Abraham Lincoln with Col. Custer. Robinson, pp. 60-61. One of the other Arikara scouts who accompanied Custer was named Fred Girard, who also survived. Robinson, p. 164 and p. 205. Joe Culbertson may have meant Fred Girard.    [79]Joseph Culbertson, p. 49; Miller, p. 270; Robinson, p. 184.

The army threw all their resources into pursuing the Indians who had defeated Custer. In December, General Frank Baldwin offered eighteen-year-old Joe Culbertson a scouting position. Joe hesitated, but his father encouraged him to take the job.[80] While Alexander Culbertson probably would have preferred that his son not fight against the natives, he realized that few jobs besides government scouts existed for mixed-bloods. During the next few months, Joe would be involved in four skirmishes against his friend Sitting Bull before the Hunkpapa chief finally escaped into Canada.[81]

The sons who had kept Culbertson tied to the upper Missouri now had their own lives. After operating a trading post for Leighton and Jordan at the Big Bend of the Milk River,[82] Jack homesteaded a ranch north of the upper Missouri near what would become the town of Culbertson, Montana. In addition to running Durham cattle, Jack operated a roadhouse for weary travelers, hunters, and soldiers including cavalry troops from nearby Fort Buford.[83]

In the spring of 1878,[84] Culbertson took one last trip with Joe. They left Poplar with White Feather, a Sioux, to search for the Yanktonai camp. Joe and White Feather rode horseback while Culbertson "drove a team of horses attached to a light spring wagon." While fording the Missouri, Culbertson got caught in the current but, despite his advanced age, managed to swim safely across. That night, Joe spotted a lone Indian heading their way. With many hostiles in the region, the group reacted cautiously. The supposed warrior, however, turned out to be Sitting Bull's half-sister and the men directed her to her family before parting peacefully.

The Culbertsons and White Feather found the Yanktonais near the present town of Malta, Montana. The warriors, fresh from battle, were dancing the scalp dance when the men arrived. As the dancers performed "their grotesque steps with frantic abandon," women outside the circle mourned their lost relatives. The men remained in the camp for several days before returning to Poplar. A few days later, Alexander Culbertson said good-bye to his son and headed downriver for the last time.[85] He left

---

[80]Joseph Culbertson, "Fighting Sitting Bull." 1879 newspaper clipping probably from *The New North-West*. "Joseph Culbertson" VF, MtHS.

[81]Joseph Culbertson, "Fighting Sitting Bull"; Robinson, pp. 309-312.

[82]Joseph Culbertson, p. 55.     [83]Segars, p. 38.

[84]Joe Culbertson gives the date as 1879 but this seems unlikely to the author.

[85]Joseph Culbertson, "Joseph Culbertson, 'Son of a King.'"

with Joe the journal he had kept throughout his years in the fur trade, a decision he would regret for the rest of his life.[86]

In Orleans, Nebraska, Alexander Culbertson lived with Julia and her husband.[87] He regaled their friends with stories of his years in the fur trade and, as was customary among the traders and Indians with whom he had spent his life, he presented them gifts. Janet McGeachin, Julia's close friend, received a variety of Indian artifacts, including a buffalo robe Culbertson said he had received from Sitting Bull.[88]

Culbertson probably also rode out to the empty prairie west of Orleans to visit the new townsite which Roberts had convinced the developers to name in honor of his distinguished father-in-law.[89] He may also have visited the buffalo hunters in that area.[90]

Finally, on August 27, 1879, at the age of seventy, Alexander Culbertson died of enteritis at Julia's home. Julia and Fannie were with him,[91] but Natawista, who had pledged in her impassioned speech on the eve of the 1853 railroad survey to be with him until they died, was far away in Canada.

George Roberts wrote the *Omaha Republican* to announce his father-in-law's passing: "Although we had expected his death, the bereavement was none the less terrible when it came, and we shall sadly miss the genial smile and kindly companionship of the noble old man who has gone to his rest."[92]

---

[86] Joe Culbertson to Charles Kessler and Julia Culbertson Roberts to Charles Kessler. KP, UCLA. Historians also must regret this decision as the journal ended up being destroyed by Joe's children who tore out pages and drew on its remaining pages.

[87] Exactly when Culbertson left the upper Missouri is unclear. Broomfield says he left "toward the end of the winter in 1878-79," while Joe Culbertson, "Joseph Culbertson Was 'Son of a King,'" says he left in the spring of 1879. Taylor, "The Major's Blackfoot Bride," p. 47, says he spent "the last few years of his life" at Julia's home. An item from Fort Buford written on 27 Sep 1877 by a man identified only as "Rex" which appeared in the 1 Oct 1877 *Bismarck Tri-Weekly Tribune* suggests to the author that Culbertson was no longer on the upper Missouri at that time. If this conclusion is accurate, then he probably went to live with Julia in mid-1877. However, there are also suggestions that he was trading at Willow Rounds in 1877. See, for example, Kennedy, p. 154, and Holterman, p. 196.

[88] Peggy McGeachin Vestal, Janet McGeachin's granddaughter, to the author. The artifacts are now housed in a small museum in Orleans, Nebraska. Mrs. Vestal believes her mother donated the buffalo robe, which used to grace their upper hallway in Orleans, to the House of Yesterday Museum in Hastings, Nebraska, but they have no record of the gift.

[89] "Hitchcock County," OPL.
[90] Hutt, OPL.
[91] Berglund, SC 414, MtHS, p. 52.
[92] "Death of Alexander Culbertson."

Chapter Twenty-Eight

## *"they yielded the palm to Madame"*

Natawista quickly discovered that life in the Indian camps, at least those of the early 1870s, did not suit her. Within a year of leaving Culbertson, she took up with Henry Alfred "Fred" Kanouse, another white trader. More than twenty years younger than Natawista, Kanouse was born in New Jersey in 1847. His family moved to Peoria in the early 1860s where he probably met Natawista. In 1868, when the Culbertsons returned to Fort Benton, Jacob Kanouse, Fred's father, settled on a ranch nearby.[1]

In 1869, Fred Kanouse began working for Carrol and Steell, Fort Benton outfitters.[2] He became Chouteau County deputy sheriff,[3] but complained that law enforcement offered few opportunities for personal enrichment: "there is no encouragement whatever for me to do work where there is no prospect of pay."[4]

Knowing how to make money, Kanouse took a leave of absence from his official duties in the spring of 1871. With whiskey, rifles, and assorted trade goods supplied by pioneering whiskey traders, John Healy and Alfred Hamilton, Kanouse headed north. At Fort Whoop-Up, he was joined by three white men and "an Indian woman." At the confluence of Elbow and Bow Rivers, the group established another Healy and Hamilton whiskey post.[5]

The otherwise unidentified "Indian woman" was almost certainly Natawista. Kanouse, like Culbertson before him, understood the benefit of aligning himself with a prominent Indian family. For Natawista, Kanouse offered an escape from the drunken Indian camps and the

---

[1]Information on the Kanouse family from David Kanouse, Los Angeles, California, in correspondence with the author. David Kanouse is the third cousin, four times removed of H.A. "Fred" Kanouse.   [2]Dempsey, "Kanouse."
[3]Overholser, p. 226, says Kanouse was "sheriff" while Dempsey, "Kanouse," calls him "deputy sheriff."   [4]Overholser, p. 226.
[5]Dempsey, "Kanouse."

opportunity to regain social standing and financial rewards. With benefits for both, Natawista married Kanouse in the Indian fashion.[6]

Natawista's second marriage differed fundamentally from her first. It is doubtful that she found, or expected to find, love with Kanouse. Originally, she and Kanouse may even have planned a partnership with Culbertson, with the old trader handling the proposed enterprise in Montana. If so, the arrangement fell apart when Culbertson moved to Fort Browning.

From his trading post on the north side of Elbow River, Kanouse carried on a brisk trade with the Bloods. While profits were good, Kanouse, whom the Indians called Blood Indian Man,[7] quickly discovered the risks. During his first season, a band of Bloods led by White Eagle[8] came to trade. One of Kanouse's traders argued with a young warrior and struck him with a six-shooter. The Bloods, after carrying off their wounded comrade, returned to the post and opened fire, killing one trader and wounding both Kanouse and Natawista.[9] Kanouse returned fire, killing White Eagle, before fleeing inside. The enraged warriors surrounded the fort, holding it under siege for three days.

Kanouse, another trader, and Natawista kept the Bloods at bay while a third trader "huddled fearfully in a shallow trench in the windowless storeroom." Kanouse bribed an Indian to go south to secure help from another of the ever-multiplying whiskey forts. The posse of southern traders drove off the Bloods. After Kanouse and Natawista recovered, Kanouse took his returns to Fort Benton while Natawista, most likely, remained behind.[10]

While Chouteau County's good citizens might have disapproved of their deputy sheriff pursuing illegal profits from the whiskey trade, Kanouse received no such remonstrance. Instead, he was promoted to sheriff after which Kanouse returned to his Elbow River trading post.[11]

En route to Fort Benton the next spring, Kanouse got into another confrontation, this one involving a white Montana resident. Near the Marias River, Kanouse and Jim Nabors quarreled over a horse. While

---

[6]Ramsey. Copy of article received from David Kanouse is undated and unsourced. It was probably written in the 1970s for the Fernie (Alberta, Canada) *Free Press*.

[7]Dempsey, "Kanouse," gives his Indian name as Kainah-kwan.

[8]Dempsey, "Kanouse," gives his Indian name as Petah-ksiksinum.

[9]Joseph Culbertson, draft manuscript, KP, UCLA, p. 47, talks about the wounding of Natawista although it is not entirely clear that it happened in this fight.

[10]Dempsey, "Kanouse"; Liddell.

[11]Dempsey, "Kanouse."

Kanouse asserted that Nabors fired first, Nabors ended up dead. Not everyone accepted Fred's claim of self-defense.

Although Kanouse was allowed to return to Elbow River that fall, questions about the killing continued to surface. The case bounced around the courts as lawyers argued over jurisdiction. By the time the courts decided where the case should be tried and issued an arrest warrant, Kanouse was safely across the border where he remained, at least in part, to escape judicial sanction.[12]

For the 1872-1873 trading season, Kanouse built a log house near Fort Macleod.[13] But, soon after his return, the Bloods killed another white trader, Dick Berry, convincing Kanouse that, despite his marriage, the region was too dangerous. He severed his ties with Healy and Hamilton and moved south to the Oldman River to open another trading post.[14]

The following spring, Kanouse again found himself in trouble with the Blackfeet. While Kanouse was visiting Sol Abbott's Fort Whoop-Up saloon, several Blackfeet entered and began shooting, wounding three, including Kanouse, this time seriously. He endured an agonizing trip to Helena where his badly damaged shoulder was repaired.[15]

Convinced now that he needed to remove himself entirely from the Blackfeet territory, Kanouse opened Fort Warren near Waterton Lakes to trade with the mountain Kootenais.[16] The Kootenais, initially friendly, grew increasingly agitated. A few months after Kanouse established his post, a chief threatened to kill a trader. Instead, Kanouse killed the chief. Once again, Kanouse's fort came under siege. The traders eventually ran off the Kootenais but not before several more had been killed.

The Fort Whoop-Up traders rushed to Fort Warren to help Kanouse when they heard he was again under siege. Although they arrived after the siege ended, Kanouse's traders could not resist re-enacting events. When they reached the climactic point where Kanouse shot the chief, an enthusiastic trader fired his gun. The shot ignited an open keg of gunpowder which blew out the side of the fort. Kanouse apparently considered this a fitting end for Fort Warren.[17]

---

[12]Overholser, p. 227; Dempsey, "Kanouse."
[13]Ramsey. Today, the house is part of the Fort Macleod Museum compound.
[14]Dempsey, "Kanouse." [15]Overholser, p. 227.
[16]Dempscy, "Kanouse"; Liddell. It may be through Natawista's association with Kanouse during this time that some Blackfeet refer to Janet Lake as Lake Natawista. See Schultz, *Signposts of Adventure*, p. 185.
[17]Liddell; Overholser, p. 348; draft biography of H.A. "Fred" Kanouse by David Kanouse.

By now, Natawista must have realized that Kanouse completely lacked the diplomatic skills of Culbertson. During all his years as a trader, Culbertson is never reported to have killed a single Indian. Natawista was probably already reconsidering her marriage when, quite literally, the Royal Canadian Mounted Police came to the rescue.

In the spring of 1873, the Canadian government, recognizing the deleterious effects whiskey was having on the Indians, established a western police force. That winter, the first contingent of the North-West Mounted Police (NWMP) marched west. The Bloods watched with trepidation as three hundred soldiers advanced; they had not forgotten what the coming of soldiers, under Major Baker, had meant for the Piegans four years earlier. They had heard rumors that the "red coats" intended to drive out the whiskey traders, but the traders claimed the soldiers planned to seize their land.

At Oldman River, the NWMP began to erect a fort. A Blood messenger appeared to ask, "Do you mean peace or war?" The soldiers responded they had come in peace to halt the whiskey traffic. Suspicious Indians slowly filtered in to the fort to assess these new white men. When one Blackfeet reported whiskey traders to the north, the NWMP's rapid reaction laid to rest the tribe's doubts. After five long years of misery, the NWMP stopped whiskey from flowing through the Blackfeet territory north of the "medicine line."[18]

For the whiskey traders, time had run out. In later years, when asked if he was around when the North-West Mounted Police arrived, Fred Kanouse replied proudly, "Son, I was the reason they came."[19] But he defended the American traders: "A trader in those days would outfit with flour, blankets, and goods and would then put in a stock of liquor. None of us were simple whiskey runners."[20]

Kanouse still hoped to make a living in the Indian trade without whiskey; at least, he had to try since he still faced charges in Montana Territory for shooting Nabors. Thus, Kanouse and Natawista returned to live in the log house near Fort Macleod. Here, Natawista probably was

[18] Dempsey, *Red Crow*, p. 82.  [19] Liddell.
[20] Dempsey, "Kanouse."

reunited with her niece, Revenge Walker, Red Crow's estranged half-sister. Following Red Crow's 1872 killing of Kit Fox, his brothers, Sheep Old Man and Not Real Good, and his sisters, Revenge Walker and Paper Woman, distanced themselves from Red Crow's band.[21]

In early 1873, Sheep Old Man, Not Real Good, and Revenge Walker were encamped near the Fort Macleod post previously run by Kanouse. Healy and Hamilton had hired D. W. Davis to run the post after Kanouse quit[22] and Davis had begun to court Revenge Walker whose Indian husband had abandoned her. Red Crow, not knowing that his estranged siblings were in the area, came to the post with the Fish Eaters looking for whiskey.[23]

That night, as the Fish Eaters drank, one of Red Crow's relatives repeated a rumor he had heard alleging that Running Bird, Revenge Walker's husband, had given Red Crow numerous horses when Revenge Walker was still young to guarantee their future marriage. After the marriage, Red Crow did not return an equal number of horses, as custom dictated. This, according to the gossip, was why Running Bird had abandoned Revenge Walker.

When Revenge Walker heard the allegation, she rode to Red Crow's camp to confront her brother. Red Crow had already left. Furious that her brother had enriched himself from her marriage while dishonoring his family, Revenge Walker began shooting his horses. Sheep Old Man intervened. Fearing Red Crow's wrath, Sheep Old Man took his family south to a camp on the Highwood.

Several days later, Sheep Old Man went to Davis's post for liquor. When he failed to return, Revenge Walker dispatched Not Real Good to look for their brother. When Not Real Good found Sheep Old Man, he was so drunk that he mistook Not Real Good for a pursuing enemy and shot and stabbed his brother.

Revenge Walker rushed to help Not Real Good who, while alive, was seriously wounded. Not Real Good told her: "Your husband has gone. You take my advice and marry the white man who keeps the store, Davis. They must have good medicine and I may then get better." Revenge Walker, though hesitant, married Davis and, with his help, Not Real Good recovered.[24]

---

[21]Dempsey, *Red Crow*, p. 9.
[22]Dempsey, "Davis." The Indians called Davis "Tall Man," which Dempsey translates as Spit-ayna.
[23]Dempsey, *Red Crow*, p. 76.    [24]Dempsey, "Davis"; Dempsey, *Red Crow*, p. 77.

Although Revenge Walker and Davis probably shared the log cabin with Natawista and Kanouse,[25] Natawista could not effect a reconciliation of the family. The feuding siblings never made peace and, years later, after the establishment of the Blood Reserve, the estranged family members lived at opposite ends of the reserve.[26]

Nonetheless, Natawista adapted to life at Fort Macleod. With the North-West Mounted Police ensconced nearby and the whiskey traffic on the wane, her new life began to resemble that which she had shared with Culbertson. Kanouse indulged her expensive tastes and, in March 1875, she was once again turning heads. Richard Barrington Nevitt, assistant surgeon for the NWMP, described "Madame Kanouse" to his fiancée:

> The ladies came on horseback; only one, however, had a saddle and this was Madame Kanouse.
>
> You should have seen her dress. It was the Dolly Varden style, a large figured chintz just short enough to display the gorgeous stripes of balmoral petticoat which in its turn was also just short enough to show two very small feet clad in moccasins and the end of a pair of leggings beautifully worked in beads.
>
> She also had on a heavy black velvet loose-fitting overcoat and over this, a most brilliant striped shawl, the stripes being about three inches broad and alternatively red, blue, green and red, with a narrow line of yellow between each color.
>
> Her head gear consisted of a small plaid shawl. The other titled aristocrats were also dressed in gorgeous array, but perforce they yielded the palm to Madame.[27]

With Mounties at Fort Macleod and the whiskey traffickers out of business, white settlers began moving into the Canadian Blackfeet lands. To avoid the violence which had accompanied Montana's white settlements, the Canadian government moved quickly to forge a peace with the Indians.

In mid-September 1877, the Canadians convened a peace council with the Northern Blackfoot, Blood, North Piegan, Sarcee, and Stoney tribes.[28] They hoped to convince the tribes to surrender fifty thousand miles of hunting grounds; in exchange, they promised reserves equaling one square mile for every five people, annual individual payments, cattle,

---

[25] David Kanouse to the author.
[26] Dempsey, *Red Crow*, p. 197.
[27] Ramsey; Dempsey, *Red Crow*, p. 78.
[28] Ewers, *Blackfeet*, p. 264.

farm implements, and incidental tokens of friendship. Upon approval of the treaty, each tribal member would receive a $12 cash payment.[29]

Blood chief Medicine Calf, who had participated in Lame Bull's Treaty, insisted on three items: securing the Bloods' hunting grounds from enemy tribes; receiving just compensation for whites already in the territory; and, ensuring that the Indians did not "give their land for nothing."

The council opened with Indian praise for the Mounties' action against the whiskey traffickers. Then they presented their proposals, designed as a starting point for discussions. The demands startled the commissioners who did not realize the Indians had become proficient in the art of negotiation. Commissioner David Laird brusquely dismissed the Indian terms, suggesting that, instead, they should perhaps pay for the NWMP's services in eradicating the whiskey trade.

This angered Medicine Calf along with other chiefs. Concerned about short-term problems, Medicine Calf considered abandoning the treaty process. But Crowfoot, the Northern Blackfoot chief, looking to the future, argued that the Indians would need the government's help and protection when the buffalo disappeared. Following raucous debate, Crowfoot prevailed.

The Bloods received word of the pending council with indifference. Red Crow and Father of Many Children, the elderly Blood chief, did not arrive at the treaty grounds until the fourth night. Red Crow had one demand: the Crees and mixed-bloods must be kept from the Blood hunting grounds.[30]

Crowfoot briefed Red Crow on the proffered terms. The Blood chief, considering the treaty "of no great importance anyway," agreed. He trusted Colonel James Macleod since he had brought the Mounties and, with Macleod as commissioner, Red Crow assumed he could also trust the treaty. The next day, September 21, 1877, the representative chiefs accepted the document which became known as Treaty No. 7.[31]

Following the signing, the commissioners presented each chief with a uniform, flag, and medal.[32] The chiefs then designated those tribal members entitled to the $12 bonus payment and future annuities.[33] Although

---

[29]Dempsey, *Red Crow*, p. 94; Ewers, *Blackfeet*, p. 265.
[30]Dempsey, *Red Crow*, pp. 95-97.
[31]Dempsey, *Red Crow*, p. 98; Ewers, *Blackfeet*, p. 264. Dempsey gives the date as September 21 while Ewers says September 22. [32]Ewers, *Blackfeet*, p. 265.
[33]Dempsey, *Red Crow*, p. 99.

not in attendance, Natawista received her $12 bonus payment at Fort Macleod on December 4, 1877.³⁴ Although she was apparently still living with Kanouse, their marriage did not last much longer.

Other changes quickly followed. Within a year, Red Crow realized that the buffalo were disappearing. Meeting with the commissioners in 1878, he requested that a Blood Reserve be established on Belly River.³⁵ They agreed. By the winter of 1879-1880, it had become clear that, to survive, the Bloods would have to adapt to life without the buffalo.³⁶ Red Crow did not blame the white man for the buffalo's disappearance; along with many Bloods, he believed that they had somehow offended Sun who had opened a hole in the earth and driven the animals into it.³⁷

With the boundaries of the new reserve established, Red Crow constructed a log house downstream from the agency. Sixty-two other families erected permanent dwellings. With the help of John MacDougall, a farming instructor, the Bloods broke the land for spring planting while receiving daily subsistence rations of beef and flour. Before long, an Anglican missionary, Samuel Trivett, opened a small school and mission house.³⁸

Father of Many Children's winter count recorded 1879 as the year "When first—no more buffalo" and 1880 as "When we all moved camp."³⁹ By May 1881, nearly all the Bloods had settled on Belly River.⁴⁰

Natawista moved to the reserve with Red Crow.⁴¹ The Bloods, thanks to honest agents who treated them with respect,⁴² fared better than the Northern Blackfoot who battled starvation on their reserve.⁴³ Still, dissension surfaced among the Bloods over leadership.

Shortly after signing Treaty No. 7, Rainy Chief, chief of the North Bloods, died. The government asked Red Crow to recommend a replace-

---

³⁴Handwritten note in the "Treaty 7 Paysheets," Glenbow-Alberta Institute Archives. Hugh Dempsey to the author. The treaty documents list her as both Natoas-txisc-in and Mrs. H. A. Kanouse.

³⁵Dempsey, *Red Crow*, p. 106.  ³⁶Dempsey, *Red Crow*, p. 108.
³⁷Dempsey, *Red Crow*, p. 113.  ³⁸Dempsey, *Red Crow*, pp. 109-110.
³⁹Hungry Wolf, *Blood People*, p. 199.  ⁴⁰Dempsey, *Red Crow*, p. 112.

⁴¹"Information from Hugh Dempsey, Publicity Bureau, Edmonton, Alberta, Canada. 27 Jan 1954. From interview with John Cotton." Typescript notes in the "Mrs. Alexander Culbertson—Natawista" VF, MtHS.

⁴²Dempsey, *Red Crow*, p. 125.  ⁴³Dempsey, *Crowfoot*, p. 134.

ment. Red Crow suggested Running Rabbit, Seen From Afar's son-in-law. The commissioners agreed, although Running Rabbit was "patently unsuited for the role." He had spent most of his life with the Piegans, had been listed as a Piegan chief in 1875 and 1876, had not signed Treaty No. 7, and had no followers. But, to Red Crow, Running Rabbit possessed one superb quality: he posed no threat to the Blood chief.[44] Running Rabbit stayed across the border until 1881, coming north only after collecting his annuities from the U. S. government.[45] After he finally settled in Canada, Natawista joined his band.[46]

Unaccustomed to farming, the Bloods survived primarily through government rations. Then the Canadian economy went into recession and the Department of Indian Affairs summarily dropped nearly one thousand Bloods from the rolls, reducing annual annuities by $5,000 and cutting weekly rations by three and a half tons of beef and two tons of flour.[47] Although she remained on the tribal rolls, Natawista decided to go live with her sons in eastern Montana.

Joe had been deeply hurt when his mother left in 1870.[48] His attitude softened after his father's death. As an army scout, Joe had gone north to try to persuade Sitting Bull to return to the United States.[49] While there, he visited his mother[50] and, in 1883, he welcomed her into his home.[51]

Thomas Mooney remembered meeting the "kindly" Natawista at Joe's home near Fort Peck. To the young Mooney, she appeared "to be a very old woman," although she was only in her late fifties. She "dressed like a white woman" and "spoke excellent English." Painfully aware of her reduced circumstances, Natawista offered Mooney a possession she no longer needed—her purse—saying: "You have money, I have none."[52]

Natawista had returned to the Blood Reserve and was living with Red Crow in September 1885 when a reporter came west to investigate conditions. George Ham reported in the *Daily Manitoban*: "A neatly-dressed squaw, altered after the custom of some white ladies, was pointed out to

---

[44]Dempsey, *Red Crow*, p. 106.  [45]Dempsey, *Red Crow*, p. 112.
[46]Blood Reserve Treaty Payment Records, 1882.
[47]Dempsey, *Red Crow*, pp. 138-139.
[48]Joseph Culbertson to Charles Kessler. KP, UCLA.
[49]Joseph Culbertson, passim.
[50]Typescript notes, "Mrs. Alexander Culbertson—Natawista," VF, MtHS.
[51]Blood Treaty Payment Records; Typescript Notes titled "Medicine Snake Woman—NA*TA*WISTA-Iksana," "Mrs. Alexander Culbertson—Natawista," VF, MtHS.
[52]"Mrs. Alexander Culbertson—Natawista" VF, MtHS.

me as being a lady who, fifteen or twenty years ago, was a reigning belle." Ham recalled her history as "the wife—now the widow" of Alexander Culbertson, "an employee of the old American Fur Company, who was at one time reported to be very wealthy."

He related that Natawista had "moved in the best social circles," but after "[Culbertson's] wealth was squandered," she "returned to her people and leads the nomadic life from which she was taken when a girl." Ham, noting that "she speaks English fluently and is said to be well educated," found hers "a strange history, not the strangest part of which is, however, that she prefers the wild freedom of the plains to the conventionalities of society."[53]

In the *Toronto Mail*, Ham reported on Red Crow's home: "a double one, well built of logs, one storey (*sic*) high, and apparently very comfortable." The reporter had been ushered into "what is commonly known as the 'living room'," containing a large cooking stove and "two walnut bedsteads, one being covered with a clean white counterpane." The walls, covered with cotton, were "decorated with several pictures, one of which was the Lord's prayer and the ten commandments illustrated." On a small nearby table, Ham noticed "silverware which belongs to Red Crow's sister (*sic*), a Mrs. Culbertson...."

Ham's observations confirmed that Natawista had neither lost her taste for finery nor relinquished her status as Alexander Culbertson's widow. Nowhere does Ham mention her marriage to the rambunctious Kanouse; Natawista clearly preferred to be remembered as Mrs. Alexander Culbertson.[54]

But she remained restless. By October 1889, she was back with Joe on the Fort Peck reservation,[55] established three years earlier for the Teton

---

[53]Handwritten notes, titled "*The Daily Manitoban*, Sept 30/85 by George H. Ham, during visit of the Gov. Gen to the Blood Reserve." Hugh Dempsey to the author.

[54]Dempsey, *Red Crow*, pp. 160-161; *Toronto Mail*, 28 Jan 1886.

[55]Wm. Pocklington to Madame Culbertson, Poplar River, M. T., 28 Oct 1889. SC 514, MtHS. There is an unresolved mystery in Natawista's last years. When she made this trip to Poplar River to visit Joe, she apparently took with her a young girl, about ten years old, named Josephine Culbertson. Josephine was a member of the Blood tribe and was referred to in subsequent correspondence as the "neice (*sic*)" of Mrs. Red Crow. When Josephine did not return to the Blood Reserve after several years of living across the border, the Canadian officials wanted to remove her from the tribal rolls. This was eventually done in February 1895 when it was learned that she had been committed to the Insane Asylum of the State of Montana in Warm Springs. At that time, she was reported to be suffering from "acute (mania?)." She had been in the asylum for three months and had "made some improvement but [was] far from being well." The author has not been able to determine who Josephine was but suspects that she may have been a daughter of Joe's. See correspondence in SC 514, MtHS.

Sioux and Assiniboine tribes,[56] where Red Crow requested William Pocklington, the Blood agent, to forward her annuity payment.[57] If Natawista arrived in Montana before October 1888, she may have had one last visit with her eldest child, Jack, before his untimely and mysterious death.

Jack had been recorded in 1880 as a "ranch man" living near Culbertson, Montana, with his wife, Mary, a twenty-four-year-old Indian, and their three-year-old son, John.[58] In the fall of 1888, Jack visited the newly established town of Williston on the Little Muddy River and a tavern belonging to George Newton. Newton, who came to Williston in 1883, delighted in his skills as a buffalo hunter, claiming to have once killed thirty-six in a single hunt. The door to Newton's bar never closed; if there was no one to serve the customers, they helped themselves and left the money on the bar.[59]

But that night in October 1888, the bar was not empty and Jack got into an argument with a man named Gibson. Before it ended, Jack had received at least four blows to the head, "none of which could have caused death, but either of which would have caused insensibility." A coroner's jury concluded that, after being assaulted, Jack probably tried to get up but "fell insensible with his face in the dirt and smothered to death."

While conceding that Gibson was "indirectly the cause of Culbertson's death," the jury decided Gibson had acted in self-defense. The *Bismarck Daily Tribune* wryly noted that Williston had a "good old fashioned way of disposing of the expenses of trial in a murder case. Although these killing scrapes occur pretty often the ingenuity of the coroner's jury is still equal to the emergency."[60] Despite the jury's verdict, Jack's family remained convinced that he had been murdered.[61]

Natawista stayed with Joe on the Fort Peck Reservation until at least the spring of 1890 when Joe invited some of his Blood relatives, specifically Eagles Rib, designated a "minor chief" by Agent Pocklington, to visit. Pocklington and Red Crow were insistent that this not occur.[62]

---

[56] *Assiniboine and Sioux Tribes*, p. 1.
[57] Wm. Pocklington to Madame Culbertson, 28 Oct 1889. SC 514, MtHS.
[58] NAM, T9/742. Dawson County, Montana Territory.
[59] *Since 1887*, p. 29.   [60] "Smothered."
[61] Segars, p. 38.
[62] Agent Wm. Pocklington to the Indian Commissioner, 2 May 1890, and to the Indian Agent at Poplar River, Montana Territory, 1 May 1890. SC 514, MtHS.

Despite the relatively settled conditions on the Blood reserve, some young Bloods, hoping to recapture past glories, continued to conduct horse raiding expeditions against rival tribes. Throughout the late 1880s, their favorite targets had been the Gros Ventres and Assiniboines in Montana. When the exasperated tribes appealed to the American authorities for help, they permitted the Gros Ventres to go to the Blood Reserve to try to recover their property. Upon reaching the reserve, the Gros Ventres sought out Red Crow. The chief cooperated, despite protests from his warriors, helping the Gros Ventres recover some stolen animals. Red Crow's acquiescence infuriated some of his followers and the raids, with loss of life on both sides, continued.[63]

Now Red Crow worried that Joe's overtures might precipitate another round of raids. With Red Crow's backing, Pocklington refused to issue the pass Eagles Rib needed to travel to Fort Peck. Pocklington also wrote the Fort Peck agent requesting that "in the event of any of my charges arriving at your Agency I would be exceedingly obliged if you would send them off about their business."

With his letter, Pocklington enclosed a message from Red Crow to Natawista. Pocklington asked the Fort Peck agent to deliver it to her personally since Red Crow was "afraid her son [Joe] will not read it properly."[64] Red Crow asked Natawista to return to the reserve, suggesting that if she would come to either Fort Benton or the south Piegan agency, he could "send for her." But he would not go to Fort Peck, it being "too far."[65]

By the end of 1891, Natawista had returned to the Blood Reserve. One tribal member recalled that "she lived like a white lady"; her hair had even turned white.[66] She moved in with Chief Moon, Red Crow's eldest son.[67] The accommodations, "a log building, shingled roof and partitioned," did not satisfy Natawista.[68] When she complained to her daughter, Fannie,

---

[63]Dempsey, *Red Crow*, pp. 161-163 and pp. 173-177.
[64]Wm. Pocklington to Indian Agent, Poplar River, 1 May 1890. SC 514, MtHS.
[65]Wm. Pocklington to Indian Commissioner, 2 May 1890. SC 514, MtHS.
[66]Interview with John Cotton, "Natawista—Mrs. Alexander Culbertson" VF, MtHS.
[67]Wm. Pocklington to L. S. Irvine (*sic*), 21 Dec 1891. SC 514, MtHS. Pocklington says Natawista was living in "her nephew's 'Chief Old Moon's' house." Pocklington routinely, albeit erroneously, referred to Red Crow as Natawista's brother. In a letter to the author, 25 Mar 1996, Hugh Dempsey writes that Red Crow's "eldest son was Chief Moon (not Chief Old Moon). I assume Pocklington got mixed up because there was a chief named Old Moon. However, he was not related to Red Crow."
[68]Wm. Pocklington to L. S. Irvine (*sic*), 21 Dec 1891. SC 514, MtHS.

then living in El Paso, Texas, with her lawyer husband, Louis Irvin, Irvin wrote Pocklington demanding an explanation.

After making clear he had not approved Natawista's letter, Pocklington assured the Irvins that she was being well treated: "She draws the regular ration here, which is considered ample, and resides in her nephew's ... house." Pocklington acknowledged that Natawista wanted her own house, "which is only natural," but he had "none to give her, nor the materials for one."[69]

Shortly thereafter, Natawista became ill. In his March 1893 monthly report, James Wilson, the new Blood agent, reported that Natawista had recovered after "being very sick for some considerable time."[70] But her condition soon worsened, and, in early June 1893, Natawista died. The Register for the Oblate Fathers of the Blood Reserve recorded the funeral of "Nellie Culbertson, sister (sic) of Chief Red Crow" on June 14.[71]

Natawista was laid to rest in the Catholic cemetery at Stand-off, not far from where Joe Kipp, the mixed-blood child she had helped raise, once operated his whiskey post. The cemetery, located on a barren wind-swept prairie, lies neglected and overgrown with prickly brambles. Plain, unpainted, broken, and nameless wooden crosses mark most of the graves. The evident disregard may reflect old beliefs: traditional Bloods abhorred ground burials, believing they trapped the soul with the underground spirits.[72]

Although Natawista flirted with the Catholic church during her lifetime, being both married and buried according to their customs, she never abandoned her traditional beliefs. And traditional Bloods know that, when a person dies, they join all those who have gone before in the Sandhills. In the Sandhills, life goes on much as it does in this world, only in spirit rather than in form.[73] In the Sandhills, Natawista still wears her finest frocks with colorful jewels on her fingers. She still laughs and dances with abandon, while telling stories about the strange white people she has met.

And, in the Sandhills, just maybe, Alexander Culbertson is once again by her side.

---

[69]Wm. Pocklington to L. S. Irvine (sic), 21 Dec 1891. SC 514, MtHS. Since no copy of Natawista's letter to her daughter and son-in-law remains, it is impossible to know what Pocklington found so objectionable about the letter sent to the Irvins.

[70]"Monthly Report by Jas. Wilson, Indian Agent, Blood Reserve," 2 Mar 1893. SC 514, MtHS.

[71]Holterman, p. 201.    [72]Dempsey, *Charcoal's World*, p. 156.

[73]Hungry Wolf, *Blood People*, p. 228.

# Epilogue

## *"Whatever is kept in memory still endures"*

On May 30, 1951, nearly one thousand people gathered at a small public cemetery for "perhaps the greatest historical event in the history of Orleans," Nebraska.[1] The sky was dull and the wind blew briskly through the tall trees as women held their straw hats.[2] A pastoral stillness permeated the small glen as the solemn, yet joyful, ceremony began with the American Legion's presentation of colors. Following a bugle call, the Orleans High School Mixed Choir sang "Homeland" and "Westward Ho."[3]

The dedicated research of a small group of civic leaders and professional historians had brought this group together, almost seventy-five years after Alexander Culbertson's death, to mark his grave. Charles E. Hanson, Jr., of the Museum Association of the American Frontier,[4] presided. Hanson's insatiable curiosity and diligent research had made the event possible.

Julia and George Roberts had laid Culbertson to rest in the "old cemetery," one-half mile east of Orleans.[5] Twenty-five years later, the farmer who owned the land decided to use it for pasture. Recognizing the sensitive nature of displacing gravesites, F. A. Gay ran a notice in the local newspaper:

> To the Friends and Relatives of the Dead Buried on the Southwest Quarter of Section 14, Town 2, Range 19, near Orleans, Harlan county, Nebraska.
>
> This notice to inform the relatives of the dead buried on this tract of land to remove their dead to the Orleans Cemetery before Oct. 1st, 1905,

---

[1]"Dedication Memorial Day," *Orleans* (NE) *Chronicle*, 31 May 1951; "Alexander Culbertson" VF, MtHS.
[2]Charles E. Hanson, Jr., to the author, 10 Jul 1996.
[3]"Dedication of Monument," 30 May 1951, OPL.
[4]"Dedication of Monument." Hanson went on to become Director of the Museum of the Fur Trade in Chadron, NE, until his recent death.     [5]Hanson, "Marking the Grave," p. 122.

as this is not deeded for Cemetery purposes and I wish to fence the same for pasture.[6]

Julia and George Roberts never saw the notice; they had moved to Idaho in the early 1880s, a change precipitated, at least in part, by Culbertson's former employer, Charles Chouteau.

Within months of his father-in-law's death, George Roberts was forced to admit that he was on the verge of bankruptcy. With nowhere else to turn, Julia and George approached Charles Chouteau for a loan. Chouteau lent them two thousand dollars which they agreed to repay, with interest, two years later. As security, George and Julia deeded their Orleans home to Chouteau.[7]

Four years later, after Roberts had repeatedly failed to make the agreed-upon payments, Chouteau sued.[8] By then, the Robertses also owed $38.50 in delinquent taxes. To complicate matters, inspectors for Chouteau considered the "heavily dilapidated" home insufficient collateral for the debt.

George Roberts tried to forestall the lawsuit, assuring Chouteau that "there is no reason nor necessity for the employment of lawyers." Roberts, acknowledging that "no one regrets more than myself my absolute and sincere inability to meet my pecuniary indebtedness," informed Chouteau of the "mortifying" fact that he was "financially bankrupt." He was, even then, searching for a location to "commence life anew."

Roberts, like his father-in-law, had spent some money trying to provide his daughters, Caroline and Margaret, the best possible education. With his finances in disarray, Roberts confessed that "the pressing necessity of giving them advantages which I am not able to do weighs like a hideous nightmare upon me."

The former attorney general promised that he would give Chouteau "absolute possession and control of our house within 60 days or as soon before that time as I can find other quarters." But he implored Chouteau to drop the lawsuit, suggesting that the house be either rented or sold to recover the money. In the end, Roberts held up Culbertson as an example: "Your course of procedure has been different and less kindly than would

---

[6]Hanson, "Marking the Grave," p. 126.

[7]Harlan County, NE, Deed Book E, page 300. Warranty Deed from Julia C. Roberts and George H. Roberts to Charles P. Chouteau. Executed 20 Oct 1879, St. Louis, MO, and filed for record in Harlan County, NE, on 17 Feb 1883.

[8]Chas. P. Choteau (*sic*) vs. Geo. H. and Julia C. Roberts, District Court of Harlan County, NE, September Term, 1883, Docket Number 1234. Harlan County Courthouse, Alma, NE.

have been that of Maj. Culbertson—had positions been reversed—and your child instead of his been the debtor."⁹

But Chouteau, unlike Culbertson, was a shrewd businessman and his family fortune had not been amassed through kindness. Moreover, as the notes signed by George and Julia Roberts lapsed into delinquency, Charles Chouteau surely recalled that, fifteen years earlier, Alexander Culbertson had also defaulted on a debt to the Chouteaus. Despite Roberts's pleading, and a slightly less cordial missive from his wife, ¹⁰ Chouteau pressed his suit, ultimately receiving judgment for $2,906.¹¹ By then, George and Julia had taken their children¹² and moved to Idaho.

Since the Roberts family had left Orleans some twenty years before farmer Gay published his notice, the grave of Alexander Culbertson could easily have been lost forever to trampling farm animals, but in 1904, luck lay on the side of history.

During their years in Orleans, George and Julia Roberts had developed a lasting friendship with James and Janet McGeachin, pioneer settlers in Nebraska's Republican Valley. When the McGeachins heard that the old cemetery was to be abandoned, they remembered Julia's dear father who had entertained them with his exciting tales of frontier life. Knowing that Culbertson lay buried in the old cemetery, the McGeachins contacted Julia and George.

As a result, George Roberts returned to Orleans to move Culbertson's remains. On October 3, 1904, Roberts purchased lot 896 in the new cemetery for ten dollars, recording the deed in Julia's name.¹³ After overseeing Culbertson's re-internment, George returned to Idaho, again leaving the grave unmarked.¹⁴ That Christmas, he sent the McGeachins two inspirational books to thank them for remembering Culbertson.¹⁵

⁹Exhibit "I," Chouteau (*sic*) vs. Roberts.   ¹⁰Exhibit "K," Chouteau (*sic*) vs. Roberts.
¹¹Chouteau (*sic*) vs. Roberts.
¹²Their three children were Margaret, Caroline, and Alexander. According to George Taylor, Caroline's son, there was a fourth child, Mariah, who died as an infant in a pram accident involving her brother, Alexander. George Roberts never forgave Alexander for this. Taylor says that Roberts was a mean-spirited and brutal man who frequently abused both his wife and children. GTOH.
¹³Hanson, "Marking the Grave," p. 126.
¹⁴It is possible that George Roberts simply did not have the money for a marker. Roberts, according to his grandson, George Taylor, consistently squandered his money on "wine, women, and song," frequently leaving Julia in desperate straits. The Roberts family in Philadelphia bailed out the family on more than one occasion, sending the money directly to Julia because they understood George's proclivities. GTOH.   ¹⁵Peggy McGeachin Vestal to the author, 9 Aug 1995.

The only marker at Culbertson's grave might have been a lilac bush had not Charles Hanson stumbled upon a biographical sketch stating that Culbertson had died in Orleans, Nebraska,[16] contradicting noted fur trade historian, Hiram Martin Chittenden, who claimed Culbertson had died in Orleans, Missouri.[17]

After first verifying that Culbertson had once lived in Orleans, Nebraska, Hanson discovered that there had never been an Orleans, Missouri. Hanson then began talking with old-timers in Orleans, Nebraska, and searching through town records. He soon determined that the famous fur trader lay buried beneath the big lilac just west of the cemetery's Grand Army of the Republic monument.

Hanson's research excited the local residents who decided that Culbertson deserved a permanent memorial. Mary Parker, Orleans high school teacher and Junior Historical Society advisor, began researching the fur trader's life. Mrs. William Lennemann, an official with the Republican Valley Chapter of the Daughters of the American Revolution, arranged to place fur trade histories in the local library while Jean McGeachin McLaughlin, daughter of Julia and George's friends, chaired the committee to select a marker.

On Memorial Day, the crowd gathered to listen as Dr. James C. Olson, Superintendent of the Nebraska State Historical Society, delivered the dedication address, paying tribute to both Culbertson and Natawista. Mrs. Lennemann, in presenting the monument, recalled a DAR precept: "Nothing is really ended until it is forgotten. Whatever is kept in memory still endures and is real."[18]

The organizers had hoped that Margaret Roberts, George and Julia's daughter whom Culbertson referred to as "Maggie" in 1875, would be present to accept the memorial on behalf of the family. Roberts, known as the "petticoat governor of Idaho" for her work on behalf of women's suffrage,[19] had confirmed Hanson's findings by recalling her father's trip to Nebraska for the reburial. But ill health prevented her from attending[20] and Elmer C. Ott, mayor of Orleans, accepted the marker on behalf of the Culbertson family and all pioneers.[21]

---

[16]McDonnell, *MHSC*, Vol. X, p. 242.  [17]Chittenden, *Fur Trade*, Vol. I, p. 386.
[18]"Dedication Memorial Day."
[19]Penson-Ward, *Idaho Women*, Vol. I, p. 187; Penson-Ward, *Who's Who*, p. 30. Margaret Roberts headed the Idaho State Traveling Library for many years.
[20]Hanson, "Marking the Grave," p. 125; miscellaneous materials in OPL. Ms. Roberts died a year later in Boise. *Idaho Sunday Statesman*, 25 May 1952.   [21]"Dedication Memorial Day."

As the crowd looked on, the marker was unveiled. So long delayed, the memorial reads:

> MAJOR ALEXANDER
> CULBERTSON
> BORN PENN. MAY 20, 1809
> DIED ORLEANS, NEB. AUG. 27, 1879
> AN IMPORTANT FIGURE IN THE DEVELOPMENT OF THE WESTERN FRONTIER, ASSOCIATED WITH THE FUR TRADE. ENTERED SERVICE OF THE AMERICAN FUR COMPANY 1829. BEGAN CAREER ON UPPER MISSOURI, 1833. IN CHARGE OF FORT M'KENZIE UNTIL 1840, THEN FORT UNION, AND SENT TO FORT LARAMIE, A SPECIAL ASSIGNMENT TO RE-ESTABLISH FUR TRADE AND SAVE FORT FROM ABANDONMENT. SUPERINTENDENT OF UPPER MISSOURI OUTFIT, WHICH INCLUDED ALL FORTS ON THE YELLOWSTONE AND UPPER MISSOURI RIVERS, 1847. ESTABLISHED FORT BENTON, THE FIRST PERMANENT SETTLEMENT IN MONTANA. MARRIED NA-TA-WIS-TA-CHA, A BLACKFOOT MAIDEN, ABOUT 1840. ACTED AS INTERPRETER AND AS SPECIAL AGENT OF THE U.S. GOVERNMENT IN MAKING TREATIES WITH THE INDIANS, SUCH AS THE ONE WITH BLACKFEET AND GROS VENTRES IN 1855 PERMITTING THE SURVEY THROUGH THEIR TERRITORY FOR A PACIFIC RAILROAD. BLAZED TRAILS ON HIS TRIPS FROM FORT TO FORT AND TO INDIAN CAMPS WHICH WERE LATER FOLLOWED BY SETTLERS AND, TODAY, ARE THE ROUTES OF HIGHWAYS. FOR NEARLY HALF A CENTURY HIS HIGH CHARACTER AND ABILITY ENABLED HIM TO MAKE MAJOR CONTRIBUTIONS TO THE DEVELOPMENT OF THE MISSOURI BASIN.[22]

It is a fitting tribute.

---

[22] Author's own observations.

# Bibliography

### BOOKS

Abel, Anne Heloise, editor. *Chardon's Journal at Fort Clark: 1834-1839* (Pierre: State of S. Dak., 1932)
Albers, Patricia and Beatrice Medicine. *The Hidden Half: Studies of Plains Indian Women* (Wash., DC: Univ. Press of America, Inc., 1983)
Ambrose, Stephen E. *Undaunted Courage: Meriwether Lewis, Thomas Jefferson, and the Opening of the American West* (N.Y.: Simon & Schuster, 1996)
Anthony, Ross Orlando. *A History of Fort Laramie: A Thesis Presented to the Department of History* (Los Angeles: Univ. of So. Cal., 1930)
Assiniboine and Sioux Tribes. *Fort Peck Reservation Centennial Years: 1886-1888, 1986-1988* (Fort Peck: Ft. Peck Tribal Archives/NAES College, 1986)
Audubon, Maria R. *Audubon and His Journals: Volume II* Notes by Elliott Coues (N.Y.: Dover Pubs., Inc., 1960)
Bennett, Ben. *Death, too, for The-Heavy-Runner* (Missoula: Mountain Press Pub. Co., 1982)
*Biographical Directory of the United States Congress: 1774-1989* (Wash., DC: G.P.O., 1989)
Bodmer, Karl. *Karl Bodmer's America* (Lincoln: Univ. of Neb. Press & Joslyn Art Museum, 1984)
Boller, Henry A. *Among the Indians: Eight Years in the Far West, 1858-1866* (Chicago: R.R. Donnelley & Sons Co., 1959)
Bonney, Orrin H. and Lorraine G. Bonney. *Battle Drums and Geysers: The Life and Journals of Lt. Gustavus Cheyney Doane* (Chicago: Sage Books, 1970)
Bradley, Lt. James H. *The March of the Montana Column* (Norman: Univ. of Okla. Press, 1961)
Buckley, Cornelius M., S.J. *Nicholas Point, S.J.: His Life and Northwest Indian Chronicles* (Chicago: Loyola Univ. Press, 1989)
Bullchild, Percy. *The Sun Came Down: The History of the World as My Blackfeet Elders Told It* (San Francisco: Harper & Row, 1985)
Burlingame, Merrill G. *The Montana Frontier* (Bozeman: Big Sky Books, 1980)
Burns, Robert Ignatius, S.J. *The Jesuits and the Indian Wars of the Northwest* (Moscow: Univ. of Idaho Press, 1966)
Campbell, Maria. *Halfbreed* (Lincoln: Univ. of Neb. Press, 1973)
Catlin, George. *Letters and Notes on the Manners, Customs and Conditions of N. American Indians* (N.Y.: Dover Pubs., Inc., 1973)
Chamberlain, Andrew B. *Historic Furnishings Report: Indian Trade House and Strong Room* (Harper's Ferry: National Park Service, 1993)

Chittenden, Hiram Martin. *History of Early Steamboat Navigation on the Missouri River: Life & Adventures of Joseph La Barge* (N.Y.: Francis P. Harper, 1903)

———. *The American Fur Trade of the Far West* (Stanford: Academic Reprints, 1954)

Chittenden, Hiram Martin and Alfred Talbot Richardson. *Life, Letters & Travels of Father Pierre-Jean DeSmet, S.J., 1801-1873* (N.Y.: Francis P. Harper, 1905)

Conrad, W. P. *From Terror to Freedom in the Cumberland Valley* (Greencastle: Lilian S. Besore Memorial Lby., 1976)

Culbertson, Joseph. *Joseph Culbertson: Famous Indian Scout Who Served Under General Miles in 1876-1895, True Stories of Camp Life in Early Days* (Wolf Point: copyright, Frank Delger, n/d)

Culbertson, Lewis R., M.D. *Genealogy of the Culbertson and Culberson Families: Revised Edition* (Zanesville: The Courier Co., Printers and Binders, 1923)

Culbertson, Thaddeus A. *Journal of an Expedition to the Mauvaises Terres and the Upper Missouri in 1850* (Wash., DC: U.S. G.P.O., 1952)

Cummings, Hubertis M. *Scots Breed and Susquehanna* (Pittsburgh: Univ. of Pittsburgh Press, 1964)

Daugherty, James. *Trappers and Traders of the Far West* (N.Y.: Random House, 1952)

De Jong, Josselin P. B. De. *Blackfoot Texts: From the Southern Piegans Blackfoot Reservation Teton County Montana* (Amsterdam: Johannes Müller, 1914)

DeMallie, Raymond J. and Alfonso Ortiz, eds. *North American Indian Anthropology: Essays on Soc. and Culture* (Norman: Univ. of Okla. Press, 1994)

DeVoto, Bernard. *Across the Wide Missouri* (Boston: Houghton Mifflin Co., 1947)

DeVoto, Bernard, ed. *The Journals of Lewis and Clark* (Boston: Houghton Mifflin Co., 1953)

Defenbach, Byron. *Idaho: The Place and Its People* (Chicago: The American Hist. Soc., Inc., 1933)

Dempsey, Hugh A. *Charcoal's World* (Lincoln: Univ. of Neb. Press, 1978)

———. *Crowfoot: Chief of the Blackfeet* (Norman: Univ. of Okla. Press, 1972)

———. *Red Crow: Warrior Chief* (Lincoln: Univ. of Neb. Press, 1980)

Denig, Edwin Thompson. *Five Indian Tribes of the Upper Missouri: Sioux, Arickaras, Assiniboines, Crees, Crows* (Norman: Univ. of Okla. Press, 1961)

Ege, Robert J. *"Tell Baker to Strike Them Hard": Incident on the Marias, 23 Jan 1870* (Fort Collins: The Old Army Press, 1970)

Erlanson, Charles B. *General Miles: The Red Man's Conqueror and Champion: General Miles' Campaign Against Lame Deer* (copyright, Charles B. Erlanson, 1969)

Ewers, John C. *Blackfeet Indians: Ethnological Report on the Blackfeet and Gros Ventre Tribes of Indians* (N.Y.: Garland Pub. Inc., 1974)

———. *Indian Life on the Upper Missouri* (Norman: Univ. of Okla. Press, 1968)

———. *The Blackfeet: Raiders on the Northwestern Plains* (Norman: Univ. of Okla. Press, 1958)

Farr, William E. *The Reservation Blackfeet, 1882-1945: A Photographic History of Cultural Survival* (Seattle: Univ. of Wash. Press, 1984)

Felt, Margaret, ed. *Daughters of the Land: Collected Short Stories of Courageous Native American Women* (Bend: Maverick Pubs., 1988)

Flandrau, Grace. *The Story of Marias Pass* (Great Northern Railway, n/d)

# BIBLIOGRAPHY 379

Foley, William E. and C. David Rice. *The First Chouteaus: River Barons of Early St. Louis* (Urbana: Univ. of Ill. Press, 1983)

Ford, Alice. *John James Audubon: A Biography* (N.Y.: Abbeville Press, 1988)

Gagnon, Gregory and Karen White Eyes. *Pine Ridge Reservation: Yesterday and Today* (Interior: Badlands Natural History Assoc., 1992)

Garraghan, Gilbert J., S.J., Ph.D. *The Jesuits of the Middle United States* (N.Y.: America Press, 1938) 3 volumes

Grinnell, George Bird. *Audubon Park: The History of the Site of the Hispanic Society of America and Neighbouring Institutions* (N.Y.: Printed By Order of the Trustees, 1927)

———. *Blackfoot Lodge Tales: The Story of a Prairie People* (N.Y.: Charles Scribner's Sons, 1923)

Hafen, LeRoy R. *The Mountain Men and the Fur Trade of the Far West.* (Glendale: The Arthur H. Clark Co., 1965-1972) 10 Vols.

Hafen, LeRoy R. *The Mountain Men and the Fur Trade of the Far West.* (Lincoln: Univ. of Neb. Press, 1982) One Volume.

Hafen, LeRoy R., Ph.D., Litt.D. and Francis Marion Young, A.B. *Fort Laramie and the Pageant of the West* (Glendale: The Arthur H. Clark Co., 1938)

Harris, Edward. *Up the Missouri with Audubon: The Journal of Edward Harris* (Norman: Univ. of Okla. Press, 1951)

Harrod, Howard L. *Mission Among the Blackfeet* (Norman: Univ. of Okla. Press, 1971)

Havens, Paul Swain. *Chambersburg, Frontier Town, 1730-1794* (Chambersburg: The Craft Press, Inc., 1975)

*History of Franklin County, Pennsylvania: Containing a history of the county, its townships,* (Chicago: Warner, Beers & Co., 1887)

*History of Idaho: The Gem of the Mountains* (Chicago: The S. J. Clarke Pub. Co., 1920)

Holterman, Jack. *King of the High Missouri: The Saga of the Culbertsons* (Helena: Jack Holterman with Falcon Press, 1987)

Hungry Wolf, Adolf (Gutohriein). *The Blood People: A Division of the Blackfoot Confederacy* (N.Y.: Harper & Row, 1977)

Hungry Wolf, Adolf & Beverly. *Indian Tribes of the Northern Rockies* (Summertown: Book Pub. Co., 1989)

Hungry Wolf, Beverly. *The Ways of My Grandmothers* (N.Y.: Quill, 1982)

Innis, Ben. *Sagas of the Smoky-Water: True Stories Reflecting Historical Aspects of the Missouri-Yellowstone Confluence Region, 1805-1910* (Williston: Centennial Press, 1985)

Jackson, Donald. *Voyages of the Steamboat Yellow Stone* (Norman: Univ. of Okla. Press, 1985)

Josephy, Alvin M., Jr. *The Civil War in the American West* (N.Y.: Alfred A. Knopf, 1991)

Kappler, Charles J. *Indian Affairs: Laws and Treaties* (Wash., DC: G.P.O., 1904)

Kane, Lucille M., editor & translator. *Military Life in Dakota: The Journal of Philippe Regis de Trobriand* (Lincoln: Univ. of Neb. Press, 1951)

Kane, Paul. *Wanderings of an Artist Among the Indians of North America* (Toronto: The Radisson Soc. of Canada, Limited, 1925)

Kehoe, Alice B. *North American Indians: A Comprehensive Account* (Englewood Cliffs: Prentice Hall, 1992)

Kennedy, Margaret A. *The Whiskey Trade of the Northwestern Plains: A Multidisciplinary Study* (N.Y.: Peter Lang, 1997)
Killoren, John J., S. J. *"Come Blackrobe": De Smet and the Indian Tragedy* (Norman: Univ. of Okla. Press, 1994)
Kinietz, W. Vernon. *John Mix Stanley and His Indian Paintings* (Ann Arbor: Univ. of Mich. Press, 1942)
Kurz, Rudolph Friederich. *The Journal of Rudolph Friederich Kurz: The Life and Work of this Swiss Artist* (Fairfield: Ye Galleon Press, 1969)
Ladner, Mildred D. *William de la Montagne Cary: Artist on the Missouri River* (Norman: Univ. of Okla. Press and Tulsa:Gilcrease Inst. of Amer. Hist. and Art, 1984)
Larpenteur, Charles. *Forty Years a Fur Trader on the Upper Missouri* (Lincoln: Univ. of Neb. Press, 1989)
Lavender, David. *Let Me Be Free: The Nez Perce Tragedy* (N.Y.: Harper Collins, 1992)
Laveille, E., S.J. *The Life of Father DeSmet, S.J.* (N.Y.: P.J. Kenedy & Sons, 1915)
Lazarus, Edward. *Black Hills, White Justice* (N.Y.: HarperCollins, 1991)
Leyburn, James G. *The Scotch-Irish: A Social History* (Chapel Hill: The Univ. of N. Carolina Press, 1962)
Lowe, Percival G. *Five Years A Dragoon: ('49 to '54) And Other Adventures on the Great Plains* (Norman: Univ. of Okla. Press, 1965)
Manzione, Joseph. *"I Am Looking to the North for My Life": Sitting Bull, 1876-1881* (S.L.C: Univ. of Utah Press, 1991)
Mattes, Merrill J. *Fur Traders and Trappers of the Old West* (Yellowstone Lby. & Museum Assoc., 1944)
———. *The Great Platte River Road* (Lincoln: Univ. of Neb. Press, 1969)
Miller, David Humphreys. *Custer's Fall: The Indian Side of the Story* (Lincoln: Univ. of Neb. Press, 1985)
Murray, Robert A. *Fort Laramie: "Visions Of A Grand Old Post"* (Fort Collins: The Old Army Press, 1974)
*Nez Perce Country: Official National Park Handbook* (Wash., DC: U.S. Dept. of the Interior, 1983)
O'Meara, Walter. *Daughters of the Country: The Women of the Fur Traders and Mountain Men* (N.Y.: Harcourt, Brace & World, Inc., 1968)
Olson, James C. *Red Cloud and the Sioux Problem* (Lincoln: Univ. of Neb. Press, 1965)
Overholser, Joel. *Fort Benton: World's Innermost Port* (Fort Benton: Joel Overholser with Falcon Press, 1987)
Penson-Ward, Betty. *Idaho Women in History: Big and Little Biographies and Other Gender Stories* (Boise: Legendary Pub. Co., 1991)
———. *Who's Who of Idaho Women of the Past* (Boise: Idaho Commission on Women's Progress, 1981)
Pfaller, Louis, o.s.b. *Father De Smet in Dakota* (Richardton: Assumption Abbey Press, 1962)
Point, Nicolas, S.J. *Wilderness Kingdom: Indian Life in the Rocky Mountains: 1840-1847: The Journals & Paintings of Nicolas Point* (N.Y.: Holt, Rinehart and Winston, 1967) Joseph P. Donnelly, S.J., translator
Ramenofsky, Ann F. *Vectors of Death: The Archaeology of European Contact* (Albuquerque: Univ. of N.M. Press, 1987)

# BIBLIOGRAPHY

Richards, Kent D. *Isaac I. Stevens: Young Man in a Hurry* (Provo: B.Y.U. Press, 1979)
Robinson, Charles M., III. *A Good Year to Die: The Story of the Great Sioux War* (N.Y.: Random House, 1995)
Sandoz, Mari. *The Beaver Men: Spearheads of Empire* (Lincoln: Univ. of Neb. Press, 1964)
Schultz, J. W. *My Life as an Indian* (N.Y.: Doubleday, Page & Co., 1907)
Schultz, James Willard. *Blackfeet Tales of Glacier National Park* (N.Y.: Houghton Mifflin Co., 1916)
—————. *Recently Discovered Tales of Life Among the Indians* (Missoula: Mountain Press Pub. Co., 1988)
—————. *Signposts of Adventure: Glacier National Park as the Indians Knew It* (Boston: Houghton Mifflin Co., 1926)
Schultz, James Willard (Apikuni). *Blackfeet and Buffalo: Memories of Life Among the Indians* (Norman: Univ. of Okla. Press, 1962)
—————. *Why Gone Those Times? Blackfoot Tales* (Norman: Univ. of Okla. Press, 1974)
Segars, Lorretta. *100 Years in Culbertson: 1887-1987* (privately published, 1987)
Sharp, Paul F. *Whoop-Up Country: The Canadian-American West, 1865-1885* (Helena: Hist. Soc. of Mont., 1960)
Shemorry, Bill. *The Story of Williston and Area* (self-published, n/d)
*Since 1887: The Williston Story* (Williston: Souvenir Book Committee, n/d)
Smiley, H.D. *Harvesting Shadows: Untold Tales from the Fur Trade* (Manhattan: Sunflower Univ. Press, 1990)
*Southern Revenge!: Civil War History of Chambersburg, Pennsylvania* (Shippensburg: White Mane Pub. Co., 1989) Notes by Ted Alexander and others.
Stevens, Hazard. *The Life of General Isaac I. Stevens* (Boston: Houghton, Mifflin and Co., 1900)
*Story of Fort Union and Its Traders* (Williston: The Elks Lodge of Williston, ND, n/d)
Sunder, John E. *The Fur Trade on the Upper Missouri: 1840-1865* (Norman: Univ. of Okla. Press, 1965)
Thomas, Davis and Karin Ronnefeldt, eds. *People of the First Man: Life Among the Plains Indians in Their Final Days of Glory* (N.Y.: E.P. Dutton & Co., Inc.,1976)
Thompson, Erwin N. *Fort Union Trading Post: Fur Trade Empire on the Upper Missouri* (Medora: Theodore Roosevelt Nature & History Assoc., 1986)
Thwaites, Reuben Gold, LL.D. *Early Western Travels, 1748-1846* (Cleveland: Arthur H. Clark Co., 1906)
Trimble, Michael K. *An Ethnohistorical Interpretation Of The Spread Of Smallpox In The Northern Plains Utilizing Concepts Of Disease Ecology* (Lincoln: J&L Reprint Co., 1986)
Uhlenbeck, C. C. *Original Blackfoot Texts: From the Southern Peigans Blackfoot Reservation Teton County Montana* (Amsterdam, Johannes Müller, 1911)
—————. *A New Series of Blackfoot Texts: From the Southern Peigans Blackfoot Reservation Teton County Montana* (Amsterdam, Johannes Müller, 1912)
Unrau, William. *White Man's Wicked Water: The Alcohol Trade and Prohibition in Indian Country, 1802-1892* (Lawrence: Univ. Press of Kansas, 1996)
Utley, Robert M. *The Lance and the Shield: The Life and Times of Sitting Bull* (N.Y.: Henry Holt and Co., 1993)

Vestal, Stanley. *Mountain Men* (Boston: Houghton Mifflin Co., 1937).
Viola, Herman J. *Diplomats in Buckskins* (Wash., DC: Smithsonian Inst. Press, 1981).
Welch, James with Paul Stekler. *Killing Custer: The Battle of the Little Bighorn and the Fate of the Plains Indians* (N.Y.: W. W. Norton & Co., 1994).
Wissler, Clark and D. C. Duvall. *Mythology of the Blackfoot Indians* (Lincoln: Univ. of Neb. Press, 1995).
Wissler, Clark. *Anthropological Papers of the American Museum of Natural History: Vol. VII: Social Organization and Ritualistic Ceremonies of the Blackfoot Indians* (N.Y.: Published by Order of the Trustees, 1912).
——————. *Anthropological Papers of the American Museum of Natural History: Vol. VII, Part II: Ceremonial Bundles of the Blackfoot Indians* (N.Y.: Published by Order of the Trustees, 1912).
Wissler, Clark, ed. *Anthropological Papers of the American Museum of Natural History: Vol. XVI: Sun Dance of the Plains Indians* (N.Y.: Published by Order of the Trustees, 1921).
Wooster, Robert. *Nelson A. Miles & the Twilight of the Frontier Army* (Lincoln: Univ. of Neb. Press, 1993).

JOURNAL ARTICLES

Atkins, C.J. "Log of the Steamer *Benton* from St. Louis, Missouri to Fort Benton, Idaho," *Coll. of the State Hist. Soc. of N. Dak.* 2 (1908): 285-313.
Bagley, Will. "Lansford Warren Hastings: Scoundrel or Visionary?" *Overland Journal* 12, no. 1 (1994): 12-26.
Boller, Henry A. "Journal of a Trip to, And Residence in, the Indian Country, Commenced Saturday, May 22, 1858" *N. Dak. History* 33, no. 3 (1966): 260-315.
Brackett, William S. "Bonneville and Bridger" *Cont. to the Hist. Soc. of Mont.* 3 (1900): 175-200.
Bradley, Lt. James H. "Affairs at Fort Benton" *Cont. to the Hist. Soc. of Mont.* 3 (1900): 201-287.
——————. "Arrapooash" *Cont. to the Hist. Soc. of Mont.* 9 (1923): 299-307.
——————. "Blackfoot War With the Whites" *Cont. to the Hist. Soc. of Mont.* 9 (1923): 252-255.
——————. "Characteristics, Habits and Customs of the Blackfeet Indians" *Cont. to the Hist. Soc. of Mont.* 9 (1923): 255-287.
——————. "Fur Trade of Upper Missouri River" *Cont. to the Hist. Soc. of Mont.* 9 (1923): 317-335.
——————. "Sir George Gore's Expedition" *Cont. to the Hist. Soc. of Mont.* 9 (1923): 246-251.
——————. "St. Peter's Mission" *Cont. to the Hist. Soc. of Mont.* 9 (1923): 315-316.
——————. "Sun River Stampede, 1866" *Cont. to the Hist. Soc. of Mont.* 9 (1923): 251-252.
——————. "The Oregon Trail: Capture of an Emigrant Train by the Piegan Chief, Little Dog" *Cont. to the Hist. Soc. of Mont.* 9 (1923): 335-340.
Chaky, Doreen. "Bad Bread and Bullets" *True West* (March 1996): 15-21.
——————. "Fossils and the Fur Trade: The Chouteaus as Patrons of Paleontology" *Gateway Heritage* 19, no. 1 (1998): 22-31.

# BIBLIOGRAPHY 383

Clarke, Helen P. "Sketch of Malcolm Clarke: A Corporate Member of the Hist. Soc. of Mont." *Cont. to the Hist. Soc. of Mont.* 2 (1896): 255-268.

Connolly, James B. "Audubon At His Best" *N. Dak. History* 31, no. 4 (1964): 223-229.

―――. "Father DeSmet in North Dakota" *N. Dak. History* 27, no. 1 (1960): 4-24.

DeGirardin, M.E. "A Trip to the Bad Lands in 1849" *S. Dak. Hist. Review* 1 (1936): 51-78.

Dempsey, Hugh A., editor. "Alexander Culbertson's Journey to Bow River" *Alberta Hist. Review* 19, no. 4 (1971): 8-20.

Dempsey, Hugh A. "The Amazing Death of Calf Shirt" *The Montana Magazine of History* 3, no. 1 (1953): 66-72.

Dixon, Ben F. and Alice L. "The Family of David Culbertson of Lincoln County, KY" Family Historians Brochure #7, n/d.

"The Encampment at Horse Creek in Indian Territory," *The Wind River Rendezvous* 12 (1982).

Ferch, David L. "Fighting the Smallpox Epidemic of 1837-38: The Response of the American Fur Co. Traders" *Museum of the Fur Trade Qtly.* 19, no. 4 (1983): 2-7 and 20, no. 1 (1984): 4-9.

"Fort Benton Journal, 1854-1856." *Cont. to the Hist. Soc. of Mont.* 10 (1940): 1-98.

Garber, Jess. "History in a Church: The Rocky Spring Presbyterian Church" *Kittochtinny Hist. Soc.* 9, no. 8 (1993): 3-4.

"Governor Edgerton's First Message to the First Legislative Assembly of the Territory of Montana" *Cont. to the Hist. Soc. of Mont.* 3 (1900): 341-348.

Hamilton, Hans. "Letter" *Pennsylvania Archives: Selected and Arranged from Original Documents* First Series, Volume 2 (Philadelphia: Joseph Severns & Co., 1852): 611-612.

Hamilton, William T. "A Trading Expedition Among the Indians in 1858" *Cont. to the Hist. Soc. of Mont.* 3 (1900): 33-123.

Hanson, Charles E., Jr. "Marking the Grave of Alexander Culbertson" *Neb. History* 32 (1951): 120-129.

―――. "The Fort Pierre-Fort Laramie Trail" *Museum of the Fur Trade Qtly.* 1, no. 2 (1965): 3-7.

Kennerly, James. "Diary of James Kennerly" *Missouri Hist. Soc. Coll.* 6, no. 1 (Oct 1928).

"Major Alexander Culbertson and His Lady" *Culbertson, Mont. Centennial Book, 1887-1987* (1987).

Mattison, Ray H. "Fort Union: Its Role in the Upper Missouri Fur Trade" *N. Dak. History* 29, no. 1 & 2 (Jan-Apr 1962): 181-210.

Mattison, Ray H., ed. "The Letters of Henry A. Boller: Upper Missouri River Fur Trader" *N. Dak. History* 33, no. 2 (Spring 1966): 106-219.

McCann, Lloyd E. "The Grattan Massacre" *Neb. History* 37, no. 1 (Mar 1956) Reprint booklet.

McDonnell, Anne. "Notes and References" *Cont. to the Hist. Soc. of Mont.* 10 (1940): 239-305.

Orr, John G. "Culbertson's Row" *The Kittochtinny Hist. Soc.* (Feb 1899-Feb 1901): 113-135.

Pfaller, Louis. "Charles Larpenteur" *N. Dak. History* 32, no. 1 (1965): 4-17.

Prout, Hiram A. "Description of a Fossil Maxillary Bone of a Paleotherium, from near White River" *The American Journal of Science and Arts* 3, Second Series (1847): 248-250.
Reid, Russell and Clell G. Gannon, editors. "Journal of the Atkinson-O'Fallon Expedition" *N. Dak. Hist. Qtly.* 4, no. 1 (1929): 5-56.
Ronan, Peter. "Discovery of Alder Gulch" *Cont. to the Hist. Soc. of Mont.* 3 (1900): 143-152.
Santucci, Vince. "Significant Badlands Fossil Rediscovered" *Park Paleontology* 1 (Winter 1991): 1.
Schemm, Mildred Walker. "The Major's Lady: Natawista" *The Montana Magazine of History* 2 (Jan 1952): 5-15.
Steckelberg, Jamie L. "Medicine Snake Woman of the Blood (Blackfeet) Indian Tribe" in *Daughters of the Land:* 53-59.
Stevens, O.A. "Maximilian in North Dakota, 1833-1834" *N. Dak. History* 28, no. 4 (Oct 1961): 163-169.
Taliaferro, Lawrence. "Autobiography of Maj. Taliaferro" *Minn. Hist. Soc. Coll.* 6.
Taylor, Dabney. "He Hated the Blackfeet" *Frontier Times* (Feb-Mar 1969): 32-33, 40.
———. "The Major's Blackfoot Bride" *Frontier Times* (Dec-Jan 1969): 26-29, 44-49.
Vickers, Chris. "Denig of Fort Union" *N. Dak. History* 15, no. 2 (1948): 134-143.
Walton-Raji, Angela Y. "The Night the Stars Fell: My Search for Amanda Young" *The Frontier Freedman's Journal: An African-American Genealogical & Hist. Journal* 2, no. 1 (Spring/Summer, 1993): 6-11.
Wilson, Wesley C. "The U.S. Army and the Piegans: The Baker Massacre on the Marias, 1870" *N. Dak. History* 32, no. 1 (1965): 40-58.
Wischmann, Lesley. "Alexander Culbertson: The Legacy Lives On" *The American West* 28, no. 4 (Fall, 1990): 32C-D.
Wood, Garvey C. "Fort McKenzie (24CH242): A Study in Applied Hist. and Archaeological Methods" *Archaeology in Mont.* 18, no. 1 (1977): 43-62.

NEWSPAPER ARTICLES

"An Interesting Marriage Ceremony" *Peoria Daily Transcript* 12 Sep 1859.
"An Old Newspaper" *Peoria Daily Transcript* 25 Apr 1859.
"Another Pocahontas" *Peoria Weekly Republican* 16 Dec 1953.
Broomfield, Joan F. "Alexander Culbertson" *The Herald News* (MT) 28 Aug 1969.
Culbertson, Alexander. "A Winter Trip Across the Rocky Mountains" *Peoria Daily Transcript* 9 Feb 1859.
———. "The Indians of the Upper Missouri" *Peoria Daily Transcript* 10 Mar 1859.
Culbertson, Joseph. "Joseph Culbertson, Son of A 'King of the Upper Missouri,' Tells of Father's Last Trip Among the Montana Indians" *Plevna* (MT) *Herald*, n/d.
———. "Fighting Sitting Bull Described by Scout for Miles" probably *The New North-West* 1879.
*The Daily Manitoban* 30 Sep 1885.

"Death of Alexander Culbertson" *Omaha* (NE) *Republican* 5 Sep 1879.
"Dedication Memorial Day" *Orleans* (NE) *Chronicle* 31 May 1951.
Dempsey, Hugh A. "D.W. Davis Operated Post Here in 1872; First M.P." *The Calgary Herald* 2 Jun 1957.
———. "Fred Kanouse: Calgary's First Businessman" *The Calgary Herald* 31 May 1957.
East, Ernest E. "Ancient Mansion Near Limestone is Background for Early Romance and Tragedy of a Shattered Fortune" *Peoria Journal* 25 Jul 1936.
———. "Colorful Story of Early Peoria Is Recalled by Woman's Death in West" *Peoria Journal* 24 Feb 1939.
"Fire" *Peoria Daily Transcript* 2 Feb 1860.
"From the Mountains" *Springfield* (MO) *Advertiser* 25 Jul 1848.
"Funeral Rites for Mrs. Irvin Here Thursday" *Great Falls* (MT) *Tribune* 7 Feb 1939.
"General Roberts, Pioneer Idahoan, to Lie in State" *The Idaho Statesman* 17 Jun 1922.
Grill, "Mon Tana Lou." "Fifty-Five Years Ago..." *Choteau* (MT) *Times* 1 Jan 1936.
"Gone" *Peoria Daily Transcript* 8 May 1857.
"Head of Navigation" *Peoria Daily Transcript* 4 Jul 1857.
"Hitchcock County" *Beatrice (NE) Express* 18 Sep 1873.
Hutt, Joe W. "Letter to the Editor" *Culbertson* (NE) *Progress* 28 Jul 1932.
"In Costume" *Peoria Daily Transcript* 14 May 1857.
"The Indian Country" *The Chicago Tribune* 3 Feb 1870.
"The Indian Trade Again" *Helena* (MT) *Herald* 18 Mar 1871
"Joe Culbertson, Historic Character, Linking Past With Present, Is No More" *The Opheim* (MT) *Observer* n/d.
"Joseph Culbertson Was Son of 'King of the Upper Missouri'" (newspaper unknown) 12 Feb 1934.
Liddell, Ken. "Furrows and Foothills" *The Calgary Herald* 23 May 1956.
"Lost or Stolen" *Peoria Daily Transcript* 31 Oct 1859.
"Miscellaneous" *Rocky Mountain News* 29 Jan 1870.
*Missouri Republican* 19 May 1855
"Mrs. Frances C. Irvin Dies Here on Sunday Night" *Great Falls* (MT) *Tribune* 5 Feb 1939.
*The New North-West* 4 Feb 1870.
"Old Fort Union, Dominant Trading Post of the Upper Missouri River, Place Where Life Was Held Cheaply" *The Fairview* (MT) *News* Dec 1921.
*Peoria Daily Transcript* 26 Jun 1857; 22 Sep 1858; 17 Aug 1860; 31 Aug 1860; 19 Sep 1860; 23 Oct 1860; 12 Oct 1861; 9 Dec 1861; 4 Jul 1862; 16 Dec 1862; 8 Jan 1862; 28 Jan 1863; 19 Jun 1863.
"Personal" *Peoria Daily Transcript* 1 May 1857.
"Pioneer of West, Mrs. J.C. Roberts, Dies at Home Here" *The Idaho Statesman* 17 Mar 1929.
Plassman, Martha Edgerton. "How Major Culbertson Outwitted the Gros Ventres and Saved Little Force of Whites Besieged at Fort McKenzie" *The Grass Range* (MT) *Review* 8 Apr 1924.

Ramsey, Bruce. "Natawista Must Have Been Some Lady" probably *Fernie* (Canada) *Free Press* n/d.
Rex. *Bismarck Tri-Weekly Tribune* 1 Oct 1877.
"Rocky Mountain Correspondence" *Peoria Daily Transcript* 1 Jul 1857.
"Scarce Article" *Peoria Daily Transcript* 6 Nov 1857.
"The Slaughter of the Piegans" *The New York Times* 24 Feb 1870.
"Smothered" *Bismarck Daily Tribune* 24 Oct 1888.
"Sons of Pennsylvania Attend!" *Peoria Daily Transcript* 31 Jan 1860.
Taylor, Suzanne D. "First Attorney General of Idaho Once Fought in Battle of Gettysburg" *The Idaho Sunday Statesman* 8 Dec 1963.
"Ten Dollars Reward" *Peoria Daily Transcript* 31 Oct 1859.
*Toronto Mail* 28 Jan 1886.
"Welcome Home" *Peoria Daily Transcript* 2 Nov 1857.
"Works of Art at the Fair" *Peoria Daily Transcript* 1 Dec 1859.

Government Documents

Appropriations for Sioux Indians, House Exec. Doc. 102 (42$^{nd}$ Congress, 2$^{nd}$ Session) 1511, 1872
Blackfeet Indians: Memorial of the Legislative Assembly of Montana Terr., House Misc. Doc. 38 (40$^{th}$ Congress, 2$^{nd}$ Session) 1349, 1867
Estimate of Appropriations, House Exec. Doc. 5 (44$^{th}$ Congress, 1$^{st}$ Session) 1605, 1875
Expedition Against Piegan Indians, House Exec. Doc. 185 (41$^{st}$ Congress, 2$^{nd}$ Session) 1418, 1870
Indian Claims Commission, The U.S. v. Blackfeet Tribe, 1855-1950, Docket No. 279-D
Letter from the Secretary of the Interior, House Misc. Doc. 59 (33$^{rd}$ Congress, 1$^{st}$ Session) 741, 1854
Message of the President of the United States, Senate Exec. Doc. 49 (41$^{st}$ Congress, 2$^{nd}$ Session) 1406, 1870
National Archives Microfilm 619/711. Letters Received by the Office of the Adjutant General, 1869
National Archives Microfilm, M234/30. Blackfeet Agency, Letters Received by the Office of Indian Affairs, 1855-1869
National Archives Microfilm M234/754. St. Louis Superintendency, Letters Received by the Office of Indian Affairs, 1846-1847
National Archives Microfilm M234/755. St. Louis Superintendency, Letters Received by the Office of Indian Affairs, 1848-1849
National Archives Microfilm M234/884. Upper Missouri Agency, Letters Received by the Office of Indian Affairs, 1836-1851
National Archives Microfilm, M234/885. Upper Missouri Agency, Letters Received by the Office of Indian Affairs, 1852-1864
National Archives Microfilm M833/3. Records of the Mont. Superintendency of Indian Affairs, 1867-1873: Letters sent
National Archives Microfilm M653/217. 1860 Census, Peoria County (part), Illinois

National Archives Microfilm M593/827. 1870 Census, Mont. Terr.
National Archives Microfilm M593/799. 1870 Census, Platte County, Missouri
National Archives Microfilm T9/742. 1880 Census, Mont. Territory
Piegan Indians, House Exec. Doc. 269 (41st Congress, 2nd Session) 1426, 1870
Report of the Commissioner of Indian Affairs, House Exec. Doc. 1 (33rd Congress, 1st Session) 710, 1854
Report of the Commissioner of Indian Affairs, Senate Exec. Doc. 1 (33rd Congress, 2nd Session) 746, 1855
Report of the Commissioner of Indian Affairs, House Exec. Doc. 1 (34th Congress, 1st Session) 840, 1856
Report of the Commissioner of Indian Affairs, House Exec. Doc. 1 (35th Congress, 1st Session) 942, 1857
Report of the Commissioner of Indian Affairs, House Exec. Doc. 1 (35th Congress, 2nd Session) 997, 1858
Report of the Commissioner of Indian Affairs, House Exec. Doc. 1 (40th Congress, 3rd Session) 1366, 1868
Report of the Commissioner of Indian Affairs, House Exec. Doc. 1 (41st Congress, 2nd Session) 1414, 1869
Report of the Commissioner of Indian Affairs, House Exec. Doc. 1 (42nd Congress, 2nd Session) 1505, 1871
Senate Exec. Doc. 1 (27th Congress, 3rd Session) 533, 1843
Senate Exec. Doc. 19 (34th Congress, 1st Session) 815, 1855
Stevens, Isaac I. "Report of Exploration of a Route for the Pacific Railroad," House Exec. Doc. 129 (33rd Congress, 1st Session) 736, 1854

UNPUBLISHED RESOURCES

Berglund, Theresa. "Reminiscences of Fannie Culbertson" Small Coll. 414, Mont. Hist. Soc., Helena, Mont..
Clifford, Myrtle. *Three Women of Frontier Montana* (Master's Thesis, State Univ. of Mont., 1932)
Culbertson, John A. "Jack." Unpublished biography. N. Dak. Hist. Soc..
Culbertson, John Moodey. Diary of 1856 Journey to Upper Missouri. In possession of Wilma Murray, Ohio.
"Dedication of Monument Marking the Grave of Major Alexander Culbertson," 30 May 1951. Cordelia B. Preston Memorial Lby., Orleans, Neb..
East, Ernest E. "Flemming, John interview" Peoria Public Lby., Peoria, Illinois.
———. "History of Peoria" Peoria Public Lby., Peoria, Illinois.
———. "Tripp, Stephen interview" Peoria Public Lby., Peoria, Illinois.
Gibson, Stan. "Missing Parts: Notes on the 1870 Marias Massacre" Unpublished article. Author's coll.
Huey, Harriet J. Baird. "One Revolutionary Family" Speech given to Philadelphia Daughters of the American Revolution, 17 Jan 1896. Culbertson Coll., Missouri Hist. Soc..
Irvin, Fannie S. Culbertson. Unpublished biographical notes. Peoria Public Lby., Peoria, Illinois.

"John Mix Stanley, 1843-1868, Scrapbook." Archives of American Art, Microfilm Reel OAM. Smithsonian Inst..

Jordan, Florence R. "Historic Rocky Spring" Unpublished speech. Kittochtinny Hist. Soc., Chambersburg, Penn.

Kanouse, Henry Alfred "Fred." Unpublished biography by David Kanouse. Author's coll.

Marsh, Elias J., M.D. "Trip Up the Missouri River from St. Louis to Fort Benton, June and July and August, 1859 on the steamers 'Spread Eagle' and 'Chippewa'," Missouri Hist. Soc..

Schimmel, Julia Ann. *John Mix Stanley and Imagery of the West in Nineteenth-Century American Art* (Ann Arbor: Univ. Microfilms International, 1983)

Toomer, Edith E. "Biography—Major Alexander Culbertson" Microfilm 250, Reel 16. Mont. Hist. Soc., Helena, Mont..

Van Horne, William R. "Our Van Horne and Culbertson Forebears" Unpublished manuscript. Kittochtinny Hist. Soc., Chambersburg, Penn.

Welch, Hugh. Miscellaneous Blackfeet stories. Author's coll.

Wingerd, Edmund C. "Spirit of Rocky Spring" Unpublished speech. Kittochtinny Hist. Soc., Chambersburg, Penn.

ARCHIVAL COLLECTIONS

Bradley Univ., Cullom-Davis Library, Peoria, Illinois

The special collections at Cullom-Davis include the collections of the Peoria Historical Society. Especially important in this collection are the abstracts of newspaper articles from the 1800s.

Cordelia B. Preston Memorial Library, Orleans, Nebraska

A file of materials on Alexander Culbertson covers primarily the events surrounding the 1951 marking of his grave. Collection also includes a rough draft of the article by Charles E. Hanson, Jr., which subsequently appeared in *Nebraska History*.

Fort Benton Public Library, Fort Benton, Montana

The library has some general reference materials relating to Culbertson and the early history of the town, as well as some materials regarding the American Fur Co..

Fort Laramie National Historic Site, Fort Laramie, Wyoming

Collection includes copies of letters written by and to Alexander Culbertson during his years with the American Fur Co..

Fort Union Trading Post National Historic Site, Williston, North Dak.

Collection includes a variety of materials about affairs at Fort Union, affairs on the upper Missouri, and business correspondence of the American Fur Co.. The Ben Innis collection contains a variety of historical materials from the western North Dak.-eastern Montana region. The author's own research papers will also be housed at Fort Union. Notable among these papers are the personal correspondence between the author and David Kanouse, relative of H. A. "Fred" Kanouse, and the Blackfeet stories of Hugh Welch, including the recollections of his great-grandmother, Caroline Connoyer, who worked for the Culbertsons in Fort Benton.

## Idaho Historical Society, Boise, Idaho

Alexander Culbertson and Natawista's daughter, Julia Culbertson Roberts, moved to Idaho in 1883 and lived the rest of her life in that state. The archives contain some information about her life in Idaho. Of special interest is the 19 Oct 1996 oral history conducted by Rosemary Wimberly of George H. R. Taylor, Bethesda, Maryland, the grandson of Julia Culbertson and George Roberts, housed at the Idaho Oral History Center.

## Kittochtinny Historical Society, Chambersburg, Pennsylvania

Collection includes information about the early Culbertson family, Culbertson's Row, and the Rocky Spring Presbyterian Church.

## Missouri Historical Society, St. Louis, Missouri

Collection includes a wealth of information about the Chouteau family, the American Fur Co., and Alexander Culbertson. Of special interest are the Culbertson Papers, the Chouteau Collection (including Chouteau-Walsh, Chouteau-Maffitt, Chouteau-Papin Collections), the Andrew Drips Papers, the microfilmed Collection of Fur Trade Ledgers, the *Fort Union Letter Books, 29 Oct 1833-10 Dec 1835*, microfilmed copies of old St. Louis newspapers, and letters received by the Office of Indian Affairs on microfilm.

## Montana Historical Society, Helena, Montana

Collection includes much valuable information on the Culbertson family. Of special interest are the vertical files on Alexander Culbertson, Natawistacha-Iksana (Mrs. Alexander Culbertson), John "Jack" Culbertson, and Joseph "Joe" Culbertson. Also: Alexander Culbertson Papers, Small Collection 586; Thaddeus A. Culbertson Journal, Small Coll. 286 (also at the Missouri Hist. Soc.); Mollie Sedgwick Papers, Small Coll. 1386; Fort Belknap Journal, Small Coll. 251; Lewis Henry Morgan Diary, Small Coll. 525 (also at the Missouri Hist. Soc.); Myrtle Clifford's thesis, Microfilm 115; Joseph Culbertson's manuscript, *Famous Indian Scout*, PAM 1191; Canadian Indian Service, Blood Agency Records, Small Coll. 514; Theresa Berglund Coll., Small Coll. 414; the James H. Bradley papers, Manuscript Coll. 49; Julia Schultz Reminiscence, Microfilm 159; Philippe T. de Trobriand Papers, Small Coll. 5; U.S. Bureau of Indian Affairs, Blackfeet Indian Agency Records, Small Coll. 891; U.S. Bureau of Indian Affairs, Montana Superintendency Records, Microfilm 75 and Microfilm 358; Heavy Runner Records, Microfilm 53; U.S. Bureau of Indian Affairs Records, Microfilm 53c; Horace Clarke Reminiscences, Small Coll. 540; Helen P. Clarke Papers, Small Coll. 1153; U.S. Office of Explorations and Surveys Records, Microfilm 30; Edwin A. C. Hatch Papers, Small Coll. 810 and Microfilm 73c; Samuel Papin Letter, Small Coll. 619; Montana Writers Project Records, Reel 16, Microfilm 250; Pierre Chouteau, Jr. and Co. Records, Manuscript Coll. 4; T. C. Powers Papers, Manuscript Coll. 55.

## River Press, Fort Benton, Montana

At the time that the author was researching this book, Joel Overholser still maintained his files at the *River Press* office in Fort Benton. Overholser is the recognized authority on Fort Benton history and anyone who investigates a related historical subject will quickly be referred to him. Through his more than fifty years of researching the town's history, Overholser has gathered extensive files on many topics, including an impressive collection of materials on Alexander Culbertson.

State Historical Society of North Dak., Bismarck, North Dak.

There is little in the State Historical Society of North Dakota archives on Alexander Culbertson. The Orin C. Libby Papers, A 85/32/12, contain references to Culbertson's 1864 trek downriver. Also, the Henry Boller papers include photographs of the Culbertson family.

Peoria Public Library, Peoria, Illinois

Collection at the reference desk includes a large file on the Culbertson family with many items pertaining to the family during their time in Peoria, much of it gathered by Ernest East in the 1930s.

William Andrews Clark Memorial Library, Univ. of California, Los Angeles

The Charles Kessler papers include much material gathered from Joseph Culbertson and Julia Culbertson Roberts in the early 1900s. The papers also include a copy of Thaddeus Culbertson's journal as well as a draft copy of Joseph Culbertson's book. This last item is significant for the number of differences it contains when compared to the manuscript subsequently published under the copyright of Frank Delger. In particular, it is interesting that none of the derogatory material pertaining to Indians, such as the use of the term "Injun," appears in the Kessler copy of Culbertson's manuscript. Additionally, the Kessler version contains more information about Natawista than is to be found in the Delger version.

# Index

Abbott, Sol: 359
Academy of the Visitation convent school (St. Louis): 278-279, 287
Alexander (Flathead): 256, 258
*Amelia* (steamboat): 214
American Board of Commissioners for Foreign Missions: 144
American Fur Company (AFC): 14, 23, 24, 25, 26, 33, 34-35, 36, 38, 39, 43, 44, 45, 46, 54, 56, 63, 66, 67-68, 71, 72, 79, 80, 82, 97, 98, 106-107, 109, 111, 114-116, 119, 120, 121n10, 122-126, 141, 142-143, 146, 154-155, 158, 161-164, 166-169, 171, 174-175, 177, 181, 183, 189-191, 193, 211, 213-214, 224-225, 229, 231, 243-245, 248, 250-252, 259-260, 263, 266, 268, 269-270, 272, 277, 282-283, 285n1, 286, 288, 291-296, 303, 308, 310, 312, 314, 321, 328, 335, 366, 375; Upper Mississippi Outfit, 33; liquor trade with Indians, 127-140; support for scientific explorations, 172-173, 184, 218, 261; trade with the Crows, 185-187; Upper Missouri Outfit, 270n11, 271-272, 375
Arapaho Indians: 73, 196, 202-204, 207
Arikara Indians: 29n18, 68, 73, 165, 182-183, 192, 202, 209, 226, 285, 288, 290, 353n78
Arnold, John (Dr): 274n36, 282, 286-288
*Assiniboin* (steamboat): 36-37, 140
Assiniboine Indians: 38, 45-47, 70, 73-75, 102, 103, 104, 133, 157, 192, 202, 209, 211-212, 214-215, 225, 244, 249, 257, 285, 297-298, 300, 345, 347-348, 350, 367-368
Atchison, Donald R (Sen): 229
Atkinson-O'Fallon expedition: 29-30, 183
Audubon, John James: 21, 47n55, 62n16, 73n32, 101n20, 116-117, 136, 172-173, 212, 290; visit to Fort Union, 98-107; *The Birds of America*, 98, 116; *The Viviparous Quadrapeds of North America*, 98, 117

Badlands (Mauvaises Terres): 172-173, 180-182, 217-218, 281
Baird, Spencer: 172, 174, 183-184
Baker, Eugene M (Maj): 328-334, 336n49, 360
Baker Massacre. See Marias Massacre (1870)
Baldwin, Frank (Gen): 354
Bannack (MT): 297, 306-307, 352
*Banner State* (steamboat): 213
Bear Chief (Piegan): 44, 47n59, 56-57, 323-324

Bear Child (Piegan): 320
Bear Paw mountains: 47, 213
Bear's Rib (Hunkpapa): 295, 346
Bear's Shirt (Gros Ventre): 258
Beaver Child. See Culbertson, Alexander.
Bell, John: 98, 102
Bellevue: 136-137, 169, 177, 188-191
Belly River: 72, 86, 123, 329, 335, 339, 364
*Benton* (steamboat): 352
Benton, Thomas Hart (Sen): 134, 161, 312
Benwire, William: 348
Berry, Dick: 359
Berger, Jacob: 38, 120-121, 124-127, 141, 159-160
Bidwell, John: 146
Bidwell-Bartleson Party: 194, 199
Big Canoe (Flathead): 256, 258
Big Feather. See Big Plume.
Big Head (Assiniboine): 297-298
Big Head (Teton Lakota): 298
Big Horn (Piegan): 330n18, 331
Big Horn River (& basin): 185, 193
Big Leg (Piegan): 327, 329
Black Moon (Teton Lakota): 346
Big Plume (Blood): 92n35, 258, 265, 318, 343-344
Big Road (Blood): 77-80
Big Snake (Blood): 111, 114
Big Swan (Northern Blackfoot): 123-124
Bird, James: 251
Bitterroot Valley: 144, 146, 148, 231
Black Bear (Blood): 92n35, 343
Black Bear (Piegan): 324
Black Bear Woman (Piegan): 43n39, 296
Black Elk band (Blood): 309
Black Fish (Teton Lakota): 348
Black Hawk (Oglala): 204
Black Kettle (Cheyenne): 333
Black Moon (Teton Lakota): 346-347
Black Robes. See Jesuits.
Black Weasel (Piegan): 322, 324
Blackfeet agencies (Ft. Benton & Sun River): 296, 307, 314, 318-319, 325-327
Blackfeet Indians (see also Blood, Piegan, Northern Blackfoot): 18, 26, 38, 41, 43-45, 53, 57, 64-65, 79, 86n4, 87, 92, 97, 104, 105, 107, 109-110, 111n14, 113-116, 119-126, 130, 137, 141, 142-143, 148, 153-154, 159-161, 162n11, 163, 164, 165, 173, 181n60, 185,

187, 192, 204, 209, 211-212, 221, 222n12, 224, 231-233, 244, 260, 263, 277, 285, 288-289, 291-292, 295, 300, 306-307, 314-316, 318-321, 326-328, 334, 337, 340-341, 343, 351, 359-360, 375; smallpox epidemic (1837), 18, 70-72, 75; tribal divisions, 22, 38n16, 56; creation legends, 49-51; child rearing practices, 88-90; religion of, 149-153; 1853 Northern Pacific Railroad Survey, 217-220; treaty (1855), 19, 248-253-261, 269, 289, 291, 307, 309, 316, 363; treaty (1865), 309-310, 316, 318; treaty (1868), 318-319
Blackfeet missions (Jesuit & Presbyterian): 143, 148, 154, 156, 159-160, 262-263, 296, 313-314
Blackfeet Sioux Indians: 29n18, 181-182, 203n16, 244, 247, 249, 266-267, 292, 301, 346n34
Blackfeet "war": 306-327
*Blackfoot* (mackinaw): 225-227, 229
Blackfoot Indians. See Blackfeet Indians and Northern Blackfoot Indians.
Blacksnake Hills: 67, 175
Blood Indians: 18-19, 21, 38, 39, 43, 56-57, 61-62, 64, 65, 77-78, 80, 81, 84, 86-87, 91, 92, 93-95, 111n16, 122-123, 153, 155, 157, 159-160, 248, 255-256, 258, 260, 265, 308-310, 313-315, 318-322, 323n62, 325, 327, 329, 335-336, 337n52, 337n53, 338-344, 358-360, 362-365, 366n55, 367-369; smallpox epidemic (1837), 70-73; Fort McKenzie massacre (1844), 111, 112n22, 113
Blood Reserve (Canada): 21, 280n73, 323n62, 362, 364-365, 366n55, 368
Bodmer, Karl: 36-37, 40, 42, 47, 188
Boller, Henry: 300-301, 303, 307
Bonneville, Benjamin L E (Capt): 186
Bouis, Anthony: 142
Bourdeau, M J: 119
Bozeman, John: 316
Bozeman Trail: 193-194, 316
Braddock, Edward (Maj Gen): 27
Bradley, James (Lt): 21, 62n16, 83n22, 92n35, 114n30, 123n18, 166n31, 169n39, 171n1, 190n39, 254n69, 289n25, 351
Brave Bear (Oglala): 204
Brazeau, John: 70
Bridger, Jim: 199, 204, 265
Brown, B Gratz: 199
Bruguière, Jacques: 128-129, 177-178
Bruguière, James: 164
Brulé (Sioux) Indians: 197, 203-204, 245-247, 259
Bryan, Electa: 296
Buffalo Followers band (Blood): 61, 258
Bull's Back Fat (Blood): 72, 258; daughter of, 61-63
Burris, N W: 308, 309n79

Calf Shirt (Blood): 92n35, 309, 318-319, 321
Camp Cooke: 316
Campbell, Colin: 168
Campbell, Robert: 142, 196, 199-200, 243-244, 271
Canada: 56n33, 341-342, 354-355, 362, 365, 366n55; Department of Indian Affairs, 365
Carrol and Steell: 357
Carson, Charley: 308, 315
Carson, Kit: 308-309, 315
Cary, William de la Montagne: 294
Cass, Lewis: 76
Catlin, George: 35-36, 104
Cayuse Indians: 144
Cerré, M S: 131-132
Chambers, A B: 196, 199, 203, 205n28, 207
Chambersburg (PA): 13, 14, 25-26, 31n25, 34, 115n36, 171, 172n9, 174, 176, 184, 213n24, 224n21, 229-230, 272n24, 279, 281
Champaigne, Michel: 163
Chapman, Augustus: 315
Chardon, Francis: 67, 69, 98, 101-102, 107, 109-110, 111n19, 119, 120, 125, 127, 137-139, 165-166; Fort McKenzie massacre (1844), 111-116
Cheyenne Indians: 29n18, 170, 196-197, 201-204, 207, 245, 259
Chief Rabbit Runner (Northern Blackfoot): 258
Chief Moon (Blood): 368
Chilton, (Maj): 199
China: 261-262, 281; Ningpo, 261; Shanghai, 261
*Chippewa* (steamboat): 291, 306
Chittenden, Hiram Martin: 14, 16, 206n31, 374
Chouteau, Auguste: 101n20, 120, 133
Chouteau, Charles: 261, 272, 288, 308, 311, 372-373
Chouteau family: 33, 35, 101n20, 111n19, 243, 293
Chouteau, Pierre: 23, 25-26, 35, 36, 72, 79, 81, 82, 83, 98, 101n20, 107, 115-116, 142, 261, 269-271, 272; liquor trade with Indians, 128, 130, 132-134, 137-140
Civil War: 115n36, 213n24, 224n21, 282, 286n4, 293, 304, 306, 318, 327, 334, 352
*Clara* (steamboat): 260
Clark, William (Gen): 29, 55, 128, 132-133
Clarke, Helen: 81n18, 322-324
Clarke, Horace: 322-324, 329, 333
Clarke, Malcolm: 81-82, 84, 120-121, 124-127, 141, 142-143, 154, 159, 163, 164, 183, 222, 292, 314; killing of, 321-324, 327-328
Clarke, Nathan: 329
Coats, James: 63
Cobell, Joe: 296-297, 328-331
Cody, "Buffalo" Bill: 267, 294
Coeur d'Alene Indians: 147
Collins, John: 103-104

# INDEX 393

Columbia Fur Company: 39
Columbia River: 213, 216
Connoyer, Caroline: 43n39, 290, 296-297, 320n46
Conquering Bear (Brulé): 205, 245-246
Cooper, (Col): 199
Cornoyer, Clement: 308
Council Bluffs (IA): 67, 120, 130, 133, 145, 166, 176-177
Cowen, Benjamin R: 348
Craighead, John (Rev): 30
Cree Indians: 136, 147n44, 255, 257, 285, 315, 363
Crow Creek: 166, 168, 179
Crow Indians: 18, 19, 29n18, 66, 73, 79, 122, 146, 153, 155, 185-187, 192-193, 202, 205, 244, 257, 260, 265, 285, 287, 292, 300, 307n62, 315, 319, 323; siege of Ft. McKenzie (1834), 61-65, 80
Crowfoot (Northern Blackfoot): 323n62, 363
Culbertson (MT): 354, 367
Culbertson, Alexander (1714-1756; Capt): 13, 15, 17, 27-28, 34
Culbertson, Alexander: 13, 17, 32, 46-47, 51, 56, 57, 59, 66, 94n47, 112n22, 114n30, 115n36, 117, 119-121, 123n18, 125-126, 134, 141n5, 142-143, 153-165, 166n31, 166n32, 166n36, 171n1, 171n4, 173n18, 174n21, 175-183, 185-190, 210n9, 211-213, 215-216, 230n43, 233n58, 243-245, 247, 259-260, 267-268, 270n11, 271n17, 274n36, 277n57, 285-298, 300, 303-304, 328-329, 335-342, 344, 352-355, 357-358, 360, 362, 366, 369; partner in AFC, 14, 163, 252, 270; as diplomat, 17, 20, 165-169, 225-228, 325-326; early demonstrations of bravery, 18-19, 24, 77-79; leaves home, 25-26, 30-31; birth of, 26-27; childhood of, 28-30; offered job with AFC, 33-34; meets Kenneth McKenzie, 35, 37; description of Prince Maximilian, 37; posted to Fort McKenzie, 18, 38-40; meets Seen From Afar, 43; first marriage, 45; 1834 siege of Fort McKenzie, 60-65; 1837 smallpox epidemic, 70-75; problems with Alexander Harvey, 79-84; courtship and marriage to Natawista, 91-95; entertains Audubon, 97-107; 1844 Fort McKenzie massacre, 109-116; establishes Fort Lewis, 121-124; liquor trade with Indians, 129-130, 135-138, 141; health problems, 169-171; scientific explorations of, 172-174, 184; Fort Laramie treaty conference (1851), 191-195, 199, 202, 204, 206, 209-210, 214; Northern Pacific Railroad Survey (1853), 217-224; lobbying in Washington, DC, 229-233; Blackfeet treaty conference (1855), 248-252, 254-255, 258; Presbyterian Mission to the Blackfeet, 261-263; Sir St. George Gore, 264-267; retires from AFC, 269-272; life in Peoria, 274-284; bankruptcy of, 276n56, 284, 310-312; attack at Tobacco Garden, 301-302; Blackfeet "war," 307, 310, 313, 315n13, 316-317, 319-321, 327; employment with government, 345-351; death of, 355; marking of grave, 371-375
Culbertson, Anna: 274
Culbertson, Anna Mary: 34
Culbertson, Cyrus Duncan: 34
Culbertson, Ferdinand: 166n36, 183-184
Culbertson, Frances "Fannie" (daughter): 25-26, 34n40, 106n46, 115n36, 188, 213, 224n21, 230, 272-274, 278-279, 280n73, 290, 295, 311-312, 316-317, 337n52, 353, 355, 368-369
Culbertson, Frances Stuart (stepmother): 17, 30, 32, 34, 171-172, 175, 188, 230, 278
Culbertson, James: 174, 274n35
Culbertson, Jane "Janie" (daughter): 94n47, 95, 272, 278-280, 310
Culbertson, John: 367
Culbertson, John "Jack" (son): 106-107, 115, 123, 180, 182, 213, 272, 278, 280n73, 281-283, 290, 294, 300, 303, 311, 350, 367
Culbertson, John Craighead: 29-33, 82, 171, 174n22, 183, 261n42
Culbertson, Joseph (1720-1794; great-grandfather): 15, 27, 28
Culbertson, Joseph (father): 15, 25, 26, 30, 171, 172n9, 173, 183n66, 230, 277, 278
Culbertson, Joseph "Joe" (son): 164n22, 277, 280n73, 295, 300, 303-304, 311-312, 315n13, 316-317, 320, 336n51, 337, 338n56, 339-342, 345-348, 350-351, 353-355, 365-368
Culbertson, Julia (daughter): 95n50, 101n20, 115n36, 119, 123, 160, 180, 182, 213, 230n45, 272, 277-280, 311, 336n51, 352-353, 355, 371-374
Culbertson, Lewis: 15
Culbertson, Maria. See Culbertson, Mariah (daughter).
Culbertson, Mariah (daughter): 94n47, 95, 154, 272, 278, 311, 317n28, 350
Culbertson, Mary: 367
Culbertson, Mary Dunlap: 261-262
Culbertson, Mary Finley (mother): 26, 30, 31, 230
Culbertson, Michael Simpson: 216, 261-262, 281
Culbertson, Nancy (daughter): 170, 180, 182, 213, 272-273
Culbertson, Nancy Agnes: 15
Culbertson, Nancy McCulloh: 273, 280-282, 293n60
Culbertson, Natawista or Nellie. See Natawista.
Culbertson, Robert (Col; grandfather): 15, 28, 31, 337

Culbertson, Robert (1722-?): 27
Culbertson, Robert Simpson: 317, 318n32, 318n34, 319
Culbertson, Samuel (Col): 15, 28
Culbertson, Samuel ("Tanner"): 15
Culbertson, Samuel (1715-1789): 27
Culbertson, Thaddeus: 171-185, 230, 269
Culbertson, William: 273, 281, 293n60
Culbertson's Row (PA): 27-28
Cullen, William J: 318
Cumberland Valley (PA): 27-28, 34, 36
Cumming, Alfred: 227, 243, 259-260, 266-267, 278; Blackfeet treaty conference (1855): 249-255, 257-258
Custer, George Armstrong (Gen): 353-354
Cutting Off Head Woman (Piegan): 321-322
Cypress Hills: 222, 338

Dakota Indians: 203n16, 226-228, 303n39
Daughters of the American Revolution (DAR): 15, 31n25, 374
Davis, D W: 361-362
Davis, Jefferson: 217
Dawson, Andrew: 262, 294
De Smet, Jean Pierre (Rev): 19, 76, 143, 145-148, 153-155, 158n44, 160, 165, 188n20, 189-190, 213, 262, 265, 268, 273, 291n47, 295-296, 299, 304-305, 314, 316; Fort Laramie treaty conference (1851): 192-195, 199-200, 204-210, 212n21
De Trobriand, Philippe (Brig Gen): 319n41, 327-333
Delaware Indians: 13, 27
Denig, Edwin Thompson: 36, 74n45, 83, 103, 104, 106, 114n30, 124, 128, 130, 158, 183-184, 186-187, 211n13, 292
Deschamps family: 66
Dickinson College (Carlisle, PA): 172
Distant Bear (Piegan): 47
Doane, Gus (Lt): 331-333
Dodge, Augustus C (Sen): 229
Donelson, Andrew Jackson: 217
Doty, James: 217, 251, 255
Doucette (AFC): 41
Double Strike Woman (Piegan): 332
Dougherty, John: 134
Douglas, Stephen (Sen): 282
Drips, Andrew: 135, 137, 146
Drouillard, George: 55
DuBarry, Beekman: 217
Duncan, (Capt): 199
Durfee and Peck: 345

Eagle Feather (Blood): 91
Eagle's Rib (Piegan): 323-324
Eagles Rib (Blood): 92n35, 323n62, 367-368
Earth Woman (Mandan): 328
Ebbetts, Cutting and Kelsey: 134-135

Edgerton, Sidney (Gov): 309, 313
*El Paso* (steamboat): 182-184, 187
Elbow River: 357-359
Eldridge, Charles (Rep): 334
Elliott, (Lt) & Mrs.: 199
England: 128-130, 136
Evans, John: 180n49, 182, 189-190, 217-218

Fanton, W H (Maj): 350
Fat Horses band (Blood): 309
Father of Many (All) Children: 86n5, 258, 363-364
Fields, Reuben: 55
Fillmore, Millard (President): 216
Finch, (Capt): 167
Finley, James: 31, 230
Fish Child (Northern Blackfoot): 309
Fish Eaters band (Blood): 43, 86, 91, 92, 94, 155-156, 163, 258, 309, 335, 343, 361
Fitzpatrick, Thomas: 196-197, 199-201, 203-204, 206-207
Flathead Indians: 144-148, 153, 156-157, 164, 231, 255-257, 289, 314, 315
Flathead mission: 213, 289, 291n47
Fleming, Hugh (Lt): 246
*Flora* (keelboat): 40-42, 44
Floyd, Charles (Sgt): 177
Floyd's Bluff: 177, 215
Fool Bear (Assiniboine): 192, 211-212, 214-215, 244
Fort Abraham Lincoln: 353
Fort Alexander: 146, 154-155, 186-187
Fort Belknap: 46, 350-353
Fort Benton (see also Fort Lewis): 112n22, 121, 161-165, 170, 174n21, 181n60, 187-189, 213, 218, 222-223, 225, 229, 231-233, 245, 248, 250-253, 260, 262-263, 265, 267-268, 271-272, 279, 287, 289, 290-292, 295-297, 303, 307-310, 313-315, 317-321, 323, 325, 328, 332, 335-336, 337n52, 338, 341-342, 344-345, 349-351, 357-358, 368, 375
Fort Berthold: 165, 209, 226, 267, 288, 293, 301
Fort Browning: 345-349, 358
Fort Brûlé: 113
Fort Buford: 354, 355n87
Fort Campbell: 142, 162
Fort Cass: 185
Fort Clark: 67-69, 82, 98, 107, 109, 119, 135, 146, 165, 182, 226, 247, 288, 290
Fort Edmonton: 313
Fort FAC: 113-115, 119-121, 124
Fort George: 127
Fort Hall: 146
Fort Hawley: 316
Fort Honoré: 122
Fort John. See Fort Laramie.
Fort Kearny: 169-170, 196
Fort Laramie: 106-108, 114, 115, 119, 145, 169-

# INDEX  395

170, 171, 173, 187, 245-246, 264, 272, 375; treaty conference (1851): 19, 23, 191, 193-209, 211, 212n21, 214, 216-217, 224, 244-245, 252, 269, 273
Fort Leavenworth: 67, 169
Fort Lewis: 122-124, 138, 142-143, 153-155, 157-160, 161, 164, 165
Fort Lookout: 154
Fort Macleod: 359-362, 364
Fort McKenzie: 26, 38, 40, 41, 44, 45, 47, 56, 59, 66, 71-72, 75, 76, 77, 79, 80, 81, 83, 84, 92, 93, 97, 98, 101, 107, 109-110, 111n19, 115n34, 121, 131, 134-135, 162, 350, 375; massacre (1844), 14, 18, 19, 111-114, 120, 123, 137-138, 142, 165, 337; Crow siege (1834), 19, 60-65, 80
Fort Mortimer: 103-104
Fort Peck: 323n62, 345-346, 348-349, 353, 365-368
Fort Piegan: 39-40
Fort Pierre: 37, 59, 66, 76, 107, 114, 115, 119, 120, 121, 125-126, 135, 142, 143n15, 146, 164, 165n30, 166, 170-171, 173, 180-182, 188, 191, 214, 218, 227, 245-247, 259-260, 262, 266, 288, 290, 295, 300, 304
Fort Randall: 305
Fort Rice: 327
Fort Sarpy: 187, 192-193, 209, 244, 288
Fort Shaw: 316, 327-328, 330, 332
Fort Snelling: 33
Fort Stand-off: 342
Fort Stevenson: 327
Fort Sully: 304
Fort Totten: 327
Fort Union: 18, 35-39, 59, 60, 65-66, 69, 70, 74, 77, 79, 82-83, 94, 98-99, 102-104, 108, 114-115, 119-120, 123-124, 128, 130-131, 136-138, 142-143, 146, 154, 162-164, 170-171, 183, 185-188, 192, 209-211, 213-215, 217-218, 220, 221, 225, 244-245, 248, 250, 262-263, 266, 272-273, 276, 280, 288, 292, 301-304, 306-307, 328, 351, 375
Fort Van Buren: 185
Fort Vancouver: 289
Fort Walla Walla: 291
Fort Warren: 359
Fort Whoop-Up: 341n1, 342, 344-345, 357, 359
Fort William: 66, 70, 120
Four Bears (Hidatsa): 192
French and Indian War: 13, 15, 27
Frightening Bear. See Conquering Bear.
Fringe (Piegan): 315

Galbraith, Thomas: 299
Galpin, Charles: 260
Gantt, Thomas: 138-141
Gay, F A: 371, 373
*General Brooke* (steamboat): 138

Gibson: 367
Gladstone, William: 308
Gore, Sir St George: 264-267
Grant, Ulysses S (President): 349
Grattan, John (Lt): 246-247
Grattan Massacre: 245-247, 259
Gray Eyes (Blood): 92n35, 319, 327
Gray Wolf (Piegan): 330
Great Father or Great White Father. See United States government.
Green River rendezvous: 144-146
Gros Ventre Indians: 41, 56, 65, 73, 84, 153, 192, 221-224, 226, 248, 255-256, 260, 306-307, 309, 315, 345, 347-348, 350, 368, 375
Grove, Henry: 311
Grover, Cuvier (Lt): 217
Gruard (Grouard), Frank: 353
Guèpe (AFC): 101

Hall, James: 218
Halsey, Jacob: 69
Ham, George: 365-366
Hamel, Augustin: 81, 163
Hamilton, Alfred: 341-342, 357, 359, 361
Hamilton, Hans: 28
Hamilton, James Archdale: 37, 64n26, 65, 72, 74, 80, 129
Hamilton, Joseph Varnum: 137
Hanson, Charles E Jr: 210n9, 371, 374
Hardie, James Allen: 328-329
Harney, William (Gen): 259-261
Harris, Edward: 98, 102-104
Harrison, William Henry (President): 134
Harvey, Alexander: 36, 63, 70, 77-78, 83n22, 98, 109-110, 121, 125-127, 138-139, 160, 162-164, 165, 173n18, 250, 321; pugnacious character of, 80-84, 110-111, 168; Fort McKenzie massacre (1844), 111-116; attacked by AFC employees, 119-121, 124; forms opposition company, 141-143
Harvey, Primeau and Company: 142, 162, 164, 168, 173n18, 182, 211, 243, 250, 272
Harvey, Thomas: 140-141, 168, 191
Hastings (Lt): 199
Hatch, Edwin A C: 250, 260, 262-263
Hatton, William S: 214
Hawkins, Jim: 174
Hawley, Alpheus: 308
Hayden, Ferdinand Vandeveer: 218
He That Looks at the Calf (Piegan): 56
Healy, John: 341-342, 357, 359, 36
Heavy Runner (Piegan): 319, 327, 329-334, 336n49
Helena (MT): 315, 320, 321, 333, 359
Henry, Alexander: 127
Hidatsa Indians: 29n18, 73, 165, 192, 202, 209
High Forehead (Miniconjou): 245-246
Hodgkiss, William D: 170, 303, 307

Hoecken, Adrian (Rev): 291
Hoecken, Christian (Rev): 189-190
Holy Snake. See Natawista.
*Honduras* (steamboat): 229
Horse Creek: 106, 195, 197-199, 202, 209
Horse Creek treaty conference (1851). See Fort Laramie.
Hubbell, James: 308
Hudson's Bay Company: 38, 39, 76, 116n38, 144, 308, 341; liquor trade with Indians, 127-129, 136
Hunkpapa (Sioux) Indians: 29n18, 203n16, 244, 247, 249, 266-267, 292, 294-295, 301, 345, 346n34, 354
Hunt, Jane Culbertson. See Culbertson, Jane "Janie" (daughter).

I G Baker and Company: 341
Idaho Territory: 304, 307, 372-374
Imoda, John (Rev): 334
Ingersoll, Bob: 282
Intercourse Laws. See liquor in the Indian trade.
intertribal trade: 54, 222, 226, 345
intertribal warfare: 45-47, 53-54, 56, 57, 61, 65, 104, 109, 122, 135, 138, 155, 157, 167, 169-170, 197, 201, 209, 210, 211-212, 219, 221-222, 244, 249, 257, 260, 285-286, 292, 315, 320, 346-348, 350, 354, 368
Iowa (Yankton): 166-167
Iowa, Sac, and Fox Indians: 215
Iron Bear (Arikara): 192
Iron Dog (Teton Lakota): 346
Iron Shirt (Blood): 44, 57
Iroquois Indians: 144
Irvin, Frances "Fannie" Culbertson. See Culbertson, Frances "Fannie" (daughter).
Irvin, Louis: 353, 369

Jackson (Piegan): 322
Jackson, Andrew (President): 82
James River: 171, 179, 288
Jefferson, Thomas (President): 54
Jemison, Mary: 17
Jesuits: 76, 143-149, 153-157, 159-160, 289, 291, 314, 338
Judith River: 70, 113, 253, 255, 263, 278, 316

Kah-ta-Nah (Blood/Gros Ventre): 84
Kainah Indians. See Blood Indians.
Kanouse, Henry Alfred "Fred": 357-362, 364, 366
Kanouse, Jacob: 357
Kellogg, (Judge): 282
Kennerly, Henry: 320
Ketchum, (Capt): 195
Kettelle, George H: 277
*Key West* (steamboat): 291, 294
Kipp, James: 14, 39-40, 60, 79, 80, 138, 142-143, 164, 166n32, 170, 250, 277-278, 328, 350
Kipp, Joseph "Joe": 328-333, 342, 369
Kipp, Julia: 95n50, 278n63
Kipp, Mariah Culbertson. See Culbertson, Mariah (daughter).
Kipp, Samuel: 278, 317n28, 350n59
Kisenaw: 280-281, 339n59
Kit Fox (Blood): 343-344, 361
Kootenai Indians: 359
Kurz, Rudolph: 188-190, 209-210, 211n13, 211n16, 212-213, 250

La Barge, John (Capt): 288
La Barge, Joseph (Capt): 99, 166n36, 167, 301-302
La Vérendrye, Pierre: 54
Ladies' Soldiers Aide Society of the Second Presbyterian Church (Peoria, IL): 282
Laidlaw, William: 79, 80, 81, 82, 107, 128, 137, 170
Laird, David: 363
Lambdin, Robert B: 215
Lame Bull (Piegan): 257-258, 260, 263
Lame Bull's Treaty. See Blackfeet: treaty (1855).
Lander, Frederick: 217
Larpenteur, Charles: 66, 69, 70, 74, 75, 80, 82, 83, 114n30, 114n33, 120, 124-125, 128-129, 137, 142-143, 154-155, 164-165, 185-186, 215, 283
Latour, Jean: 162
Latta, Samuel: 293, 295, 300-302, 307
Leavenworth (KS): 129, 130, 136
LeDouck (AFC): 70-71
Lee, James: 120-121, 124-127, 141, 160
Lee, Jason: 144
Leighton and Jordan: 354
Lennemann, Mrs. William: 374
Lewis & Clark expedition: 13, 21, 29, 54-55, 91, 123, 177
Lewis, Meriwether: 19, 42, 54-56, 122
L'Heureux, Jean: 338
Lincoln, Abraham (President): 282, 293, 299
liquor in the Indian trade: 36, 39, 41, 127-140, 166, 214, 307, 338, 341-345, 357, 360-363
Little Chief (Cheyenne): 202
Little Crow (Santee): 299
Little Dog (Assiniboine): 70
Little Dog (Piegan): 92n35, 222, 245, 256, 258, 292, 297, 309, 313, 315, 328, 336
Little Soldier (Gros Ventre): 258
Little Wolf (Piegan): 327
Little Wound (Teton Lakota): 346
Locust Grove (Peoria home of Culbertsons): 274-277, 281-282, 310
Logan, John (Rep): 334
Long Dog (Teton Lakota): 346
Long Hair (Assiniboine): 46, 350
Looking Glass (Nez Perce): 258

# INDEX

Loretto (AFC): 81
Low Horn (Piegan): 223
Lowrie, Walter (Sen): 261
Lowrie, Walter Macon (Rev): 261
Lukins, Peter: 320

MacDougall, John: 364
Mackey, Elkanah (Rev): 21, 261-264, 269
Mackey, Sarah Armstrong: 261-264
Maclay, Eleanor "Ellen": 34
Macleod, James (Col): 363
Maffitt, William: 271-272
Magri, Vincent (Br): 291
Man Afraid of His Horses (Oglala): 246
Mandan Indians: 29n18, 30, 39, 43, 54, 60, 109, 130, 165, 192, 202, 209, 285, 288, 328; smallpox epidemic (1837): 67-69, 73, 109, 165
Many Shot (Blood): 343
Manypenny, George: 229-232, 247, 258
Marias Massacre (1870): 329-335, 338
Marias River: 40, 46, 55, 78, 95n50, 163, 308, 330, 358
Marsh, Elias (Dr): 290-291
*Martha* (steamboat): 162, 166-169, 214
Martin, Henry: 309n79
*Mary Blane* (steamboat): 174-175
Matlock, Gideon C: 166-168, 179
Maximilian, Prince of Wied-Neuwied: 36-38, 40-43, 45-47, 57, 74, 99, 130-131, 172-173, 188, 317
McClellan, George (Gen): 217
McClellan, John: 313
McClelland, R: 232, 267
McCord's Fort: 13, 15, 28
McCormick, Silas: 353
McCulloh, Robert: 280-281
McCulloh, Thomas: 293, 310-312
McGeachin, James: 373
McGeachin, Janet: 355, 373
McKay, Walter (Pvt): 331
McKenzie, Kenneth: 14, 35, 36-40, 43, 59-60, 64n26, 65, 66, 69, 79, 100, 103, 321; liquor trade with Indians, 128-133, 138n58
McKenzie, Owen: 100, 103, 105, 180, 321
McLaughlin, Jean McGeachin: 374
Meagher, Thomas (Gov): 315-316
Medicine Bear (Teton Lakota): 348-349
Medicine Calf (Blood): 363
Medicine Snake. See Natawista.
Medill, William: 139
Meek, Fielding Bradford: 217
Meldrum, Robert: 186-187, 192n47, 193, 202, 205, 292
Métis: 147n44, 214
Mexican War: 188, 216
Mexico: 30, 146, 188
M'Gillivray, Duncan: 127

Milk River: 41, 163, 183-184, 213, 221, 248, 251-252, 262, 297, 335, 338, 345-346, 354
Miniconjou (Sioux) Indians: 203n16, 245-247, 259, 295, 301
Minnesota: 33, 217, 299, 304, 345, 346n34
Mississippi River: 33, 35, 173-174, 217
Missouri River: 13, 17, 18, 19, 29, 33, 35, 36, 38, 40-42, 54, 57, 65, 67, 68, 71, 73, 76, 79, 80, 82, 83, 95, 97, 98, 103n30, 104, 105, 108, 111n19, 113, 114, 117, 120, 121, 130, 133, 134, 135, 137-138, 140, 145, 146, 149, 156, 160, 161, 163, 168, 171, 172, 173, 184, 187, 188, 191, 213, 214, 224, 225, 231, 233, 260, 264, 270, 272-273, 276, 280, 285, 286, 288, 293, 294, 296-297, 299, 304, 308-309, 312, 313, 315, 335, 347, 349, 350, 352, 354, 375
Mitchell, David: 14, 18, 40-41, 43-44, 46-47, 56-57, 59-60, 64, 73n32, 79, 134-135, 214-215, 243; Fort Laramie treaty conference (1851): 191-192, 195-197, 199-207, 209, 210n9, 212n21
Mo-kwee (Gros Ventre): 135
Moncravie (AFC): 80
Montana Territory: 43n39, 55, 56n33, 144, 281, 307, 320, 324, 326, 329, 332-334, 340-341, 345, 358, 360, 362, 365, 375
Mooney, Thomas: 365
Moravian Seminary for Young Ladies (Bethlehem, PA): 188n20, 279-280, 311
Morgan, John: 314
Morgan, Lewis Henry: 92
Mountain Chief (Piegan): 43n39, 258, 316, 318, 320, 322-324, 328-329, 334
Mouse (Sans Arc): 295
Mullan, John (Lt): 217, 231-232, 245, 291
Mullan Road: 291, 349
Murray, James: 186
Musselshell River: 256, 316

Nabors, Jim: 358-360
Napi (legendary): 49-51, 85-86, 86n4, 149-151
Nasselle (AFC): 177
Nataska (tribe unknown): 287
Natawista (Blood): 20, 21, 24, 86n5, 92n35, 94n47, 100-101, 103-107, 115, 123, 155, 159-160, 162-163, 170, 180, 182, 187-188, 210, 213, 222, 225, 230, 245, 248, 257-258, 262-265, 273, 276n56, 280n73, 286, 288-290, 295-296, 300, 303-304, 306, 310-313, 315n13, 316, 319, 320n46, 323n62, 328, 338, 340-341, 343-344, 351, 355, 366-369, 374-375; courtship and marriage, 91-95; name variants, 23, 91n31, 91n32; Northern Pacific railroad survey (1853), 218-224; life in Peoria, 274-283; ability to speak English, 290-291, 365-366; attack at Tobacco Garden, 301-302; returns to live with Bloods, 335-337; life with Fred Kanouse, 357-362, 364

Natoyist-siksina'. See Natawista.
Nevitt, Richard Barrington: 362
New York (NY): 115-116, 119, 130, 170, 262, 289
Newton, George: 367
Nez Perce Indians: 144, 153, 255
Nicholas (Piegan): 148
Nicollet, Jean Nicolas: 173
*Nimrod* (steamboat): 137-138
North West Company: 35
North West Fur Co: 308, 319, 328, 330, 341
North-West Mounted Police: 360, 362-363
Northern Blackfoot Indians: 21, 38n16, 56, 73, 112-113, 123-124, 142, 153, 255-256, 258, 308-310, 315, 320n44, 323n62, 325, 341, 343-344, 362-364
Northern Pacific railroad survey (1853): 19, 216-224, 250-251, 269, 275, 337
Norwood, James: 214-215
Not Real Good (Blood): 361

O'Fallon, Benjamin (Maj): 29
Officer, Rebecca: 15
Oglala (Sioux) Indians: 29n18, 203n16, 204, 245-247, 259
Old Ignace (Iroquois/Flathead): 144-145
Old Man (legendary). See Napi.
Old Woman (legendary): 49-50, 85-87
Oldman River: 72n30, 342, 359-360
*Omega* (steamboat): 98-99, 101, 136
Ophir (MT): 308-309, 314
Oregon Territory: 116n38, 194
Oregon-California Trail: 146, 169, 191, 194-195, 200, 316
Orleans (NE): 336n51, 352, 355, 371-375
Orr, James (Rep): 230
Osage Indians: 109, 204, 215
Ott, Elmer C: 374
Otter Woman (Blood): 335
Owl Child, Pete (Piegan): 322-324, 327n2

Painted Bear (tribe unknown): 204
Paper Woman (Blood): 361
Parker, Ely: 327
Parker, Mary: 374
Parker, Samuel (Rev): 144
Parkville (MO): 277, 278n63, 317n28, 350
Pawnee Indians: 29n18, 169-170, 182
Pease, William: 332-334
Peigan Indians. See Piegan Indians.
Pend d'Oreille Indians: 255
Peoria (IL): 188n20, 273-274, 276-282, 285-287, 289-290, 310, 335, 339n59, 352, 357
Philadelphia (PA): 109, 271
Philadelphia Academy of Natural Sciences: 172n9, 173
Picotte, Honoré: 114-115, 119-120, 122, 125-126, 129, 138, 142-143, 163, 167, 182, 188-190

Picotte, Joseph: 119, 126, 142, 211
Piegan Indians: 19, 21, 38-39, 45-47, 55-56, 112n22, 113, 122, 127, 142, 148, 153, 155, 222-223, 245, 248, 255-256, 258, 260, 263, 265, 290, 292, 296, 307-310, 314-316, 318-320, 323n62, 325, 332, 338-339, 351, 360, 362, 365, 368; smallpox epidemic (1837), 70-73; killing of Malcolm Clarke, 321-324, 327; Marias Massacre (1870), 329-334
Pierce, Franklin (President): 216, 230, 251, 260
Pierre's Hole: 41, 146, 186
Pikuni Indians. See Piegan Indians.
Pilcher, Joshua: 73, 133-134
Plains Indians (see also specific tribes): 51-53, 55, 57, 68, 75, 102, 197, 203, 215
Platte River: 33, 106, 115, 137, 169-170, 197, 204, 208
Pocklington, William: 323n62, 367-369
Point, Nicholas (Rev): 19, 143, 146-148, 153-162, 165
polygyny: 90, 93, 158, 223
Ponca Indians: 29n18
Poplar River: 120, 170, 183, 183n70, 306, 366n55
Potawatomi Indians: 145, 189
Potts, Andrew: 135
Powder River: 193, 265
Powell, L E: 169
Pratte, Bernard: 67-68
Presbyterian Board of Missions: 261-264
Pretty Woman (Blood): 42-43
Primeau, Charles: 126, 142
Princeton Theological Seminary: 171, 261-262
Prout, Hiram: 173

Rainy Chief (Blood): 364
Randell (AFC): 179
Red Coat. See Culbertson, Alexander.
Red Crow (Blood): 92n35, 323n62, 343-344, 361, 363-369
Red Deer Woman (Blood): 86, 91, 92
Red Horn (Piegan): 330n18, 331
Red Stone (Assiniboine): 347-348
Red River: 144, 147n44, 214
Redfield, Alexander: 288-289
Reed, Henry H (Rev): 295-297, 300, 306-307
Reese (AFC): 111; James, Joseph, 111n19
Rem, Jack: 66
Revenge Walker (Blood): 361-362
Revolutionary War: 13, 28, 29, 30, 337
Reynolds, Charlie: 353
Rhett, (Capt): 199
Rides on the Clouds (Cheyenne): 202
Riplinger, John: 308, 310, 330, 337n53
River Crow Indians: 316, 345, 350
*Robert Campbell* (steamboat): 217-218, 280, 300-301
Roberts, Alexander Culbertson: 373n12

# INDEX

Roberts, Caroline: 372-373
Roberts, George H: 115n36, 290, 336n51, 352-353, 355, 371-374
Roberts, Julia Culbertson. See Culbertson, Julia.
Roberts, Margaret "Maggie": 352, 372-374
Roberts, Mariah: 95n50, 373n12
Robidoux, Joseph: 67, 175
Rock Old Man (Blood): 320
Rocky Mountain House: 127
Rocky Spring Presbyterian Church: 30-31, 230
Rosati, (Bishop): 145
Rosebud River: 185, 193
Rotten Belly (Crow): 62, 65-66
Round Iron. See Meldrum, Robert.
Running Bird (Blood): 361
Running Rabbit (Blood/Piegan): 365
Running Wolf. See Harvey, Alexander.

Sacagawea (Shoshone): 20, 91
Sacred Heart Mission: 147
Sacred Woman (Blood): 92n35
*St. Ange* (steamboat): 189-191, 195
St. Joseph (MO): 174-176, 188-190, 229, 277, 279
St. Louis (MO): 25, 33, 34, 36, 37, 67, 79, 80, 81, 82, 83n22, 97, 98, 99, 119, 120, 125, 126, 127, 128, 132, 133, 137, 138, 141, 142, 144-146, 154, 157, 162, 163, 164, 166n32, 169, 171, 173, 174, 180, 184, 189-190, 195, 199, 213, 214, 215, 217-218, 224, 226, 229, 232, 233, 243-244, 249, 250, 259-260, 262, 266, 268, 278-279, 280n77, 286, 287, 288, 290, 294, 298, 300, 335, 348
*St. Mary* (steamboat): 250, 261-262
St. Mary's River: 72, 335, 342
St. Mary's Mission: 146-148, 153, 165
*St. Peters* (steamboat): 67-70
Sandoval, Isidoro: 72, 77, 83-85, 321
Sanford, John F A: 36, 38, 270-271
Sans Arc (Sioux) Indians: 203n16, 295
Santee (Sioux) Indians: 203n16, 299, 346n34
Sarcee Indians: 315, 362
Sargent, Aaron (Rep): 334
Sarpy, John: 125, 126, 167, 270-272
Sarpy, Peter: 138n58, 177
Sata (Flathead/Blackfeet): 165
Saxton, Rufus (Lt): 217, 225-228
Scanlon, Thomas (Rev): 277
Schoonover, Bernard: 292-293
Scollen, Constantine (Rev): 343
Sebastian, William (Sen): 230
Secret (Santee Sioux): 347
Seen From Afar (Blood): 42-43, 92-95, 122-123, 155-157, 163, 257-258, 260, 275, 276n56, 313, 315, 318-319, 335-336, 343, 365
Shaw, John: 271
Sheep Old Man (Blood): 344, 361
Sheridan, Philip H (Lt Gen): 326, 328-329

Sherman, William Tecumseh (Gen): 316, 326, 334
Shields, James (Sen): 229
Shonkin Creek: 84, 296
Shoshone Indians: 20, 91, 197, 201-202
*Shreveport* (steamboat): 300-301
Sibley, Henry (Gen): 299, 304
Sideling Hill (PA; battle of): 13-14, 28
Siksika Indians. See Northern Blackfoot Indians.
Silverthorne, John: 267-268
Simmons, Andrew J: 345-349
Sioux City (IA): 177, 290, 300, 348n42
Sioux Indians (see also specific bands): 23, 76, 107, 109, 145, 168, 169, 177-179, 181n60, 185, 196, 202, 203n16, 204-205, 209, 211, 214, 227, 244, 259, 285, 289-290, 292, 294-295, 298, 300, 303-306, 328, 345, 348, 351, 352, 354
Sire, Joseph: 136, 138, 270
Sitting Bull (Hunkpapa): 294, 345-348, 354-355, 365
Sitting Eagle (Teton Lakota): 346
smallpox: 272, 332, 334-336, 342-343; epidemic (1837), 14, 18, 67-76, 92, 94n47, 109, 165
Small Robes band (Piegan): 148, 153
Smith, Charles: 167, 169
Smithsonian Institution: 172n7, 172n9, 184, 217-218, 287
Smutty Bear (Yankton): 167-168
Snake (Oglala): 204
Society of Jesus. See Jesuits.
Sohon, Gustavus: 275n54
Spalding, Henry (Rev): 144
Spokane Indians: 289
Spotted Eagle (Nez Perce): 258
Sprague, Isaac: 98, 101n20
*Spread Eagle* (steamboat): 287-288, 294-295, 300
Squires, Lewis: 98, 101, 103, 105
Standing Buffalo (Santee Sioux): 347
Stand-off (Alberta, Canada): 369
Stanley, John Mix: 217, 222-223, 233, 275-276, 277n57, 281, 310; Barter for a Bride, 276; Last of their Race, 276
Stevens, Charles (Dr): 261
Stevens, Isaac: 19, 21, 216, 221n3, 222n12, 225, 228, 229, 231-233, 243, 245, 261, 278, 289, Northern Pacific railroad survey (1853), 217-224; Blackfeet treaty conference (1855), 248-259, 290
Stoney Indians: 362
Stuart, James: 349
Sublette, William: 133
Sully, Alfred (Gen): 304-305, 320, 325-329, 331
Sun dance: 43, 91
Sun River: 292, 296, 313-314, 316, 341, 349

Terra Blue (Brulé): 197-198, 203

Teton Sioux (Lakota) Indians: 29n18, 203n16, 297, 346-349, 366-367
Teton River: 111, 161, 291, 309, 318, 325
Thompson, David: 56
Three Bulls (Northern Blackfoot): 258, 318
Tilton, (Col): 174
Tinkham, Abiel: 217
Tobacco Garden: 301-302, 306
Tongue River: 193, 265
Townsend, E D (Bvt Maj Gen): 326
*Trapper* (steamboat): 82-83
Treaty No 7 (1877): 363-365
Trivett, Samuel (Rev): 364
Two Kettles band (Sioux): 203n16, 300
Two Medicine River: 43, 55
Two Suns (Blood): 43, 86, 91-93, 94n47, 155
Three Forks: 18, 72, 148
Three Suns (Piegan): 315

Union Fur Company: 103
United States government: 20, 76, 91, 116n38, 127, 129, 134, 166-167, 171, 191, 196, 200-201, 203, 208-210, 214, 218, 223, 227-228, 231-233, 243, 246-247, 250, 255-258, 264, 271, 278, 288, 295, 305, 310, 313, 316, 325-327, 334, 346-347, 350, 365, 368, 375; Bureau of Indian Affairs: 29, 139, 168, 217, 222, 267, 334; Secretary of War (see also specific individuals): 30, 76; Congress: 76, 191, 195, 206n31, 225, 229-231, 247, 261, 316; Superintendent of Indian Affairs (see also specific individuals): 128, 133, 140, 154, 191, 215, 216, 243, 249, 251, 320, 327, 344n24, 345; Indian agents (see also specific individuals): 131, 133-134, 214; Office of Indian Affairs (St. Louis): 134, 137; Geological Survey: 182, 189; Commissioner of Indian Affairs (see also specific individuals): 210n9, 224-225, 229, 247, 250, 266, 309-310, 326, 327, 344n24, 345, 349; Engineer Corps: 216-217; Coast Survey: 217; War Department: 222, 249, 334; Secretary of Interior (see also specific individuals): 232, 267; Department of State: 276n56; Interior Department: 307, 334
United States military: 29-30, 33, 136, 171n1, 191, 196, 197, 199, 206, 209, 217, 246-247, 249, 289, 291, 295, 297, 299-300, 303-304, 307, 315-316, 318, 326-334, 336, 339, 345-347, 354, 365
Upham, Hiram: 315
Upper Missouri River. See Missouri River.
Upson, Gad: 307, 309-310
Urbin dit Bolduc, Joseph: 162
Utah Territory: 176, 194, 197, 278

Van Vliet, Stewart (Capt): 169
Vaughan, Alfred: 210n9, 215, 227, 243-244, 246-247, 249, 259, 261-262, 265-266, 279, 288, 291-292, 303-304, 307, 316
Vermillion Post: 178
Viall, Jasper: 344n24, 345, 347
Victor (Flathead): 153, 258
Virginia City (MT): 306-307
Voorhees, Daniel (Rep): 333

Walker, Mariah Culbertson Kipp. See Culbertson, Mariah (daughter).
Wallace, John: 303
Warren, Gouverneur K (Lt): 261
Washington, DC: 129-130, 139, 200-202, 209, 216-217, 224-225, 229-230, 232-233, 245, 249, 259-260, 270-271, 274n36, 288, 291, 297, 315, 318, 346-349
Washington, George (President): 34, 281
Washington Territory: 216, 289, 291
Water Bird (Blood): 344
Waterton Lakes: 359
Watts, John: 135
Weasel (Piegan): 135
Weasel Horse (Gros Ventre): 258
Weasel Tail (Blood): 52
West Point: 82, 216, 261, 278n67, 321
Westport (MO): 146-147
Wheeler, Joey & Lonny (Orleans, NE): 352n70
Wheeler, W F (Marshal): 324, 327-328
White Bear (Mandan): 109
White Buffalo (Piegan): 45, 47
White Cow (Assiniboine): 103-104, 106
White Eagle (Blood): 358
White Feather (Sioux): 354
White Man's Horses (Blackfeet): 221
White Wolf (Mandan): 192
White Earth River: 106, 178
Whitfield, J W (Maj): 245
Whitman, Marcus (Rev): 144
Whitman, Narcissa: 144
Willow Rounds: 163, 330, 355n87
Wilson, James: 369
Wolf Tail (Piegan): 331
Wolle, Francis: 280, 311
Wood, Jane Culbertson Hunt. See Culbertson, Jane "Janie" (daughter).
Woodbury, Daniel (Lt): 169
Wyeth, Nathaniel: 131-133

Yankton Indians: 29n18, 166-169, 180, 205, 227, 247, 249n34, 288, 347
Yankton Post: 178
Yanktonai (Sioux) Indians: 29n18, 203n16, 249, 259, 354
Yellowstone expedition. See Atkinson-O'Fallon expedition.
Yellowstone River: 35, 55, 133, 146, 153, 185, 187, 192, 375
*Yellow Stone* (steamboat): 35-37, 130
Young Sun (Blood): 343

www.ingramcontent.com/pod-product-compliance
Lightning Source LLC
Chambersburg PA
CBHW022058150426
43195CB00008B/178